MAKING A DIFFERENCE

MAKING A DIFFERENCE

Speeches by

RT HON. DR DENZIL L. DOUGLAS
Prime Minister of St Kitts & Nevis

THE SECOND TWO TERMS
OCTOBER 2004 - FEBRUARY 2015

Edited and Introduced by
KENNETH G. TILLEY

IAN RANDLE PUBLISHERS
Kingston • Miami

First published in Jamaica, 2024 by
Ian Randle Publishers
16 Herb McKenley Drive
PO Box 686
Kingston 6
www.ianrandlepublishers.com

National Library of Jamaica Cataloguing-In-Publication Data

Name: Douglas, Denzil L., author.
Title: Making a difference : speeches by Rt. Hon. Dr. Denzil L.
    Douglas, Prime Minister of St. Kitts and Nevis : the second two
    terms October 2004 to February 2015.
Description: Kingston, Jamaica : Ian Randle Publishers, 2023.
Identifiers: ISBN 9789768286963 (pbk). | ISBN 9789768286970
    (hbk). | ISBN 9789768286970119 (ebook).
Subjects: LCSH: Speeches, addresses, etc. | Saint Kitts and Nevis –
    Politics and government – 21st century. | Saint Kitts and Nevis –
    Economic conditions – 21st century. | Saint Kitts and Nevis –
    Social conditions.
Classification: DDC 972.973 -- dc23.

Cover Design by James Bailey
Book Design by Ian Randle Publishers
Printed and Bound in the United States of America

CONTENTS

THE ECONOMY

~ CONTENTS ~

EDUCATION AND SKILLS TRAINING

INFORMATION AND COMMUNICATIONS TECHNOLOGY

NATIONAL SECURITY

HIV/AIDS, NCDs AND HEALTH CARE

HOUSING AND LAND

NEVIS

REGIONAL AFFAIRS

INTERNATIONAL AFFAIRS

POLITICS: ST KITTS-NEVIS LABOUR PARTY (SKNLP)

POLITICS: ST KITTS-NEVIS TRADES AND LABOUR UNION (SKNTLU)

Foreword

Coming Of Age, a collection of speeches given by the Rt Hon. Denzil L. Douglas during his first two terms as prime minister of St Kitts and Nevis, fully prepares enquiring minds for this second compilation of speeches to learn how his two subsequent terms enabled Dr Douglas to fulfill his lifelong mission of *Making A Difference* in his native land. That is precisely what he accomplished by abolishing the last vestiges of the age-old plantation system to create instead a competitive and service-oriented economy within a modern, democratic society.

A diligent pupil and hand-picked protégé of the revered Robert Bradshaw, a privileged beneficiary of the tutelage of the silver-tongued Paul Southwell, Dr Denzil Llewellyn Douglas brought to the political craft that remarkable combination of fervour for social upliftment, intellectual rigour, abundant energy, and extraordinary flair for effective communication at differing tiers which enabled him to successfully address the innumerable challenges that confront the leader of every small island state.

Despite the country's limitations of size and its vulnerability to natural disasters, the comprehension and systematic approach of Dr Douglas resulted in numerous commendable policies including a massive land and housing empowerment programme, education and skills training, technology and telecommunications development, environmental sustainability, and health care reform. The publication of these prime ministerial addresses will serve as a permanent record of the facilities for tourism, cruise ports, airport expansion, road infrastructure, sports, and culture that he built during his productive incumbency.

My many years of associating with him, as a colleague head of government, permit me to attest readily to the steadfast purpose and exemplary quality of his regional leadership commitment. Dr Douglas was chosen as the CARICOM prime minister responsible for the Health HIV/AIDS portfolio and immediately proceeded to persuade us to appreciate the medical aphorism 'the health of the region is the wealth of the region.' Whether dealing with HIV/AIDS or NCDs as PANCAP chair (Pan Caribbean Partnership Against HIV/AIDS), the able leadership role of Dr Douglas is unquestioned. This book reflects how and why his vast experience and abundant wisdom are widely acknowledged throughout the Caribbean and our hemisphere. His articulation, his comprehension, and the grit so evident in his persuasive utterances, are highly regarded on the entire global stage.

Denzil Douglas has proven unequivocally that a microstate with progressive policies at home, enhanced by engaged participation and active cooperation in the broader world, can bring real, transformative benefits to its people. He invariably asserted the right and competence to articulate with credibility the peculiar problems and interests of small island developing states in whatever fora he participated.

Making A Difference is an impressive selection of speeches and public statements by Prime Minister Douglas on a wide range of issues and topics. This compelling book will give readers an opportunity to follow the progress made and understand how social harmony and economic development were successfully promoted in this small but vibrant and alluring Caribbean jewel during the period of his memorable leadership.

Most Hon. P. J. Patterson, ON, OCC, OE, KC
6th Prime Minister of Jamaica (1992–2006)

BIOGRAPHICAL NOTES

RT HON. DR DENZIL L. DOUGLAS
Second Prime Minister of the Federation of St Kitts and Nevis
July 1995–February 2015

Born in the north island village of St Paul's, Capisterre on January 14, 1953, Denzil Llewellyn Douglas had a modest upbringing in the heart of sugar country and the embrace of the St Kitts-Nevis Labour Party (SKNLP).

An excellent student, Dr Douglas received his secondary education on a Bradshaw Scholarship to the grammar school and continued his studies at The University of the West Indies receiving his BSc. in 1977 and his medical degree in 1984. In 1979, while still a student, he became the first Young Labour representative to sit on the party's national executive. Following his medical internship in Trinidad, he returned to St Kitts in 1986 and established a private practice.

In 1987, Dr Douglas became deputy chair of the SKNLP. In the March 1989 national election he was elected from Newton Ground/Harris (#6) to the National Assembly where he has remained the member of parliament for more than thirty years. Later that same year, he became the Political Leader of the SKNLP and leader of the opposition.

As Political Leader, Dr Douglas steered a course that restructured and re-energised the Labour Party. In the 1993 general election, the party won four of the eight seats on St Kitts and laid the groundwork for its decisive 1995 victory when it won seven seats and formed a majority government. In the 2000 election, the SKNLP was re-elected with a resounding mandate winning all eight St Kitts seats in the National Assembly. The party won its third straight victory in 2004, winning seven seats, and won an unprecedented fourth term in 2010 with six seats. The SKNLP won only three seats in the 2015 election and became the official opposition in the new parliament. Dr Douglas stepped down from his role as Political Leader in 2021.

When the Labour Party was returned to government in 2022, Denzil Douglas assumed the role of Senior Minister and was appointed

Minister of Foreign Affairs; International Trade, Industry, Commerce, and Consumer Affairs; and Economic Development and Investment.

INTRODUCTION

This second collection of speeches by the Rt Hon. Dr Denzil L. Douglas covers his third and fourth terms as Prime Minister of St Kitts and Nevis from October, 2004 to February, 2015.

After two terms in office, the Labour government was seasoned and experienced and on most fronts, the overall quality of life of Kittitians and Nevisians was steadily improving year by year. St Kitts and Nevis had recently moved up on the United Nations Human Development Index from #51 to #39, top spot in the OECS and second only to Barbados in the wider Caribbean region. In the latest Country Poverty Assessment (CPA), extreme poverty in St Kitts and Nevis fell from 11 per cent in 2000 to 1.4 per cent in 2009. Douglas proudly attributed this welcome advancement to his government's 'progressive social and economic policies.'

Nearing the end of his second term, Douglas called a national election for October 25, 2004. The Labour Party subsequently won seven of the eight seats on St Kitts (the Labour Party does not contest the three seats on Nevis) and formed a majority government with a clear mandate to end the 350-year-old sugar industry and move the nation to a service-oriented economy with tourism as its main pillar. The country went to the polls again on January 25, 2010 when the Labour majority was reduced by one to six seats.

Despite the many achievements of the previous two terms, as always there were a myriad of challenges, some old, some new, facing a government embarking on a fresh mandate.

The speeches/statements in this volume are generally shorter than most of the speeches in Volume 1, *Coming Of Age*. It's not clear whether this is a result of tighter, more succinct messaging by Dr Douglas or a growing recognition that audiences in today's instant communication environment want shorter, pithier communications from their politicians and statesmen. It's probably some combination of both.

While the sections in Volume 2 mostly mirror those of Volume 1, there are some noteworthy changes reflecting evolving priorities, both locally and regionally, in the broader, ever more connected world.

For example, 'Housing and Land' and 'Nevis' have fewer entries this time than in Volume 1 primarily because these two topics are mature, successful policy files that continue to move forward positively on their own momentum.

Policy areas that grew in importance in terms three and four were 'The Economy,' 'Regional Affairs,' 'Politics,' and a new category, 'The Environment and Sustainability,' which reflected growing concern about increasing global climate change and the urgent need for new sources of sustainable energy and development.

These changes in priorities point clearly to increasing participation by St Kitts and Nevis and her fellow CARICOM members in the world beyond the Caribbean basin and a growing recognition that the entire world, from micro-states like St Kitts and Nevis to the globe's most advanced economies, is more interconnected and linked together than ever.

Changing priorities also point to Denzil Douglas's growing belief as the region's senior statesman that full interaction with world organisations and institutions is the only way to help St Kitts and Nevis and the other CARICOM members tackle the increased challenges of the twenty-first century including trade liberalisation, environmental destruction, AIDS and NCDs, and economic turbulence. These crises are not caused by smaller states, especially Small Island Developing States (SIDS), but they nonetheless often bear the brunt of the downstream results without the tools and the funding to mitigate or adapt to them.

As in Volume 1, the selected speeches and pronouncements were chosen from the hundreds given by Dr Douglas during his second two terms in office from 2004–2015. They are organised thematically and presented chronologically and will hopefully provide readers with the information and context to determine for themselves the extent of the impact the Douglas Labour government had on the welfare of the citizens of St Kitts and Nevis, the region, and beyond during the second half of its twenty-year administration and whether, indeed, it did make a difference.

Kenneth G. Tilley
October 2023

Acronyms

The list of acronyms used in the speeches in *Making A Difference* is almost twice as long as it was in *Coming Of Age*. I have no plausible explanation as to why that is except that all governance bodies, whether local, regional, or international are awash in acronyms and their usage seems to be increasing. It is often almost impossible to read their communications without a comprehensive acronym list at hand. Apologies.

ACP	Africa, Caribbean and Pacific Group
ACS	Association of Caribbean States
ALBA	Bolivarian Alliance for the Peoples of Our Americas (Venezuela)
ART	Anti-Retroviral Treatment
ARVs	Anti-Retrovirals
AVEC	Advanced Vocational Education Centre
BPOA	Barbados Programme of Action
CAIC	Caribbean Association of Industry & Commerce
CANA	Caribbean News Agency
CAPE	Caribbean Advanced Proficiency Examination
CARDI	Caribbean Agricultural Research & Development Institute
CAREC	Caribbean Epidemiology Centre
CARICOM	Caribbean Community
CARIFORUM	Caribbean Forum of African, Caribbean and Pacific (ACP) States
CARPHA	Caribbean Public Health Agency
CARTAC	Caribbean Regional Technical Assistance Centre (IMF)
CBI	Citizenship By Investment Programme
CBSI	Caribbean Basin Security Initiative
CBU	Caribbean Broadcasting Union

CCH	Caribbean Cooperation in Health
CCM	Concerned Citizens Movement
CDB	Caribbean Development Bank
CEC/CXC	Caribbean Examinations Council
CEHI	Caribbean Environmental Health Institute
CELAC	Community of Latin American and Caribbean States
CFBC	Clarence Fitzroy Bryant College
CFNI	Caribbean Food and Nutrition Institute
CGCED	Caribbean Group for Cooperation & Economic Development
CGF	Commonwealth Games Federation
CHA	Central Housing Authority
CHART	Caribbean HIV/AIDS Research & Training Initiative
CHRC	Caribbean Health Research Centre
CHTA	Caribbean Hotel & Tourism Association
CHOGM	Commonwealth Heads of Government Meeting
CIC	Chamber of Industry and Commerce
CID	Criminal Investigation Department
CIDA	Canadian International Development Agency
CKLN	Caribbean Knowledge and Learning Network
CMO	Chief Medical Officer
COFCOR	Council for Foreign and Community Relations
COTED	Council for Trade & Economic Development (CARICOM)
CPA	Country Poverty Assessment (CDB)
CPHA	Caribbean Public Health Agency
CRN+	Caribbean Regional Network of People Living with AIDS
CSME	Caribbean Single Market & Economy
CTU	Caribbean Telecommunications Union
CUPIDE	Caribbean Universities Programme for Integrated Distance Education
CVQ	Caribbean Vocational Qualifications
CXC/CEC	Caribbean Examinations Council
DFID	Department for International Development (UK)
DBSKN	Development Bank of St Kitts and Nevis
ECA	Eastern Caribbean Assembly
ECCA	Eastern Caribbean Currency Authority

ECCB	Eastern Caribbean Central Bank
ECCU	Eastern Caribbean Currency Union
EC$	Eastern Caribbean Dollar
ECEMP	Eastern Caribbean Economic Management Programme (Canada)
ECHMB	Eastern Caribbean Home Mortgage Bank
ECLAC	Economic Commission for Latin America & the Caribbean
ECSM	Eastern Caribbean Securities Market
ECTEL	Eastern Caribbean Telecommunications Authority
EDF	European Development Fund
EPAs	Economic Partnership Agreements (EU)
ESG	Environmental, Social, and Governance (non-financial factors increasingly considered by investors)
EU	European Union
FAO	Food and Agriculture Organisation
FATF	Financial Action Task Force
FBINAA	FBI National Academy Associates
FTAA	Free Trade Area of the Americas
GATS	General Agreement on Trade in Services
GDP	Gross Domestic Product
GFATM	Global Fund to Fight AIDS, TB and Malaria
GNI	Gross National Income
GNP	Gross National Product
GSEII	Global Sustainable Energy Islands Initiative
HFO	Heavy Fuel Oil
HIPC	Highly Indebted Poor Countries
HIV/AIDS	Human Immunodeficiency Virus/ Acquired Immunodeficiency Syndrome
HTA	Hotel and Tourism Association
IADB	Inter-American Development Bank
ICS	Institute of Caribbean Studies (US)
ICT	Information and Communications Technology
IDA	International Development Association
IDB	International Development Bank
IICA	Inter-American Institute for Cooperation on Agriculture
ILO	International Labour Organisation

IMF	International Monetary Fund
IMPACS	Implementation Agency for Crime & Security
INTERPOL	International Criminal Police Organisation
ITU	International Telecommunications Union
JVC	Joint Venture Company
M&E	Monitoring and Evaluation
MDGs	Millennium Development Goals (UN)
MAA	Mutual Assistance Agreement (FBI Academy)
MOU	Memorandum of Understanding
MTCT	Mother-to-Child Transmission
NCM	No Confidence Motion
NCDs	Non-Communicable Diseases
NDC	National Democratic Congress (Grenada)
NEMA	National Emergency Management Agency
NGO	Non-Governmental Organisation
NHC	National Housing Corporation
NHIC	National Health Insurance Commission
NIA	Nevis Island Administration
NRP	Nevis Reformation Party
NTRC	National Telecommunications Regulatory Commission
OAS	Organisation of American States
OECD	Organisation for Economic Co-operation and Development
OECS	Organisation of Eastern Caribbean States
OPIC	Overseas Private Investment Corporation (US)
PAHO	Pan American Health Organisation
PAM	People's Action Movement
PANCAP	Pan Caribbean Partnership Against HIV/AIDS
PDVSA	Venezuelan state-owned oil and natural gas company
PECA	PetroCaribe Energy Cooperation Agreement
PEP	People Employment Programme
PEPFAR	President's Emergency Plan for AIDS Relief (US)
PLHIV	People Living with HIV
PLWA	People Living With AIDS
RNM	Regional Negotiating Machinery
ROC	Republic of China (Taiwan)
RSS	Regional Security System

RSKNPF	Royal St Kitts and Nevis Police Force
RGSM	Regional Government Securities Market
SBA	Stand-By Arrangement (IMF)
SCASPA	St Christopher Air and Sea Ports Authority
SEDU	Small Enterprise Development Unit
SELF	Student Education & Learning Fund
SGDs	Sustainable Development Goals
SIDF	Sugar Industry Diversification Foundation
SIDS	Small Island Developing States
SKANTEL	St Kitts and Nevis Telecommunications Limited
SKELEC	St Kitts Electricity Company
SKIPA	St Kitts Investment Promotion Agency
SKN	St Kitts and Nevis
SKNANB	St Kitts-Nevis-Anguilla National Bank
SKNDB	St Kitts-Nevis Development Bank
SKNDF	St Kitts-Nevis Defence Force
SKNLP	St Kitts-Nevis Labour Party
SKTA	St Kitts Tourism Authority
SKNTLU	St Kitts-Nevis Trades and Labour Union
SLDI	Special Land Distribution Initiative
SMEs	Small- and Medium-sized Enterprises
SPV	Special Purpose Vehicle (SKNANB)
SSMC	St Kitts Sugar Manufacturing Corporation
STEP	Skills Training Empowerment Programme
SVEs	Small Vulnerable Economies
The UWI	The University of the West Indies
TLE	Tertiary Level Education
TLIs	Tertiary Level Institutions
TRIPS	Trade-Related Intellectual Property Rights
TVET	Technical and Vocational Education and Training
UDC	Urban Development Corporation
UK	United Kingdom
UN	United Nations
UNAIDS	Joint United Nations Programme on HIV/AIDS
UNDF	United Nations Development Fund
UNDP	United Nations Development Programme
UNESCO	United Nations Educational, Scientific and Cultural Organisation

UNGA	United Nations General Assembly
UNGASS	United Nations General Assembly Special Session
UNIDO	United Nations Industrial Development Organisation
US/USA	United States of America
USAID	United States Agency for International Development
USDA	United States Department of Agriculture
USF	Universal Service Fund
UVI	University of the Virgin Islands
UWI	The University of the West Indies
WB	World Bank
WHO	World Health Organisation
WTO	World Trade Organisation
YES	Youth Empowerment Through Skills
ZBC	ZIZ Broadcasting Corporation

The Economy

THE ECONOMY

⟨◆⟩

The most significant decision Denzil Douglas had to make as prime minister was the closure in 2005 of the almost 350-year-old sugar industry. King Sugar was dead. It was a momentous decision that ended a fundamental part of Kittitian and Nevisian national and personal identity. Closure would also have a long-lasting impact on the economy and the well-being of Kittitians (Nevis had abandoned sugar some years earlier) with no one, including Douglas, knowing for certain what the eventual outcome would be. Douglas agonised over the decision but believed that the closure of the sugar industry, while problematic in a considerable number of ways, would none-the-less open up a number of new twenty-first century opportunities for the Federation's people. He also knew that the economy had to be transitioned thoughtfully and carefully from sugar to services, focused primarily on tourism but also including international financial services, information and communications technology, and offshore tertiary level education providers.

Development of a new economy led by tourism became the government's primary concern following the closure of the sugar industry and included providing infrastructure for more hotel rooms; ensuring (and often paying for) reliable airlift into the country; generating construction activity; creating more jobs in the hotels and hospitality sector; and increased destination marketing in key North American and UK markets.

Perhaps the two most important initiatives with the greatest positive effect on post-sugar economic readjustment were the Sugar Industry Diversification Foundation (SIDF) and the Citizenship By Investment (CBI) programme.

SIDF was established by the government to help transform the post-sugar economy by funding new enterprises that would help build the Federation's human capital and support economic growth. SIDF embraced a broad, wide-ranging interpretation of its mandate which allowed it, for example, to fund and support the government's People Employment Programme (PEP).

The Citizenship By Investment (CBI) programme had a history dating back to the 1980s but it was restructured and reinvigorated by the Douglas government to encourage much needed foreign investment. Reputable non-citizens invited by the government to make a significant investment in the country in approved real estate such as hotels and golf courses (US$350K at the time) or in Sugar Industry Diversification Foundation (SIDF) projects (US $200K), could then qualify for SKN citizenship and a well-respected international passport. With effective regulation, due diligence, and good management, CBI became very successful and an international best practices model and through its real estate and SIDF portfolios, shouldered much of the burden for ensuring the viability of the economy through those difficult times.

The St Kitts-Nevis-Anguilla National Bank (SKNANB) also played a major role during the recession through its land for debt exchange initiative whereby government loans could be exchanged for available unused sugar lands which could then be sold to the private sector for development and the national debt reduced accordingly.

Other initiatives that helped to improve the economy included scaling-down and restructuring the enormous non-SKNANB debt from the sugar industry closure through a debt exchange offer to creditors; participation in the PetroCaribe alliance whereby Venezuela provided oil to a number of Caribbean countries on conditions of flexible financing and preferential payment; creation of the St Kitts Investment Promotion Agency (SKIPA) to streamline the setting up of new businesses in the Federation by both locals and foreigners; and urgent exploration of alternative energy sources including solar, geothermal, and wind.

After having achieved considerable success transitioning the SKN economy from sugar to tourism and other services, Douglas became the spokesperson for the Commonwealth on the economic challenges facing small, vulnerable, highly indebted middle-income states. He had been making the argument for some years that removal or reduction of protectionist barriers and differential treatment was a major economic blow to small states, island or otherwise. SKN's high per capita GDP meant it had 'graduated' from nearly all concessionary funding, putting it into a 'higher bracket than reality supports,' unable to reach its maximum potential in the global economy.

By June 2014, the debt to GDP ratio was down 67 percentage points from over 145 per cent pre-restructuring to 78 per cent, with a projected further decline to 60 per cent by the end of the year.

Closure of the Sugar Industry Parliamentary Address
National Assembly, Basseterre, July 29, 2005

Madam Speaker, it is not merely coincidental that I am addressing Parliament on the closure of the sugar industry just a few days before we celebrate the emancipation of our forebears from the hardship and horrors of slavery. Indeed, the closure of the sugar industry is yet another milestone in our long and arduous struggle to make emancipation and freedom truly meaningful. I believe that in 1834 after the bells and drums of emancipation had petered out and the celebrations had ended, our forebears must have faced many anxious and depressing moments when they thought of returning to the cane fields and sugar factories.

Moreover, when they did return to the sordid working conditions of the sugar estates, they must have wondered what freedom really meant. It must have been truly shocking when they came face to face with the reality that, for most of them, emancipation was essentially the freedom to choose between their demise outside the estate and their continued trauma and travail inside the estate. Today, our sugar workers can decide to walk away from the cane fields or the sugar factory, and at the same time, secure a happy and progressive future for themselves and their families. This is possible because the Labour Party has prepared the way for life after sugar.

From the moment that the PAM administration lost office in 1995, they have been singing one chorus in unison: 'Sugar is dead! Close the industry! Away with the SSMC!' They knew that they had literally raped the industry through their lack of interest in the plight of the sugar workers and had brought the industry to the point of no return. They had done everything possible to end sugar production during their term of office but they were afraid to carry the process through to completion.

They were truly fearful. They knew that the working people of this country would not sit idly by and allow a heartless group with a bourgeois mentality to bring an end to their livelihood without providing alternative means of subsistence. They were determined, however, that

Labour should carry out their dirty work. Hence, from 1995 onwards, they have agitated relentlessly for the premature closure of the industry. They even tried to fool the sugar workers by promising them all sorts of goodies which they knew they could not deliver.

But the sugar workers were not fooled, and my government was determined that they would not be forced out of employment in the sugar industry until we were satisfied that the economy had been sufficiently transformed to provide alternative work for them and to cater to their social and economic needs. We were also determined that a decision of such monumental proportions as the closure of an industry that had dominated the economic life of our islands for over 350 years, must be based on extensive consultations with our people. Hence, while PAM continued to sing their chorus and to clamour for a hasty end to the production of sugar, we were actively listening to our people and preparing the foundation for the transition from sugar through the creation of a truly diversified service-oriented economy.

In consulting with the people of our Federation, we ensured that they were provided adequate information on which to base their views and opinions. In 1999, we commissioned a report by SABAS, an international consulting firm, on the prospects for the sugar industry and, based on that report, we organised a series of public meetings and consultations to determine 'the way forward in respect of the sugar industry.' A special committee was then formed to review the reports of the public meetings and consultations and to provide appropriate advice to the government. This special committee was reconstituted as the St Kitts Sugar Manufacture Redevelopment Committee with four sub-committees that were mandated to deal with issues relating to land use, diversification, finance, and retirement.

At that same time, the government ensured that the international community was kept abreast of the developments in our sugar industry. In April 2004, we convened a symposium with local, regional, and international participants to discuss the sugar industry in St Kitts and Nevis. Since then, there has been a range of other meetings with international and regional donors to discuss ways in which the regional and international community could be of assistance to St Kitts and Nevis as we proceeded with our programme of economic transition. Since the decision to end the production of sugar, we continue to build partnerships with international and regional donors and we have been meeting sugar workers to ensure that their concerns are given due consideration and effectively addressed.

Despite the agitation of PAM for a hasty end to the sugar industry, I am convinced there was no short cut to the stage we have reached today. Any attempted short cut would have created anxiety and tension among our people and would have heightened the risk of chaos and confusion in our society. Moreover, the period of consultation has given us the time required to implement our programme of economic transformation and to build the capacity of the government to carry out its responsibilities to the displaced sugar workers.

In particular, notwithstanding the series of hurricanes that we have faced, notwithstanding the dramatic increases in oil prices, notwithstanding the impact of international terrorism and war on our tourist industry, notwithstanding the gyrations of international capital and foreign exchange markets, notwithstanding the continued uncertainty in respect of the growth prospects of the USA and other advanced economies, we have steered our economy to a path of enhanced economic growth and expansion. In 2004, our economy recorded an impressive rate of real economic growth of 6.41 per cent, the highest rate of increase in economic activity that we have recorded since 2000.

What is even more remarkable is that we have achieved this level of growth in a year when the output of sugar as a percentage of GDP fell. In fact, over the period that my government has been in office, the contribution of sugar to GDP in constant prices has fallen from 4.01 per cent in 1995 to 2.49 per cent in 2004. Over the same period, sectors such as hotels and restaurants, construction, manufacturing, and banking and insurance have increased their share of GDP. In other words, my government's strategy for diversifying our economy and reducing our reliance on sugar has been bearing fruit. Consequently, the impact of the loss of the sugar industry at this time is far less than it would have been if we had succumbed to the pressure of PAM and closed the industry in an earlier year.

The improvement that we have seen over the past decade will only accelerate in the years ahead. Port Zante is developing at a rapid rate and there is a range of hotels and other tourism-related facilities scheduled for implementation over the next twelve months. These include the luxurious Auberge Hotel project that will convert the southeast peninsula into a world-class, environmentally sensitive luxury resort facility, the

La Vallee Golf Course Villa and Commercial Development, the Cable Bay Hotel and Villa Resort Development, and at least three major hotel projects at Whitegate. Our tourism product will also be enhanced by the construction of a world- class water theme park at the Marriott, a dolphin park and hotel at Friars Bay, and a horse racing and entertainment facility at Whitegate. Indeed, over the next few years, the entire economic landscape of St Kitts and Nevis will be dramatically transformed and all of our people, including our sugar workers, will reap great benefits from this unprecedented level of economic growth and expansion.

Before we could bring down the curtain on sugar production, we also had to ensure that our banking sector, and our key financial institutions in particular, were equipped to meet the financial needs of sugar workers and our people generally. We are proud that today, the bank of our people, the St Kitts-Nevis-Anguilla National Bank, is by virtually any measure, the largest bank in the OECS with assets of over $1.4 billion. Moreover, by virtually any measure – profitability, liquidity, or asset base – our National Bank, which is owned and controlled by our people, is stronger than ever before and is well placed to play a major role in the transition process.

The period of consultation has also given us the opportunity to strengthen the government's fiscal position that had been dealt some severe blows by a series of hurricanes. Over the past three years, we have been implementing a fiscal stabilisation programme that has been helping to contain government expenditure and boost revenues. Indeed, in 2003, we underwent a massive fiscal adjustment of some 8.9 per cent of GDP, which brought us much closer to our goal of eliminating current account deficits. We are confident that in 2005 we will consolidate this achievement and move the current account to a surplus position.

When I delivered my budget address late last year, I projected that in 2005 we would achieve a current account surplus of $13.9 million. I am pleased to advise that by the end of June this year we had already achieved a current account surplus of over $5 million and we are confident that over the rest of the year we will continue to build on this surplus to reach the budgeted current account surplus of $13.9 million. We are also projecting that the continued enhancement of the growth rate, the implementation of our privatisation strategy, and the reduction of deficits will cause the debt to GDP ratio to fall for the first time in over a decade.

Of course, the debt of the SSMC will be of particular concern at this time. We are pleased to advise, however, that we are currently in discussions with the National Bank in respect of the implementation of a proposal to exchange/retire the debt of the SSMC, including any additional debt arising from the closure costs, for government debentures. We are also giving consideration to the establishment of a land management company with the participation of government, National Bank, and social security. The land management company would purchase sufficient lands from the government to facilitate the redemption of the debenture and would carry out operations to develop and sell real estate on a commercial basis.

We are of the view in light of the current prices of land, that government will be able to sell the land management company sufficient lands to facilitate the early repayment of the debt and still maintain the majority of the lands currently owned by the government. In any event, to the extent that all of the major participants in the land management company, including the National Bank, are controlled and at least majority-owned by the government of St Kitts and Nevis, then it will still be possible for government to exert sufficient influence to ensure that the operations of the land management company adhere to high standards of transparency and accountability and that land development sales will be consistent with the development and land use policies established by the government.

Moreover, the lands retained under the control of government or its statutory bodies will continue to be available for housing, the expansion of villages, agricultural development, and social and economic infrastructure. We are also determined to put in place appropriate mechanisms to ensure that all land distribution by government entities is fair and transparent and gives priority to the people of this country. We have always welcomed foreign investors to our shores but we will not allocate lands to their projects unless they pay the full commercial price for such lands and they demonstrate that, through the level and nature of their investment, their projects will bring meaningful benefits to the people of this country. Our lands are not for speculators. Our lands must be used to advance the quality of life of our people.

We consider the management of our land resources as critical to the continuing growth and development of our Federation. Consequently, among projects that we are pursuing with regional and international donors is a land use analysis to be carried out by the Ministry of Sustainable Development in association with Vanderbilt University. This project will produce a range of maps and statistics that will provide scientific input into the feasibility studies and reports in respect of land use changes and the proposed activities on the sugar lands.

We also intend to work with Vanderbilt University to implement an integrated land system that will produce various critical outputs including a geographic information system (GIS) framework to coordinate and standardise the management of spatial information, a land cadastral map, a land ownership database that will support the establishment of a modern land registry, and an updated and fully annotated land use map. Of course, in all of our activities relating to land use management, the protection of the environment, including soil conservation, will be give considerable emphasis. In this regard, we will continue to devote resources to soil conservation activities and to the minimal maintenance of sugar cane on the landscape while we pursue with private investors the development of sugar cane-related enterprises such as rum distilling, co-generation of electricity, ethanol production, and the production of animal feed.

I am convinced that non-sugar agriculture in this country will make a quantum leap over the next few years and I encourage our people, especially our sugar workers, to take full advantage of the opportunities that will be created in agriculture. We are currently pursuing a range of projects that will ensure that we can feed ourselves and our many tourists and at the same time enhance our agricultural exports to neighbouring islands such as St Maarten and Anguilla with substantial tourist industries but limited agricultural capability. Among the projects that are currently under implementation is a small farmers agricultural diversification project that will include the development and expansion of commercial and semi-commercial fruit tree orchards, increased pineapple production for domestic and export markets, extension of vegetable production from six to twelve months per year through the establishment of irrigated farms, the establishment of a packing house facility, the strengthening of farmer organisations, the establishment of a core group of livestock farmers, the expansion of the Basseterre abattoir, the engagement of an agricultural marketing specialist with international experience, the establishment of a tropical plant nursery, and the importation and multiplication of plant genetic material for tree cropping and forestry.

To support these activities, the Ministry of Agriculture will also implement an agricultural resource management project that will involve the construction of storm drains, the terracing of sloping lands, ghaut stabilisation, and the drilling and commission of wells to provide water for the irrigation of agricultural lands. International donors including the

CDB, the FAO and IICA have expressed great interest in these projects and we are confident that our own efforts and resources will be complemented by financial and technical assistance from these agencies.

In charting the way forward after sugar, we have placed considerable emphasis on ensuring that the sugar workers join the mainstream of economic growth and expansion in this progressive country of ours. In particular, the transition office has procured technical assistance to implement a change management project aimed at helping sugar workers cope with any stress that may arise from the need to change the way of life that many of them have known since they entered the workforce or even since birth.

In addition, the Ministry of Social and Community Development, along with the Basic Needs Trust Fund, AVEC, and CFBC is implementing a post-sugar social reconstruction project estimated to cost US$6 million that will support, re-skill, and prepare SSMC employees for employment in the new growth sectors of the economy including tourism, telecommunications, and information technology. The project will, among other things, deliver skills training, provide financial subsidies for persons involved in retraining, provide counselling in savings and investment, prepare sugar workers to take up entrepreneurial opportunities, and conduct a labour market survey to help in fashioning strategies for re-incorporating sugar workers into the work force.

The minister of Labour and National Security will outline the very generous severance payment package that we have approved for sugar workers, but there is also a range of other supporting measures that we will put in place to ensure that our sugar workers continue to thrive and prosper, and are not pushed below the poverty line. These measure include the following:

- Medical care will be provided to the sugar workers by the national health programme after they have been severed;

- A housing scheme will be implemented for workers who do not own a home but have served the industry for more than twenty years and whose income level places them below the poverty line;

- SSMC pensioners will be transferred to the social security scheme with the guarantee that they will be no worse off in regard to the amount of pension receipts;

- A programme of training and re-orientation shall be elaborated for the severed workers and during the course of such programme a weekly stipend will be provided to the trainees;

- The Ministry of Agriculture shall accommodate interested severed workers in the pursuit of non-sugar agriculture by making agricultural lands and extension support available to them. The Ministry of Agriculture will also provide land preparation services and other inputs to farmers for one year;

- The government will expand the pool of bus and taxi operators and waive or soften the existing experience requirements to allow new entrants to enjoy duty and tax concessions;

- Banks and other financial institutions will be encouraged to create special packages for sugar workers who are interested in farming, fishing and small business;

- Duty-free concessions will be provided in respect of farming tools, equipment, and materials for sugar workers who move into farming;

- Corporation tax and traders tax will be reprieved for a period of five years for businesses established by sugar workers;

- Water for irrigation and irrigation equipment will be provided free of cost to sugar workers entering into agriculture;

- Exemption from consumption tax will be added to the existing exemption from duty enjoyed by fishers and farmers for a period of five years.

I am sure you will agree that my government has converted a potentially devastating problem into a massive opportunity for our people to build new and more prosperous lives for themselves. By our careful and consultative approach, we have enlisted the support of the entire regional and international community. Last week, in a meeting of donors spearheaded by the European Union, a range of international and regional donors undertook to provide assistance to St Kitts and Nevis in the implementation of the project and a range of other projects with a total estimated cost of over US\$20 million. My recent visits to the presidents of the Republic of China and Brazil, the prime ministers of Thailand and India, and the governor of Japan have all borne fruit that will specifically assist the sugar workers and generally, the citizens of St Kitts and Nevis.

In addition, we are in the process of negotiating a substantial support package with the European Union as part of the accompanying measures for sugar protocol countries affected by the proposed changes in the sugar protocol. St Kitts has taken the lead in moving out of sugar and has mobilised considerable support in its quest to obtain EU assistance. In particular, the United Kingdom has been making strong representation to the Europeans on our behalf and it seems very likely that we will benefit considerably from a European financial package aimed at assisting us to accelerate the economic transition and transformation process.

As you can see by the extent of the reconstruction programme I have outlined, the problems relating to the transition from sugar did not sneak up on us like a thief in the night. We carefully laid the groundwork over many years to secure the livelihoods of our people. The utterances of the past administration suggest that they viewed the closure of the sugar industry as a simple process that could have been achieved by the stroke of a pen. There was no thought given to the hundreds of workers who stood to lose everything they had worked for over their entire lives However, for a Labour Party that was formed by the people for the people, the welfare of the people of our country had to be paramount, and we were prepared to wait as long as it was necessary to ensure that appropriate mechanisms were put in place to protect our workers.

We feel that we have reached the stage where we are well prepared to cope with the challenges of the transition from sugar production. Indeed, we are convinced that with the programme I have outlined here today, that the future for sugar workers and for the people of this country as a whole is brighter than ever before. We are able to take this momentous decision today because the government has done its homework, it has done its assessment, and it has already determined the conditions.

The Labour government which I have the honour and privilege to lead at this time in our ever-evolving socio-economic and political development, has been able to decide on the way forward because it has treated the sugar workers and the citizens of this country with humaneness and social justice. One great ancient philosopher said: 'Humaneness and justice are the means by which to govern properly. When government is carried out properly, people feel close to the leadership and think little of dying for it.' Time and time again I have asked sugar workers and fellow citizens to walk with me, march with me, and let us face the brighter future together unafraid. We have decided on the season/weather, and this is the right season to close the industry. We cannot wait one more second, one more minute, one more hour, one more week. We must not wait one more month, one more year. We must not wait. The time is now. Now is the time!

The conviction of our decision is also reinforced not only by assessing the way and the timing, but also the outcome, which already has been predetermined. We are aware from our assessment that this period of transition can be a traumatic one, full of all the apprehension and uncertainties of change, even though it is change for good, and even in cases where retrenched sugar workers are being quickly employed in new jobs. That's why our post-sugar national Marshall Plan includes not only:

i.   a handsome severance financial package; but also

ii. continuous professional counselling and guidance of workers;

iii. basic, intermediate and advanced level certification of workers from a national vocational qualification programme; and

iv. a national manpower service in which labour market assessment of economic sectors becomes critical for job creation.

I further emphasise that we are able to take this momentous decision today because of the quality of leadership of this country. According to the classics, the way of the ancient kings considered humaneness foremost in leadership. Alternatively, for another group of leaders, they considered intelligence foremost. But over the last ten years that Labour has returned to political office, the leadership of this country has relied upon humaneness, intelligence, trustworthiness, courage, and sternness at necessary times in dealing with the sugar workers as we grappled with the socio-economic and political issues of the failed sugar industry and the transformation of the national economy.

We boldly declare today the end of one chapter and one era in our development as a people and proudly declare today the beginning of a new chapter that is brighter than the one of yesterday, a new era because we know that we have the discipline to survive the transition and to succeed in our national economic transformation. I call on all our citizens to become focused. Let those of our youths and our people generally who are misguided turn from their paths of lawlessness and crime to those of peace and enhanced lifestyles that will generate respectable and respected citizens with their attention fixed on things good, honest, noble, and just. Let us be our brother's keeper, and let us remember today in this House, that it is not only the sugar workers who are affected. All of us are affected, all of us are in this together.

It was Solomon, speaking to us through Proverbs, which is very practical and specific in its challenges to us in our everyday life, who penned these immortal words:

> Listen to your father, who gave you life, and do not despise your mother when she is old. Buy the truth and do not sell it. Get wisdom, discipline and understanding. The father of a righteous man has great joy; he who has a wise son delights in him. May your father and mother be glad; may she who gave you birth, rejoice!

I want to close now with an appeal to our youths, the human resource of this nation and for whom in particular this courageous decision has been taken. I am reminded of my youth, of my humble birth, of my upbringing and grounding in the village of St Paul's situated in picturesque Capisterre at the north-western tip of the island in the heart of the sugar belt. It is a place they call 'Back a de land.' I am the son, proud son, of a deceased sugar cane worker, a seasonal worker, the 'checker' at the Belmont siding during the crop season for over fifty years. He was a tailor by trade in the dull season, and a preacher on Sundays in the local Wesleyan Holiness Church. His name was Charles Bedford Douglas. My mother, who predeceased my father when I was only one year old, was an ordinary housewife who at age thirty-one already had six children alive. Her name was Laurette Adina Douglas. I did not have the privilege of knowing her. But through some natural ability, honed by discipline and hard work, I was awarded in 1965 at age twelve, the Robert Llewellyn Bradshaw Scholarship to the St Kitts-Nevis-Anguilla Grammar School, back then the elitist colonial school of the country. I taught at the Basseterre High School, studied in Barbados and in Jamaica, interned as a medical doctor in Trinidad and Tobago, and returned to serve in 1986, to serve the sugar workers, their children, fellow citizens, and residents of St Kitts and Nevis.

I believe I have been blessed. But despite this blessing I remain a proud St Paulian. I remain the son of a sugar cane worker. I remain Douglas, of the village of St Paul's and not one of the West Farm Estate Yard. Douglas of St Paul's village, and not one of Wingfield Estate Yard or of Sir Gilles Estate Yard. I remain Douglas of St Paul's, the son of a sugar cane worker, who laboured for twelve hours per day at the siding in Belmont and who knew no overtime. I was not the son of the manager of the sugar cane estate.

My beginnings, my grounding, and my experiences have all prepared me for the action we debate in parliament today. I believe my noblest cousin before me, my benefactor who was responsible for my preparation for this task, the late Right Excellent Sir Robert Llewellyn Bradshaw, National Hero, is smiling down on us in parliament today. His legacy is being passed on. His vision is no longer a vague and amorphous form for it has taken a solid shape. It is real. The sugar workers are being empowered, and Mr Bradshaw must be a proud man today.

In the past I have asked the citizens of this country to march with me and they marched with me. I now ask my fellow citizens/sugar workers to walk with me. Walk boldly with me to a brighter future. Walk courageously with me and be strong with your chest out and your head held high. I say to you today, do not shed any tears. Do not cry for sugar. Women of Newton Ground, St Paul's, Dieppe Bay, Parsons, Saddlers and Harris, and women of the sugar industry, no cry. King Sugar is dead. Long live the future of St Kitts and Nevis because there is life after sugar. That is why I am not afraid. And so you must not be afraid of our courageous decision as a nation to close the sugar industry. The King is dead, but long live the King!

I think it was Joshua who put it so well about 3,400 years before today, 1,400 years before the birth of Christ, when he recorded the commands he received from the God of the Israelites as they prepared to move to the promised land: 'Have I not commanded you? Be strong and courageous, do not be terrified; do not be discouraged; for the Lord your God will be with you wherever you go!'

The spirit of our African ancestors who survived the terrible journey in the smelly holds of the slave ships across the Atlantic are here among us in this our promised land. God Almighty is also with us. In closing, may He bless us as a nation, may He bless the citizens of this country, may He bless the sugar workers, their children and their families, may He bless you to the end.

May it please you, Madam Speaker.

National Consultation on the Economy 2006

St Kitts Marriott Resort, October 25, 2006

It is my distinct pleasure to address you on the occasion of our annual National Consultation on the Economy as we participate in the 2007 budget planning process. We continue our tradition of consultation with our economic and social partners as we believe that sustained engagement is necessary in order to ensure ownership of the policies which will guide our course as we move forward on our path to sustainable development. Our discussions today will centre on the very important theme 'Empowerment, Transformation – Securing Our Future.' The area of focus that has been selected as the main subject matter for discussion indicates two of the primary goals of the government's medium-term economic strategy – empowerment and transformation. It is our government's firm belief that the transformation of our economy is only possible and sustainable through the empowerment of our people.

We are living in a time when new and innovative responses are required because the challenges which confront us are not like those we have encountered before, particularly in the post-independence era. The environment in which we are now required to operate does not allow us to remain passive and at the same time achieve and sustain economic growth and development. A people-focused approach is therefore necessary at this juncture in our development. I refer specifically to changes in the international environment by which we are now forced to compete directly in foreign and domestic markets due to the removal or reduction of protectionist barriers and differential treatment which we had grown accustomed to over the years. We are currently experiencing the direct impact of the change in the European Union Sugar Protocol which has caused us to exit from sugar manufacturing. Consequently, one of the main items on the agenda today will be the presentation of our proposed medium-term response to the new EU sugar regime. We invite your participation in this very important dialogue on the adaptation strategy.

Other areas which will require the kind of innovative response which I referred to earlier include the preparation of our economy for the OECS Economic Union and the CSME. These important regional initiatives have necessitated a re-look at our tax system in order to ensure that we remain competitive within the region. This issue of competitiveness and the fear of personal loss of jobs have caused many of our citizens to lose sight of many of the benefits and opportunities that can be derived from operating in the considerably larger market that these unions will produce.

Failure to address these issues in the context of a comprehensive programme of tax reform could result in a fall in government's revenues and, consequently, in its ability to provide the services which our citizens expect and demand. In my 2006 budget address I indicated that the issue of tax reform would be further pursued during this year. I am pleased to report that with the assistance of development partners we continue to look at our tax system with a view to ensuring its coverage, simplicity and efficiency. For this reason we have had assistance from CARTAC in introducing the relevant public officials to the basics of the value added tax and we have requested their assistance in carrying out a feasibility study on a more broad-based transaction tax for St Kitts and Nevis. It is also expected that the feasibility study will examine issues related to the need for our Federation to further reduce its import taxes and move to phase four of the Common External Tariff.

We have also had to deal with the effect of our high per capita income that has caused our Federation to be graduated from nearly all sources of concessional finances, which in the past have supported our development. This has in some instances constrained our ability to implement all of the necessary capital investment projects. At the very least, the premature graduation of our Federation from concessional funding has contributed to the higher cost of our development and translated ultimately into higher debt. In addition, shocks in the international markets, which we refer to as globalisation, have the potential of exerting a devastating and lasting toll on our domestic economy. The impact of the September 11th terrorist attacks in the United States is indelibly imprinted on our minds. We are still dealing with the security and financial market requirements which emanated from this.

In addition, it appears that the current impact of high oil prices on our already strained resources will be an issue that we must confront on an on-going basis and for which we are expected to also develop creative solutions. I therefore invite your input and suggestions concerning the very important area of energy conservation.

There is a myriad of other issues that we must continue to address in the short- to medium-term because of their impact on the transformation process and their considerable influence on the rate at which our people are empowered. These include the wide range of issues relating to our strategic response to chronic communicable disease like HIV/AIDS, chronic non-communicable diseases like diabetes and hypertension, and other significant health matters that affect the quality of life of our people; population aging issues which could begin to exert pressures on our health care system, pensions and social security system; the protection of our environment which requires special focus especially as it relates to the sustainability of our tourism product; the need to strengthen the business environment to ensure our competitiveness; land management issues including the continued implementation of a transparent and definitive land management strategy; and the continued focus on the maintenance of law and order which is a vital necessity for the safety of our people and for growth and development. Our policy responses to these challenges will resonate down through the ages and history will reflect whether our decisions on these issues were sound and appropriate. It is not just the government that future generations will judge. It is not just the Chamber of Industry and Commerce or the various church organisations that will be subjected to the scrutiny of future historians. It is our entire generation that will be blamed for compromising the livelihood of our children and succeeding generations if we fail in this most noble enterprise of transformation and empowerment. We must therefore take these consultations very seriously and put aside petty differences with a view towards arriving at concrete solutions to many of the developmental challenges and problems that we face as a nation.

In spite of the scope and severity of the challenges which confront us, we must retain our resolve to maintain sound macro economic policies that will promote a stable economy, characterised by steady and sustainable growth. All of the aspects of sound economic management, including sound fiscal policies, we expect will translate into manageable fiscal deficits and levels of domestic demand that will be consistent with the ability of our economy to deliver. Indeed, we must progressively enhance the capacity of our economy to deliver improved standards of living for our people by fostering a culture of excellence that will enhance the competitiveness of the goods and services produced by our people and our enterprises. These important elements of development are critical to our continued survival and progress as a nation and we simply cannot entertain any compromises in these important areas. I therefore urge that you focus your interventions on these important issues and on any other issues you deem critical to the transformation of our economy and the empowerment of our people.

Our theme for today imposes a requirement for us to make a critical assessment of the approaches which we as a nation will develop as a means of securing our future in the global economy. I believe that we will all agree that operating in the current global economy is challenging, to say the least. We must deal with the erosion of trade preferences, increased competitiveness, changes in the areas of information and telecommunications technology, modification of international linkages in trade, and as I indicated before, dramatic declines in the availability of concessional financing. Indeed, our economy has been significantly affected by the general climate of uncertainty and fluctuations in the global economy and the economy of the United States in particular. Our manufacturing and tourism sectors, which exert significant influence on the level of economic activity in our Federation and on revenue collections, are particularly vulnerable to changes in the global economy.

This vulnerability to global events is exacerbated by our small size which, according to the 'Report on Small States' prepared by the Commonwealth/World Bank Joint Task Force, predisposes us to remoteness, insularity, susceptibility to natural disasters, limited institutional capacity, limited diversification, and a high degree of openness. That same report makes several recommendations for the consideration of small states in adjusting to the changing global regime. I will present several of these recommendations for your consideration. The report suggests that small states should shift their attention to designing and implementing aggressive outward-looking, export-based development strategies. This will require efforts to reposition the economy which will entail an increased effort to exploit or create comparative and competitive advantage in the services sector including tourism, finance, insurance, health, education, internet services, and e-commerce. The report admitted that there would be certain scale disadvantages which would require special attention.

Increasing competitiveness and improving the investment climate with emphasis on securing property rights, simplifying the tax regime, enacting appropriate competition legislation, providing an adequate physical infrastructure, enhancing education and health infrastructure, and improving governance were viewed as an integral part of this outward looking development strategy. In light of our country's recent ranking in the World Bank's 'Doing Business' report, we will need to examine carefully our performance with respect to best practices in certain of these key areas in order to ensure that we continue to be attractive and competitive. My government is committed to the elimination of red tape and the simplification of administrative processes with a view to making it easier to do business in the Federation. However, it is important to note that the world rankings were also based on an assessment of the length of time it takes to procure professional services required for the commencement and operation of business. Hence, any improvement in our rankings will require the effort of both the private and public sectors. We stand ready to collaborate with the private sector in this important endeavour.

The small states report also suggested that small states would do well to harness the considerable potential of their diaspora communities because this will help to provide finances, entrepreneurship, and markets for private sector development. As we are all aware, several developed countries have benefited considerably from the migration of our trained and talented people. This phenomenon that is often referred to as the 'brain drain' has been devastating to many of our economies but we must learn to convert problems into opportunities. We must therefore find creative ways of attracting and utilising the skills, knowledge, and resources acquired by our people who are resident overseas.

We are not deterred or discouraged by our small size. We have proven over and over again that what our country lacks in geographical expanse is compensated for by the immense talents and capabilities of the people that make up our relatively small population. Hence, we continue to cope with every challenge thrown up in the global environment. Indeed, our recent macro-economic outcomes are encouraging with strong growth led by the construction sector. Economic growth has continued to improve since 2003 when we experienced negative growth of –1.3 per cent. In 2004, real economic growth rebounded to 7.3 per cent and recorded another impressive performance in 2005 at an estimated 4.1 per cent. The 2006 real GDP growth rate is projected at around 4 per cent. In 2005, the tourism sector was the lead contributor to economic growth boosted by increased promotion and marketing of the destination and increased airlift and diversification of the tourism product. A deceleration of growth by 0.6 per cent was noted in the manufacturing sector and this was chiefly as a result of the decline in sugar manufacturing. The non-sugar manufacturing sub-sector however increased moderately in 2005 influenced by an improved US economy.

With respect to our fiscal performance, which we are aware is a primary concern of our social and economic partners, I am pleased to report that our fiscal balances have strengthened significantly. For the first time in a decade, the primary fiscal balance moved into surplus in 2005 and it is anticipated that we will outperform this accomplishment in 2006. The primary balance at the end of 2005 was 3.6 per cent while it is projected that the balance at the end of 2006 will stand at 6.8 per cent. You will recall that in my 2006 budget address I gave the commitment of the government to the attainment of a primary surplus of 8 per cent of GDP by 2010. I am pleased to report that we are on our way to achieving this target. This accomplishment is particularly commendable given the severance payments that had to be made to former SSMC workers in 2005 and the pressures from rising oil prices. This is truly a testimony to the efforts at fiscal stabilisation being spearheaded by the Ministry of Finance. Underpinning this performance is a marked improvement in revenue collection as a result of administrative reforms in both the customs and inland revenue departments of the Ministry of Finance. The Customs Modernisation Programme included training in fraud detection and risk profiling as well as the introduction of the TRIPS customs management system. In the inland revenue department, training in auditing and other significant areas has borne great fruit.

Expenditure restraint has also contributed to improved fiscal performance. Wages and salaries as a percentage of GDP have been declining since 2002 and it is projected that this will stand at 9.9 per cent of GDP at the end of 2006, moving from 11.9 per cent of GDP in 2002, a drop of two percentage points. The overall fiscal balance has also been improving as government continues its efforts in prioritising capital projects with the aim of focusing on those which will bring financial and economic returns.

Despite this marked improvement, the fiscal situation remains challenging particularly as the government begins to undertake a number of activities formerly undertaken by SSMC and to service the SSMC debt. On the positive side, however, we are fortunate that for a number of years now we have been spared the ravages of hurricanes that literally tormented us during the latter part of the nineties and the early part of this century. Consequently, we have been able to move forward with our plans to tackle the fiscal imbalances and excessive debt that resulted from the hurricanes. In my 2006 budget address I outlined the measures that were being taken to address the debt situation. I assure you that we are on track with our fiscal stabilisation programme and that the government is still steadfastly implementing its programme to bring our debt to acceptable levels over the medium-term. You will be provided with more details of the work that is on-going in the fiscal report to be delivered later today.

Despite our challenges we continue to see on a daily basis the confidence that investors both domestic and foreign have in the potential of St Kitts and Nevis by virtue of the high level of investment taking place in our country. A number of private sector developments are currently being pursued at varying stages in the development process. These include the Cable Bay Resort, La Vallee Development, Kittitian Heights, development at Port Zante, the Ritz Carlton Hotel, the Marriott Vacation Club, Beaumont Park, and the Auberge project. These developments will result in well over EC$1 billion in investment in our economy over the medium-term. There is clearly no doubt that the growth potential of our economy is strong and that we need to continue to create an environment that is conducive to strong and sustained economic growth and attractive to both foreign and domestic investments. To this end, a large amount of resources have been expended on infrastructure development to foster growth. Partnership with the private sector is crucial to the continued sustainable development of our economy. Therefore, continued dialogue such as today's consultations must remain an integral part of the development process.

I encourage your participation and commitment to the strong vision that we will outline for a transformed economy. We can only build a strong, vibrant economy if all of us take ownership of our various roles and come together to ensure that there is cohesiveness. This sort of unified and mutually agreeable approach is the only way by which we will be able to achieve success. However it is not a popular approach, as it requires commitment, leadership and sacrifice. This will be difficult for those who are insincere, disloyal and who only pay lip-service to nation-building. This task that I have outlined here today is not for the faint-hearted and pessimistic. When we look at the daunting task ahead of us, we must conclude that the only way we will be able to build our nation is if all of us join together, pool our resources and confront the enormous challenges which lie ahead with our collective wisdom. I urge all of us gathered here today to embrace the spirit of our national motto 'Country Above Self,' as we seek to transform our economy to ensure sustained macro-economic stability and improvement in the quality of life for all our citizens.

PetroCaribe Energy Co-Operation Agreement

Fort Pine Depot, Basseterre, December 6, 2007

(PetroCaribe is an oil alliance of a number of Caribbean states with Venezuela to purchase oil on conditions of preferential payment).

This launch is the culmination of a very long journey which began in June 2005 at the first meeting of heads of state and government of the Caribbean on PetroCaribe held in Puerto La Cruz and the second meeting of energy ministers of the Caribbean held in Montego Bay in August 2004.

By October 2005, the then chairman of the Conference of the Caribbean Community requested information on the capability of the PetroCaribe Agreement within the context of the Revised Treaty of Chaguaramas. The PetroCaribe Agreement is mainly two-fold consisting of the Energy Cooperation Agreement together with several bilateral energy documents. The preamble to this revised treaty envisaged the necessity for member states to coordinate their trade policies with third states or groups of third states.

As a government which is part of a larger region, we have considered among other things the geopolitical and speculative factors that cause serious distortions in energy markets and have recognised that the high cost of imported energy is having a debilitating economic impact which threatens to undermine the socio-economic fabric, particularly in oil-deficient Caribbean countries like ours.

It was therefore quite prudent for us to consider PetroCaribe as a catalyst for the introduction of alternative approaches to market access, product distribution and retail, and correction of the various pricing inequities that prevail through creative business and financial arrangements and social programmes.

Recognising the diversity of energy resources among Caribbean countries, the continued importance of petroleum and natural gas as fuels, and the capabilities of different countries, it is inevitable for us to conceive the development of PetroCaribe as a multilateral framework that reflects shared social responsibility among countries through an exchange of experiences that facilitate the transfer of benefits to the less favoured social sectors. This, I am certain, will include provision for the establishment of bilateral, multilateral, and commercial arrangements that will foster investments in exploration and production activities, refining, transportation, storage, distribution, and the retailing of petroleum products.

This PetroCaribe Agreement has been signed and implemented in a number of countries including Antigua and Barbuda, the Bahamas, Belize, Cuba, Dominica, The Dominican Republic, Grenada, Guyana, Jamaica, St Vincent and the Grenadines, St Lucia, St Kitts and Nevis, and Suriname.

The PetroCaribe Energy Cooperation Agreement recognises the need for urgent assistance in the fight of Caribbean societies to cope with the high price of fuel and the need to urgently transform our societies. This agreement therefore complements other strategies to cushion the effects of such high oil prices on the lives of ordinary men and women in this beloved country of ours.

For the past two and a half years, the Ministry of Public Utilities has vigorously pursued the implementation of this initiative. During those thirty months, numerous meetings were held on both sides. One of the greatest drawbacks to the actualisation of this initiative was the absence of adequate storage capacity. We have managed to achieve this milestone today partly because of the offer of acceptance by Sol to provide the necessary storage in the short- and medium-term.

It is, however, important to inform you that the government of Venezuela has made a commitment to construct a storage tank farm across the harbour to my right. The tank farm will consist of:

- two 12,000 bbl HFO tanks (heavy fuel oil);
- one 5,000 bbl jet aviation fuel tank;
- two 5,000 bbl gasoline tanks;
- one 2,140 bbl LPG tank;
- one 5,000 bbl water tank; and
- an additional 12,000 bbl diesel tank at the Needsmust Power Station.

Bids have already been received for this project and by the end of this month the contract will be awarded to commence work.

The local St Kitts company, PDV St Kitts-Nevis Ltd, has already been incorporated and the joint venture company is now in the process of establishing offices in Basseterre. This office will be fully staffed to take charge of the business of fuel importation and distribution logistics. The government has realised that the ever-increasing price of oil on the world market affects the movement of the surcharge and your government being the caring government that it is will continue to monitor the situation with a view to bringing some relief.

The receipt of PetroCaribe fuel however, does not make the fuel any cheaper but provides flexible financing mechanisms and compensations to enable the government to develop a variety of social programmes that will improve the quality of life of our people, particularly the elderly and single-parent families.

Freight expenses arising from these operations will be charged at cost price, thus representing additional savings from this agreement. Furthermore, there is a guaranteed direct trade relationship without intermediaries in the supply process, an arrangement that will assist in generating additional savings, not to mention the construction of storage facilities and terminals that will be owned and controlled by the government upon completion.

The terms of payment for the fuel are flexible and take the form of either:

a. long-term financing

b. short-term financing

c. deferred payments

The payment period will be based on the price per barrel. Should the price per barrel exceed $40, the payment period will be extended to twenty-five years including a two-year grace period specified at 1 per cent interest. These financing terms certainly complement my government's fiscal agenda. In 2007, over $48 million was budgeted for fuel for our power station. Now, with one new additional generator and another expected shortly, the 2008 budget has been increased to $55 million. Government paid over $4 million per month for fuel from its local service provider and if this money is not paid in a timely manner, we can face serious difficulties. The PetroCaribe arrangement has provided that breathing space that will augment government's cash flow. This is indeed a remarkable achievement and I must commend the Ministry of

Public Utilities for its aggressive pursuit in achieving the well-deserved success witnessed here this afternoon.

I have been informed that because of our small storage capacity, thanks to the management of Sol, we at this time will only focus on shipments of diesel for our power station, but as our storage capacity increases, the expanded list of products will include LPG, gasoline, aviation fuel, etc. It is hoped that the effects of this small beginning here today will be felt throughout the Federation and that in the years to come, PetroCaribe fuel will be an integral part of the landscape finding its way into every sector of our society.

St Kitts and Nevis uses huge quantities of diesel in its generating division and the overall operation of projects. The increasing cost of crude oil on the world market and the gradual erosion of our revenue-generating bases resulting from globalisation and trade liberalisation have forced small islands like St Kitts and Nevis to take full advantage of treaties, conventions, and protocols aimed at fostering conditions to improve the quality of life of our people.

The development agenda of my government is rife with capital projects, all of which will require a reliable and sustained power supply which we must seek to produce in an efficient and cost-effective manner. The cargo that is now being delivered by Ocean Breeze sitting off Fort Pine across from my right will have a multiplier effect and provide the appropriate catalyst to drive infrastructural development and create opportunities for social advancement within our communities. You have heard the minister indicate that the generation division uses 575 barrels of diesel per day, which is 17,250 per month. This has increased following the commissioning of the new 4MW generator and will increase further following the receipt and commissioning of the second new generator to be delivered within three weeks time.

My government is fully aware that this arrangement is but a temporary facility because our dependency on small diesel generating sets will continue to pose serious challenges in this volatile international oil market. Consequently, my government has taken concrete steps to find long-term sustainable solutions to our dependency on fossil fuel

Following the general elections of 2004, my government established an Energy Task Force under the able leadership of the minister of state in the Ministry of Finance, Sustainable Development, Information and Technology. I am pleased to report that the task force is pursuing its mandate and just three weeks ago updated the cabinet on its work with the assistance of the OAS and other consultants. To date the government has received numerous proposals for the development of renewable energy including biomass, wind, ethanol, solar, and geothermal. The task force is engaged in crafting an energy policy with the assistance of OAS for the consideration of cabinet.

And so, this event must be seen in the context of your government responding to what is a complex challenge as the price per barrel of oil continues to increase. I take this opportunity to call on all households to play their part in conserving energy at the household level.

In conclusion, I wish to thank all who have helped to bring this project to the point of receiving our first shipment of diesel. I extend solidarity and support to the government and people of the Bolivarian Republic of Venezuela for their zeal, commitment, and forthrightness in assisting the government and people of St Kitts in this tangible way.

Long live the Bolivarian Republic of Venezuela!

Long live the people of the Bolivarian Republic of Venezuela!!

Long live President Hugo Chavez!!!

SKIPA LAUNCH (ST KITTS INVESTMENT PROMOTION AGENCY)

St Kitts Marriott Resort, December 11, 2007

I am indeed very honoured and I would venture to say relieved to be able to launch the St Kitts Investment Promotion Agency that you have been hearing so much about recently. Over the last few years we have heard a great deal said about the development of a 'One Stop Shop' and as more persons both locally and from abroad attempt to establish businesses here in St Kitts, the need for an agency such as this one became more and more apparent. Persons trying to establish a business have in the past been referred from one department to another only to be referred back to the first department when they are trying to find out information about setting up a business or applying for incentives. However, with the launch of this new IPA, to be more familiarly referred to as SKIPA, I feel confident that those days are now behind us.

The potential impact that SKIPA can have on the economy and people of St Kitts is immeasurable. The agency with its four broad areas of responsibility for investment facilitation, investment promotion, policy advocacy, and image-building will enhance the investment climate here in St Kitts.

The Agency's role in investment facilitation which so many persons have cried out for will improve initially with

- dissemination of information to investors about government processes and concessions that are available for certain types of projects;

- streamlining of procedures by having one agency act as liaison between the investor and the various government departments involved in the processing of applications submitted by investors;

and eventually after the second phase of the development of the IPA has been completed,

- expediting the processing of some basic applications as the agency will have a more involved role in concessions management and the processing of some licences.

There will still be a few matters that the agency will have to continue to rely on the substantive government departments to deal with, but the overall efficiency in processing applications will be greatly improved.

Another great benefit that SKIPA brings with it is its mandate to deal with both local and foreign investors. For too long locals have complained that foreign investors are given preferred treatment when they are trying to establish a business here in St Kitts. Although we may argue that this could be a misperception, the very fact that there are currently multiple points within government that local investors may attempt to initiate an inquiry or application to start a business removes the element of control and consistency in dealing with these persons and the information that they may receive. Therefore this new Investment Promotion Agency which will now be the single point of entry for all investors, both local and foreign, should ensure that any investor trying to establish a business here is accorded the same treatment and provided with the same information.

Upon completion of the required legislative reform and further public-private sector consultation during the first half of next year, the IPA will be responsible for managing concessions and some licence applications for investors as mentioned earlier. There will be a transparent piece of legislation that clearly outlines what an investor is entitled to once the investment meets certain criteria. Hence, there will be a level playing field for all investors and concessions will be managed by a board comprised not only of public sector representatives but private sector persons as well. A level playing field is not a strange concept for St Kitts because we ask for it on a regular basis from the larger and more powerful countries in the global community in their dealings with us and other small developing countries, particularly in relation to trade in services. Countries like St Kitts with scarce natural resources can only rely on the services that can be offered by our people who are in reality our most valuable resource.

One of the most important points that I would like to highlight is that the board of the IPA will be comprised of representatives of key government ministries as well as private sector organisations and groupings. This in itself is a major shift in policy with respect to dealing with investment because the private sector will now be actively and integrally involved in the investment promotion and facilitation process here in St Kitts. This is indeed a very progressive move that can only serve to improve communication and the overall partnership between the government and the private sector. With the board of the IPA being not only a public and private sector partnership, but also apolitical, there can be no allegations of interference in the investment approval processes. Further, with the severe penalties outlined in the IPA Act to deal with board members who do not disclose conflicts of interest, the professionalism and objectivity of the IPA board members should be unquestionable.

The agency's role in investment promotion is also an extremely critical development. No longer will the various government ministries be responsible for promoting their own strategic sectors in isolation. The St Kitts Investment Promotion Agency will be conducting coordinated and targeted marketing to attract investors to develop industries or businesses in sectors that the government has identified as sustainable and viable for the country to be engaged in. With this properly planned and coordinated approach, investors that are found to be able to add value to the development of our country will be researched and targeted so that presentations can be made to them about the opportunities available here in St Kitts. Further, this coordinated approach to promotion will allow the agency to capitalise on any overlap or linkages that exist between various sectors to enable more effective and efficient marketing strategies to be adopted.

The IPA will also have an important role in developing and improving the overall image of St Kitts, not only locally but internationally as well. Therefore, in addition to actually disseminating positive information about investment opportunities in St Kitts, the agency will also be responsible for directly and indirectly spreading the word that the ease of doing business in St Kitts has dramatically improved and continues to be enhanced through constant dialogue and partnerships between the public and private sector. The other important indirect way for the IPA to relay positive information about St Kitts is by this agency ensuring that persons who have established businesses in St Kitts have only positive experiences to share with other potential investors.

Finally, all of the work to be done by the IPA centres around one essential purpose, which is to empower our own people by providing the environment for them to establish their own businesses and by promoting linkages that can arise between large investments that come to the island and the spin-off opportunities that can emerge as a result. However, we must recognise that not all persons are cut out to be entrepreneurs, but have a lot of skill, experience, and intelligence to offer to businesses that develop on the island. The IPA will not only be actively involved in ensuring that businesses that are successfully established here continue to have facilitation services available to them but the agency will be involved in surveying the needs of these businesses and ensuring that our local labour force is suitably trained and prepared to take up their rightful places at all levels within these established enterprises.

Every single person in St Kitts will be impacted in some way by this new Investment Promotion Agency and it is my sincere hope that this day, December 11, 2007, will go down in our history books as one of the major milestones reached by this country and will be celebrated in years to come as a major positive turning point for the investment climate and all the people of St Kitts.

Citizenship By Investment (CBI) Conference
Henley and Partners and HSBC
Hong Kong, November 19, 2008

It is my pleasure to share with you some of the broad policy considerations that have helped to shape and guide the development of the St Kitts and Nevis Citizenship By Investment (CBI) programme, which was established in 1984 as the first such programme anywhere in the world, and has grown into one of the most reputable and well-regulated global citizenship by investment programmes. My country has always suffered from the problem of emigration of our young, talented, and educated persons to larger, more developed countries where they are often lured by more lucrative jobs or other opportunities.

The brain drain that results from this and its impact on our dynamic young workforce has left us with no alternative but to develop policies and programmes to attract persons to our shores who are willing and able to contribute meaningfully to the development of our economy and our country. It is in this context that we welcome people from around the world to share in our development and to contribute to the progress of our people through our Citizenship By Investment programme.

Like many developing and developed countries around the world, St Kitts and Nevis provides the opportunity for persons to make a significant investment in our country and to qualify for citizenship on the basis of such investment and other critical criteria relating primarily to character and reputation. In St Kitts and Nevis, the minimum investment that enables a person to apply for citizenship is US$350,000 in approved real estate or a contribution of at least $200,000 to our Sugar Industry Diversification Foundation (SIDF), which has been playing a critical role in the transformation of our economy from a sugar monoculture to a modern, dynamic, service-oriented economy and which has been bringing much needed relief to the displaced sugar workers who were pushed out of their jobs when our sugar industry succumbed to the forces of globalisation and trade liberalisation.

Indeed, some 10 per cent of the workforce of the country were forced to join the ranks of the unemployed in 2005 when our sugar industry collapsed and many of the protections our sugar enjoyed in European markets were removed in response to pressure from the World Trade Organisation (WTO) to free-up global markets for agricultural produce. Ironically, notwithstanding the WTO, agricultural producers in developed countries continue to enjoy a considerable degree of protection and subsidisation.

Fortunately, my government immediately implemented a comprehensive plan to transform our economy and to mitigate the impact of this dramatic loss of export earnings. In particular, notwithstanding the loss of the sugar industry that dominated the economic landscape in St Kitts and Nevis for some four hundred years, our economy was not pushed into recession. It has continued to grow and this year, just three years after the closure of the industry, it is now estimated that our unemployment rate has dropped from over 16 per cent in 2005 to about 7 per cent. Our programme of economic transformation was comprehensive and extensive and it involved numerous elements including the Citizenship By Investment programme which has provided liquidity to our banking system, promoted investment in hotel, villa and condominium projects that were deemed approved projects for the purposes of citizenship by investment, and facilitated a number of projects in environmental protection and business development through the activities of SIDF.

Foreign direct investment has been an important element of our strategy for economic transformation and growth. Indeed, foreign investors have taken full advantage of our friendly investment climate which includes the absence of personal income tax and capital gains tax; the absence of death and inheritance taxes; generous corporate tax holidays including exemptions from corporation taxes and from border taxes in respect of investments in key sectors of the economy; and legislative provisions for a range of corporate and business vehicles including trusts, foundations, and exempt companies to facilitate effective international tax planning.

Our efforts in respect of investment promotion have borne much fruit. Just before I left home to attend this conference here in Hong Kong, I participated in a ground-breaking ceremony to mark the commencement of construction work in respect of a Tom Fazio golf course as the first element of a major hotel resort project which will include a marina village to accommodate luxury yachts, a resort community with hundreds of luxury villas and residential units, and two five-star hotels including a Mandarin Hotel which is in the advanced planning stage and should be under construction by the middle of next year. Moreover, just after I return I will be participating in a signing ceremony with the Ritz Carlton in respect of a major resort project which is expected to break ground during the course of next year. And here attending this conference are the chairman and sales director of the Kittitian Hill Resort which is an approved project for our Citizenship By Investment programme.

What is particularly striking about these developments is that they are taking place in the midst of a fearsome global recession that has dried up credit flows and has undermined personal wealth as asset values plunge in capital markets all over the globe. Indeed, developers of the Mandarin Hotel have been pleasantly surprised at the level of sales of their villa plots with prices averaging well over US$1 million. Moreover, they have already started to record sales in respect of marina slips although work in respect of the marina village is not expected to start until next year. I believe that these investors have learned an important secret. That is, in these difficult and perilous times, an investment in St Kitts and Nevis is perhaps the best way to safeguard your assets.

I should emphasise, however, that an investment in an approved project in St Kitts and Nevis does not guarantee citizenship. It only qualifies a person to apply for citizenship. All applicants must go through an extensive background check which is carried out on behalf of the government by an independent third-party agency. They must also undergo appropriate medical examinations by their physicians and they must declare that they have not been involved in any criminal activities, and that their investment funds were not derived from any criminal activities. If any of these declarations turns out to be false at any time, then the citizenship certificate may be revoked. Of course, the entire process is transparent and fair and the decision to issue the citizenship certificate is not arbitrary. Any person meeting all of the requirements will usually obtain citizenship within a period of three months.

The marketing of the programme is also very well regulated. In particular, authorised persons in St Kitts and Nevis involved in the programme are required to seek approval for promotional materials making references to our Citizenship By Investment programme. In addition, we have engaged the international firm, Henley and Partners, to assist in the development of the SIDF component of the programme and to create greater awareness of the entire programme internationally.

These measures may seem somewhat strict to some of you who are more familiar with economic citizenship programmes in large first-world countries where such rigorous background checks are quite often not part of the procedure to obtain citizenship. However, because of the size and vulnerability of a country as small as ours, every precaution is necessary.

Notwithstanding our extensive screening procedures, we are quite open to immigration of persons who are skilled or who can contribute meaningfully to the development of our Federation. Indeed, St Kitts and Nevis is a party to the Caribbean Community Treaty which provides for the progressive removal of restrictions to the free movement of people throughout the Caribbean. This means that persons who become citizens of St Kitts and Nevis will, over time, find it possible to move and work freely around the Caribbean and to establish businesses in other Caribbean countries with the same rights and privileges as nationals of such countries. Only last week my government signed a new visa waiver agreement with the EU that will allow our citizens to travel freely to the agreed European countries without visa restrictions. This agreement becomes operational within the first and second quarters of next year.

We are persuaded that the world is now a village and the days when distance and oceans separated countries and people are now behind us. We must be prepared to welcome the world to our shores as investors, visitors, residents, and citizens. Of course, as a democratic nation governed by rules, we expect that such rules will be upheld at all times and that the history, culture, and concerns of our citizens will always be respected.

I close by personally inviting each of you to visit our Federation and experience paradise for yourself. You will find that in St Kitts and Nevis you can avail yourself of many investment opportunities and at the same time enjoy yourselves by beholding our breathtaking scenic vistas, experiencing our rich history and culture, and bathing in the warmth of Kittitian and Nevisian hospitality.

POVERTY ASSESSMENT STUDY NATIONAL CONSULTATION

St Kitts Marriott Resort, April 24, 2009

I stand before you today with great pride and a sense of accomplishment as the results of the 2007/2008 Country Poverty Assessment (CPA) are presented to the public in the spirit of partnership and continuous dialogue.

On behalf of the government of St Kitts and Nevis I would like to express appreciation to the Caribbean Development Bank for their very strong support for our development agenda. CDB deserves commendation for providing the financial and technical resources for the conduct of such a study for a second time. Appreciation is also extended to the members of the national assessment teams on both islands for coordinating the activities of the Country Poverty Assessment. The findings of this assessment have provided evidence of the accomplishments that have been made by our people in the fight towards the alleviation of poverty, and dare I say, the eventual eradication of poverty in our Federation. It also highlights the work that remains in order to realise our goals of continuous improvement of the living standards of every Kittitian and Nevisian and to further secure our position among the countries of the world with a high rate of human development.

Poverty reduction has been identified as a core development issue, not only in St Kitts and Nevis, but in all countries worldwide. This is evidenced by the inclusion of the eradication of extreme poverty and hunger within the Millennium Development Goals (MDGs) agreed upon in September 2000 at the United Nations Millennium Summit. Well in advance of the official establishment of the MDGs, St Kitts and Nevis has long considered the fight against poverty a top priority developmental challenge. Our own experience here in the Federation has proven that the subject of poverty is multi-faceted requiring a holistic approach to the problem. Consequently, the MDGs have been a part of government's overall agenda in the areas of education, health, and social development over the past few decades. Various initiatives or 'safety nets' have been established, as well as the reorganisation and development of institutional structures to ease the economic and financial burdens of our people and to provide new opportunities for the most vulnerable persons in our society.

Our Federation became a pioneer over four decades ago with the provision of free universal primary and secondary education. However, in order to ensure that all persons are able to achieve their potential and provide for themselves and their families, we have re-assessed and improved the services to include the widespread provision of preschool programmes and the upgrade and expansion of secondary and tertiary level education programmes which include technical/vocational training and second-chance opportunities. These elements are considered critical to the fight against poverty as they provide options for child care which enable parents, particularly our single mothers, to secure employment as well as the opportunity for all our citizens to complete or improve their level of certification making them labour market-ready.

Acknowledging that hunger is a barrier to learning, the School Meals Programme, which was initially provided on a limited scale, has been expanded to all primary schools and most secondary schools in St Kitts. School uniforms are provided to our students based on need, overseas examinations are provided free of cost to students enrolled in the secondary schools, and access to books is provided through the Student Education and Learning Fund (SELF). The Youth Empowerment through Skills (YES) programme, launched on February 13, 2009, is another initiative which focuses on skills development, employment opportunities, and career and social development through work experience and job placement. This innovative programme specifically targets young people who lack the requisite skills and/or wish to become certified in their area of proficiency. At the heart of this programme is government's desire to stamp out poverty, inequality, and social exclusion.

Living conditions are also considered in the context of accessibility to quality health care. The Federation's health policy continues to be focused towards ensuring that the population has adequate access to quality health care services at an affordable cost. The health status of the citizens of St Kitts and Nevis has improved considerably which is evidenced by a reduction in infectious and communicable diseases and those that are caused by nutritional deficiency. It has been determined that the major health challenge for our Federation is the increased incidences of chronic lifestyle diseases and HIV/AIDS. In order to combat the ravages of these diseases, the government has ensured that primary health care is provided free of cost to vulnerable groups and has undertaken measures to mitigate the cost of secondary care in order to make services and medication affordable. In 2000, a Health Promotion Unit was established within the Department of Health in order to educate the public regarding preventative and managed care, and to provide counselling services to promote positive mental well-being. These services are brought to communities through the media and the various health centres. A men's health campaign will also be undertaken as the Department of Health has found that women tend to be more proactive regarding their health with the men remaining more focused on work. This campaign will be the beginning of an initiative to provide extended hours at health centres thus making the services more readily available at a time that is more convenient for those who work from 8:00 a.m. to 4:00 p.m. and find it difficult to obtain leave during the normal work day.

Research has shown that poor housing conditions, which are usually found among individuals in the lower socio-economic group, is linked to incidences of physical and mental distress. Recognising the need for quality housing, the government embarked on an ambitious housing initiative in 1996 which has provided houses for low income families. The housing programme, spearheaded by the National Housing Corporation, continues to provide adequate shelter for hundreds of families across the island of St Kitts. This has not only totally changed the landscape of the island but has facilitated higher levels of home ownership and has instilled a sense of accomplishment and empowerment among our citizens.

These are only a few of government's initiatives which have transformed the lives of our people from ones consumed by deprivation and malaise. Over the past decade these initiatives have proven to be beneficial as illustrated by the results of the 2007/2008 Country Poverty Assessment. St Kitts was found to have a poverty rate of 23.7 per cent, a reduction of almost 7 percentage points from the 30.5 per cent recorded in the 1999/2000 assessment. The indigence level plummeted by almost 10 percentage points during the period to 1.4 per cent. Nevis experienced an even greater reduction in the incidence of poverty with a rate of 15.9 per cent a significant decline of 16 percentage points while the indigent population was recorded at zero, a substantial drop from the 17 per cent recorded in the survey of 1999/2000. Indeed, this is a laudable performance. Permit me to remind you that all this was accomplished in spite of the fact that the country was facing the unprecedented challenge of responding to the closure of the over three hundred-year-old sugar industry in St Kitts. Imagine the additional gains we would have accomplished in the absence of such a major localised challenge.

As leader of this proud nation, I give you today my government's and my own commitment that even though we are encouraged by these results, we will not become complacent. As a Small Island Developing State (SIDS) with an open economy, we are vulnerable to the impacts of external shocks, the most recent being the global economic and financial crisis. We are also susceptible to internal upheaval such as the recent upsurge in violence and crime. These factors and others could derail the achievements that have been made and significantly reduce future prospects for development as we work to transform the economy from one dominated by mono-crop cultivation to one that is primarily service-oriented and anchored in tourism, agriculture, ITC, financial services, and light manufacturing. In the midst of all the global turmoil, my government will not be deterred. Instead, we will continue to seek out every opportunity that lays within these challenges. We recognise the role that government can play in helping to build social cohesion. Therefore we are pursuing a national transformation agenda which is rooted in sound macro-economic policies and improved public financial management so that our systems can become more fair and progressive.

While some persons share in the philosophy and belief that a person should, as President Obama puts it, 'Pull yourself up by your own bootstraps, even if you don't have boots … ,' the government of St Kitts and Nevis has never and will never ascribe to that view. We will continue to institutionalise initiatives geared towards improving the living conditions of the masses while mitigating anything that threatens to spread and deepen poverty in the Federation. We will endeavour to promote the integration and participation of all citizens in the social and economic life of St Kitts and Nevis. There is no doubt that our policies on education, health, and social protection are substantial. However, we must find ways to make sure that these policies are implemented so that they have a much greater impact on the welfare of the most vulnerable persons in our communities. One sobering fact, that is central to our future success, is that the challenges that lay ahead will not be solved solely by government programmes, but by the willingness of the private sector and civil society to truly partner with the government and the willingness of our people to capitalise on every opportunity made available to them. The road ahead will not be easy and sacrifices may be required as a nation and at the individual level. As we listen and make recommendations, let us set our goals in the context of our economic and social circumstances.

NATIONAL CONSULTATION ON THE ECONOMY 2009
Youth Development at the Core of our National Priorities
St Kitts Marriott Resort, September 10, 2009

I am always delighted to participate in the annual national consultation exercise that has grown from strength to strength over the years and continues to provide a most meaningful forum for discussion and exchange of views on the economy among the government and its partners in development. I expect that this year's theme, 'Youth Development at the core of our National Priorities,' will generate considerable interest and debate because of the critical importance of youth development issues to the progress of our nation. Indeed, I contend that if we can successfully resolve all of the issues affecting our young people, we will significantly quicken our strides along the path of social and economic development.

The issue of youth development is a cross-cutting issue that affects and is affected by activities in all sectors of our economy. Indeed, much of government's activity in stimulating the economy during this challenging period of global economic malaise takes full cognisance of the impact of sluggish or negative growth rates on young people. We are keenly aware that young people all over the face of the globe carry a disproportionate share of the burden of unemployment. In periods of economic downturn, they leave school in large numbers to find that the labour market is not particularly welcoming and they must wait for extended periods before they find jobs. In addition, in nearly all countries of the world, young people represent a high percentage of the employees who lose their jobs during an economic downturn or who are forced to reduce their hours of work and their weekly wages as employers restructure their operations and struggle to survive.

My government has therefore acted swiftly and definitively to combat the impact of the global recession on our economy and all the evidence suggests that, notwithstanding some reduction in economic activity and some layoffs, to date we have been spared the brunt of the global economic recession. We know that the sector that is most vulnerable to the economic fallout of the global crisis is the tourism sector. Hence, we quickly approved packages of concessions for small hoteliers and for stand-alone restaurants that permits them to import food and wine and some items of equipment and furniture free of duty. We also extended concessions to small start-up businesses and many of our entrepreneurs, including young people, continue to benefit week after week from this important initiative to the benefit of the economy as a whole. Moreover, we have been monitoring the economy with a view to intervening wherever and whenever necessary to ensure that we remain on track to the attainment of our goal of enhanced economic activity, job creation, and increased incomes.

We have also taken a keen interest in the major investment projects that contribute to national growth, and we believe that our package of assistance and concessions has helped tremendously in facilitating the continuation of work or the advancement of plans in respect of major investments at Christophe Harbour, Cockleshell Bay, Ocean's Edge Resort, Port Zante, Silver Reef, and the Marriott development at the site of the former Angelus Hotel. We recognise that construction is a leading contributor to growth and we have therefore extended our assistance to contractors with a view to promoting construction activity in all sectors including the housing sector, the business sector, and the commercial real estate sector.

Of course, we continue to tackle the specific problems of our young people directly and frontally. Our special land initiative has catered specifically to first-time landowners, the vast majority of whom are our young people. We are determined that they will not carry the label of landlessness that our forefathers carried. We also expect that they will put the land to good use and use it as security for the loans they require to build homes, start businesses, and pursue educational opportunities. Indeed, we are convinced that the effective use of the land provided to our people under the special land initiative will contribute to growth, employment, and overall economic development in our Federation for many decades to come.

The government has also committed huge sums towards the education of our young people. Earlier this month we committed to pay The University of the West Indies some $6.2 million in respect of the annual economic cost of our students studying there. In addition, the Development Bank of St Kitts and Nevis continues to provide hundreds of student loans to our young people without regard to their political affiliation.

The recently constructed Saddlers School will play an important role in the implementation of strategic plans for educating our young people. In particular, it will offer students the opportunity to prepare themselves even more effectively for the workforce by acquiring a range of practical skills even as they also pursue various academic subjects. Moreover, the school will be available for the education of adults after the usual school hours and will provide the opportunity for inter-generational interaction and for the transmission and perpetuation of the values that have served our communities so well over the years.

But we understand that the needs of our young people are immediate, especially in the context of the global recession. We therefore introduced the very progressive YES programme that has trained or provided attachments to over one thousand students and has helped to prepare them to take up more secure positions in the workforce. We are convinced that as we create new opportunities for our young people to acquire skills and earn decent incomes for themselves, the lure of criminal activity will lose much of its appeal.

The government understands that youth crime and gang violence is an issue that we must continue to address in a definitive way. Of course, we understand that the problems we face in this regard are similar to the problems encountered by many Caribbean countries. I therefore took the lead in organising a Regional Summit on Youth Crime and Gang Violence during which countries from around the region as well as our international partners shared experiences and developed ideas for dealing with this issue. Even as we concretise many of these ideas and include them in our action plans, we at the same time continue to increase the frequency and coverage of patrols, step up the activities of the anti-gun and strike force units, and significantly enhance our overall law enforcement capability. But, ultimately, we must attack the root cause of youth crime if we are to build a peaceful, secure, and harmonious society. It is clear that the family unit, which was traditionally the primary instrument of social control in our communities, has undergone significant changes, mainly as a result of teenage pregnancies, the holding of multiple jobs by young parents, and the dismantling of the extended family and the consequent marginalisation of the role of grandparents in bringing up children. Some of these changes are not reversible.

Consequently, we must refashion other existing institutions to more effectively cater to the needs of our young people in our changing society. In particular, our churches can no longer wait for the family to send the children to Sunday School. They must expand their outreach programmes and play more proactive roles in bringing them to Sunday School and exposing them to appropriate values. Our children in school must be provided moral education and when they leave school for any reason whatsoever they must be monitored and provided a helping and guiding hand in times of need or difficulty.

In this regard, we must give serious consideration to proposals for the establishment of an internship or orientation programme aimed at preparing our young people for the workplace and for playing more meaningful and constructive roles in our society. Our youth at risk must be identified long before they get into trouble and they must be exposed to special training to bring them from the fringes of society. In addition, all of our social and economic programmes must be properly tailored to ensure that our young people are given reasonable and fair access to the fruit of our continuing economic development, and that they are empowered to attain decent standards of living for themselves and make meaningful contributions to society.

We must also refrain from stereotyping all our young people on the basis of the criminal activity of a misguided minority of young people. The achievements of many of our young people are substantial. We must therefore encourage the top performers among our young people and hold them up as examples to the others. I was particularly pleased by some of the stunning performances of our students in the recently held CXC examinations. As a nation, we are truly proud of these students. We are also proud of our debating team that earlier this year won the Leeward Island Debating Championship. We are proud of our netball team that won the OECS Under-23 Netball Championship. We are proud of our athletics relay team that participated in the Central American and Caribbean Champions Games and brought home gold.

So, even as we spend time during these consultations deliberating on the problems of our young people, let us also reflect on their achievements and seek to devise ways of giving each and every young person the opportunity to realise his or her fullest potential. This is the surest way of accelerating our march to that peaceful, harmonious, and progressive society that we are building here in St Kitts and Nevis.

Much has been happening over the past months, locally, regionally and internationally, which I am sure you will want me to touch on tonight. I am reminded that it was just over five months ago that my Labour Party successfully contested the January federal election. I believe that the resounding vote of confidence that we received from the people of St Kitts and Nevis at that time is testimony to my government's track record of a balanced and inclusive approach to pursuing development initiatives while keeping a close focus on protecting the more vulnerable in our society.

I believe, also, that the recent election results represented a vote of confidence in my government's people empowerment programmes, including those directly related to facilitating private enterprise and wealth creation. I also believe that the voters of this country were aware of how hard my government has worked, and continues to work, to facilitate appropriate private investment in our country, and to sustain a healthy investment climate in general.

Tonight, therefore, I intend to focus on a few important elements pertinent to the country's socio-economic well-being, and I promise to be as brief as I can.

ECONOMIC OVERVIEW

Indeed, the global economic and financial crisis has severely impacted the economy of St Kitts and Nevis as well as the other member states of the Eastern Caribbean Currency Union (ECCU). The crisis has resulted in a severe decline in tourist arrivals, remittances, construction, and related foreign direct investments. The Federation was especially hard hit by the closure of the Four Seasons Resort in October 2008 after the passage of Hurricane Omar. These factors resulted in a contraction of 9.6 per cent of real output in 2009. The construction sector declined by an estimated

25 per cent due to the downturn in private sector development projects as demand fell off for long-term investments. Activity in the tourism sector also contracted by 20 per cent as increased international airfares and high unemployment in our major source markets influenced the industry. It should be noted, however, that the cruise industry remained vibrant and actually expanded by 13.5 per cent as the industry continued to benefit from negotiations with cruise lines and strategic marketing campaigns by the tourism authority.

The way forward points to the opportunity for St Kitts and Nevis to refine its mode of doing business, to improve levels of efficiency and productivity throughout the public and private sectors, and to set new standards in all areas of economic activity.

FISCAL MATTERS

The government has been experiencing a decrease in its revenues and, as such, has only limited fiscal space to respond to the crisis. Recognising that more space had to be created so that assistance could be given where needed, the government has exercised further fiscal restraint and prioritised expenditure to those areas that will spur growth. As is well known, we have provided a stimulus package to small hotels, stand-alone restaurants and small and medium enterprises through the provision of tax and duty concessions. The unemployed youth in the Federation were also targeted through the Youth Empowerment through Skills (YES) programme. All of these elements, when taken together, will have positive impact in the short- and medium-terms.

Recognising that these are difficult times throughout the world, government has had to implement coping measures to prepare the country for the challenges ahead. These measures include streamlining discretionary tax exemptions, introducing a value-added tax, improving the regulation of duty-free stores, containing expenditure on goods and services, and reprioritising capital expenditure. A wage and hiring freeze will also be implemented. This will form part of government's wider public sector reform that is aimed at increasing productivity while at the same time contributing to government's efforts at reducing expenditure. The collection of outstanding amounts owed to government is also a priority. Our high level of debt remains an issue and therefore the debt strategy that was formulated in 2009 will be further elaborated and implemented in 2010.

Obviously, hard decisions have had to be made in order to navigate the crisis but be assured that the most vulnerable in our society will be protected, that the circumstances present opportunities to restructure and create a new and productive economic environment.

INVESTMENT

As a small island developing state, it is important that we deal with our challenges while staying committed to the building of a modern country and society and to encourage the quickest possible return to economic growth.

One of the fall-outs of the prevailing global situation is the reduction of investment flows into the Federation. This emphasises the need to generate further domestic savings but at the same time there is still the need for foreign investment inflows. Recently I visited Canada and Europe on a mission to stimulate investment interest in St Kitts and Nevis. Over the years we have built up an infrastructure that is conducive to investment and that is why there is great importance in attracting new investment from local and foreign sources alike. I strongly encourage our private sector companies to engage in innovative and positive ways to invest in the economy of our country. Doing so will certainly help stimulate our economy into the medium-term. This is a time to be bold and to lay the groundwork in anticipation of the recovery of the global economy.

My government has been paying particular attention to investment facilitation and promotion and we intended to improve the process significantly by creating the St Kitts Investment Promotion Agency. In a relatively short space of time this agency has demonstrated substantial effectiveness. Since its inception, SKIPA has performed extremely well in the area of investment facilitation, receiving 242 inquiries for investment projects in 2009 alone.

SKIPA has facilitated the establishment of a number of new local businesses including Spice Mill, Sky Safari, and the MV Sea Surfer. The agency has also facilitated the expansion and modernisation of a number of local businesses through initiatives such as the Small Hotels Incentive Package which allows hotels to refurbish 20 per cent of their facility duty-free, annually, over a five-year period. In the meantime, a number of large investment projects, both local and foreign, are currently being processed by the agency and these are expected to have a positive impact on the economy of our Federation. Indeed, SKIPA has worked assiduously over the last year to strengthen its facilitation services with an aim to reducing the processing time of applications and this has been quite satisfactory. SKIPA is an agency that is evolving and will, in time, provide level three services to the tremendous benefit of our country.

TOURISM

Global economic and financial conditions have resulted in substantial challenges in our tourism industry, especially in terms of hotel occupancy, visitor expenditure, investment, and job sustainability. While it is a time for careful management of our various enterprises and resources, it can be considered, as I said before, a time to reorganise and strategise for the future.

It is strongly believed that the recovery of the world economies will bring a more discerning traveller who, among other things, wants greater value for money spent. That is to be expected. It is important for us to pay attention to the establishment of quality standards in various areas of the industry, maintain and improve our authenticity as a Caribbean destination, address the issue of attitudes toward tourism, improve the aesthetics of communities on the island, address environmental challenges, and maximise proficiency and productivity at every level.

There is little doubt that tourism will remain for the foreseeable future an essential tool for addressing poverty alleviation through opportunities for entrepreneurship. It provides an avenue by which many of our people can be empowered in ways that lead to improvements in their quality of life. As stakeholders in this industry, we must ensure that we employ every possible means within our resources to market our product and we must be prepared to use some non-traditional methods to reach potential clients. Technology must play a greater role in our communications and interactivity is critical in reaching a broad spectrum of potential travellers. I wish to emphasise that securing our tourism industry has much to do about building strong public and private sector partnerships that are fundamental for achieving success in the future.

CRIME AND SECURITY

Most of our efforts to develop a sustainable economy will be very limited if our citizens, residents, and business community feel insecure. Throughout the Caribbean there has been an increase in the level of crime,

St Kitts and Nevis being no exception. All of us desire, need and want a country in which we can live and do business and achieve personal and national aspirations. I wish to affirm that government is addressing the crime situation and that it is a high priority on our national agenda. It is with this in mind that we approached and secured over €3.8 million in funding from the European Union to tackle crime-fighting issues on several indentified fronts. They include but are not limited to the following:

1. Introducing the use of effective international best practices and appropriate technologies to improve the prevention, reduction, and detection of crimes;

2. Upgrading the curriculum of the police training school;

3. Improving recruitment practices and enhancing staffing policies and working conditions for the police in order to attract more graduates into the service;

4. Providing training at regional and international institutions in the areas of forensic sciences, criminology, management, and administration;

5. Rehabilitating, upgrading, and refurbishing police stations, the police training school, and the coastguard facilities;

6. Formulating an inter-ministerial approach to crime-fighting through collaboration among ministries such as Education, Youth, Justice and Legal Affairs, and Social and Community Development, among others.

Our new approach to law and order will involve strengthening the management framework of the various units that are mandated to deliver on programmes that are action-oriented with a results-based approach. The Ministry of National Security has proposed, after consultations with INTERPOL, the restructuring of the intelligence unit that has been given a revised mandate to drive the operations, crime detection, and information-gathering initiatives of the Police Force.

The introduction of a homicide unit, another new initiative for the Police Force, takes into consideration the need for focussed attention on improved crime detection and conviction rates. With the increased emphasis on the use of forensics in crime detection, the establishment of a forensic lab in the sub-region will allow for increased access by police forces in the smaller islands of the Eastern Caribbean to the technology and will enhance their crime detection capabilities. The Police Force will require a dedicated unit with the expertise to ensure an effective outcome.

St Kitts and Nevis and other members of the Caribbean Community will see the materialisation of a plan of action and framework for cooperation on security as a deliverable of the United States government's regional support initiative. St Kitts and Nevis led the discussions on behalf of CARICOM that will be formalised in Washington this month when the draft declaration and plan of action will be signed as a show of political support to strengthen the Caribbean–United States security cooperation strategic mechanism. This provides for, inter alia, a balanced and integrated approach that incorporates effective law enforcement with youth crime prevention and intervention and the provision of viable options for rehabilitation and reintegration for youth who leave gangs. In collaborating with the region on the issue of illegal firearms, there is strong cooperation in the area of combating illicit trafficking, development of investigative techniques, and improvement of the conviction and detection rates of firearms traffickers.

Time does not permit me to expand further. However, I take this opportunity to thank the members of the private sector for the support provided over the years to our law enforcement institutions. Equally, we express our appreciation for the assistance we are receiving from foreign governments and international institutions. Fighting crime must involve all of us doing our part to improve the quality of life in the Federation. Let us commit to closer collaboration on this matter as well as to all the other issues that affect the development of our country.

I thank you for your continuing support, as we strive to build a stronger nation in the midst of severe challenges. Let us work together to achieve a better society.

MILLENNIUM DEVELOPMENT GOALS REVIEW SUMMIT

United Nations, New York, September 22, 2010

It is indeed a pleasure for me to represent the government and people of St Kitts and Nevis as we undertake this very necessary and important collective review of progress made toward achieving the Millennium Development Goals.

These are significant goals, to which we agreed a decade ago, to free our peoples from want. I would like to take this opportunity to share with you the extent of my government's work and its ongoing commitment to human security and the dignity of all people; to reiterate our call for structured and meaningful global partnerships and cooperation to tackle the many challenges confronting our peoples; and to remind countries to fulfil their pledges.

I need not remind this assembly that St Kitts and Nevis is the smallest independent nation in the western hemisphere with a population just under fifty-thousand and a land mass of 104 square miles. Yet smallness has never been a deterrent to our progress nor an excuse not to adhere to the highest standards of democratic governance, strict observance of human rights, sound economic principles, and commitment to a high standard of living.

I am pleased to say that since the late 1990s we have implemented internal mechanisms and policies which, coupled with citizen engagement, have allowed us on an ongoing basis to make real progress in fulfilling our own development needs which coincide with the MDGs.

According to the latest Country Poverty Assessment, extreme poverty in St Kitts and Nevis fell from 11 per cent in 2000 to 1.4 per cent in 2009.

Since 1972, St Kitts and Nevis has enjoyed compulsory universal access to primary and secondary education.

St Kitts and Nevis was among the first in the western hemisphere to establish a Ministry of Women's Affairs. And even before political independence twenty-seven years ago, women have been occupying high offices and decision-making roles. Today, women empowerment and participation at all levels of policy-making and governance is the norm and gender is not a limiting factor in assigning persons to key posts in St Kitts and Nevis.

Our infant mortality rate in the last decade has shown an appreciable downward positive trend and maternal mortality has been negligible during the period under review due to my government's steady investment in the health sector including capacity-building consistent with its commitment to improve the quality of life of its citizens.

In terms of environmental sustainability, determined policies have resulted in implementation of geothermal and wind energy projects.

PANCAP, the pan-Caribbean partnership on HIV/AIDS of which St Kitts and Nevis is a member, is regarded as a WHO best practice centre in combatting HIV/AIDS. It is also renowned for its practices in prevention, treatment, and care, and also as an advocate for the elimination of all forms of discrimination against people affected by the disease.

On the issue of global partnerships, due to diminishing Official Development Assistance (ODA), St Kitts and Nevis has had to fund and sustain MDG programmes mainly from the scarce resources of the state. Therefore, we welcome the contribution of the government and people of Taiwan to our national efforts to meet the MDGs through their investment in agriculture, food security, and technology. Such partnership could be a model for developed countries some of whom have failed to live up to their commitments.

Our progress towards achieving the 2015 MDGs is the result of careful planning and prudent management. However, we live in complex times with myriad challenges where despite our very carefully calibrated macro-economic policies, fiscal prudence and financial programmes, our best efforts and best practices are often undermined by external forces as we have witnessed since the 2008 onset of the global financial crisis and economic meltdown.

Likewise, progress made through costly investments can be blown away in a matter of minutes leaving our small vulnerable economy to the mercy of an already tight financial market and the unavailability of grants or concessional loans. This has been exacerbated by the unfair calculation of our per capita GDP which places St Kitts and Nevis in a higher bracket than reality justifiably supports. Like other nations, despite our careful efforts to craft and implement our own stimulus packages, this issue of per capita GDP remains a major handicap, one that predates the global financial and economic crisis. It is unfair, arbitrary, indefensible, and economically destabilising. We manage our affairs responsibly, efficiently, and competently, yet we are still denied access to crucial concessional loans.

In the case of St Kitts and Nevis, the crushing burden of the high costs of borrowing, economic and social dislocations resulting from the closure of the sugar industry five years ago, the downturn in the global economy and the drying up of investment capital, the assault on our service sector, and the rising level of commercial indebtedness, all threaten to undermine our progress in fulfilling the MDGs and to unravel the success of our small yet vulnerable country.

In addition to this and the impact of the economic downturn, as we speak hurricanes swirl throughout this hemisphere. The regularity and ferocity of floods, hurricanes, the incidence of sea level rise, and other catastrophic events are bold reminders that the consequences of climate change are real.

The fact that we are this concerned about the unravelling of the progress made at this point in our review, five years before the target date for the achievement of the MDGs, is not consistent with the spirit of the Millennium Development Goals. I am not convinced that this is in any way indicative of the constructive multilateral collaboration we have spoken about so boldly for the last ten years.

I hereby encourage nations assembled for this review summit process to take action, whether in their legislative bodies or in multilateral agencies, to promote the kind of collaborative efforts which advance the common good and place partnership above parochialism and move our peoples further along the path to personal growth and the fulfilment of their individual potential.

THE DEBT CHALLENGE IN SMALL AND VULNERABLE STATES
Commonwealth Finance Ministers Meeting
St Kitts Marriott Resort, October 8, 2010

The interconnectedness of our global economy imposes an obligation for all of the parts to work cohesively in order to ensure that a problem in one area does not cause contamination in the entire system. The current crises have taught us that financial and economic contagion can spread very rapidly. This phenomenon has driven home quite forcefully the reality that whenever there is a problem in one area of the global economy others who may not be directly impacted cannot claim to be immune.

We therefore cannot turn a blind eye to the serious debt issues of small and vulnerable economies as experience has shown that events in small economies can reverberate throughout the international economic and financial markets.

I wish to emphasise, having the benefit of experience, that countries which are battling debt sustainability issues are virtually caught between a rock and a hard place. The frequent choices that one has to make between repaying debt for past development and funding current developmental needs can be devastating to a country's economy and ultimately impact the poor and vulnerable in that society.

I must provide you with a bit of our history in order for you to fully grasp the present reality of St Kitts and Nevis. You will be able to see how important it is to assist all small vulnerable economies in avoiding debt problems or to assist them in tackling these problems at an early stage. Having recognised the need to exit its four-hundred-year-old sugar manufacturing industry due mainly to loss of preferential treatment under the European Union Sugar Regime, the government and people of St Kitts and Nevis began the process of transforming the economy even prior to the actual closure of the industry. When our people took the reins from the planters in the 1970s, the industry was already in very poor shape, but sugar was the only thing that the vast majority of our workers knew, and there were hardly any other options available to them at that time.

Through a lengthy process of engagement with our people, advice from the international community and an examination of relevant experiences, we arrived at a consensus to transform the economy into one anchored in the provision of services, especially those related to tourism, as well as light manufacturing, agriculture, and information technology. We therefore set out to build the appropriate infrastructure, empower our people, and begin the process of institutional transformation. This meant in practical terms the modernisation of our air and seaports, building of road networks and health facilities, power generation and distribution plant upgrades, and telecommunications systems and educational facilities development, all of which necessitated financing.

However, the passage of several hurricanes, storms, flash floods and the onset of a series of events in international markets such as the 9/11 event in the USA, the food crisis, the oil crisis, and financial and economic crisis have resulted in the nullification of our efforts over and over again. The result is high debt levels as our investment in the sugar industry was unrealised due to premature abandonment of the agreed regime, the cost of investment in transformation, the cost of building and rebuilding infrastructure, and the graduation from concessional financing which was done without any regard for our vulnerability, consequently forcing us to use very costly borrowings to finance basic development.

What is significant and to some extent worrisome about the graduation process is that nowhere in this international system of rating a country's eligibility for aid did any warning bell go off or any red light flash to say 'stop, this is a vulnerable country, this is a small state with structural vulnerability challenges.' This system which we continue to adhere to not only failed to foresee the risk of graduating such a country as St Kitts and Nevis but even after the toxic combination of graduation and vulnerability has caused the risks to become a reality, the system continues to mount its deadly pressure by asking this country to accelerate the repayment of its IDA credits because its GNI had reached some nebulous number agreed upon years ago when the country was eligible. This said number having the same significance for a world power as it has for St Kitts and Nevis. Therefore St Kitts and Nevis having been graduated from concessional financing must now also accelerate the repayment of its IDA credits. This is not to comment on the amount of the repayment but the principles upon which the internationally accepted system of deciding countries' fates are based and to point to the inflexibility and lack of insight of such a system in an evolving global economy and to emphasise the need for urgent reform.

I speak to the need for reform in the way in which highly indebted small middle income countries are graduated from concessional financing because graduation leads to higher debt. I emphasise the need for recognition by the international community that vulnerability to natural disasters or other exogenous shocks expressed by a vulnerability index is an important criterion in assessing small economies. I am also asking for reform in the way in which structural impediments to growth such as the impediments of small size are viewed by the international community and I also wish for such reform to take cognisance of the reality that debt to GDP ratios in small states are not declining because there is a problem with growth in small states and this must be studied and addressed.

It is because of the foregoing that St Kitts and Nevis (and I believe in the wider OECS) supports the four options put forward by the Commonwealth Secretariat for debt relief to address the existing solvency and liquidity issues of small vulnerable economies. The four well-designed alternatives are:

1. Multilateral debt reduction for climate change adaptation and mitigation;

2. Extension of the IDA Debt Reduction Facility to provide relief on the commercial debt burdens of Small Vulnerable Economies;

3. Development of a Commonwealth Debt Relief Mechanism;

4. A temporary debt moratorium.

I must sound the warning, however, that these options must never be designed in the 'one size fits all' manner in which the current system operates. For while we agree with transparency and even-handedness, we also believe that any system which does not include some possibility for flexibility when the need arises can be compared to a man who has no soul and as such has lost his essence and real meaning for existing. In devising such a system the types and structure of conditionalities must also be carefully devised so that we do not defeat the purpose of the facility by making it impossible for those who are in need to qualify. We must also ensure that whatever the pledged resources that they can genuinely be realised. We are not insensitive to the fact that donor countries are experiencing their own problems and we wish to express our appreciation for their continued partnership. However, we wish to encourage the donor community to be committed to delivering resources. When this is not realised it further contributes to the problem of fiscal instability and unsustainable debt burdens in small countries. Reform of the aid allocation system must not exclude the participation of small vulnerable economies. Measures, which take into consideration vulnerability, must be used in setting the criteria for eligibility and this should allow access to middle income vulnerable countries.

We therefore support the policy options put forward by the Commonwealth Secretariat with respect to the future financing of SVEs to address the debt sustainability challenge. We agree with the two proposed new variables, namely: (i) measuring structural economic vulnerability, and (ii) measuring human capital development and adding these measurements to the current performance-based allocation formula. We believe that this new method of assessing countries' eligibility for aid would greatly improve the support that countries need in dealing with exogenous shocks.

St Kitts and Nevis also supports the establishment of an automatic shock facility with low or no conditionality for the purpose of providing an automatic, efficient and sufficient financial response to match the scale of the impact of shocks. With respect to the latter we wish to emphasise that the quota system is flawed as it has no relationship to the level of need of countries and therefore proves insufficient when large scale shocks occur.

In moving forward, the multilateral development banks and bilateral donors must be engaged in high level dialogue on these issues aimed at achieving buy-in and bringing urgent reform to the system of aid allocation. Certain time frames must be set by which implementation of some of these reform proposals, especially those that we have control over such as the Commonwealth Debt Relief Initiative, can be expected. There are certain low-hanging fruits which may not be very costly or complex which can be achieved in the short- to medium-term and these must be pursued. Other reforms must form part of an agreed timetable for implementation over the medium- to long-term. We do not have the luxury of time as the problems which SVEs face must be dealt with immediately otherwise we risk catastrophic breakdowns in the economic and financial systems of our Commonwealth.

In closing I wish to applaud the Commonwealth Secretariat for the valuable work which it has accomplished at the request of ministers and I trust that this effort will not be in vain. I believe that with much dialogue and follow-through we will be able to achieve the objectives of ministers in assigning this important task of exploring options for dealing with the debt of small vulnerable economies to the Secretariat and I wish to encourage continued research in this area.

St Kitts-Nevis-Anguilla National Bank 40th Anniversary

St Kitts Marriott Resort, April 9, 2011

May I suggest that we get straight to the point and begin this evening by giving an enthusiastic and well-deserved round of applause to the founder and managing director of the St Kitts-Nevis-Anguilla National Bank – Sir Edmund Wickham Lawrence.

And, as we reflect on what this institution has meant to the advancement of our nation, let us give an equally heart-felt round of applause to the board, management, and staff of this outstanding symbol of our country's financial competence and competitiveness, not only at home, but globally as well.

Finally, let us applaud the people of all classes, ages, races, and occupations in St Kitts and Nevis whose confidence, patronage, and solid partnership with the St Kitts-Nevis-Anguilla National Bank (SKNANB), combined with the leadership of Sir Edmund, his board, management and staff, explain the unquestioned and unrivalled success of this bank over the past four decades.

I don't have to tell you that we have been living in perilous times. Ireland. Greece. Portugal. France. The United States. The UK. All of these nations and so many more have been rocked by economic stresses and strains that have had reverberations all across the globe.

And, as we reflect on the state of the world, I must ask: When was the last time that you took a really careful look at a world map? Not a regional map, but a world map. It is difficult to reconcile who we are and how we feel as that infinitesimal little speck among the massive land masses that represent so many other countries across the globe, isn't it?

And then, apart from the matter of territory, there is the matter of population. Sometimes, as we go about our business here in the Federation, it is easy to forget just how small our blessed country really is. Indeed, stadium attendees at many sporting events across the globe would far exceed – sometimes by twice as much, sometimes by three times as much – the fifty-thousand persons that represent our entire population.

Yet, we in this blessed Federation have made it clear, time and time again, that neither land mass nor population can trump drive, initiative, focus and, indeed, God's blessings. The theme of the bank's 40th Anniversary celebrations, 'Vision, Resilience, Stability,' speak directly to this point, and I will explain in a minute why I raised the issue of where St Kitts and Nevis ranks *vis-à-vis* the rest of the world where population and size are concerned.

We in St Kitts and Nevis in general, and the St Kitts-Nevis-Anguilla National Bank in particular, have made incredible strides. In 2010, the publication *The Banker* compiled a listing of all of the banks in the world – banks in the United States and banks in Japan; banks in Russia and banks in Brazil; banks from Senegal to Germany to Australia and all points in between. Every single bank operating on the face of the earth was listed. This exercise established that there are some 1,000,006 banks worldwide. And these banks were then ranked. The people of St Kitts and Nevis need to know that the St Kitts-Nevis-Anguilla National Bank ranked 1,089 when compared to the 1,000,006 currently operating in the world.

In other words, this institution that we are here to honour this evening, this institution in this tiny country, this institution that was established and was built and has grown as a result of the skills, the drive, and the confidence of the people of St Kitts and Nevis ranks in the top .001 per cent of all banks worldwide. Put another way, 99.999 per cent of the banks in the world are ranked lower than what we here in the Federation refer to as 'National Bank.'

Congratulations, once again to National. Congratulations, indeed, to us all. We know what we have. We value what we have. And we shall protect what we have.

This institution has demonstrated the importance of establishing goals, putting plans in place to achieve those goals, and steadfastly, competently, professionally implementing the established plans in order to achieve the desired success. And so this institution has earned our respect. It has conducted its affairs with competence and honour. And, we say with pride, 'It is ours.'

Begun with share capital of $164,000 and total assets of $440,000 in 1972, the National Bank Trust Company was then established as a wholly-owned subsidiary. One year later, the National Caribbean Insurance Company Limited was also established as a wholly-owned subsidiary of the Trust Company. And, at the dawn of this century, in 2001 to be exact, yet another milestone was reached with the establishment of the St Kitts and Nevis Mortgage and Investment Company Limited, another wholly-owned subsidiary of National. In addition, as you may know, National recently joined forces with three other banks in the Eastern Caribbean Currency Union to establish the East Caribbean Investment Corporation.

This, I think we would all agree, is an outstanding record of growth and expansion. Most importantly, however, it is an impressive demonstration of the prudent financial management, the effective strategic planning, and the acute attention to the needs of customers on the part of Sir Edmund that has made National the outstanding institution that it is today.

But the milestones did not end there.

In 2003, National listed on the East Caribbean Securities Exchange. Today, it has thousands of shareholders. And it has paid dividends every single year since 1972.

These have not been easy times. Banks have been experiencing real difficulty throughout the region, and indeed throughout the world. Yet the National Group of Companies in 2010 reported an operating income, before taxes, of EC$48.6 million, and a net income for the year of EC$41.6 million. That deserves a round of applause.

I should also say, as many of you know, National Bank has paid particular attention on increasing shareholders' value by providing shareholders with a solid return on their investments. As a result, between June 1999 and June 2009, National was able to increase shareholder equity by 584 per cent – that is, from $EC 62 million to EC$446 million.

Is this impressive? Or is this impressive?!?!

And, on the most remote of chances that I still have not managed to convey to you what an extraordinary success story National represents, I want to remind you that St Kitts and Nevis is the smallest nation in the OECS. Yet National is the largest indigenous bank in the OECS.

In all humility, I must say that Kittitians and Nevisians have always been extraordinary people, and in this institution, we have certainly proved this to ourselves, and to the world, yet again.

But we're here tonight to discuss so much more than banking in general, or the National Group of Companies in particular. We are here to honour National as a shining example, with countless lessons for us all, not only in the realm of business but in our private lives as well, in the functioning of our communities, in what we owe to each other and to our nation.

You must admit that when Sir Edmund decided to establish National Bank in 1972, when the field was dominated by international banking giants that had been in these islands forever, it took enormous courage. Enormous vision. Enormous determination. And an enormous sense of commitment and dedication.

The success of the bank today, despite the seemingly insurmountable challenges of forty years ago, should be instructive to us today. And I say this, as I reflect on the deeply distressing news reports of this past week, which have placed in sharp focus the fact that greater cohesion – not less – is needed in our society.

My government has ensured that our security forces have been getting essential training. We have ensured that they have been receiving additional equipment. We have been collaborating with regional and international law enforcement partners. Stops. Searches. Heightened patrols.

All of this we are doing and shall continue to do. Solving the challenge of youth violence will require government and society to function as a strong and vibrant partnership and I want to commend the general public for having taken a clear decision in recent months to speak out more, to share more, to assist the security forces more than ever before. This is key, and for this we are truly grateful because, as I just said, what this moment demands is greater social cohesion, not less.

The violence that we have witnessed in some Caribbean youth tells us that whatever technological advances our societies have experienced in recent years, there is something for which there is no substitute and that is old-fashioned family cohesion. While the government is addressing itself to identifying and apprehending existing criminals, society must begin to see, with new eyes, the importance of more contact and interaction – not less – between our nation's parents and our nation's children. And we must become more sensitive to the extent to which an over-emphasis and over-valuing of an electronic culture can slowly and steadily eat into, and undermine, the humanising benefits of interaction between parent and child.

As our incomes have grown and our material security expanded, our families' need for, and dependence on, other families is nowhere

where it used to be. Our families can, in many ways, get along just fine without other families *materially*, but the human soul needs interaction if it is to be healthy. The human soul needs a sense of community if it is to thrive. The human soul needs to know that it is a part of something bigger and larger and embracing and so, even though our own particular children may be alright, and even though the children of our friends may be alright, every single one of us needs to 'interfere' more – not less – in the lives of children we do not know but whom we encounter as we go about our daily lives.

Let us remember that human interaction is humanising. Let us, then, have more interaction. Let us have more 'interference':

More 'interference,' not less, in the form of, 'Little boy, don't push.'

More 'interference,' not less, in the form of, 'Little girl, it is not nice to behave this way in public.'

More 'interference,' not less, in the form of, 'Little boy, it is 10:30 in the morning. You should be in class no matter how boring you say school is. Let me tell you why.'

More 'interference,' not less, in the form of 'Little boy, little girl, say "Please." Say "Thank you." Say "Excuse me."'

More 'interference,' not less, in the form of calling the police on your cell phones to let them know that there are under-age persons at certain night spots.

More 'interference,' not less, in terms of telling the owners of bars or clubs that you will withdraw your business if they continue to admit underage persons.

More 'interference,' not less, in terms of quietly sharing words of caring help and guidance with young, inexperienced, and inept mothers who, while in public with their young children, are doing and saying everything wrong.

Was it not the ancient Africans who told the world that 'it takes a village?' Was it not they who warned that adults who are concerned only about their own children, and only about the children of their friends, are sowing the seeds of social chaos and dysfunction? And was it not this idea that was so powerful that the wife of a former US president, now the US secretary of state, Hillary Rodham Clinton, used it as the title of her best-selling book?

Sir Edmund did not conclude forty years ago that the challenge was too great, and the risk of failure too daunting, as he looked at all it would take to build a financial institution that could stand tall vis-à-vis any on the world stage. And now, as we see violence ripping apart the lives of so many throughout our region, neither must we. Sir Edmund's sense of self, and his national pride, told him that not only did we as a people deserve to have a bank of our own, but that the time had come for us to step forward and build it ourselves. Step by step.

So, too, as we examine the causes and meaning of the youth violence must we now similarly commit ourselves to steadily and bravely mending those seams of our society that have become so sadly frayed. You can count on my government to continue to do its part. My government will be counting on you to continue doing yours.

The St Kitts-Nevis-Anguilla National Bank was founded on a clear and admirable *vision*. Its proven ability to withstand global economic shocks, cyber-threats, and other challenges has proven its *resilience*. And our very presence here bears testimony to its *stability*. This bank that we are here to honour tonight has a great deal of which to be proud. We, in St Kitts and Nevis, have a great deal of which to be proud. Together, let us continue the journey forward on the impressive path that for forty years we have proudly trod, undeterred and walking towards the sun.

Congratulations, and three cheers for the St Kitts-Nevis-Anguilla National Bank!

Land Exchange Agreement
Between St Kitts-Nevis-Anguilla National Bank and the Government of St Kitts and Nevis
Lodge Community Centre, October 24, 2012

In July 2011, the government entered into a Standby Agreement (SBA) with the International Monetary Fund (IMF). One of the terms of that agreement called for the government to reduce the national debt. Notably, prior to entering this agreement with the IMF, the government had already set for itself a goal to reduce its debt through a variety of means and these proposals were accepted without major adjustment by the IMF.

One of the major holders of government debt was, and still is, St Kitts-Nevis-Anguilla National Bank Limited (SKNANB). The government and the bank came together and agreed to a plan that would substantially reduce the national debt and help set St Kitts and Nevis on a sustainable course of fiscal health.

We should remember here that the government did not enter into this agreement with just any institution. This is a bank that since its inception has shown that it will, within the scope of its business model, work diligently and unequivocally with the people of St Kitts and Nevis to move this country forward.

What was agreed was for the Federation, which is rich in lands, to offset the debt to National Bank by transferring certain land assets at least equivalent in value to the debt to National Bank, thereby extinguishing the debt to the bank.

But more was required. The government could not simply transfer lands to the bank and the bank could not simply remove the debt from its books. There are rules and regulations. The bank is a business, and the government conducts the business of the people. The bank had, in some way, to be given cash back for the cash borrowed and the government had to ensure that the people of St Kitts and Nevis were given good value for their lands.

What was then further agreed between the parties was that a Special Purpose Vehicle (SPV) would be established. This SPV would be a company incorporated in partnership between the bank and the government. At the date of incorporation, each party – government and bank – would hold equal shares. At this point, the government holds one-hundred thousand shares in the Company and the Bank owns one-hundred thousand shares in the Company. That ratio will never change except in favour of the government and people of St Kitts and Nevis but that will be explained a little later.

After the transfer of the lands to the bank, the debt owed to the bank would be transferred to the SPV. Also, the bank which has entered into an exclusive agreement with the SPV, would give the SPV exclusive rights to sell the lands. Any money that is realised from the sale of the lands would be used first to defray the costs of sale and secondly, to reduce the Company's debt.

Here is how the shareholding arrangement works in favour of the people of St Kitts and Nevis.

The bank owns 'A' shares in the Company. The government owns 'B' shares in the Company. The main purpose of these different classes of shares is to clarify the redemption value and priority of the shares. The designation of classes of shares does not mean that the bank has more power or authority in the Company than the government. What it means is that when the lands are sold, the bank's shares will be paid out before the government's shares are paid. And this is the way it should and has to be. The bank lent the cash, the bank must get back its cash.

So as the lands are sold, and the monies from the sales reduce the Company's debt, the bank's 'A' shares will eventually be redeemed. The government will continue to hold all its 'B' shares in the Company even after the bank's shares have all been redeemed. That means that the bank's shareholding will eventually come to zero and the government (and therefore the people of St Kitts and Nevis) will at the end of the day hold one hundred percent of the Company. Holding one hundred percent of the company means that the government will hold one hundred percent of all the remaining assets of the Company. And the agreement of the parties, and the structure of the Company, is designed to ensure that there will be no, or no significant, liabilities of the Company at the end of its purpose. Because that is what a Special Purpose Vehicle is designed to do. It will carry out its purpose – in this case to sell lands and extinguish a debt – and at the end, having achieved its purpose, the assets will be distributed and the company will be dissolved.

Therefore, if there are any lands that were transferred to the bank under the terms of the agreement, and those lands were not needed to be sold to satisfy the Company's debt, those lands will be returned to the people of St Kitts and Nevis. The bank will not have a choice. The government will not have a choice. They have to be returned.

Even further, if there is any excess money left over from the sale of lands after the bank has been fully paid, that money also will be turned over to the people of St Kitts and Nevis.

Neither the government nor the bank can transfer, assign or dispose of the shares they own to any third-party unless the other shareholder agrees to such a transfer in writing.

Neither the government nor the bank can pledge, mortgage, charge or otherwise encumber any of the shares that they own in favour of any third-party unless the other shareholder agrees in writing.

Therefore you, the people of the Federation, will always know the persons having power and authority over the sale of our lands. This further ensures that no third-party without a genuine interest in, or an emotional tie to, the lands of this Federation will ever hold the power to sell these lands.

The people of St Kitts and Nevis are protected further. In the Company, there will be six directors. Three will be appointed by the bank. Three will be appointed by the government. The chairmanship of the board will be rotated annually between the shareholders, with one of the government's appointed directors being the first chairman. When it comes to voting, the directors have equal voting powers and the chairman does not have a casting or deciding vote. The government will always have equal say in what happens in the Company.

There are more benefits to the people of the Federation. Once the government loan is transferred to the Company, the interest rates reduce from an average commercial rate of 8.6 per cent per annum to the extremely favourable rate of 3.5 per cent per annum. This new, lower rate was not just handed over to the government by the bank. This rate was negotiated by the government who said that at all times the value of the people's land must be recognised. A reduced interest rate ultimately means that fewer lands will have to be sold to satisfy the debt because the overall debt will be reduced.

It should be understood that the SPV will be run like any other well-established private sector company. There will be directors as explained earlier. There will be professional staff hired and operating from brick and mortar premises. There will be secretaries and managers. There will be auditors appointed. The rules governing companies in the Federation will apply to it. Annual returns will be filed. It will have retained accountants and legal counsel.

Further, the land sales process will be transparent and apparent. The lands have been valued by an independent valuation agent agreed between the parties and a minimum of three real estate agents selected through a competitive tender process will assist the Company with the sale of the lands. They will only assist however in accordance at all times with any licences or permissions granted to them by the Company. The company will continue to have the sole and exclusive right at all times to sell the lands. It is the sole and exclusive agent for the marketing and sale of the lands in accordance with the agreements made between the Bank and the government.

The bank, as legal owner of the lands, will sign the transfers of the lands to the prospective buyers. The government will always have an equitable interest in the lands by virtue of its shareholding in the Company and the relationship between the transferred debt and the sale of lands.

At the end of the day, we have every confidence that the land exchange process will prove to be a boon to the Federation. The entire process from the date the Company becomes fully functional to the date that the Company's debt is fully paid out is calculated to last three years with provisions for an extension if that becomes necessary. We do not expect it to become necessary.

It is the conversion of one asset to another – the change from land to cash. It has the benefit of reducing the Federation's debt by 33.3 per cent instantly. It has the further benefit of reducing the interest cost to the country instantly.

Throughout the process your government will continue to oversee the lands that are the birthright of the people of this Federation and ensure that they will be used for purposes that ensure to the benefit of the people of this nation.

Debt Exchange Offer
National Broadcast, ZIZ Broadcasting Corporation, February 27, 2012

Today a pivotal moment in St Kitts and Nevis's debt restructuring process has arrived with the launch of the government's offer to exchange bonds and certain commercial loans for new instruments that will be far more in line with the country's current capacity to pay. The launch of the Exchange Offer marks the conclusion of an intense and ultimately successful period of negotiations between the government and its key commercial creditors.

I am very pleased to report that late last week the critical mass of affected commercial creditors confirmed their support for the restructuring terms that are at the heart of our exchange offer, allowing us to proceed to launch. We have listened to the feedback provided by creditors during the consultation and incorporated their views into the terms to the extent possible as we have worked to decisively place our debt on a sustainable footing.

For example, in response to creditor recommendations, the government has decided to include two options within the exchange offer so as to enable creditors to choose their preferred method for delivering debt relief. Affected creditors will therefore be able to choose between:

- a new discount bond entailing a 50 per cent reduction in the face value of existing claims, with repayment made over twenty years and interest rates set initially at 6 per cent and dropping to 3 per cent after four years, or
- a new forty-five-year par bond with a 1.5 per cent interest rate and a fifteen-year grace period on principal.

Creditors who participate in the exchange offer by tendering their instruments within the specified time frame will be entitled to receive a one-off 'goodwill' payment one month after the issuance of the new bonds in lieu of accrued interest.

The Caribbean Development Bank, in full support of our efforts to achieve debt sustainability, has agreed to guarantee the payments that will become due under the new discount bond up to a cap of US$12 million. This feature will provide additional value to creditors electing the discount option.

Certain debts of the NIA and its public sector constitute eligible claims under the exchange offer and will effectively be restructured into new federal bonds. The NIA and the federal government will therefore be entering into a parallel agreement under which the NIA will reimburse the federal government for the debt service due under these restructured facilities. As has already been confirmed by the government on a number of occasions, the treasury bills issued by the federation and by the NIA fall outside of the scope of the debt restructuring and are therefore not eligible claims under the exchange offer.

Although the terms of the restructuring remain tough, they reflect the debt relief requirements of St Kitts and Nevis as implied in the short- and medium-term macroeconomic projections undertaken by the IMF as well as the realities of the ongoing global economic downturn. Our determination to find a once-and-for-all solution to our debt overhang is supported not just by the IMF and the CDB, but also by the key creditors holding the critical mass of debts eligible under the exchange offer.

Affected creditors wishing to accept the terms of the exchange offer must submit their tenders by no later than the close of business on Wednesday, March 14, 2012. The exact procedures for doing so are specified in the documentation that they will be receiving shortly. The closing of the transaction is scheduled to take place on or around March 28, 2012. This is the only offer that will be made by St Kitts and Nevis in respect of the eligible claims. Furthermore, the government does not intend to resume the servicing of any existing claims that are not validly tendered into the exchange offer.

SUGAR INDUSTRY DIVERSIFICATION FOUNDATION (SIDF) REPORT
St Kitts Marriott Resort, May 30, 2012

At no time in human history have the social and economic circumstances that govern the affairs of nations remained static. In recent years, however, heightened levels of global economic uncertainty have brought with them levels of apprehension not seen since the Great Depression.

Not only have nations across the globe found themselves in the economic doldrums, but the relative standings of various nations have changed as well and indeed continue to do so. Nations that we have traditionally understood to be dominant economic forces globally have not been quite so dominant in terms of growth in recent years. And nations that just a few decades ago were struggling to achieve basic levels of growth and stability are now exhibiting ascendant trajectories that few could have predicted fifteen or twenty years ago.

As a result, much of the world now finds itself in an economic space that is highly fluid and unpredictable, to say the least. Throughout it all, however, in these most trying of times, as a result of the unwavering determination of my government, and despite the very real challenges involved due to the fact that our economy is interwoven with those of hard-hit Europe and North America, our management of the economy has won positive appraisals from international financial institutions. We have managed to do what many in the region and beyond have found to be almost impossible – to protect civil service jobs, to keep development projects moving forward with all the socio-economic benefits attendant thereto, and to reduce our debt by some fifty percent. Our primary engine of growth, tourism, has repeatedly earned leading rankings in a range of categories by a variety of impartial international entities.

Nonetheless, global uncertainties persist.

And what this means, or at least what we in St Kitts and Nevis should take this to mean, is that even as we seek important new alliances, and even as we reinforce and expand existing ones, our primary and undergirding mantra must primarily be one of self-reliance. And for this mantra to mean anything in the real world of economics, it must be fired by imagination, application, determination, and collaboration. And this is what makes the Sugar Industry Diversification Foundation (SIDF) so timely and so relevant to our forward movement as a nation at this juncture in our history.

In urging 'self-reliance,' I am not advocating that St Kitts and Nevis 'go it alone.' Indeed, I am not certain that 'going it alone' is even possible in this interconnected world. What I am instead calling for is the firing of our own imaginations by our undertaking vital research and by engaging in the requisite analysis in order to put forward viable ideas that will stimulate economic activity, expand options for those ready to help move our country and themselves forward, and advance the type of economic diversification that promotes social and economic stability the world over.

SIDF was designed 'to transform the economy and society by building human capital, nurturing the spirit of enterprise, and spurring economic growth.' As a result, Kittitians and Nevisians have been, are being, and will continue to be given the opportunity to develop viable project ideas in a range of key sectors, encouraged by the fact that whatever traditional sources of funding may exist, there has now been created for the people of St Kitts and Nevis, by the people of St Kitts and Nevis, a new and important source of possible alternate funding. In an era of acknowledged uncertainty and at a time when funding sources are not in great abundance, the potential impact of SIDF on the entrepreneurial profile and prospects of our nation and our people should not be underestimated.

We in St Kitts and Nevis have demonstrated our competitiveness in a range of endeavours at both regional and international levels. What we, as a people, are now tasked with is to stir within the national psyche a keener appreciation of the importance of entrepreneurship and of independent and productive enterprise.

SIDF, on the other hand, is tasked with ensuring the efficient allocation of funds among competing alternatives. In late May, 2012, SIDF provided a detailed report on the projects which it has already funded in keeping with its overall goal of building human capital, encouraging a spirit of enterprise, and stimulating growth within the Federation. In each case, funds were applied for because funds were needed and SIDF was positioned to step forward and, following careful analysis, meet that need. The benefits have been substantial, both to the entities involved and to our nation as a whole.

Even as we have now learned about the actual impact of SIDF thus far, let us think ahead to areas of possible future need and impact in education, economic diversity and food security, recreation, sports and culture, tourism and hospitality, and alternative energy, for these constitute the key areas of economic activity in the Federation today. Informed, enlightened, and viable ideas is what SIDF needs and what our nation needs. Let us then go forward with this in mind as we strive to change St Kitts and Nevis for the better.

PEOPLE EMPLOYMENT PROGRAMME (PEP) LAUNCH

Bank Street, Basseterre, December 21, 2012

I am very pleased to be here this morning to express the strong support of both the Office of the Prime Minister as well as the Ministry of Finance, for the very well-named PEP – the People Employment Programme – a most constructive and visionary initiative. And I must publicly thank three Ministries: the Ministry of Education, in particular the National Skills Training Programme; the Ministry of Public Works; and the Ministry of Social and Community Affairs for their collaboration with the Sugar Industry Diversification programme to bring to fruition this youth-focused, employment-focused, people-focused programme.

It was only on Tuesday of this week, while addressing the Chamber of Industry and Commerce's annual luncheon, that I reminded the nation of the ways in which both the public and the private sectors here in the Federation have been adversely affected by the global financial crisis, a crisis that began as a 2008 American housing crisis but soon spread to nearly every nation and sector within the global economy leaving a trail of unemployment, business failures, crushing public debt, fiscal mayhem and economic despair, a trail of trauma that lingers on some four or five years later.

Everyone here sees on the nightly news how even the great United States of America has been humbled by this crisis. America's debt has risen above 100 per cent of GDP, and it is now struggling to avoid yet another crisis that threatens to plunge its economy into yet another recession. And I do not have to tell you what the consequences of that would be for the rest of the world. All our lives we have read about the marvels of Greek civilisation and we all know of the days when Spain dominated this hemisphere, yet today these countries and others like them are struggling with huge fiscal imbalances and massive escalations in debt. Particularly tragic is the fact that in both Greece and Spain, for example, youth unemployment has now shot up to some 50 per cent. In other words, half of the young adults in those countries are completely unable to find work.

Almost every country of the world has been severely affected by this debilitating crisis. Indeed, even we here in the Federation have had to make our own sacrifices to defend ourselves and our country, to prevent this Federation that we all love from falling off the type of precipice that so many others have fallen over. And so, we fight. And think. And plan. And push new policies and programmes that will stabilise our nation and protect our people.

Today then, with Christmas just around the corner, I am very grateful, as leader of our beloved nation, that we have been able to demonstrate the fortitude that has enabled St Kitts and Nevis to rein in the global threats and to put our fiscal house in order. I am very grateful that we had the vision and the discipline to slash our nation's debt by half, bringing it dramatically down – from some 200 per cent of GDP to some 100 per cent of GDP today. As a result, the debt of St Kitts and Nevis is today on a manageable and sustainable path. Added to all of this, my government continues to develop and offer initiatives to stimulate both foreign direct investment as well as local investment. Of paramount importance to us, however, is ensuring that we put forward initiatives to enable our young people to become gainfully employed.

And so today, I commend this appropriately youth-focused PEP programme which will empower the young people of the Federation, enhance their income-generating skills, improve their entrepreneurial capacity, and place them on the path to sound, independent decision-making in order to be productive participants in the development of our country. PEP is an important example of my government's determination to improve the earning power of our nation's women and to correct the types of social imbalances that are found in countries all over the world, but which we wish to correct here.

We, in St Kitts and Nevis, have made important sacrifices. But we have also put forward the types of policies that promote economic growth in a balanced manner. Because at the same time that we are facilitating business expansion and business creation, we also recognise the importance of developing a cadre of young people positioned both to seize opportunities created by business expansion as well as to carve out and implement innovative investment ideas of their own.

A significant amount of time was spent on the development of PEP in order to ensure that it was both broad-based and comprehensive. And

I am particularly pleased by how well the six areas on which it focuses fit into the economy that my government has worked so arduously to build. It provides, to the already-qualified, opportunities to advance themselves through real world, practical assignments. In addition, there are two central programmes of PEP that are designed specifically to enable women in the small enterprise sector to break into and advance in the male-dominated construction trade. PEP also focuses on the critically important areas of agriculture infrastructure improvement, training, and entrepreneurial development, all in order to advance the interests of our citizens and our economy.

I want therefore, to encourage every young person within the sound of my voice – whether present here today, or who is getting this message via radio or the internet – to move right away to register for this programme. There are one thousand positions to be filled, and all who are interested should move now to seize this important opportunity.

As prime minister, I am extremely optimistic about the future of St Kitts and Nevis. And everyone in our country should not only take pride, but indeed be quite grateful to our Maker that we have been able to withstand this most turbulent period in world history. This should imbue us with the strength and the confidence to move forward in a spirit of faith and positivity because St Kitts and Nevis is poised for another take-off and this is why it is so important to us that we have as partners qualified, ambitious, and eager young participants. The PEP programme was designed to get us precisely there. And so, I once again urge our nation's youth to step forward and equip themselves to take their rightful place in the land of their birth, via this programme.

To the ministries involved, to all of the young people who have already begun to show such great interest, and to the PEP programme itself, I express commendations and I stand most confident in your success.

Citizenship By Investment (CBI) Programme

Jumeirah Carlton Tower Hotel, London, England, October 30, 2013

I am very pleased to be here this morning and welcome the opportunity to share with you the details of the St Kitts-Nevis Citizenship By Investment Programme (CBI) – its evolution, its current status, and the role it plays within the social, political, and economic fabric of our Federation.

The Citizenship By Investment Programme in St Kitts and Nevis is some thirty years old. However, the programme that is in place today is not the programme that was introduced in 1984.

Indeed, in 2005, faced with the vagaries of a rapidly changing global trading environment, and increasingly mindful that our three-hundred-year reliance on sugar exports had no chance of underwriting the development vision that we had for our people, my government decided that the time had come to re-assess and refine the Citizenship By Investment Programme that had been first implemented some twenty-one years earlier. The programme had, we could say, 'reached the age of majority,' and so major improvements were in order.

Our objectives were clear. We wanted a programme that would

i.   advance the social and economic interests of the people of St Kitts and Nevis;

ii. be managed in a manner that was both efficient and transparent;

iii. be structured so as to attract persons of sound character and reputation who were interested in obtaining dual citizenship, and were also capable of making our pre-set level of investment.

Today, some eight years after the restructuring of our programme, and thirty years after its initial introduction, St Kitts and Nevis has the longest-lasting programme of its kind in the world. However, not only is ours the longest-lasting, but it is among the most well managed, reputable and stable. As a result, interest in and the demand for the St Kitts and Nevis programme has remained consistently high.

Why is this?

First of all, there is the matter of the country itself. St Kitts and Nevis is endowed with a natural beauty that is, in all humility, quite breathtaking. For that, however, we admit that we can take no credit. And natural beauty is not enough.

Equally important, simply as a matter of responsible decision-making by those interested in attaining dual citizenship, is the fact that St Kitts and Nevis is a very well-managed, politically stable, high-income nation with a solid tradition of parliamentary democracy.

It is also significant that for almost fifty years now, our country has had universal, mandatory, and free elementary and secondary education and this has a major impact on the feel and potential of a place.

In addition, St Kitts and Nevis is well-known for our innovative *and* responsible approach to governance, strengths that have resulted in clear advantages to those considering dual citizenship. Airlift between St Kitts and Nevis and North American and European cities, for example, is easy and convenient. We have a telecommunications infrastructure that is second to none because at the same time that we decided in 2005 to switch from a mono-culture, sugar-based economy to one fuelled by tourism, agriculture, light manufacturing, and financial services, we simultaneously committed ourselves to ensuring that St Kitts and Nevis had a telecommunications infrastructure that would make 21st century global communications of all types standard fare for all who live or work in the Federation.

To place our country in context, however, I should mention that St Kitts and Nevis is a part of a nine-state archipelago referred to as the Eastern Caribbean States and within this grouping, the innovative yet responsible governance style to which I referred earlier, has resulted in St Kitts and Nevis achieving the top-ranked performance in terms of manufactured exports to the United States, per capita GDP, direct foreign investment, and IMF 2013 growth projections, to mention just a few of the metrics that one tends to assess when interested in dual citizenship possibilities. Even beyond the Eastern Caribbean, however, our educational and health care delivery systems are such that the life expectancy in St Kitts and Nevis is on par with that of the wealthiest nations on earth. And this, too, is significant.

And then there is the matter of energy, that factor that is so key to both comfort and productivity, and over which wars have been, are being, and will continue to be fought. We in St Kitts and Nevis wish to extricate ourselves from the type of uncertainty that fossil-fuel reliance creates so we have committed ourselves to becoming the world's first sustainable island state. Our emphasis is on green energy, a green economy, a green development philosophy. And we can afford to embark upon this path because St Kitts and Nevis is one of the sunniest nations on earth. There is the constancy of our trade winds. And our volcanic geological origins have endowed us with the potential for geothermal energy.

In keeping with our commitment to becoming the world's first sustainable island state, from our street lighting to our government facilities, and from our air and seaports to our housing programmes, the emphasis is now on solar power. Indeed, determined to encourage the embrace of solar power throughout the rest of the region, we are already moving forward as the first solar-panel manufacturing nation in the Eastern Caribbean.

I provide these details as a means of conveying the ethos of forward-thinking focus and delivery that define governance in St Kitts and Nevis. Because it is these important governance factors, combined with the exquisite topography of our islands, that have caused St Kitts and Nevis to remain a top-tier, highly sought-after choice where investment programmes of the type being discussed here today are concerned.

I must stress, however, that in addition to all that I have said thus far, if I had to identify the one feature that truly sets St Kitts and Nevis apart and explains the strength and appeal of the St Kitts and Nevis programme throughout these many years, I would have to point to our meticulous attention to effective regulation and due diligence.

I am aware that, since the establishment of the St Kitts and Nevis programme in 1984, and particularly our refinement of it in 2005, there have been many attempts at replication. Indeed, we may be sending intellectual property infringement penalties in several directions pretty soon! Seriously though, these programmes require very careful management and oversight or the consequences – for the host country, the citizens by investment, and regular citizens as well – can be less than pleasant. We are aware, for example, that some nations which have established similar programmes but which did not have the requisite management and oversight infrastructure in place, have had a number of unpleasant experiences such as the misfortune of having visa waiver agreements withdrawn and so on.

It is because of St Kitts and Nevis's absolute aversion to outcomes such as these that we have placed such emphasis on regulation and due diligence to the lasting benefit of both our nation, those who have applied for and been granted citizenship of St Kitts and Nevis, and those who are citizens by birth or naturalisation.

When one applies for economic citizenship in St Kitts and Nevis, one can choose to invest in real estate or contribute to the Sugar Industry Diversification Foundation (SIDF) – a public charity that then funds social and economic development projects ranging from agriculture to tourism, and from entrepreneurship to education and beyond. A listing of the approved real estate options is provided on the St Kitts and Nevis Citizenship By Investment website, as are details about the Sugar Industry Diversification Foundation, a list of persons authorised to assist you in your application process, and a wealth of information pertaining to the application and approval processes.

In closing, I should mention that there is no income tax in St Kitts and Nevis. And there also is no requirement to be resident in the Federation after obtaining citizenship by investment, thereby eliminating the risk of one's citizenship being withdrawn for not meeting residency requirements.

Most importantly, the Citizenship By Investment Programme in St Kitts and Nevis, as I explained at the beginning, was designed to advance the social, economic, and political interests of the people of St Kitts and Nevis while providing a dual citizenship opportunity for persons of sound character and reputation. Our programme has been rated highly not only by those who are interested in obtaining St Kitts and Nevis citizenship but, most importantly, by leading nations of the world.

The past five years have been a period of economic trauma and instability for much of the world. Industrialised and non-industrialised nations have felt both the shocks and the aftershocks of the 2008 financial crisis. Because of astute financial management and discipline, however, St Kitts and Nevis was spared the trauma experienced by many of its neighbours, and indeed, the world. Being a part of a globalised world, we have not been completely immune but responsible governance has certainly helped to insulate us.

As a result, throughout the duration of the crisis, direct foreign investment continued to flow to our Federation. Major development projects continued moving forward while in the region and further afield, many projects were forced to close.

It is often difficult to find St Kitts and Nevis on a world map – we are that tiny. Once you are actually in the Federation, however, nothing about it feels tiny at all. Surrounded by our majestic topography on the one hand, and feeling the confidence and calm that is possible only when there is good governance on the other, you will understand why, with so many other options to choose from, persons of sound reputations and character who are interested in citizenship by investment, time and again, choose the nation that I am honoured to lead.

TOURISM

TOURISM

Tourism was always an important part of Labour's SKN development strategy but after the closure of the sugar industry in 2005, tourism became the main driver of the economy.

The first two terms of the Douglas administration had seen the Port Zante cruise ship terminal rebuilt after the natural disaster of five hurricanes in five years; the airport upgraded and rebuilt; and the opening of the flagship Marriott Resort in Frigate Bay.

The agenda in terms three and four was to build on this foundation and market the SKN tourism product aggressively in the Caribbean's major tourism markets in the US, Canada, the UK, and Europe. New products were added to the tourist offering and the number of new hotel projects kept increasing including Ocean's Edge, Christophe Harbour, Silver Reef, Marriott Vacation Club, Kittitian Hill, Park Hyatt, Koi, Pirate's Nest, Ramada, and Imperial Bay, among others.

When the worldwide financial crisis took hold in 2008, tourism everywhere took a hit. The high cost of energy meant less airlift and higher prices for would-be tourists and fewer visitors. However, the Douglas government did not lessen its tourism development efforts during that time but continued to build, renovate, and improve so that the Federation would be ready when the crisis was over.

The total number of visitors to the Federation in 1995, the first year of the Douglas administration was two hundred and eighty-seven thousand. By 2005, the number had risen to five hundred and five thousand, and by 2015 the number of visitors had exceeded one million at, one million, one hundred and fifty thousand.

TOURISM AWARDS BANQUET
St Kitts Marriott Resort, October 27, 2007

We have just completed a very successful Tourism Awareness Month and I must also take this opportunity to express my sincere appreciation to all the hard-working employees of the Tourism Authority who did so much to make it a success. Special thanks are also due to all those who served with such dedication on the many committees that had to be established in order to pull it all off. The private sector in general, and those businesses directly involved in tourism in particular, were also key to this month's success and I thank you all for your participation. To all who continue to highlight the importance of tourism, to all who have been energising this sector, and to all who are showing the people of St Kitts and Nevis how they and their families can advance economically and socially as a direct result of tourism, I salute you.

I have said over and over, and I can never say it enough, the social, economic, and political security of St Kitts and Nevis demands that we build and manage, with wisdom, a strong, diversified economy. This is key if we are to register not simply economic growth, but, indeed, economic development. This is key if we are to boost not only our macro-economic indicators, but also the quality of life for our people.

Tourism is an expanding industry globally. It is important therefore, that we in the Caribbean use our competitive advantage to ensure that we share in that growth in a manner commensurate with the unique attributes, characteristics, and possibilities that we bring to the global tourism table.

In St Kitts and Nevis, we are equipping ourselves to generate revenues for years to come by creating not only a diversified economy, but indeed, a diversified tourism product. To this end, we recognise the importance of preserving and promoting our cultural heritage for this has great value. We recognise the importance of establishing and astutely managing sports tourism for the potential in this area is also great. We are exploring possibilities in the area of community tourism for it is essential that we constantly search for new ways and more ways for our people to benefit directly from this sector in which my government has invested so much of our nation's resources.

The challenge, therefore, is for all of us to ensure that our tourism industry encourages and facilitates the emergence of wide-ranging, viable entrepreneurial initiatives throughout St Kitts and Nevis, both large and small. The challenge is for us to demonstrate and prove to our people that within the tourism industry, opportunities for them abound.

Tourism, at its most elemental level, is about human interaction, isn't it? It presents opportunities for learning and exposes both the visitor *and* the visited to new experiences. Well managed and properly run, tourism can result in a rejuvenation of the body *and* the mind for the visitor, and an improvement in the economic and social prospects of the visited.

Tourism however is, after all, a business, whether for the government or for the individual operator. And all businesses must be managed so as to maximise benefits and minimise costs. Tourism all over the world must be managed so as to maximise the economic and other benefits while keeping the associated social and other costs under control. St Kitts and Nevis is no different. And on this we must remain vigilant.

If we want our people to be emotionally invested in this sector that is so important to everyone in this room, we will have to commit ourselves to providing them with the training that they need to be competitive, the training they need to be able to spot and benefit from business opportunities associated with the industry, and the training they need to understand the essential components of being successful in any field, a commitment to excellence, respect for self and others, initiative, dependability, business *savoir faire*.

And this desire to have more Kittitians and Nevisians benefit directly from this sector leads me to the matter of community-based tourism and the economic opportunities offered therein. Community-based tourism offers communities a special opportunity to showcase themselves not simply as pleasant hosts, but also as visionary, competent, business people. Yes, we must impress upon our people the importance of welcoming visitors in a calm and pleasant manner, but we must with equal dedication impress upon them the importance of acquiring the skills and the insights to spot and successfully pursue viable business opportunities, whether through the creation of products or the provision of services. This is the only way to ensure that local people in our smaller communities will warmly welcome and enthusiastically celebrate the tourism industry that we are all here to praise and promote this evening.

Around St Kitts and Nevis, there are communities that exhibit unique and positive cultural, historical, or environmental characteristics. We must help the people who live in them to understand the business potential inherent in their communities. We must help them to understand what about the place that they have been seeing day after day all their lives, that place that does not in any way seem special, would indeed be very special to a visitor. And we must explain to these people the ability of their community's unique and special traits to make life easier for them economically and socially.

And then there is the matter of our environment. In the Caribbean, our environment is our product. There are many spin-offs of course, but the initial pull, our key and essential magnet, is our environment. And so the care, protection and preservation of our natural and physical environments, both by us and by our visitors, must be paramount. We must constantly think of imaginative and effective ways to impress upon us all – the public sector, the private sector, the cruise ships, our people, and our visitors – that protecting our environment is not optional. We have a sacred and inescapable duty and responsibility to protect and to preserve where our God-given and essentially fragile special natural environment is concerned. And that is a message that must go far and wide.

Although our immediate responsibility is the protection of our local environment, we must also develop greater awareness of and concern about the global environment because this too has long-term implications for us in these parts of the world. Global warming, for example, may seem for many like a distant issue that has no bearing on us. But that is not exactly true. We actually serve our own best interests by being more concerned about some of these seemingly abstract environmental issues. Indeed, if we decide that global warming is someone else's problem, and if the whole world shrugs and adopts this attitude, our grandchildren may one day end up with their Bay Road right in front of the Washington Archibald High School! Our land, our water, and our environment must attract from us more attention and more concern.

St Kitts and Nevis will be successful in establishing its own niche in the global tourism industry when the Ministry of Tourism, those businesses that are now involved in the sector, and the people of St Kitts and Nevis enter into more frequent and in-depth exchanges as to how the tourism pie can best be expanded so that as many of our people benefit from tourism as possible. From the dawn of time, self-interest has been a powerful motivator. And to the extent that we can demonstrate to more and more of our people that our tourism product holds economic opportunities for them, not only as employees, but also as entrepreneurs, then the 'attitude problem' to which many often refer will melt away like butter in the sunshine.

Private sector practitioners, public sector officials, members of the audience, ours is a small and intimate nation and there are a number of issues, challenges, and opportunities associated with this industry. The greater the involvement of our people and the more successful we are at expanding the definition of 'stakeholder,' the more successful St Kitts and Nevis will be in creating and maintaining a tourism industry that is stable, a tourism industry that is competitive, a tourism industry that stays on a positive trajectory.

As we work together to create the type of tourism landscape that we think will best serve the interests of this nation, let us remember how very important it is for us to maintain and enliven the dialogue and how beneficial it will be to us all if we are able to expand the number of parties to that dialogue. When the various segments of our nation are singing from the same sheet music, when we truly share a common vision across the length and breadth of this country, then will this industry provide for all of us the tremendous economic, social, and other benefits which we know it is so very capable of delivering.

Let us leave here tonight committed as a government, and committed as members of the private sector, to finding ways to ignite and unleash an entrepreneurial spirit amongst our young people. Let us leave here tonight committed to ensuring that they will feel and know that in St Kitts and Nevis there are opportunities for them to transform sound business ideas into tangible, viable, lucrative products and services. In that optimism, in that personal faith in the industry, lies our nation's ability to hold its own on this highly competitive global battleground.

To this end, Caribbean nations will continue to collaborate on various aspects of our regional tourism product and the Caribbean Tourism Organisation and the Caribbean Hotel Association will continue to be valuable partners in that regard. Let us move forward with vision and commitment, with the social and economic advancement of the people of the Caribbean in general, and the advancement of the people of St Kitts and Nevis in particular, uppermost in our minds.

SUPPLYING LOCAL AGRO-PRODUCE TO THE MARRIOTT RESORT

St Kitts Marriott Resort, November 3, 2007

I am very delighted that we are here this evening to participate in an important development between tourism and agriculture. My government has been intensifying the thrust to enhance the linkages between the two sectors because it is a critical component for our economic growth and development.

This country imports an enormous amount of food products for the size of its economy. We must modify this substantially so that much of the food we need is sourced from local farmers. This development between the Farmer's Cooperative Society and the St Kitts Marriott is a significant start and my hope is that all concerned will work diligently to ensure that this early phase is a success and that it will lead to additional opportunities for farmers on our islands.

Enhancing agricultural output has been occurring as a result of collaborative approaches including farmers and the Department of Agriculture as well as institutions such as the FAO, IICA, and CARDI. In addition, we have been fortunate to have a long-standing relationship with the Agricultural Mission of the Republic of China that has been instrumental in improving the productivity of our farms. This combination of technical support coupled with an increased number of farmers, particularly following the closure of the sugar industry, has created a foundation that must be strengthened and upon which new endeavours can be pursued for the benefit of the economy.

I wish to express my appreciation to the management of the St Kitts Marriott for the confidence they have placed in our farmers. It must be understood that this is an opportunity to demonstrate to the tourism sector the ability of our farmers to meet the criteria for supplying fresh produce to our hotels and restaurants. I am convinced that the developing hotel plant on the island will create important markets for our local farmers. I urge our farmers and those who have interests in agriculture to approach the sector as you would any other business. Management, structure, processes, standards, reliability, and quality are all important ingredients for success in expanding agriculture and creating further linkages between tourism and agriculture.

I wish to assure our farmers that the government will continue to work in their best interests and we certainly invite further collaboration and cooperation. I have great pleasure therefore, in wishing this venture, which is symbolised through the signing of the Memorandum of Understanding, every success for all involved.

CARIBBEAN HOTEL & TOURISM ASSOCIATION RETREAT

St Kitts Marriott Resort, October 1, 2008

I am pleased to welcome you to the Federation of St Kitts and Nevis and to extend my best wishes for a productive retreat of member small hotels of the Caribbean Hotel and Tourism Association (CHTA). You are meeting at a time when there are significant challenges facing Caribbean tourism as a result of global influences over which unfortunately we have little or no control.

The sharp increase in the cost of energy globally over the past year has been the biggest enemy of our regional economies. Tourism in the Caribbean has been one of the victims with wide-ranging negative impacts including reduced airlift capacity to several destinations and rising airfares.

As hoteliers you are also affected by the increased costs of energy and food and the general cost environment in Caribbean tourism can be described as serious. The uncertainty and decline in confidence caused by recent developments in the financial markets of the United States will not help matters. Rather, it is likely to affect the travelling patterns of many North Americans who will be extremely cautious concerning their spending patterns in the short-term. This ripple is spreading to other important markets in Europe that are important feeders to Caribbean tourism.

Your gathering in St Kitts and Nevis at this retreat is a timely event that must be used to help small hoteliers develop the best possible response to the current economic environment. I believe we all agree that we can best respond to a regional concern when we collaborate on a regional scale, when we bring regional expertise together and act in the interest of the region.

Of course, a retreat like this enables all of us to brainstorm about solutions together rather than leave each of us to struggle with major problems individually. As the single most important economic sector in the Caribbean, the challenges being faced today by the tourism sector require significant and urgent cooperation between trade associations such as yours, other industry stakeholders, and government agencies and departments. Clearly this is a time for focused talk and targeted action. But it is also a time for innovation and I expect that your time in our beautiful twin-island Federation will produce new innovations which will be acted upon at the earliest possible time if we are to overcome the challenges that face this great and important tourism industry.

My government is very clear about the need for partnerships in economic development and all of our initiatives and interventions in the tourism sector have been derived from the input of a mix of private sector stakeholders and public sector technicians. For example, the St Kitts Tourism Authority has a mandate from my cabinet to actively engage the local private sector in all of its programmes and it has worked supportively with the St Kitts-Nevis Hotel and Tourism Association in its bid to host this crucial retreat.

The fact that the nine-member board of directors of our tourism authority only includes one public sector employee is further evidence of our commitment to engage the private sector as early as possible in the process of policy and programme formulation in tourism.

Through good times and tough times, small hotels have been in the forefront and have given a unique ambience to the local tourism product. Investment in our local and regional hotel sector has been rising with a number of major projects now being implemented. The Investment Promotion Agency (IPA) that we recently established will make the process much easier for potential investors and will enhance the already positive tourism investment climate in the Federation.

In spite of global challenges that affect us at this time, the investment climate in St Kitts and the Caribbean remains upbeat and the IPA reports a steady interest from potential investors. I am pleased to report that the IPA is progressing with the drafting of a new policy document that will be approved and implemented shortly. This policy will revolutionise the relationship between small hotels, classified locally as 100 rooms or less, and our government. Specifically, the policy introduces a Special Incentive Package for Small Hotels. The policy will address the issue of improving small hotel properties through an incentive system that will be tied to qualitative conditions.

Under the draft policy, gaining access to incentives will be associated with programmes aimed at improving customer service, expanding the use of locally-grown agricultural produce, encouraging the use of energy-efficient equipment, and improving collaboration with the tourism authority in marketing programmes. Small hoteliers will benefit from a package of improved fiscal incentives enabling physical and aesthetic improvement to properties while requiring that there be improvements to management and service quality in general.

While there is clearly a need for governments in our region to do more to support the small hotel group, we must also make it clear to all hoteliers and other tourism stakeholders that the challenges we now face globally mean that it cannot be business as usual. Standards and global competitiveness must be in the driving seat of government's investment programmes and concessions must no longer be seen as a handout from government. Those businesses on the receiving end of government concessions must also be on the delivering point of improved productivity through quality service to customers and responsible empowerment of employees

Even in the absence of a specific small hotels policy, my government has always been very supportive of the local hotel sector. From January this year to date, the Ministry of Finance has already approved duty and tax concessions amounting to over EC$13.7 million in value, this coming as a response to the prevailing global conditions that are affecting the industry.

In spite of these emerging challenges in the tourism sector, we believe that our exit from sugar production was timely and necessary. What it did was inject the opportunity to transform our economy and create increased opportunities for our people. Today, we are very much in pursuit of a diversified service-oriented economy inclusive of ICT services, financial services, tourism and allied services, and of course, we well understand the necessity to enhance resources for the development of non-sugar agriculture. The exit from sugar production also meant the ability to provide better resources for more profitable endeavours and as a result, strengthen the investment and economic climate in the country.

In the current situation, time will be our best friend if we use it wisely. If we do nothing or are ineffective in new strategies, then we will bear the consequences. Tourism, in general, is a resilient industry. Long-term prospects remain very good. It is the short- and medium-terms that will be most challenging. The key issue is how well we can market our tourism products led by a new sense of innovation and creativity, energy conservation, and quality service. What is certain, as I have indicated earlier, is that there has to be a highly interactive approach to tourism planning, product development, and marketing inclusive of all stakeholders.

Activities need to be coordinated and decisions based upon accepted national strategies for the development of tourism in each of our countries and these must be linked and coordinated with regional approaches. The era of ad hoc tourism development is over and the region now needs to project itself onto the world stage as a serious player in quality tourism with the distinctive Caribbean flavour and the unique essence of each island.

Finally, what is also clear is that it is a time for the region's stakeholders to demonstrate good leadership, to explore beyond the confines of our national boundaries, and to come up with new directions that will be of value to the socio-economic aspirations of the people of the Caribbean region. I am confident that the region will survive the storm and I perceive that this is a golden opportunity to redefine the values of our tourism for a successful tomorrow.

St Christopher National Trust Launch

National Museum, Basseterre, October 1, 2009

This evening's event is likely to go down in the history of St Kitts as one of the most profound and proud moments in the untiring work to preserve the heritage of our island. The launch of the St Christopher National Trust is a significant turning point in the preservation of our history and culture.

As a result of legislation passed in our National Assembly earlier this year, the St Christopher Heritage Society has transitioned into the St Christopher National Trust and is now charged with the responsibility of preserving our heritage sites and artifacts, and the conduct of research as well as the pursuit of other relevant activities that support its work.

A number of persons have contributed to such efforts over the years on a voluntary basis. As a non-governmental organisation (NGO), the St Christopher Heritage Society has had its share of challenges but it persevered through the dedicated commitment of many of its volunteers. Over the years, we have seen this organisation expand its capacity and capability and it has been a front line organisation among its peers in the Eastern Caribbean, although without the legal authority of a Trust.

There are many persons who could be identified in the work of heritage preservation on the island but most would agree that Ms Jacqueline Armony has played a pivotal role over the years, an anchor around which many of the developmental activities occurred. She must be commended for her dedication.

The establishment of the St Christopher National Trust can be viewed as a natural progression along the path of national development and certainly it brings greater focus on its role in the growth and development of our country. More than a society ever could, the National Trust will have the foundation and the legal instrumentalities to be more assertive in its work.

The National Trust will definitely be a complement to the development of tourism in our country. In fact, we expect it to play a significant role in that regard given that this country, with its substantial historical assets, heritage sites, and natural environmental attractions, along with its people, together constitute the basis for sustainable tourism development now and in the future.

I call on all citizens and nationals to be supportive as the St Christopher National Trust embarks on an important journey that will benefit the entire nation.

AGRO-TOURISM DEMONSTRATION FARM

Sandy Point, St Kitts, January 31, 2012

What a fascinating moment. This government, which I am honoured to lead, has long proclaimed its commitment to green energy, to agriculture, to tourism, and to constructive collaboration with the Republic of China on Taiwan. And today, at this ground-breaking ceremony, all of us assembled here – our minister of agriculture, our minister of energy, our minister of tourism, and our bilateral partner of long-standing, the Republic of China on Taiwan – are coming together in order to ensure the simultaneous, interwoven flowering of all of these priorities including agriculture, green energy, tourism, and bilateral cooperation, in one, well thought-out, and innovative project for the benefit of Kittitians and Nevisians for decades to come.

We in the Labour government decided long ago that we would be in no way deterred by our lack of 'natural resources' in the traditional sense of the word – no natural gas, no copper mines, no endless sea of timber. And the reason we've not been deterred is that we have also long understood and been grateful for the fact that we have indeed been blessed with the most important 'natural resource' of all – an imaginative, determined, and enterprising populace. And we in the government know and understand that *that* is what is key to all human advancement everywhere.

But in addition to our human gifts, we also have a country that is breathtakingly beautiful and a land where fertile soil abounds. What better way to marry the botanic, touristic, green energy, and bilateral potential then than in a project such as the one we are here to move forward today, this unique and multi-faceted Agro-Tourism Demonstration Farm Project.

Our minister of agriculture is forever exploring expanded opportunities to marry the fertility of our soil with the imagination of our people. Our minister of energy is doing all in his power to move the Federation away from its traditional fossil fuel dependence in the direction of green energy. Our minister of tourism is constantly seeking innovative ways to make the Federation's tourism offering more intriguing and more competitive. And St Kitts and Nevis and the Republic of China on Taiwan are forever seeking new opportunities through which, together, we can advance the interests of our respective countries and peoples. This project is an intriguing culmination of all our efforts and all our objectives.

And, may I say here, as we look at the tourism potential of this idea, that the international visitor is not monolithic. Even the international visitor who comes to St Kitts and Nevis is not monolithic. Some are interested only in sea and sand. Others in history and architecture. Still others seek 'escape' in revelry. There is a significant segment of travellers however that are interested in nature, in traditional herbs and medicines, in the flora and fauna of the countries that they visit. And this Agro-Tourism Demonstration Farm was designed specifically with that segment of the international travelling community in mind.

However, as is the case with all we do, this Agro-Tourism Project will have another equally important use as well. It will present to the young people of this Federation yet another face of agriculture, yet another use to which our precious lands can be put, yet another way in which planting and growing can be an important and meaningful source of revenue and inspiration.

This project had its genesis in a mission that I led to Taiwan last year in search of expanded opportunities for Kittitians and Nevisians. Today, that mission has borne fruit. And as a result, some twenty acres has been set aside for this magnificent project that will draw nationals from across the Federation and travellers from around the world to learn from and enjoy the wonders of nature in this carefully laid out facility. Today, after almost a year of meticulous planning and preparation, we open the preparatory office.

In the future, indigenous plants from St Kitts and Nevis will be showcased alongside indigenous plants from Taiwan. And special plants whose medicinal properties were long known by our ancient African forebears will be growing alongside plants whose medicinal properties were long known by the ancient Asian forebears of our Taiwanese partners. Friendship and partnership at its best.

Sugar, the plant so indelibly woven into our history, will also have a place here, a place of fun and challenge in the carefully designed cane field labyrinth, shaped like our two countries, through which locals and visitors alike will try to find their way.

Ours is a government of vision. For us, liberation means expanded opportunities and empowerment means broadened horizons for Kittitians and Nevisians in *all* fields of endeavour. And this project pushes forward this very important mandate.

KITTITIAN HILL RESORT
SOFT OPENING
St Paul's, Capisterre, St Kitts, July 11, 2014

This is a great day for Kittitian Hill, for Capisterre, and for the Federation. We have known for months now that there was going to be a soft opening in July, and that day is now here. If we have eyes to see, there is very little that I need to say. Just look around. Everything that we see here is the result, first of the vision of Mr Val Kempadoo, the individual in whose heart and mind this project originated, and the person who, over the course of many meetings, convinced the government of the power and potential of this project.

And everything that you see around you is the result of the hard work, the dedication, and the skill of local carpenters, local stonecutters, local electricians, local plumbers, local plant experts, local gardeners, other local tradesmen, and local financial and other experts who, at the end of all of countless days and weeks and months, created all that we see before us today.

Every single person associated with Kittitian Hill, from the developer to the newest employee, deserves a wonderful, a thunderous, and a tumultuous applause. I have repeatedly made clear my commitment to ensure that developments that take place in this country will take place all over this country. Not just in one area. Not just in Basseterre, not just in Frigate Bay, not just on the South-East Peninsula. But all across the country.

In years gone by, how many of us have seen our fellow Kittitians who live in Saddlers, in St Paul's, in Newton Ground, and throughout this part of the country in general, having to head on a daily basis all the way to Basseterre, all the way to Frigate Bay, all the way to the Industrial Site, simply to find work? With Kittitian Hill, and with the other developments underway in this part of our country, those days will be no more. With Kittitian Hill and other developments planned for this region, the people of Capisterre will be able to work where they live. And people from other parts of the country just might begin choosing to travel to this region of our country in order to make use of the employment and other opportunities that developments like Kittitian Hill make possible.

As beautiful and as impressive as Kittitian Hill already is, this is just the beginning. This is just Phase I. And yet, this beginning has already injected some EC$282 million into our economy. Already, at this very early stage of Kittitian Hill's existence, EC$38 million has been spent with local contractors. At this early stage of this project, which has not yet even been completed, some $42 million has already been spent with local suppliers. As of today, when we are simply marking the soft opening of Kittitian Hill, and not the official opening, some seventy-seven local suppliers have already benefited from the revenue streams that have begun flowing as a result of Kittitian Hill's existence.

Kittitian Hill, as we know, is no ordinary development. My government is totally committed to the notion of sustainable development, and Kittitian Hill is very much in keeping with this. My government has been stressing the importance of developers recognising and relying on the vast array of local resources and Kittitian Hill is a development which relies, to an extraordinary extent, on local plants, local suppliers, local resources. The government of St Kitts and Nevis is resolute in our commitment to green energy and green energy is a priority here at Kittitian Hill.

Already some 550 construction workers have been employed here at Kittitian Hill. Within a matter of months, by the end of this year to be exact, fourteen villas will be open and operational. There will be 174 hotel rooms. And there will be 324 of our fellow nationals working here.

Newton Ground, St Paul's, Saddlers, Dieppe Bay – this entire northwestern region of the country – is a place of spectacular beauty. It is lush. It is green. The mountains are majestic. Our breezes are like God's caress. Those of us who were born here and who have lived here have always known this. Developments like Kittitian Hill will bring more of our people here on a regular basis. And developments like Kittitian Hill will help our people to see this part of our country with new eyes.

Kittitian Hill is a tremendous asset to our country. The workers who have brought Kittitian Hill into being are jewels in our nation's crown.

Let us acknowledge and celebrate our country's stability.

Let us acknowledge and celebrate our country's promise.

Let us acknowledge and celebrate all that we, as a people, a nation, and a government, have been able to achieve because there is a great deal to acknowledge and a great deal to celebrate.

Let us celebrate all that our country has accomplished, and let us look forward to many years of positivity and growth both here at Kittitian Hill and throughout our nation at large.

The Environment and Sustainability

THE ENVIRONMENT AND SUSTAINABILITY

This section, The Environment and Sustainability, is new. In Volume 1, *Coming of Age*, environmental and sustainability concerns were subsumed under the Tourism section which dealt primarily with the monumental task of transitioning the St Kitts and Nevis economy from sugar production to the tourism and hospitality industry.

The devastating impact of five hurricanes in Labour's first five years in office, the growing global awareness of climate change, and an increasing number of environmental disasters virtually everywhere in the world, meant that St Kitts and Nevis, a microstate and the smallest country in the western hemisphere, soon found itself deeply involved in environmental and sustainability issues.

With tourism now St Kitts and Nevis's largest and most important economic sector, successful management of environmental challenges, both current and developing, became the single most important determinant of the federation's future prosperity and success. From a relatively low profile only ten years earlier, environmental and sustainability issues were now front and centre on the government's agenda.

The Douglas administration initiated a number of green sustainability programmes in St Kitts and Nevis including biofuels development; wind and geothermal energy projects; creation of a solar farm; corporatisation of the electricity department to ensure SKN citizens an efficient, affordable and reliable source of electricity; and the establishment of an Eco-Park.

Denzil Douglas took every opportunity on the international stage to point out that countries like St Kitts and Nevis are not responsible for the climate crisis but disproportionally suffer the consequences, especially Small Island Developing States (SIDS). He reiterated that small countries are not able to support environmental and sustainability research and infrastructure and consequently need technical and financial support from larger, richer countries which need to take responsibility for the climate change crisis, develop a comprehensive action plan to contain it, and find the political will to achieve the deliverables.

Bio-Fuel Technologies Presentation

Ocean Terrace Inn, Basseterre August 28, 2007

It is with great pleasure that I greet you and welcome you to St Kitts and Nevis and to this venue to participate in discussions on the challenges and opportunities for St Kitts and Nevis from the development of bioenergy and in particular biofuels as a subset of that group. For those of you who are visiting our country for this event, I can assure you that we will do everything in our power to make your stay here an enjoyable and memorable one.

Let me state at the very outset, that St Kitts and Nevis is indeed proud and extremely honoured to have been given the assistance and afforded the opportunity to be involved in this path-breaking bioenergy analysis and the ensuing US/Brazil initiative. We realise that we now have the possibility of being if not on the ground floor at least on the first or second floor of truly momentous growth and development generated by affordable and benign energy that is also environmentally sustainable.

I was particularly pleased to see that the discussions are planned to proceed in a two-step interconnected way. In the morning session there will be a stakeholders' consultation where the results of the bioenergy analysis for St Kitts and Nevis will be presented and where stakeholders will be able to give their reaction as well as highlight issues, concerns or ideas relating to biofuels and bioenergy generally.

In the afternoon session, linked to the above but primarily as part of the US/Brazil Initiative in the Americas, of which St Kitts and Nevis is one of the four pilot countries, there will be a presentation by Dr George Phillipidis on bioenergy technologies which we hope will further raise awareness in our Federation about the truly revolutionary and transformative period that the world is now entering as we pursue a future based on bio-technology and sustainable bio-based production. Participants will thus be able to use the technological context set by the afternoon session to evaluate where to locate St Kitts and Nevis given the analytical findings.

The arrangement of the two sessions also demonstrates an important feature of the new modes of bio-production. The new systems are characterised by an advanced level of integration where as far as possible one must try to anticipate and prevent unintended consequences, while having the intellectual and economic infrastructure to support the creation and production of the bio-goods. This also presupposes extensive and long-term planning and a high level of organisation at all points of development and implementation. Achieving that level of organisation and integration can sometimes be difficult for small island states like St Kitts and Nevis especially as for the most part, the country on its own is too small to support the research and other facilities that are integral to the development of these technologies.

We have all heard about Brazil, of course, and its long-term development of biofuels going back to the 1920s and earlier. I was, however, astonished to discover that the US was seriously involved in bio-based production since the 1940s when according to *Agricultural Research*, a publication of the US Department of Agriculture, four regional research centres were set up 'to discover, and develop new uses, especially industrial ones, for the agricultural abundance being produced by US farmers.'

This is, however, all good news for us here in St Kitts and Nevis. As a small island developing state, St Kitts and Nevis has been very eager to develop alternative sources of energy to fossil fuels and has been exploring in particular the feasibility of developing renewable energy resources. This has proved to be very difficult due to the lack of local technical expertise and access to appropriate technology. These factors have been exacerbated by the small size of the country which inhibits commercial development of alternatives because of high development costs that may not necessarily be offset by high future demand. The government of St Kitts and Nevis believes that the most effective way of effecting technological transfer as well mitigating the disbenefits of small size in the energy field is to take a regional approach in concert with supportive development partners. It seems to me that this is exactly what the US/Brazil biofuel initiative is intended to do.

St Kitts and Nevis is currently at the very beginning of realising any biofuels potential that it may have. St Kitts and Nevis was unique as the only African, Caribbean and Pacific (ACP) state so seriously affected by the changes to the EU's sugar regime that it had to discontinue sugar production. The expectation that former sugar lands would now be available for other economic activities has resulted in a number of investment proposals some of which include using the land for the production of ethanol or other forms of biofuels. The response of the government has been to seek technical assistance to enable the country to make the right decisions regarding one of its most scarce resources, land. I would like to thank the OAS who, in conjunction with GSEII and supported by the ESG and UNIDO, have recently overseen the completion of a bioenergy potential assessment of St Kitts and Nevis and the production of the background discussion paper that is being presented today.

The key objectives of the study were:

1. To analyse the technical, economic and socio-environmental characteristics of biomass-to-energy systems for converting the locally available biomass to energy in the context of St Kitts and Nevis, and

2. To identify key criteria to select sustainable and commercially viable biomass to energy systems in the context of St Kitts and Nevis.

The conclusion of the paper, which examined various types of biomass to energy conversion systems and analysed different scenarios for these systems through economic modelling, was that under certain conditions both electricity generation and ethanol production for the local market would be feasible in St Kitts and Nevis.

Given these conclusions, St Kitts and Nevis has good reasons to be optimistic. My hope therefore for this discussion is that it will achieve its objectives, that the discussions will be incisive and fruitful, that St Kitts and Nevis with the help of its hemispheric partners who are the acknowledged best in the world in this field, will serve as a model for what all small island states can achieve given the right support and encouragement. Given the assembled talent and expertise, I am in no doubt that we can do this. I look forward with anticipation to the outcome of your deliberations and assure you that St Kitts and Nevis will continue to work with our hemispheric family to achieve true fuel security within sustainable development.

Climate Change Summit
United Nations, New York, September 22, 2009

Climate change has emerged as a significant issue for Small Island Developing States (SIDS) as its impacts threaten to undermine all efforts to pursue sustainable development agendas and to realise global developmental targets such as the Millennium Development Goals (MDGs). Indeed, the multi-faceted repercussions of uncontrolled climate change go way beyond sea level changes and have far-reaching and destabilising consequences in such areas as desertification, food production, population displacement, refugee flows, sociopolitical destabilisation, and geo-strategic conflict. The continued increase in greenhouse gas emissions beyond 2015 is clearly untenable and earth temperature increases of some 2 per cent, relative to pre-industrial levels, destructive.

As a small developing state continuously battered by the vagaries of hurricanes that repeatedly undermine its developmental gains, St Kitts and Nevis uses this forum to join once again in registering deepest concerns regarding the slow pace at which the global community is moving to address this issue. While sessions such as this year's summit on climate change are important, permitting, as they do, the articulation of the perspectives and recommendations of nations of all socio-economic and geographic profiles, it is essential that they are seen as a means to an end, and not an end in themselves.

In the past, the alliance of small island states has made a compelling case as to the importance of dedicated and measurable progress in controlling global temperature and CO_2 concentrations. However, global warming and its attendant rise in sea levels are phenomena that pose grave and possibly irreversible dangers not only for small island nations like mine but indeed, for all low-lying coastal areas, of which there are many in some of the largest and most heavily industrialised non-island states.

Countries such as mine are not responsible for this crisis. Nonetheless, as a matter of principle, we are doing our part to reverse these troubling global trajectories. Our forests, comprising some 20 per cent of our land mass, have now been declared protected areas. In my country, our forests absorb more carbon-dioxide than we produce. In addition, we are now actively involved in the aggressive development of geothermal and wind energy capabilities on our islands – again, as a matter of principle, to do our part.

In addition, throughout the wider Caribbean region, governments have been giving this crisis the attention that it deserves. I point here to the Caribbean Planning for Adaptation to Climate Change Project, the Mainstreaming Adaptation to Climate Change Project, and the Caribbean Community Climate Change Centre which has been fully operational since 2004, the mandate of which is to provide a strategic approach to long-term action.

With sea levels continuing to rise around us, St Kitts and Nevis urges a 45 per cent reduction in CO_2 emissions by 2020 relative to 1990, and a 90 per cent reduction by 2050. In its recent summit, some of the major G8 emitters expressed their commitment to intensify climate change-related efforts. We now urge swift, effective, and principled action.

St Kitts and Nevis joins our small island partners in the call for an urgent and rapid response to the transfer of technology, robust funding for adaptation and capacity-building, and most importantly, a discussion and definitive conclusion on how we can achieve a stabilisation of carbon dioxide in the earth's atmosphere at 350 parts per million (ppm) and an increase of below 1.5°C. We are therefore urging the major emitters of greenhouse gases to make rapid reductions in their greenhouse gas emissions. We reiterate our request for financial and technical support for capacity-building and technology transfer in all SIDS and low-lying countries to be able to more effectively confront the challenges of climate change.

It is my hope that this year we shall succeed in arriving at an effective plan to overcome this climate change challenge. I fear that if we continue to squander our resources and we are reluctant to reverse our behaviour patterns toward the environment, we will irreparably damage our planet. Let us, together, strive to pool our efforts and resources to combat this threat to our countries and our peoples. Let us together unite and with concerted action contribute to a safer, cleaner earth for our children and their children's children.

Countries like mine have played no part in the creation of this crisis. Nonetheless, it is we who have been made to bear a disproportionate share of the global ecological burden. This simply is not right. Adaptation strategies, capacity-building, and the development and/or acquisition of pertinent technologies are, for us, pressing and costly priorities. It is only just and fair, therefore, that those countries which, though never intending to, nonetheless did trigger this global crisis in the process of advancing their own economic growth, now step forward to meet the cost of the aforementioned adaptation strategies, capacity-building, and technology acquisition in countries like mine.

We meet again in December in Copenhagen. I urge, however, that we act today as though we have neither December nor Copenhagen. There is too much at stake for procrastination. There is too much at stake for equivocation. Let us understand the dangers inherent in this moment. And let us act accordingly.

CORPORATISATION OF THE ELECTRICITY DEPARTMENT

Ask the Prime Minister Radio Programme
ZIZ Broadcasting Corporation, September 8, 2009

This morning I want to talk about energy. Energy, in a modern society, affects so much. It determines the extent to which today's families can carry out the normal activities associated with managing a household from electricity-based recreation, to labour-saving devices, to the so-called information super-highway that parents and children have come to rely on for the completion of academic or career-related responsibilities. Outside of the home, within industry, energy represents an important component of a company's operating costs and can affect a firm's competitive advantage, or lack thereof, *vis-à-vis* its competitors. The bottom line, then, is that in the twenty-first century a great deal of human activity, whether recreational or work-related, revolves around energy.

And so the reliable provision of reasonably priced energy is of utmost importance to my government. And this is an area in which we have been investing a great deal of effort, time, and attention. Indeed, this is so important a priority that we are careful to form strategic alliances whenever possible to ensure that as we strive to protect the nation's long-term energy interests, our analysis, our plans, and our projections are indeed sound. In this regard, therefore, I should tell you that we are currently working in conjunction with the Organisation of American States to review and fine-tune our power purchase agreement with North Star, the wind farm entity that has been given permission by the government to operate in the Belle Vue area. Testing has been ongoing for some seven months now and I am very pleased to report that the results thus far has been very favourable. A highly experienced legal expert on matters of this kind who has worked both with the OAS as well as other regional governments, is a member of our legal team, and I should also mention that as a result of this wind farm alone, my government will be able to deliver to the people of St Kitts an additional 8 MW hours of electricity by early 2010.

And then, of course, there are the geothermal energy resources in Nevis for which the federal government sought and secured OAS involvement and support for exploration. Our use of fossil fuel-based energy will not end overnight, of course. That is why the identification and pursuit of alternate energy sources is key to my government's long-term development plans. And it is this reality that explains our advances in these two key areas, wind and geothermal. And as is the case with North Star, my government will be interested in pursuing a power purchase agreement with the relevant party in Nevis to ensure that the people of the Federation have yet another source, in addition to North Star, of reasonably priced, reliable, non-fossil fuel-based energy.

The identification and development of these energy resources are key components of our development equation, but there is another part that is equally important and that is management. The delivery of these three energy components – wind, geothermal, and fossil fuels – must be coordinated in such a way as to secure and deliver a reliable supply of reasonably priced energy to the nation. With this in mind, therefore, I am pleased to report that my cabinet is putting the pieces in place to move steadily and responsibly toward the corporatisation of the electricity department. And we will do this so that the type of management structure and expertise needed, the type of coordinated delivery systems, and the quality of service that we have set as our goal in the area of energy security, are indeed available.

On the subject of corporatisation, one of the first tasks of my government will be to ensure that persons of the highest levels of technical expertise and management acumen will be relied upon to be a part of this historic step forward for the nation. And from throughout our Federation, they will be invited to serve in this important capacity. The important point is that, as I have said before, we, like people all over the world, need a reliable source of reasonably priced energy.

My government recognised the energy potential represented in our God-given trade winds and we moved with seriousness and commitment to ensure that this gift of nature, in combination with the twenty-first century technology that is producing wind energy all across the globe, does so right here in St Kitts as well. Similarly, we recognised the energy potential of the geothermal resources of Nevis and moved, again with seriousness and commitment, to secure the type of multinational support that is needed to transform this other gift of nature into a valuable source of renewable energy for us all.

Wars are being fought, way beyond our shores, over energy. It is in our best interests, as a people, to identify and pursue with vision, insight, and confidence those sources of energy that will enable our development plans to move forward, free of 100 per cent fossil-fuel dependence. This we have done. This we shall continue to do. And, as we can already see, our country and our people will be the better for it.

CLIMATE CHANGE CONFERENCE
Organisation of Eastern Caribbean States (OECS)
St Kitts Marriott Resort, September 11, 2012

Whatever the debate being waged internationally regarding the question of climate change, and however dramatic the rhetorical jousting within various circles on this issue, we in the Caribbean can attest to the radical climatic shifts that our region has undergone in recent decades.

I am fortunate enough to be completing my sixth decade of life. For most of those years, I knew nothing of hurricanes. In the last two decades, however, St Kitts and Nevis has felt their wrath like never before. Their ferocity has been shocking. Their frequency, ill-mannered and most unwelcome. But St Kitts and Nevis is hardly unique. We remember only too well the brutality of Ivan and Emily *vis-à-vis* Grenada in 2004 and 2005, despite Grenada being, we thought, safely nestled in the more southerly reaches of our archipelago. The list goes on, with multi-faceted and troubling ramifications for us all, ramifications with which both policy-makers and you, as specialists in the field, are already only too familiar.

What then, do we do? How do we protect ourselves from this global phenomenon with so many interrelated and oft-times internally discordant parts?

First of all, we must continue to impress upon the international community the hard-won insights that our own hard work and our first-hand experiences have gleaned. And we must continue to impress upon them the extreme difficulties associated with our efforts to protect our people and our nations when nothing pertaining to climate change takes place in a vacuum, and nothing stays within the confines of either its point of origin or the site of its correction. Global climate trends and patterns are now an incredibly complex Rubik's cube, an intricately interwoven and interrelated whole. The challenges we face are unquestionably complex, the need for solutions especially pressing.

Wasn't it just this year that the US National Oceanic and Atmospheric Administration diagnosed the warmest twelve-month period on record, ever? We know the implications of this for countries like ours and so we know that whatever the official title of this seminar and whatever the titles of the conferences that have both preceded and will follow this one, these sessions are, at their most fundamental level, about self-preservation. And self-preservation is the first law of nature. For us, climate change is far from an abstraction. Instead, it has an urgently existential dimension. It conjures up simple words with far-reaching implications, words like vulnerability and viability.

And so, conference participants, let me stress again just how key your presence here, and your work here, are to our region's self-preservation mandate, as regional governments strive to advance and undergird the human, infrastructural, economic, and environmental interests that are put so severely at risk by climate change. We in the OECS are islands, yes, but because we are so tiny, our coastlines, relative to the land mass between those coastlines, have a major and disproportionate bearing on almost every aspect of our existence.

Britain, we know, is an island. Zanzibar is an island. Madagascar is an island. There are many land masses which, like us, are called islands. But there, the similarities end. The impact of those islands' coastal resources on their overall well-being is far less than ours because of the vastness of their territory and, shall we say, the 'neatness' of ours.

As a result, there are a number of issues with which we, compared to them, must constantly contend:

1. the physical safety of our people who, compared to the inhabitants of those larger land masses, are never far from the coast;

2. the protection of our reefs because of their enormous significance to our fishing and tourism industries;

3. the repeated storm-related battering that our coastal public and private infrastructure must withstand;

4. the opportunity cost to our people of scarce public resources having to be spent on the repeated rebuilding and revetments necessitated by increasingly angry seas;

5. the ever-present threats to crucial maritime activities, including commerce, when storms ravage our docks, damage our ports, and disrupt our harbours.

The list goes on. It is with these inescapable realities that we must contend. And it is the need for preventive, corrective, and adaptive measures that we are called upon to address.

The ever-morphing challenges associated with climate change place special burdens on us because they demand that we be equally fluid and adaptive in our response to these ever-changing challenges. Our constantly having to respond to externally-created crises may be neither welcome nor fair, but they are reality. And that is why we must be thorough and effective in our insistence that those who created this crisis bear the associated financial burdens.

The 1987 Montreal Protocol, as we know, for example, successfully protected the ozone layer by regulating the gases used in air conditioning. This led to the use of progressively more benign gases and, as a result, older, ozone-damaging coolants have now been largely eliminated from use. The newest coolants, widely used in industrialised nations, have little or no effect on the ozone.

There is only one problem. Pound for pound, these new coolants contribute to global warming thousands of times more than does carbon dioxide, as has been widely reported, including in the *New York Times* on June 20 of this year. Not a positive development for us, and yet another example of how these challenges are forever morphing even as we strive not only to address the economic ramifications of climate change and the issues of integrated coastal areas and watershed management, but indeed as we look at the institutional mechanisms through which we address these challenges.

In closing then, let me reiterate that your task is far from routine, and the complexity of the challenges with which you must grapple, enormous. We thank you, again, for your efforts. We thank you for your commitment to our region. Rest assured that we will give the outcome of your deliberations the attention and the weight that they so fully deserve.

THE ENVIRONMENT AND SUSTAINABILITY:
The Vulnerability of Small Island Developing States
United Nations, New York, September 2012

I wish now to address a matter that is profoundly troubling to small island states like mine – and that is that the largest contributors of greenhouse gases are still not taking responsibility for the increasing temperatures, rising sea levels, coastal degradation, coral reef bleaching and decimation, infrastructural damage, and loss of life that their actions have wrought. Our people, our maritime integrity, our soils, and our infrastructure are all interrelated contributors to our overall social and economic viability, and the absence of corrective and restitutional action on the part of industrialised nations involved is neither constructive nor understandable in this highly interdependent world. The physical, psychic, and financial costs that other countries' energy usage has inflicted on countries like mine has been enormous, plunging us deeper into debt and severely frustrating our efforts to meet our Millennium Development Goals. While a shift to renewable energy will not instantly solve the myriad problems caused by a significantly fossil fuel-based global economy, the embrace of green energy will indeed help to halt the intense downward spiral into which our fossil fuel-based economies have thrust our planet, and so we strongly urge that green energy be made an absolute priority globally.

The recently held United Nations Conference on Sustainable Development set the stage for a reconfiguration of the global programme on sustainable development and, indeed, signalled a new era in the sustainable development agenda of the international community. Two decades of debate and deliberation were instrumental in our being able to frame the dialogue and envision a path for the two decades now before us, and if we are to even approach the potential of Rio+20, it will be essential that we first face up to, and then break, the strictures of indifference and narrow self-interest that have plagued us for far too long. It is therefore incumbent upon both us and future generations that we view our responsibilities as parts of an ongoing continuum, with each of our efforts both benefitting from, as well as building upon, the work that came before.

And so, St Kitts and Nevis applauds the decision to convene the Third UN Conference on Sustainable Development for Small Island Developing States in 2014. Small Island Developing States, by virtue of our size and geographic profile, are clearly among the most vulnerable nations on earth, hence the recognition of our need for special attention where sustainable development is concerned, and indeed, the importance of everyone remembering the absolutely essential nature of special and differentiated responsibilities where small island states are concerned. I therefore urge that clear targets be established now so that we can all prepare thoroughly and well for the 2014 conference at which urgently needed attention will be paid to ways in which our vulnerabilities as Small Island Developing States might best be reduced. This august body can be assured of our full participation in this process and in the post-Rio+20 sustainable development agenda.

3rd Caribbean Sustainable Energy Forum and Exhibition

St Kitts Marriott Resort, September 13, 2012

I must begin, not only by welcoming you but also, by expressing our deep appreciation to the governments of Finland, Germany, the United Kingdom, and the European Union for their sponsorship of this event. Special thanks go out as well, of course, to the CARICOM Secretariat which in conjunction with our own Ministry of Energy and Public Utilities, did so much to make this forum possible.

Throughout this region, governments continue to formulate policies and programmes to advance the social and economic well-being of our people. We enact legislation to enhance the educational standing of our students, and the competitiveness of our farmers. We empower public works specialists to improve our physical infrastructure, and health care professionals to improve our physical well-being. We give community development programmes the focus they deserve, and we compete with nations large and small to bring discerning travellers to our shores.

But no matter the area of focus, whether it be one of those I just mentioned or another such as foreign policy, national security, telecommunications, they all rely on, they all depend on, and indeed they all absolutely must have energy. And this, of course, is why we are here today. We are here because energy is a twenty-first century obsession for governments everywhere. Wars are being fought over it. Geo-strategic partnerships are based on, sustained by, and broken apart, because of it. And so every nation understands the importance of reducing its vulnerability in this regard. Every nation realises the urgency of finding ways to expand its options, secure its access, and reduce its dependency where energy is concerned. St Kitts and Nevis certainly understands this. And so do our neighbours throughout the region.

We are often told that large countries often have an advantage because of their size. That is true. But size can also have its advantages where small nations are concerned because sometimes when one is tiny, as we are, out of necessity you develop a certain alertness, a certain instinct to think ahead and protect yourself because you understand only too well how very easy it would be if one is not vigilant, to get run over in the rush. This has certainly been the case where we are concerned, and so, as the smallest nation in the western hemisphere, we place a great deal of emphasis on in-depth planning and meticulous follow-through in all areas, but especially where finite fossil fuel supplies, a warming planet, and a volatile world oil market are concerned.

How does a tiny nation like St Kitts and Nevis, then, protect itself? In a matter of days, we will celebrate our twenty-ninth year as an independent nation. Twenty-nine years may be the blinking of an eye in the context of world history, but throughout our time in office, my government has worked tirelessly both to establish and manage a respected and stable democracy, as well as to provide the types of human and infrastructural developments that will enhance our people's standing and options in this highly technological and increasingly globalised age. And each and every one of our strivings and accomplishments has expanded our need for energy. St Kitts and Nevis must, as a result, find ways to generate energy. And we must do so in a manner that is both cost-effective and reliable.

Like much of the region and much of the world, we have for almost a century been wedded to an energy generation model that does not serve our long-term interests. Our traditional reliance on foreign-based fossil fuels has left us vulnerable to the vagaries of political currents far from our shores, held us hostage to geo-strategic machinations in which we have no say, and generally caused us to be affected by far too many factors completely beyond our control. The only constant where oil prices are concerned, it seems, is volatility. In light of this, the steadfast friendship and tangible support showed to us all by the government of Venezuela, through such arrangements as PetroCaribe, simply cannot be overstated. This has made a tremendous difference as our governments have worked to build stable economies in this most unstable world, and our people have benefited tremendously from it.

It is a fact, however, as we always remind ourselves, that fossil fuel supplies are finite. And it is also a fact that for 365 days of the year, St Kitts and Nevis is in the embrace of an utterly phenomenal energy source – the sun. In addition, geography has placed us in the direct path of wonderful trade winds and our geology has bequeathed to us geothermal sources of power. We are therefore taking the only wise and responsible path open to us – we are moving to develop them all.

There is already a wind farm in Nevis, for example. Work continues with OPIC for a similar facility to be established in St Kitts. And current projections are for us to have access to locally-generated geothermal energy in two years.

The Republic of China on Taiwan, a friend and ally of long-standing, is now, as you know, the second largest producer of solar panels in the world. As they have in other areas, they have developed a special partnership with us *vis-à-vis* solar energy as can be seen in the solar lighting project along both our Kim Collins Highway as well as a our Frigate Bay Road. I am very pleased that Taiwan's leading solar panel manufacturers are represented here at the forum and will be available tell you more about their products and answer any questions you may have at the exhibition that has been arranged here for your convenience.

Indeed, solar-powered road lightings are just a part of our move toward green energy. Solar panels are currently generating energy for both our government headquarters as well as our ITC Centre, for example, and they will, from now on, be installed on all newly constructed, affordable homes in the Federation, as a means of controlling the cost of energy for our nation's families. But it is not only the government that is enthusiastic about solar energy. Our largest companies have made clear to us their determination to move in this direction as well. Indeed, they have already officially sought and received the required authorisations to do so. We commend them for their enthusiasm, vision, and leadership in this regard.

Our neighbour, Jamaica, we know, has long had a wind farm, and Barbados, our other sister-island, has long been a producer of solar panels. Caribbean governments, now more than ever, understand that green energy is the destination and that there is no turning back.

That having been said, however, and despite the absolute necessity of moving steadfastly in the direction of renewable energy, there are certain truths that must be faced. For example, even though prices may be declining for some technologies, renewable energy technologies are still not cheap to implement. There remains a pressing need for capital, for financing, for technical support. And because of the newness of this area we, as governments, businesses, specialists, and analysts must indeed do everything in our power to ensure than costly mistakes are avoided. Let us be wise, circumspect, and discerning as we move toward these important technologies. And let us all undertake the hard work, the meticulous research, the in-depth analysis that will be necessary if we are to ensure that we fully understand these new technologies and the risks that may be associated with their integration into our systems. This requirement for circumspection and discernment is not unique to us, by the way. It is incumbent upon all nations, large or small, so to do. This is simply what responsible governance and responsible management anywhere and everywhere demand.

This forum will be paying particular attention to the integration of regional energy systems which is of particular importance to us as island states. And the geothermal project in Nevis as it relates to other OECS member states, I know, will be of special interest and relevance in that regard. I urge that the special challenges of capacity, financing, and intergovernmental cooperation be kept at the forefront of your deliberations, and that proactive and innovative approaches be put forward so as to ensure that the benefits of these developments do indeed redound to our region, and in the shortest possible time.

Let us also remember, and this is of vital importance, that focusing on the technological dimensions of green energy is only a part of our responsibilities. Equally important, if not more so, if we are to truly protect the interests of our peoples and our region, will be the special regulatory framework that must go hand-in-hand with these technological advances.

And then, of course, there is the need for the broad-based education of our people on the key issues, risks, limitations, and opportunities where green energy is concerned. Something as simple as instilling in the minds of our nationals the habit of unplugging appliances when not in use could have a dramatic impact on energy consumption and expenditures in our respective countries. This and other straightforward, but important, means of 'turning our people on' to energy conservation must be made priorities.

What is so special about this conference is that it captures the depth and breadth of all that we are called upon to do where our embrace of renewable energy sources is concerned. At the same time that we must identify innovative and engaging ways to educate and involve our respective populations at the micro level, so too must we, as a region, simultaneously engage the international community at the macro level in order to establish those key partnerships that will allow us to derive from this moment, and from these opportunities, the benefits that our people so richly deserve. Let us not forget that our movement toward green energy will not only save scarce financial resources that can be far better used domestically, but this shift will also lead to the establishment of a new and dynamic energy sector with new and exciting opportunities for both business development as well as job creation.

On this march forward, we cannot afford to rest and so, just a few months ago I made a point of travelling to India in search of new opportunities and partnerships in this regard. In addition, we have now corporatised our electricity department to make it both more efficient and more effective. I look at our young students, many of whom have a fascination with science but who tend to think simply in terms of studying physics, studying chemistry, or studying some subject in the abstract. And I think of how incumbent it is upon us as parents, as teachers, as government officials, as business leaders, to find ways to encourage our young people to see themselves not simply as the consumers of technologies that are developed by individuals far away, but as individuals who can, with further study, join that forward-thinking band of scientists who are solving major challenges and delivering workable solutions to the rest of the world. We must help them to understand that there are endless ways in which they can join the highly trained innovators, by being the ones to develop energy-saving devices, by being the ones to design solar, wind, or geothermal technologies, by coming up with innovative ways to incorporate energy-efficient features into building design. In addition, we need local specialists coming up with creative ways to, for example, introduce greater efficiency in our region's transportation sectors and better inform vehicle importation policies. The possibilities are endless.

What I wish to stress however, is that your presence here today is of great value to our region. As you are aware, the Council for Trade and Economic Development in Georgetown in March of last year mandated that the CARICOM Secretariat expedite cross-border trading in electricity to help create increased energy supply, economic integration, and competitiveness.

Over the next two days, there will be a thorough weighing of the various options before us. There will be a careful assessment of the costs and benefits associated with various courses of action. And there will, at the end, be light – hopefully a floodlight, and a solar powered one at that – as to the way forward. Among your varied areas of focus will be the promise of geothermal energy, possible funding mechanisms, systems integration, the challenge of access – all very, very important.

Your recommendations regarding both geothermal energy as well as energy-efficiency enhancement, will, of course, be seriously studied as we move forward with the development of a regional action plan.

LIGHTING OF ISLAND MAIN ROAD SANDY POINT TO ST PAUL'S

Eco Park, LaValle, December 31, 2012

Today, we are here to witness the continuation of an important and ongoing project – the transformation of our nation from one that is dependent on fossil fuels to one that uses renewable energy. Anyone who has driven around our island must have noticed by now the erection of street lights that are new – and different. These street lights can be seen on the Kim Collins Highway and they can be seen on the Frigate Bay Road. What is different about these lights is that they not only provide illumination for our drivers and our pedestrians, but they do so in a responsible and an ecologically sound manner. In other words, they harness the most powerful energy source on earth – the sun – to provide us with the light that we need.

As every school child by now knows, the government of St Kitts and Nevis and the government of China on Taiwan have been partners on many important fronts. We both take the time to understand the needs and objectives of each other and we strive to the best of our abilities to help bring about the realisation of these goals. As a result, both governments have been intimately involved in advancing our goal here in St Kitts and Nevis of becoming a 'green' nation where energy is concerned. And this special partnership, combined with the vision and hard work of our minister of public works, has brought us to the point where we are today connecting Sandy Point and St Paul's in such a way that this most beautiful section of the Island Main Road, connecting areas of such historic significance in our country can, at last, be connected not only via a road but by light. I like the symbolism here. May this illumination and this light affect all that we in St Paul's and Sandy Point think, and do, and accomplish, both in the new year and as long as we shall live.

This is an important project. It took a considerable amount of work and planning. And I am very pleased to be a part of it. May the people of Sandy Point and St Paul's, and indeed the people of our entire country, travel safely and in comfort along this long-standing stretch of road which, most appropriately as we head to 2013, will be illuminated night after night for our safety and convenience, not in the way that our streets have been lit for years, not by the use of fuel that threatens the environment and costs too much, but by solar cells, by the power of the sun, by green technology. This is a great day. This is a great project. May it forever benefit Sandy Point and St Paul's.

CARIBBEAN OZONE OFFICERS REGIONAL MEETING

St Kitts Marriott Resort, March 18, 2013

It gives me great pleasure to stand here greeting you in this your twenty-fifth year of celebrating the establishment of the Montreal Protocol, a convention which demonstrates that the international community can bring its collective efforts to bear upon a common problem and arrive at effective solutions. The Montreal Protocol was drafted twenty-five years ago with the lofty goal of reducing the effects of ozone depleting substances which were causing an increasing weakening of our critical ozone layer. The sun's ultraviolet rays were penetrating through this destabilised layer resulting in increased incidences of skin cancer, cataracts, and other critical health and environmental effects. My country has recognised the importance of protecting and rehabilitating this vital shield and we have therefore prioritised this element of environmental protection by not only supporting the people who are committed to ensuring that the work is done, but also supporting and empowering our local refrigeration and air-conditioning sector. In the last twenty-five years we have been part of a process that has seen the reduction of some 98 per cent of the ozone depleting gases. This is a critical achievement. But notwithstanding how vital this accomplishment is, we cannot afford to rest upon our laurels as the challenge of dealing with HCFCs still lies ahead of us. We must continue to work hand-in-hand with refrigeration and air-conditioning personnel to help them continue their education and develop a strong, resilient, and vibrant sector.

In St Kitts and Nevis our commitment to the process has been demonstrated with the passage of 'Substances that Deplete the Ozone Layer Regulations' in 2004, which had the foresight to regulate HCFC importation long before the discussion of HCFC phase-out was started. We accelerated our phase-out of CFCs and have maintained zero percent consumption since 2008. We have assisted the refrigeration and air-conditioning sector in keeping up with the fast-moving changes in the industry through the provision of education and supply of essential equipment. We are committed to continuing to provide necessary assistance until we are no longer needed. Currently, we are implementing the HCFC Phase-out Management Plan with the goal of significantly reducing our importation of HCFCs by 2020. With the keen interest of the refrigeration and air-conditioning sector to embrace alternative technologies, I think I can boldly predict that most if not all of our HCFCs will be phased out by 2020. We intend to continue educating the general public and empowering our people to demand environmentally friendly goods and services.

Ozone preservation and protection does not operate in isolation of any of the other environmental conventions or bodies. The challenge we face today in this fragile global economic climate is to find innovative ways to stretch every dollar to be effective in multiple ways. We fully recognised that funds received from our environmental partners must not be wasted but maximised to achieve multiple goals. Ozone protection goals for 2013 and beyond should not focus on ozone protection alone but should actively embrace other environmental aspirations such as clean air and energy efficiency. In the current global warming climate, we struggle to reduce our dependence on greenhouse gases while still meeting our economic viability. Climate change has been identified as a cross-cutting and persistent crisis. I have been advised that the current replacement gases for the old refrigerant and air-conditioning technologies are now more energy efficient and have low to no global warming potential. This is the only way to go if we intend to have a healthy future and a long and meaningful existence. Theodore Roosevelt once said

> to waste, to destroy our natural resources, to skin and exhaust the land instead of using it so as to increase its usefulness, will result in undermining in the days of our children, the very prosperity which we ought by right to hand down to them amplified and developed.

Our environmental commitments do not belong to the Ozone Secretariat, Multilateral Fund, and Ozone Officers alone. They should be the fundamental principles of our people everywhere. As governments, we do our best to ensure that we are representing the interests of our people but we need the support and actions of our people as well. As knowledgeable and partnering consumers, our people need to demand that our retailers only sell the best and most environmentally friendly goods. To put it in simple words, our refrigerators, air-conditioners, and chillers need to be modernised and not be tied to obsolete technology. As consumers who have shares in our own future, we need to ensure that the person who is repairing our refrigerator or installing that long-awaited AC unit has been properly trained and is using the best available technology. We need to demand the best and lead from the front.

Phasing out ozone depleting substances, although highly successful to this point, is not a simple task. There are numerous challenges that the officers face in ensuring the environmental integrity of the work they are doing. We are confronted by the dilemma of how to dispose of used or contaminated gases. The region to this point has not yet identified a methodology to dispose of the numerous cylinders of gases currently held in country stocks awaiting destruction. Persons with fewer scruples than our technicians will simply illegally release the gases to circumvent issues of storage and the need for recovery cylinders. I urge you to address this issue as it will become more and more critical as we advance in HCFC phase-out.

Another challenge the sector will encounter or continue to encounter is the illegal trade in ODSs. Illegal trade can derail our efforts to completely phase out HCFCs in the near future. We have to develop and strengthen the partnership forged with customs, brokers, refrigeration and air-conditioning associations, and institutions. These entities are vital to the success of the work ahead. Failing to embrace or include any of these entities will lead to a weak link in the system. We in small island states are no strangers to the power of collaboration. The sheer nature of our size and economic capabilities has often formed the imperative for our coming together and thus magnifying our voice in the regional and international arena. It is a lesson that cannot be overemphasised.

The government of St Kitts and Nevis and by extension our citizenry, has benefited tremendously since joining the international community in the fight to preserve the critical ozone layer system. The international community, through the guidance of the Ozone and Multilateral Fund secretariats, has continued to provide critical financial support for project implementation and the institutional strengthening project that targets capacity development at the local level. It is through this support that St Kitts and Nevis, and let me be presumptuous in saying the entire English-speaking Caribbean ozone network, has been so successful in implementing the Montreal Protocol. It is crucial that this support be continued, as it allows us the flexibility to address the issues and will certainly be helpful in assisting us to meet the ambitious HCFC targets.

As ozone depleting substances form a critical part of our economic framework, we, along with the international community, must continue to work diligently to encourage the development of energy efficient, cost-effective technologies. Phasing out HCFCs should not be a burden to countries whose livelihoods and economies are intertwined with the industry. I call on the developed world to encourage the transfer of these technologies at a reasonable cost and further call for the establishment of a destruction facility in our region. The government of St Kitts and Nevis is wholly grateful to our partners for their invaluable technical and financial support in enabling us to make our contribution to the task of eliminating ozone-damaging gases.

We congratulate you again for twenty-five years of excellent work and wish you continued success in the future.

CARIBBEAN MAN
AND THE BIOSPHERE
INTER-MINISTERIAL CONFERENCE
St Kitts Marriott Resort, March 27, 2013

Welcome to the Federation of St Kitts and Nevis and to the Inter-Ministerial and Expert Conference on Biosphere Reserves in the Caribbean. Your being here adds a special dimension to this event, an event which many recognise as being a milestone in terms of UNESCO's Man and the Biosphere Programme in the English-speaking Caribbean.

Two years ago, as we know, St Kitts and Nevis was identified as a new site on the World Network of Biosphere Reserves Register. And we were well aware then of the relevance and indeed the importance of this initiative to the Federation, culturally, ecologically, and economically. And so we welcome this programme because biosphere reserves are such crucial components of the ongoing effort to enhance biodiversity and natural resource protections globally. Indeed, what they give to us, and what they represent, are living laboratories where conservation and the sustainable use of natural resources can be demonstrated.

The past five years have been a period of unprecedented uncertainty for even the most powerful nations on earth. And the interconnected nature of the world's economies has made it impossible, or at least most unwise, for any country be either indifferent or nonchalant where global economic conditions are concerned. And so, in countries everywhere, policy-makers and planners are combining their specific areas of expertise in the quest to provide, for their respective nations, economic growth. And so, because everyone in this room understands the potential of Biosphere Reserves to stir imaginations, stimulate entrepreneurial instincts, spur innovation, and therefore increase the level of economic activity, it is easy to see why St Kitts and Nevis welcomes this initiative.

A key selling point of biosphere reserves, as far as St Kitts and Nevis is concerned, is the fact that they do not limit involvement to any particular sector. Public sector involvement is welcome, private sector involvement is welcome, and so is everything in-between. Indeed, we are pleased by the fact that this type of effort thrives on cross-pollination as it goes about providing opportunities for involvement from a range of prospective participants. In light of the fact that we, in St Kitts and Nevis, are committed to providing an ever-evolving array of involvements for our nationals as they seek new and viable means of revenue generation, there is clearly a natural symbiosis between the ethos of biosphere reserves and the objectives of my government.

We are a tiny nation, but we are a very responsible nation. As a result of careful planning and sound economic management, for example, St Kitts and Nevis, as you may know, in recent months was classified a high income country. We therefore recognise the ability of the Man and Biosphere Programme to provide even more opportunities for our people to use their imaginations, their skills, and their energy in an ecologically responsible way, to ever advance and ever uplift the social and economic environment in which we live.

Kittitians and Nevisians have traditionally proven, time and again, that we are disciplined, we are productive, we are focused. And, as a result, for example, our tiny nation of some fifty-thousand persons on a land mass of just about 100 square miles has, year after year, ended up exporting more manufactured products than any other country in the OECS, including Barbados. In addition, the level of foreign investment that we have attracted is higher than anywhere else in CARICOM. And even on the issue of traveller satisfaction, to give just one more example, cruise passengers rated St Kitts second to only one other country in the region as far as overall satisfaction is concerned.

This not, in any way, to suggest that the world economic crisis is of no concern to us and definitely not, in any way, to be immodest, but simply to explain the mindset and the discipline, the sober choices and conscious sacrifices, the commitment, and the seriousness that Kittitians and Nevisians have always invested in any activity with which we have chosen to become seriously involved. And our Man and Biosphere Programme will be no different.

In light of all of this, we in St Kitts and Nevis very much look forward to the kind of collaboration, the sharing of ideas, and the cooperation that is always so vital to this type of initiative achieving its full potential. Climate change, for example, has long been a major preoccupation of my government. How could it not, really, in light of the implications of climate change for small island states like St Kitts and Nevis? This fact in itself should offer a clear indication of the value that my government attaches to the Man and the Biosphere Programme, because of the programme's potential to serve as an integrative tool as we strive to address such climate change-related issues as violent storms, coral reef destruction, sea level rises, infrastructural damage, coastal degradation, and so on.

And even apart from St Kitts and Nevis, *per se*, we know that, thanks to the special expertise that UNESCO brings, biosphere reserves will undoubtedly become more common throughout the Caribbean. This we all look forward to, and as is the case in St Kitts and Nevis, I anticipate that these reserves will increasingly be viewed as integral parts of the region's important planning, both in the areas of sustainable development as well as in the area's ongoing adaptation to climate change.

Biosphere reserves are very much in keeping with our economic, social, and ecological priorities, in other words, with our commitment to support development that is sustainable. Maintaining that delicate balance between economic development and the protection of our bio-diversity will, of course, remain paramount. And promoting eco-tourism, for example, while ensuring that the requisite safeguards are in place to preserve our flora and fauna, must also be non-negotiable.

Most of all, we must involve the people who inhabit this land. For this land is theirs to appreciate, theirs to protect, and theirs to manage responsibly in their ongoing quest for social and human advancement. And what we all know is that even as they do, they must, like people everywhere, remain cognisant of the environmental responsibilities that they have to those who though not yet born, will one day inhabit, as we do today, this particular section of planet earth.

750 Kilowatt Solar Farm at Bradshaw International Airport

Robert Llewellyn Bradshaw International Airport
Basseterre, March 27, 2013

Today, the St Kitts and Nevis government once again leads by example. Because in all types of settings, and in countless ways, we have been impressing upon our fellow nationals the importance of families and businesses shifting from fossil fuels to renewable energy. In order to add practical force to this general policy, we have provided duty-free access to renewable energy products. We have shifted our energy reliance on such structures as government headquarters, our IT Centre, and elsewhere. Solar power now lights our way along the Kim Collins Highway, the Sandy Point to Newton Ground Route, the Frigate Bay Road, and so on. We have committed to placing solar panels on affordable housing. And today, with the support of the Republic of China on Taiwan – our constant and outstanding partner throughout our determined march toward green energy – we step forward to undertake the construction of a 750 kilowatt solar farm here at the Robert Llewellyn Bradshaw International Airport.

With the high cost of electricity worldwide, and with the strategic importance of air and seaports the world over, it is essential that St Kitts and Nevis not only have a reliable source of electricity for our air and sea ports, but that we be able to access these energy sources in a cost-effective, and easily manageable manner. And so, having reviewed a number of proposals submitted by a number of contractors, the government was pleased to award this contract to Speedtech, a company based in Taiwan. The energy produced here will be fed into the national grid and then be offset against the energy that is used by the St Christopher Air & Sea Ports Authority (SCASPA).

In closing then, I must again make a special point of thanking the Republic of China on Taiwan for its ongoing spirit of partnership where our nation's renewable energy goals are concerned. They have been outstanding partners in every way. And I also wish to commend and thank the Ministry of Energy and SCASPA for their extraordinarily hard work which has enabled us to be here to launch the construction of the RLB solar farm today.

Education and Skills Training

EDUCATION AND SKILLS TRAINING

The St Kitts-Nevis Labour Party has always believed that the most important requirement for the nation to develop and prosper was a modern, robust, free public education system. This was even more true after the closing of the sugar industry and the transition to a service-based economy. The Labour government began by providing quality day care and early childhood education facilities throughout the island; building, repairing and upgrading both elementary and secondary schools; providing laptop computers to all students (and by extension, to their families); and offering accessible and affordable tertiary education at Clarence Fitzroy Bryant College.

By terms three and four, that ongoing effort was bearing fruit. What had been a traditional, narrow-focused education system was now taking a broader, more inclusive view of just what 'education' entails. More attention was given to critical thinking and hands-on skills training for jobs in the new economy including tourism and hospitality services, construction, landscaping, hair dressing, automotive and machinery repairs, air conditioning services, retail management, and so on.

Several innovative programmes were launched to assist youth in getting into the new economy including YES (Youth Employment Through Skills) in 2009 which encouraged qualification in the skilled trades, especially for males who often drifted into guns and gangs culture due to a lack of employment opportunities.

PEP (People Employment Programme) launched in 2012 helped find jobs for youth as well as those made redundant by the closure of the sugar industry. TVET (Technical & Vocational Training) 2013 was a government/private sector joint programme to share the responsibility and costs of providing more skills and training opportunities for SKN young people.

Another indicator of the changing and evolving view of education's role in SKN society was a recognition that more attention needed to be paid to the emotional and mental health challenges of students and the provision of 'social guidance.'

Launch of Project 'YES' (Youth Empowerment Through Skills)

Warner Park Stadium, Basseterre, February 13, 2009

We are assembled together today at Warner Park, the site in our country that over the years has been most closely associated with athletic competition and musical expression at the highest levels. Today, though, we are here to plan and dream and commit ourselves to achievement in other areas as well. We are here to remind ourselves that lasting and meaningful advancement comes through education, that precious and important opportunities come through training, and that life gives of good choices and special options when we are serious, when we believe in ourselves, when we accept and hold on to an outstretched hand.

And the YES programme is an outstretched hand. A hand of partnership, a hand of guidance, and a hand of support. It offers you the advancement you want, through education. The precious opportunities you deserve, through training. And expanded choices you long for, in a spirit of partnership.

Through the launch of this YES programme, the government of St Kitts and Nevis is going the extra mile to teach our young men how to become *Real Men*. How to be of value to themselves. How to develop a skill that is needed by the people of this country. How to earn money regularly and legally. How to hold their own and win the respect of relatives, neighbours, and everybody in this country.

Through the launch of this YES programme, the government of St Kitts and Nevis is going the extra mile to teach our young women how to protect themselves. How to provide for themselves. How to be secure and independent women in this modern world, with the skills to generate income, with the skills to find and hold a job, with the skills to start their own businesses and make their children secure. How to hold their own, and win the respect of relatives, neighbours, and everybody in this country.

This is why the YES programme was established. And this is why I commend you young people for stepping forward to seize this opportunity.

Young people –

- Do not be afraid of the future.
- Do not be intimidated by what you do not know.
- Do not be afraid that you will fail.
- Do not tell yourself that you did not do well in school and so you will not do well in this programme. Step out in faith.
- Believe and know that the YES programme is here to help you.
- Believe and know that YOU CAN MAKE IT – IF YOU TRY.
- Believe and know that the YES programme will stand by you while you try.

First, though, let me tell you something. I know that some of you must sometimes look at very successful people in this society and feel intimidated because the difference between your lives and theirs is so great. I think that the problem is that you are looking at them today but you are forgetting that they were once just as young and inexperienced as you are today. Remember that what you are seeing in these successful individuals is the result of years of dedication, of not giving up, of believing in themselves. And the success you see today is their reward. Instead of being intimidated by them, be inspired by them because many of today's successful people were just as inexperienced as you, and just as insecure as you, when they were your age.

As you think about your own dreams, and as you wonder how you will ever get where you want to go, never forget that some of the Federation's most successful bakeries got started when the owners were your age with nothing more than a five-pound bag of flour.

Never forget that some of the Federation's most successful builders got started when they were your age – by somebody teaching them how to lay bricks or do basic carpentry.

Never forget that some of the Federation's most successful automobile dealers got started when they were your age by someone teaching them how to change the oil in a car.

Never forget that some of the largest stores in town got started when the owners were your age by someone selling a few pieces of cloth, or a few cups and plates, out of a small bag they carried from door to door. This is how dreams become reality.

My point, then, is that you have taken the important first step to a good and successful life by signing up for YES. And we congratulate you. You must now follow that up in a spirit of faith and hard work and determination. Look around you at all the cars and buses rushing around the Federation. Someone has to fix them. That can be a very good livelihood, and that can be you. Look at how our people flock to the fruit and vegetable boats from the other islands. People want to buy locally-grown foods. This can produce a very good livelihood, and that too can be you.

Look at the many buildings going up around this country – they need electricians, plumbers, masons. More good livelihoods. Why not you?! Look at the many businesses in the Federation – they need tailors and seamstresses to make their uniforms, they need persons with good customer relations and computer skills. All of these positions represent good livelihoods and any of them that you wish can be you.

The YES programme has far more areas of possible training than I can even begin to list here today. Everyone has something that interests them. Everyone has a talent that can be developed. Everyone can lead a secure and stable life.

A solid, respectable future can and must be yours. And the YES program will help to make it so. Dedicate yourselves, young people. You will be rewarded.

Invest your time and energy, young people. You will be rewarded.

Remain focused, young people. You will be rewarded.

And the YES programme will show you how.

Applications are available right here today. Sign up. Take charge of your life. Give your life a new and positive beginning, today.

COMMENCEMENT ADDRESS
45th Graduating Class
University of the Virgin Islands
St Croix, USVI, May 19, 2009

In three years time the University of the Virgin Islands (UVI) will be fifty years old. That is a tremendous achievement. Last year, my country, St Kitts and Nevis, celebrated twenty-five years. That, too, was a significant achievement in our growth and development. As the class commencement speaker noted, her class is this year's stimulus package. So to all gathered here today, and especially to the 'daring, dedicated, and determined' UVI class of 2009, I want to take off from that idea of the stimulus and focus on the links between the University of the Virgin Islands and my home state, the Federation of St Kitts and Nevis. Along the way I will make some suggestions that ought to remain with you as you commence your journey of shaping the USVI, the wider Caribbean, and indeed the world.

My country's motto is 'Country Above Self.' You say that you 'specialise in futures.' Let me say that the kernel of what we have here today is a situation where our country and your future will be forever entwined. The University of the Virgin Islands, whether it was the then College of the Virgin Islands in the old days, or the University of the Virgin Islands in its present representation, has always been a place where hundreds of our nationals and perhaps thousands of Eastern Caribbean nationals have made their academic home. It is true that we have my alma mater, The University of the West Indies, but for many nationals in the Eastern Caribbean, and certainly those from my home, St Kitts and Nevis, UVI was and continues to be the institution of place and the academic sceptre of choice.

I, therefore, want to echo the sentiment that we should begin a greater coexistence between UVI and St Kitts and Nevis. Higher education is of paramount importance in the Caribbean today. Information communication technology (ICT) is the mortar that is critical to the educational edifices of our region. That is why I am absolutely delighted that UVI and Clarence Fitzroy Bryant College (CFBC) in St Kitts recently inaugurated and officially launched the UVI–CFBC telecommunications centre. This has put more feathers in the cap of UVI in our region of the Caribbean and it also means that now we, UVI and CFBC, can train our students at the master's level in education, public administration, business administration, and other fields. In time, I am sure classes will be offered in the areas of marine science, criminal justice, police science, psychology, and others.

In St Kitts and Nevis, we already have developed a comparative advantage in higher education. We have several institutions of higher education. We have a long-established veterinary school, an international nursing school, and seven medical schools of international repute. That UVI now has extended its hand of cooperation to us underscores its motto that it specialises in futures.

On this score, we recognise that while UVI continues to spread its wings in the wider Caribbean, it must at the same time consolidate its strength in the US Virgin Islands (USVI). Over the years, St Kitts and Nevis has contributed to UVI in the area of professors, administrative staff, and other staff. A current sitting member of my cabinet, the Honourable Richard Skerritt, UVI's first Rhodes Scholar; a past long-term member of a previous government, Hugh Heyliger; and a premier of our sister state, Nevis, the Honourable Vance Amory, are all graduates of CVI or UVI. So, this is not a new friendship, this is not a shot-gun wedding, this is not a courtship of convenience. This is a commitment that has had long-lasting benefits, a win-win situation for both of us. For while UVI and CFBC have started the telecommunications centre, I am mindful of the fact that UVI has also extended its programmes in the British Virgin Islands (BVI) and St Maarten and that it has plans to sign MOUs with Antigua and Barbuda, Dominica, and St Vincent and the Grenadines, to name a few. The fundamental essence of this futuristic stratagem lies in the fact that our two-year institutions can be feeder institutions for your upper-level classes. The time will come when our two-year institutions will become four-year institutions. At that time, UVI will have the opportunity to be among the other leading institutions in the Caribbean to guide us along the academic trajectory that will position us in the pantheon of the academic space.

Class of 2009, your institutional mission notes that 'the University of the Virgin Islands is a learner-centred institution dedicated to the success of its students and committed to enhancing the lives of the people of the US Virgin Islands and the wider Caribbean through excellent teaching, innovative research, and responsive community service.' I am sure they also meant responsible community service. And UVI underscored its mission by saying in the vision statement that UVI 'will be an exceptional US institution of higher education in the Caribbean dedicated to student success, committed to excellence, and pledged to enhance the social and economic transformation of the US Virgin Islands.' These are sound words that cannot be condemned, if I am to use the motto of a publication with which I am closely associated in St Kitts. While UVI is an American institution, it is imperative that it be noted, in clear and concise terms, that UVI is also a Caribbean institution. It must first provide educational leadership in the Virgin Islands but at the same time it has to provide educational guidance, in a holistic sense, to the other educational institutions in the Caribbean. All of the institutions in the Caribbean have to work systemically to enhance the educational architecture of the Caribbean region. We cannot afford to fall behind the rest of the world.

Graduates, class of 2009, the fact that UVI has been bold enough to put on record that it is an institution that is dedicated to the success of its students goes to the core of the enormous commitment and dedication of the founding fathers of UVI. Students must be first. But it should be remembered that faculty and faculty concerns, whether they are for a better ergonomic environment, better and improved salaries, unions, or shared governance, must also be on the agenda. And while I would not be brazen enough to map out an agenda for the incoming president, given the current agenda of concerns in institutions of higher learning around the Caribbean, and in North America, these and many more issues of salience will be on the agenda of the new president of UVI. In St Kitts and Nevis, I have found it to be of signal importance to be open, transparent, and clear. When you are not transparent, citizens assume that all manner of evil is being committed. I admired from afar the administration of your outgoing president. Wherever she may go, let us give her thanks and roses for guiding this institution and this class of 2009.

This brings me to another fundamental point. What you graduates are embarked on, and what UVI is doing here in the Virgin Islands and in the wider Caribbean, is emblematic of what the late Sir Robert Llewellyn Bradshaw, our first national hero, said at a West Indian solidarity conference in St Thomas on January 13, 1973. He said, and I quote:

> The economic strength [of our people] will be gained neither by shouting slogans, waving banners, nor indeed by being truculent and offensive. It will be gained only upon the basis of hard work, particularly by our youth; objective education at the highest level; systematic planning for the future; and above all, realistic unity among the various ... peoples of the Caribbean ....

You graduates, and all of us here in the region, have to craft an education development path that will ensure that all of us in this part of the world that we call home, the Caribbean, play critical roles in where our countries and where our peoples will go in the future. You, we, all have to be on the cutting edge of the transformation in education and be part and parcel of the change that education will demand of us in this century. Today there are new methods of teaching, new approaches to problem-solving, and new time-sensitive issues to be solved. Thus hard work, objective education at the highest level, and systematic planning for the future, according to the Bradshaw synthesis, have to be the core of what will get us to where we want to go.

But where do you want to go? Where do we want to go? You may wish to be the stimulus package of the Virgin Islands or the Caribbean for that matter. But in so doing be mindful of the fact that you are not an island unto yourself. Share your ideas. Share your thoughts. Share your skills. It is still true that when you share, it is like an investment. The more you share, the more you gain. That is why I am so eternally grateful to UVI's sharing of technology with us in St Kitts and Nevis. This is a win-win situation for UVI and for our CFBC in St Kitts. This is a win-win situation for our CFBC faculty to come to UVI to learn and teach, and for faculty from UVI to come to CFBC to learn and to teach. This is an opportunity for you, the daring, dedicated and determined class of 2009, to show your colours and be bold. Be bold and go where no other class has gone before to make an impact on the world. See the region and the world as your oyster.

How do you assume the mantle of action and the leadership that are implicit in what I am suggesting to you? Kenneth 'Buzz' Shaw, one of the most experienced leaders in American higher education, today gives us some gems which he calls 'buzzwords.' They are really buzz phrases. I cite five of them as you embark on your long journey to make the region and the world a better place for you, for us, and for those who will come after you, whether it is here at UVI, at the CFBC, or at any other institution of higher learning in the Caribbean and beyond.

Buzz Shaw said:

1. Know your institution's culture and respect it. But don't be so reverent that you begin to believe that change would be sacrilegious (even though some will try to convince you that would be so);

2. Do celebrate diversity, but don't apologise for the lack of perfection. Progress is not synonymous with constant harmony; progress comes from acknowledging differences, which can often be a messy process;

3. Don't assume that those who disagree with you are your enemies. When a colleague expresses a view different from yours, step back for a moment to assess how her or his perspective meshes with the institutional vision;

4. Don't take criticism to heart. Expect to be blamed for things with which you had nothing to do. Your legacy will come from the long pull, not from the incident of the moment;

5. Keep track of what you have learned and add to the body of knowledge about the elusive thing called leadership.

These five ideas pertained to leadership as a successful president of academia. But to you successful students today, they are also pivotal as you start your journey of leadership in the Virgin Islands and beyond.

Knowledge of your institution is going to be important going forward. You cannot and should not graduate from this institution and leave it to flounder. It gave you many years. You should now give it many years. Be ambassadors for your institution. Change is the only constant, so while you make changes or suggest changes in your alma mater, be prepared to get negative vibes from those who may see you as upstarts and radicals.

Remember, progress is not synonymous with constant harmony. But be prepared to make some progress. You will be criticised, you will be hammered on a number of scores, but at the end of the day, add something new to what will catapult your institution and yourselves to new heights of endeavour. All of you have gone through some trials and tribulations, I am sure, to get where you are today. The fact that you made it is of central moment. So, I end by saying share your ideas, share your knowledge, share your skills. The old Biblical maxim could be stated thus: *'cast your bread upon the waters, and it will come back to you many days later in abundance.'* Knowledge kept to oneself is knowledge destroyed. Go beyond your borders and try to advance your ideas and learn from others.

In the wider Caribbean today we are boldly moving into a Caribbean Single Market and Economy. There are hiccups but our commitment is to be on a path that will make the region a better place for all of us to live and grow.

Today, the ninety-two of you who will receive degrees are better placed than we were years ago to make an impact on the region. So with your Master of Arts in Education, your MPA, your MBA, your Bachelors of Science and Bachelors of Arts, your Associate of Applied Science (that is your Process Technology degree), and your nursing degrees, you are poised to make an impact. And if you are truly daring, dedicated and determined, you will write a chapter in the annals of education in the Virgin Islands and the wider Caribbean. And if your institution continues to stretch its hands across the waters to work with the people of the wider Caribbean, we can all say like the great Muñoz Marin of Puerto Rico, 'let us pull ourselves up by our bootstraps.'

In the final analysis, to you the daring, dedicated and determined UVI class of 2009 here at the University of the Virgin Islands St Croix campus, I wish all the best as you embark on your journey to stimulate your home, the region, and the world. Never believe that because you live on a small island that you cannot have big ideas. Dream big! Think big! Some say that you should think outside the box. I say, think as if there is no box to restrict your ideas. Move from the old approach to education and go boldly to exponential frontiers where others have dared to go. And if you dare, if you are dedicated and determined, nobody will be able to stop you.

Bon voyage and much success.

A New School Year
Education Update
Ask the Prime Minister Radio Programme
ZIZ Broadcasting Corporation, September 1, 2009

September is upon us and so therefore is a new school year with all the demands that this places not only on students but on parents, teachers, and the rest of society. After all, education in the truest sense of the word is not limited only to what happens in the classroom but is also a function of all that a young person sees and hears on a daily and ongoing basis, both within and outside the classroom. And so we, as the unofficial teachers of our nation's young, in addition to those whose official job classification is that of 'teacher,' all have our work cut out for us. And we must take this sacred responsibility seriously because although most of us will have no impact on our young peoples' understanding of geography, welding, or computer technology, we do have a major impact on who and what the nation's young people become, often without even realising it. We do this directly and indirectly. We do this via the example of our own lives. And, most importantly, we do this by what we do and do not say to the young people we encounter every day, by the guidance we do or do not provide whenever we come into contact with the Federation's six-, nine-, and fourteen-year-olds. I am talking now about children we do not know, children who are not related to us in any way. At the beginning of this new academic year, we really should reflect seriously on the ways in which we, as adults, help to steer children we encounter in one direction or the other, either through acts of omission or acts of commission, because we never know what impact the right words delivered at the right time can have on the life of a child.

Food for thought then as we stand at the threshold of the 2009/2010 academic year. And, more than mere food for thought, this is really the challenge that life in the twenty-first century has put before us in this Federation that we all love. We must meet this challenge and we must live up to its demands like responsible and visionary men and women, and as patriots.

In addition to this nation-wide responsibility however, I want to talk about some of the ways in which my government is revising and refining the very concept of education in order to ensure that our young people will have the greatest possible opportunity to develop into psychologically healthy, competent, informed, responsible, self-reliant, and professionally competitive adults.

First of all, I want to ensure that the public understands the significance of the new and innovative Saddlers Secondary School. I have talked about this school before, but as we ready ourselves for the new school year, it is important that the public understands the extent to which this school will dramatically expand the training options and therefore, the life chances of all our young people.

How is the Saddlers School different? Well, first of all, this school is a direct result of my government's successful transformation of our economy over the past four years. As our economy has become more complex and as a broader range of skills has become necessary in this newly transformed economy, it is essential that our people have the new and specific skills that this new economy demands. It is, after all, essential that the people of St Kitts and Nevis will be the ones who will receive the new and important income streams that these new investments bring. Educational specialists have long understood that there are many types of intelligence. Throughout much of the world however, educational systems have traditionally focused on one type of intelligence. If St Kitts and Nevis is to achieve its full potential, educational systems must begin to tap into the broad range of intelligence so that the full range of potential can be developed for the benefit of both the students involved and the nation at large. It is as a result of this insight and this knowledge that the Saddlers Secondary School was born.

But my government has gone beyond this as well. In light of all that the region and indeed, the world, has been facing, my government is placing great importance on our teachers expanding and upgrading their abilities to identify, and therefore arrange help for, children with emotional difficulties. We have made sure that Clarence Fitzroy Bryant College now has the capability to train the nation's teachers to recognise the warning signs that a child, for one reason or another, has emotional difficulties, and needs help. In this day and age, the value of our teachers having this very important skill, I am sure, will be clear to all.

You will remember that I began by talking about the ways in which my government is revising and refining our definition of 'education.' I want to stress that in addition to instructing children in the areas of history and woodwork, mathematics and French, we believe that there must be greater emphasis on developing the humanity and the character of our children. Mere skills acquisition is not enough in this twenty-first century. And so, beginning this academic year, the Ministry of Education will be launching a new initiative that will facilitate greater interaction between the youth of our Federation and the adults of our Federation in the form of after-school programmes. This programme has been designed specifically to calm, to strengthen, to uplift, and to encourage our young people to set their sights on a positive and upward path. This type of inter-generational interaction has great potential to shape the Federation's youth for the better while at the same time bringing great meaning and human fulfilment into the lives of older nationals as well. And so, I certainly hope that responsible adults from throughout the Federation with various skills, interests, and wisdom will reach out to the Ministry of Education offering to involve themselves in this important and timely nation-building exercise.

As the young people head back to school then, we must all impress upon them the importance of hard work and perseverance. As parents send their children out, they must remember their responsibility to encourage, to guide, and to support. And as students return to school, teachers must remember that children spend more of their waking hours in the presence of teachers than they do with their own parents. Teachers have great power to shape our children and therefore the nation. Let us, therefore, all recognise our sacred responsibilities as serious adults and patriots and let us go forward and meet them.

Technical and Vocational Education and Training (TVET) Programme

St Kitts Marriott Resort, December 6, 2013

The handing-over ceremony of which we are a part this morning represents what is best about public service and it encapsulates the true meaning and purpose of government. And I say this because the re-thinking, re-packaging, and re-marketing of the TVET programme is all about expanding options. It is about inclusion. It is about new and improved opportunities. The re-thinking of the TVET programme is about looking and seeing with new eyes. And it is about seeing strengths and possibilities and positives where we blindly did not allow ourselves to see them before.

I wish to thank the chairman of the St Kitts-Nevis TVET Council and his staff for all that they have done to bring today's handing-over ceremony into being. And I wish also to thank UNESCO for the support and collaboration without which our being here today would have been exponentially more difficult.

My government has invested an extraordinary amount of time, resources, and energy into ensuring that both local and foreign investors recognise the potential that exists within our borders. We have ensured that investors as widely divergent as hoteliers, solar panel producers, electronics specialists, and others, repose their confidence and their capital with us here in the Federation. But we do this not as an end in itself. Instead, we do this in order to create ever greater and ever better opportunities for the people of St Kitts and Nevis. And that is why this handing-over ceremony assumes the significance that it does to me, to my cabinet, and to my government. Because, as everyone who has worked so hard to bring us to this point today knows, with our new approach to TVET we are determined to change the prevailing attitudes toward the TVET programme. Secondly, we are determined to incorporate TVET into a far broader segment of our educational policy than has until now been the case. And most importantly, we are determined to upgrade, expand,

and refine the skills with which the young people of our Federation will step into the real world of work.

The investments that we have worked so hard to bring to our country have been brought here, and will continue to be brought here, primarily to improve the lives of the people of our Federation, and this new thrust by our TVET programme will make a major and lasting contribution in this regard.

Permit me to say here how pleased I am by the special emphasis that will now be placed on critical thinking skills. It is so important that young people – anywhere in the world – be able to do more than merely memorise. It is essential, in addition, that they be able to analyse, that they be able to spot significant patterns, that they be able to understand those differences in data that are important and those that are not. In other words, it is important that young people, and people of all ages really, be able to think. And this new and upgraded TVET programme will take us a long way in this regard.

TVET has, until now, been seen as primarily a governmental concern. This is no longer acceptable. The young people who are aided via this programme, the skills that are passed on via this programme, benefit the entire Federation and the private sector in particular. What we will need from this point forward therefore is a far greater sense of TVET being a shared responsibility. It is neither viable nor fair as we strive to keep St Kitts and Nevis the competitive island-state that it is, that the responsibility for skills development should be borne totally by one side while the benefits accrue dramatically and overwhelmingly to the other. There have been many areas of public-private partnership in the past that have redounded handsomely to the benefit of our nation. I am convinced that the TVET programme can be yet another in that regard and so I look forward to many years of expanded and strengthened involvement by the private sector in this very important area of human resource development.

The local private sector, UNESCO, the ILO, and the government, I am certain we will all agree, represent a dynamic and powerful combination and have a superb opportunity to continue advancing the interests of our nation and our people, and this we must all work to make a real and powerful reality.

This new push where the TVET programme is concerned is taking place at a most fortunate moment in world history. It is taking place at a time in which the electronic media and social media provide phenomenal opportunities for marketing and information dissemination. In light of the importance of this expanded program to all the people of our Federation, I am positive that I do not need to advise anyone to use electronic and social media to the maximum extent possible. I strongly support and encourage this type of outreach which I am certain is already underway.

In conclusion, let me state that the education of our youth has been a major priority of my government – and indeed my party – from the moment of our inception. The expanded and upgraded TVET programme epitomises the priorities and emphasis of my government and I am immensely proud of all that the chairman, his staff, and others have been able to accomplish in this regard. This handing-over ceremony is a red-letter day in the history or our nation and in the ongoing preparation of our young people to step forward and seize the opportunities that this government has worked so hard to create. May this new and enlightened approach redound to the benefit of us all for decades to come.

THE UNIVERSITY OF THE WEST INDIES TECHNICAL ADVISORY COMMITTEE MEETING

St Kitts Marriott Resort, February 13, 2014

Welcome to St Kitts and Nevis.

This is the second time that our country has hosted the Technical Advisory Committee meeting of The University of the West Indies Grants Committees, and we are honoured to do so once again.

We are honoured because The University of the West Indies is such a cherished symbol of our forward movement as a Caribbean people.

And we are honoured because St Kitts and Nevis has long had a fierce appreciation of the power of education to transform lives, to expand options, to counter unfairly determined social hierarchies, and to facilitate instead the full flowering of each individual through access to education.

For the benefit of the members of our audience who are not from St Kitts and Nevis and who may not be aware of the intense battles that were waged in the Federation in the 1960s over the issue of education, permit me to quickly share with you the pivotal role of education in the social and political restructuring of our nation.

In the late 1960s, St Kitts and Nevis, like the rest of the Caribbean, was still fully committed to the centuries-old tradition of limiting secondary education only to the children of families which could afford to pay. The end result of this tradition was that each year some 98 per cent of children, regardless of their intelligence and ability, were locked out of our high schools and forced at twelve, thirteen, and fourteen years of age to find their way in the world.

What a waste of human potential.

Making a fearless break with that odious tradition, however, the government of the Right Excellent Robert Llewellyn Bradshaw proclaimed that every child in this St Kitts and Nevis, regardless of the circumstances of their birth would, from that time forward, have access to free and mandatory secondary education.

Centuries of mental conditioning being what it was, there were those who were deeply offended at the very thought. And the resistance to 'equal education for all' was both swift and 'un-demure.' Premier Bradshaw, however, understood that it would not only be the children in question who would benefit from five additional years of secondary education, those children's families would also benefit from the expanded skills, insights, and knowledge that their children would acquire, and it was indeed our society as a whole that would benefit as a result of having thousands of young people who were at last being given the opportunities that their parents and grandparents deserved – and could have made excellent use of – but were nonetheless denied.

The Bradshaw government understood the importance of Kittitian and Nevisian children being awakened to their innate capabilities and of their being equipped by the state to step forward with confidence and dedication to develop their God-given talents and capabilities and to at last walk tall in the land of their birth.

As a result, the social transformation in St Kitts and Nevis has been absolutely phenomenal. As a result of the then-government refusing to buckle on this philosophically fundamental issue – free and mandatory education for all – talent and potential have been unleashed across the length and breadth of St Kitts and Nevis in ways multi-faceted and glorious, bringing forth engineers and writers, lawyers and historians, doctors and architects, artists and scientists, something their parents could never have dreamed of.

In addition, aware of the growing demand for skilled labour that always accompanies increased investment, St Kitts and Nevis has also invested heavily in both time and resources to ensure that within this country's secondary schools the twenty-first century requirements of the building trades, auto mechanics, air conditioning, and computer technology, and so on, are being addressed. We are making certain that within the secondary school environment the requirements of tailoring and seamstressing, of farming and of culinary arts, of computer technology and metalwork are imparted with insight and regularity from one year to the next. Because this is the only path to individual independence.

Expanded options and upward social mobility is what St Kitts and Nevis is all about for citizens at all strata of our society. And we are keenly aware that there are few forces in any society that possess the transformative power of education. It is because of this awareness and because The UWI so compellingly represents the forward movement of our people, that we are so honoured to once again host the Technical Advisory Committee of The University of the West Indies.

Please join me in a warm round of applause, then, for The University of the West Indies – an institution which, since its beginnings in 1962, has trained and equipped to take their places in the world over one hundred thousand sons and daughters of the Caribbean, young men and women who have taken the training acquired at The UWI and then moved forward to assume the highest levels of professional achievement in the sciences, arts, governance, and business.

For this, The UWI, we thank you.

We thank you also, for the core values that you have identified in all your official documentation. Because they are the values on which the fate of the individual, the family, the community, and the nation rest:

- Integrity
- Intellectual freedom
- Excellence
- Civic responsibility
- Accountability
- Diversity
- Equity

These values are more important today than ever before. There was a time when our Caribbean culture was very much in our own hands as a Caribbean people. We read books and magazines that were published thousands of miles away, yes. And we listened to music and saw films that had been produced far beyond our shores. Despite this, however, the influence of the family, the community, and the church remained remarkably strong. And everyone felt decidedly grounded in their 'island life,' whether here in the Federation, in Trinidad and Tobago, in Grenada or anywhere else along our Caribbean archipelago.

Today, however, that has changed. Dramatically. The speed and power of modern communications has caused many within our region to have character-based frames of reference that have little to do with our islands and their traditions. And so, the challenge falls to us all in this fast-paced twenty-first century world to help our region remember the importance of integrity which is best measured by what we do when no one is watching.

We must be proponents of

- intellectual freedom without which innovative, enlightening, and liberating insight is not possible; and
- excellence, the commitment to which rewards us with empowering self-respect and regard for our fellow man;
- civic responsibility, on which societal order, justice, and empathy rests;
- accountability, because in all areas of human endeavour, actions have consequences. And this no one can escape;
- diversity, because we must recognise and value differing but interlocking roles that the various members of our societies play in our ever-evolving nations;

And finally,

- there is the core value of equity, sometimes described as fair play, as balance.

These are not solely the values of The University of the West Indies. They are the values which allow us, as individuals, to achieve our full potential. They are the values that help families to function as healthy, cohesive, and interdependent wholes. And they are the values that enable communities to represent the type of undergirding on which stable nations stand. We, as individual nations and as a region therefore, must continue to consider the importance of these core values. And we must ensure that they are evident in our own lives and in our respective spheres of influence.

And so I end where I began, acknowledging the importance of The University of the West Indies to our onward march as a region, to our sense of psychological and political independence, and to our regional sense of nationhood. A Caribbean without this institution of higher learning, one that is so uniquely and thoroughly ours, would be, in a psychological sense, arid and desert-like indeed. Thankfully, however, we do have The University of the West Indies where the intellectual curiosity, the energy, and the firepower on which vibrant, resilient societies depend are readily found in great abundance.

Important discussions will occur here over the next two days and important insights gleaned. We have had the honour of being the site of these deliberations before and as I have said, we are pleased to have you gather in our Federation once again. Education has long been the engine that has propelled our Federation forward. And because of this, The University of the West Indies and the Technical Advisory Committee to The UWI's Grant Committees will always have a home here.

INFORMATION AND COMMUNICATIONS TECHNOLOGY

Information and Communications Technology

The subject of information and communications technology may seem dry and rather technical but it is in fact one of the primary pillars of the success of the new post-sugar diversified economy. There cannot be a strong, modern economy in a liberalised trading world without modern telecommunications and citizens who know how to use them. Denzil Douglas understood this early on and set the pace for regional reform of the telecoms sector. Reliable, up-to-date ICT is fundamental to SKN's continuing progress and economic development. It is not just a facilitator but is a generator of national income and good, well-paying jobs.

It was not enough to simply break Cable & Wireless's choke-hold on regional telecoms. The new ECTEL regime, launched in 2000, had to make telecoms services affordable and accessible for all. It was critical for sharing information among Caribbean governments and keeping citizens informed of government policies, and programmes. With the assistance of ROC (Taiwan), SKN developed a strong e-government platform that allowed citizens to communicate electronically with the government, register and receive documents, pay bills, etc., in an increasingly paperless society.

The programme with the biggest impact on ordinary citizens was the provision in 2013/14 of laptop computers to SKN schools. It was a major undertaking (again with Taiwan's help) and provided excitement, stimulation, and motivation for students and their families. The transfer of skills from students to their families and the broader community produced a functioning computer-literate society in just a few short year

Caribbean Broadcasting Union 38th General Assembly

St Kitts Marriott Resort, August 28, 2007

I am delighted to add my words of welcome to delegates to the 38th Annual General Assembly of the Caribbean Broadcasting Union (CBU). All of us must be especially proud of the success of the Caribbean Broadcasting Union and I believe that the people of the Caribbean willingly shower praises upon the CBU for the vital role it plays in Caribbean integration. Indeed, the CBU has been a key instrument in helping to maintain the vision of the Caribbean Community, giving our people a significant window for the sharing of information about each other, and hence, furthering the bonds of friendship, respect, understanding, and love among our brothers and sisters in CARICOM. I am very proud of the contributions that CBU has made and will continue to make in the years to come.

In those early years when CBU and CANA were established, there was a clear understanding that the strengthening of the community had to do a lot with how well we could infuse news and information throughout the Caribbean on a consistent basis, how effectively we could bring the major events of the community to the residents of our member countries. This was very important because, in the long run, it gave CARICOM citizens an identity that was real in all our minds.

CARICOM heads throughout the decades, but especially in more recent times, were also fully aware of the crucial role the media must play in the region in regard to the strengthening of our political democracies and helping to promote social and economic stability. By giving greater voice to our citizens, we enhance dialogue across the region and demonstrate to ourselves that freedom of expression supports development rather than being a hindrance to the processes of growth. The media is therefore a vital component in shaping the psyche of our people and creating a level of confidence that allows our people to participate in determining their own destiny.

Member countries of the Caribbean Community have several media institutions that serve domestic purposes and which have long been in the forefront of raising national awareness and involvement on a variety of interests and issues. From the Bahamas in the north to Guyana in the south, the archives of our contemporary history are recorded in the pages of our domestic newspapers and on our national radio and television stations.

Moreover, the significant exposure of our people to secondary and tertiary education over the years has quietly encouraged elements of change.

When these are taken in context with the technological revolution that has taken place in broadcasting and publishing technologies, it is not surprising that an increasing number of individuals now pursue careers in the media and significantly for some of our countries, there has been substantial capital investment in print and radio.

Today, media houses across the region are positioned well to play an even greater role in the development of people in the Caribbean Community. There is a strong desire among our national populations to enter and remain an integral part of the continuing information revolution spearheaded by the flexibility of the internet and the convenience of satellite communications. Significant changes in telecommunications legislation and regulation have opened the door to the internet for millions of Caribbean people.

It is a critical opportunity for media houses to go beyond the basic provision of news and develop creative strategies and innovations which will engage our people in the kind of positive involvement that lends itself to the enhancement of productivity, the stimulation of new ideas, and the encouragement of entrepreneurship. Media houses of the region must begin to rethink their strategies and programming and take that foundation that has been laid and build upon it. We must not wait for ideas to originate from cosmopolitan media corporations. Rather, there must be regional introspection among media houses that are prepared to lead their organisations more forcefully with new vision into the global environment without being restrained by the traditional services and products of today.

Let's not forget, also, that the media can and should be a powerful tool to present Caribbean culture and heritage to the international arena. We have seen some breakthroughs in the music industry but that is still comparatively small. It is often said that the people of the region are creative and talented, and I believe this is so. What is required is organisation, the coordination of human and financial resources and the establishment of our own distribution networks. We must gain control by working together domestically and regionally to create alliances that will take advantage of the CSME, benefitting small and large regional economies in the process.

If we can achieve these things, I envision that several benefits will accrue to the region and its people:

1. Providing greater opportunity for expression domestically, regionally, and internationally.

2. Engaging a much wider cross-section of Caribbean nationals in discussion.

3. Helping to empower our people and improve quality of life.

4. Creating new business opportunities domestically and regionally.

5. Creating new career pathways for our people.

6. Stimulating economic growth and social development.

7. Helping to engender greater pride in ourselves as a people thereby empowering ourselves to take on a greater, sustained, and positive mark in the international community.

Most of you would recognise that achieving this goes beyond the acceptance of the status quo. It calls for substantial change in the way we think and interact with each other. It calls for new and higher levels of commitment and trust at individual and corporate levels. And fundamentally, we must do it our way, a way that creates and sustains a positive Caribbean identity.

Some countries of the Caribbean Community have been developing ICT centres of excellence and this is important. ICT is, and will continue to be, a critical component in the development of the region.

The issue of access to the internet must be tackled head-on because it must be considered a major tool of economic and social development. I am of the view that the more people who have access to the internet for productive endeavours, the better it will be for the development environment in the region. Just as important is the need to examine our legislative frameworks to ensure that the media's development can be facilitated more effectively in a globalised economy.

The media of the Caribbean must continue to play its role in nation-building, fully cognisant that there must be a new vision and new levels of integration. As I leave you with these thoughts, let me remind you once more of the need for the Caribbean's media houses to step beyond the confines of traditional expectations and instead explore parallel and divergent business opportunities, especially those which can exploit more effectively the international appeal of our cultural heritage.

NATIONAL INFORMATION AND TECHNOLOGY CENTRE OPENING

C.A. Paul Southwell Industrial Park, Basseterre
October 25, 2007

Today, we open our nation's Information and Technology Centre. In so doing, we mark a special milestone in our quest to reshape and retool the economy of our beloved St Kitts and Nevis. This step is of great importance in the context of the post-sugar economy and it will deliver tangible benefits – social, economic, and political – to the people of this country for decades to come.

Today's opening was made possible due to the tremendous support of the government and people of the Republic of China on Taiwan who, like us, recognised the potential of an IT sector to strengthen and make more competitive the economy of St Kitts and Nevis. The relationship between St Kitts and Nevis and the Republic of China has always been an excellent one and our great friendship was pivotal in the development and realisation of this project.

The establishment of this centre must be seen in the context of both the wider globalised economy as well as the evolving CARICOM Single Market and Economy. Both will have a major impact on our economy for years to come. The economic security of St Kitts and Nevis depends on our ability to promote, create, and manage a fully functioning, diversified economy.

As you are aware, this Labour administration has been strengthening tourism. We have been promoting light manufacturing. We have been facilitating financial services. And we have been stressing food-based agriculture. Today, we add the information and technology sector to this mix. We understand the potential of this sector to unlock and unleash the human resource potential in our country as it gives rise to a better informed and a better educated population, both of which are key to meaningful social and economic development.

In St Kitts and Nevis, as around the world, information and communications technology has become a driving force for positive economic change. Information and communications technology helps to move educational processes forward. It increases efficiency in both public and private sectors. It boosts effectiveness in agriculture, in marketing, in production processes, in trade, in enhancing good governance, and in under-girding democracy. And today, St Kitts and Nevis takes yet another step forward in better equipping ourselves in this twenty-first century arena.

Information and communications technology (ICT) is a tool. When used imaginatively, it can be a powerful weapon in the battle against poverty. When used with insight, it can stir the entrepreneurial spirit and spur economic progress. When used with vision, it can aid and assist and strengthen a range of important economic and social activities. And we, the government of St Kitts and Nevis, intend to use the capabilities associated with this centre with imagination, with insight, and with vision.

I have spoken on many occasions about the ways in which the government of St Kitts and Nevis has been modernising our operational infrastructure so as to enhance our delivery of services to the public and private sectors. This is key to good governance. This IT Centre will assist us greatly in this regard. It will enable us to undertake more governmental processes electronically. And it will redefine, for the better, the relationship between our human resources, our technology, our processes, and the results we seek.

In a nutshell, our decision to upgrade and expand our information and communications capabilities through the opening of this centre will make St Kitts and Nevis more competitive in the realms of social and economic development. Our ability to plan soundly will be improved. Getting access to timely information will be made easier. There will be greater control over fiscal processes thereby increasing savings. Most importantly, the people of St Kitts and Nevis will have greater access to more information. This National IT Centre is for St Kitts and Nevis an instrument of positive change and constructive transformation.

I wish to remind all assembled here that the benefits derived from any technology are totally dependent on exactly how that technology is used. We can all be confident that the technology being placed at our disposal today will be superbly managed and made to serve the interests of our people under the diligent management of the Ministry of Technology.

The capabilities of this centre will be used by the government of St Kitts and Nevis as a tool to transform and enhance the quality of life for the people of this country.

It is with great pleasure that I declare the National Information and Technology Centre officially open

Caribbean Telecommunications Union ICT Roadshow

St Kitts Marriott Resort, August 24, 2009

The quest of mankind for a better way of life is older than recorded history. Mankind in spurts of discovery has moved from simple gathering and hunting to a world today characterised by complex economic relations facilitated by enormous advances in the variety and usage of technology. Much of what we take for granted now had its beginnings in the ability of man to manipulate his environment for his benefit. We see this in the history of agriculture, the industrial revolution, the steady progress of science and technology. It is difficult to fathom where human civilisation would be today had it not been for the significant discoveries and knowledge gained along the way on the path of human existence.

It is even more surprising that this tremendous pace of discovery and development occurred in relatively recent historic times, within the last century. Think of the evolution of air and sea transportation, space exploration, medical advancement, global communications and navigation, the automobile, architecture, and building construction. These are just a few examples. What is common among all these sectors is the role of technology. Conceptualisation, trial and error, and scientific research have become basic standards in human endeavour. Today, they are integral actors in commercial activity, government functioning, and social development.

The development and integration of information and communications technologies (ICT) is the major difference between global economic and social development today as compared to just fifty years ago. ICTs manage more effectively the path towards economic and social advancement, although some would argue that they have also been instrumental in mankind's destructive influence on the environment and ever-present tendency to engage in wars of all kinds.

Today, here in St Kitts and Nevis, we are indeed pleased to have the Caribbean ICT Roadshow. I see it as a tool and an opportunity for engagement and interaction among our people on the vital role that ICT is playing and will continue to play in this country's social and economic progress. The high prevalence of cell phones, the growing demand for internet connections, and the expanding access to global information has changed the social and economic landscape of Caribbean countries. For certain, this is just the beginning.

As is the case with other major technological advancements, there is no going back. I am convinced that ICT will form the basis of major discoveries in the twenty-first century and they will touch the lives of people in rich and poor countries alike, helping to fulfil their needs and aspirations. Their impact may even exceed that of the automobile on human interaction more than a hundred years ago.

For small island states like St Kitts and Nevis, the use and expansion of ICT is not an option but a necessity of the first order. Like it or not, our economic survival depends in large measure on the ready availability of high quality ICT engagement in every sector of our economy. ICT is critical for investment and crucial in support areas such as health and education. With limited financial resources, ICT integration in the public and private sectors as well as civil society, can be quite challenging. Nevertheless, it is important that small island states remain engaged in ICT to avoid or reduce economic stress derived from globalised competition for development/investment dollars.

I am very encouraged with the work of the Caribbean Telecommunications Union (CTU) as it does its part to promote dialogue and understanding of what ICT can and should do for the region's future development. It is clearly a case where the power of ICT must be harnessed to serve the Caribbean's development needs in the most cost-effective manner and in such a way as to bring the most productive benefits to the people of the Caribbean.

With all the advancements of ICT now at our disposal, can we honestly say that we are effectively using the resource for political, economic, and social change? Have we made a major impact on the use of the internet, for example, in the promotion of healthier lifestyles for Caribbean people? Have we been able to use the internet more effectively as a commercial business base? Are there enough policy and legislative frameworks to guide the internet's use and development? The honest answers to these questions would point to the fact that we have made some progress but there is a tremendous amount of work still to be done in the Caribbean region.

What I am pointing to is the fact that there exist enormous opportunities for business, government, and institutions to make greater use of ICT in all its forms, bringing greater financial convenience, improved product and service delivery, institutional facilitation, easier interaction with government offices and agencies, as well as strengthening democracy and facilitating transparency. ICT presents a unique opportunity in which large cross-sections of our populations can actively be involved in shaping its use. It has its place, for example, in schools where teachers, parents, and students can receive and provide relevant information. Communities can be empowered through the availability of ICT resources.

In St Kitts and Nevis, we committed to the pursuit of ICT as integral to sustainable development. The establishment of the ICT Centre has been pivotal in this regard. E-government has begun to take shape and we are steadily building human resource capacity to drive further achievements. The liberalisation of our telecommunications laid the foundation for healthy competition in services and has been of great benefit, for example, to tourism development and business communications. ICT is an important element of the government's post-sugar adaptation strategy. ICT can be used as an alternative avenue for income generation, particularly for our younger entrepreneurs, and we know there is scope and need to explore entertainment, culture, and heritage as sources of income generation and information dissemination.

The CTU has been engaged regionally and internationally in forging a path forward for ICT development in our countries. We have worked with international development institutions and governments to lay the foundation for future growth and development with ICT as an enabler. We are building on the strengths that we have while increasing capacity and capability through special projects and programmes. As I said before, finance is one of the most difficult constraining factors but we believe that inclusive approaches bring ideas and support that are absolutely necessary for moving forward.

I wish to take this opportunity, therefore, to add my voice of invitation to the business sector, civil society, individuals, and governmental institutions to take advantage off this Caribbean ICT Roadshow. It is an opportunity that you must hold with both hands. I invite your full participation.

UNIVERSAL SERVICE FUND LAUNCH
Eastern Caribbean Telecommunications Authority 10th Anniversary
St Kitts Marriott Resort, September 9, 2010

First of all, let me both thank and congratulate the Eastern Caribbean Telecommunications Authority (ECTEL) for its professionalism and competence as the regulatory body governing the telecommunications sectors of Dominica, Grenada, St Lucia, St Vincent & the Grenadines, and, of course, St Kitts and Nevis, over these past ten years. It seems like just yesterday that the ECTEL treaty was being signed in our sister-island of Grenada, but yet our calendars and the telecommunications strides that our respective nations have made since then make it clear that a decade has in fact already sped by.

Let me commend you, also, for the programme of activities that you so insightfully put together to mark this anniversary. I am particularly heartened by the emphasis that you have placed on the youth of St Kitts and Nevis. Your special efforts to include and involve young people bears testimony to your appreciation of the fact that as St Kitts and Nevis, and indeed the rest of the OECS, continues to strengthen its capabilities to function in a technologically advanced and highly competitive globalised world, it will be essential that the next generation of our people understands, is involved in, and is positioned to master the challenges and complexities of a rapidly changing telecommunications landscape. And so I must also make a special point of stressing how very important it was that one of your fora focused not merely on the technological or technical aspects of the telecommunications industry, but also on the nation's young people 'making positive use of ICT for personal development.'

Technological advances throughout the history of mankind have made many great things possible. They have facilitated more efficient modes of travel, developed more reliable forms of communications, and empowered us to do more with less and more quickly. Indeed, they have often created within mankind a sense that we really just might be creeping ever closer to truly being masters of our own destiny.

However, each and every technological advance, with all its advantages, has also caused thoughtful, visionary, and responsible members of societies all over the world to be forever mindful of the fact that every benefit has a cost, and so it is always in the best interest of all societies, not just St Kitts and Nevis, to be keenly aware of the possible social and other costs associated with all technological advances, and to wisely and boldly put measures in place to mitigate the impact of these costs to society.

Let me hasten to stress that this cost/benefit duality is in no way unique to the telecommunications industry. Our acknowledging this duality in no way equates to our being negative. On the contrary, it underscores the fact that we, as thinking people, are keenly aware of the impact of technological advances on societies throughout history, for better or for worse. It is evidence of our confidence in ourselves as a people. It is evidence of our determination to remain sensitive to possible costs in advance and pre-empt them. And, most importantly, it is an affirmation of our awareness that we must be protectors of our social space, our economic prospects, and our region's future.

The telecommunications sector in St Kitts and Nevis, the Caribbean, and indeed throughout the world, has revolutionised who can study where, and what. It has forever changed who can enter any particular line of business and exactly who their potential market will be. Thanks to the marvels of telecommunications, there are now heretofore unheard-of opportunities for trans-border cooperation and collaboration in the area of health care, in real time. It has dramatically enhanced civil aviation, maritime operations, and so forth and so on. It has dramatically reduced, and has sometimes even eliminated, the disadvantages that have long been associated with small states like ours, and the challenge of distance. It is not an exaggeration to say that the changes in telecommunications have forever changed the world.

As we look at the impact of technological advances on mankind throughout the ages and our responsibilities in the face of rapid technological change, let us consider, for example, the impact of Henry Ford's bringing to the mass market for the first time his now-famous Model T in 1908. That was, without any question, a technological and manufacturing breakthrough that forever changed the face of America and the world. For the first time in human history, ordinary men and women, previously dependent on a horse, mule, or donkey, could own this new and dramatic mode of transportation called an automobile. It changed where people lived and how people lived. It changed where they went, and when they went there. It changed so very much about life as it existed until then, and it all seemed to change almost overnight. Not unlike the dramatic changes that modern telecommunications have brought into our lives in this, the twenty-first century.

But as magnificent as the automobile was – and it was! – the wise and the visionary recognised the need for certain safeguards in the public interest as the possible costs associated with this technological marvel became better understood. And so, years after people had been buying automobiles by the thousands, those who were concerned about the public good and public safety made the case for rear-view mirrors because they realised that drivers focusing only what was ahead of them, and only on where they wanted to go, was not in the public interest. Drivers, the thinkers of the day argued, should also know what was coming behind them. And so we got rear-view mirrors.

Then, those who were concerned about the public good and public safety again, long after thousands of cars had already been sold, made the case for speedometers, because they realised that everyone driving as fast as they wanted without even being aware of how fast they were driving, was not in the public good either. There needed to be standards and there needed to be a certain degree of self-management throughout society, hence the introduction of the speedometer.

I am making these references to highlight and emphasise the importance of thinkers and visionaries in any society in which there is rapid technological change. And I am saying this because I know that this region is filled with outstanding minds that will work together to ensure that the people of this region get the very best, and work to resist any of the downsides associated with rapid technological change.

One last example that highlights the importance of vision to the well-being of a technologically advanced society. Those who were concerned about the public good and public safety, seventy years after the first mass-produced automobile, and after millions of them had been sold, once again stepped forward to make the case for seat belts because they realised that permitting highway deaths and maimings to continue to mount was simply not acceptable in a humane and civilised society.

These then are just some of the ways in which those concerned about protecting the public good, while welcoming positive and impressive technological advances, remained alert to any threats to social order, social progress, societal health and stability, and acted accordingly. Today, we know, there are those who are determined to use modern telecommunications to undermine and destabilise the societies that we throughout the Caribbean, and people throughout the world, have been diligently trying to build. The challenge to us all then, even as we hail the tremendous positive opportunities made possible by the advances in telecommunications, is to think and talk and exchange ideas with each other as to how, both here and abroad, societies might best protect themselves, in a democratic and socially acceptable manner, from those who would wish to use the marvels of telecommunications to undermine good and stable societies.

ECTEL was established because the signatory governments were desirous of creating a competitive environment for telecommunications in the region. We wanted the benefits of universal telecommunications services to be realised by the people of this region. We were determined to provide affordable, modern, efficient, and competitive telecommunications service to the people of this region. We believed that a harmonised and co-ordinated approach within the region was key and we were convinced that a liberalised and competitive telecommunications sector was essential for the economic and social development of our people. This emphasis on the economic and social development of our people must be, in the final analysis, the be all and end all of all that we do in government. It must also be the be all and end all of all that ECTEL does in this region as well.

And with those broader, societal observations as a backdrop, I want to now focus on the real reason that we are here this evening and that is the official launch of the Universal Service Fund (USF). This ceremony is very significant, not only to the National Telecommunications Regulatory Commission (NTRC), but also to my government as it signals the creation of a new facility to promote the expansion of telecommunications services throughout the Federation.

The Universal Service Fund is a facility that will fund the extension of telecommunications services to geographic areas that may not be financially attractive to telecommunications providers. This fund then will ensure a more equitable distribution of telecommunications services throughout the Federation and this is only fair. We certainly do not wish to have any segment of this Federation feeling in any way left behind and now, because of the fund, there will be no need for any areas to feel this way.

I am pleased to be able to state that the NTRC will undertake the analysis that is needed to identify those sectors of our society that are in need of services. Relevant projects will be developed and implemented. I urge the Federations' telecommunications providers, who already have important insights into the areas of need, to work closely with the NTRC in this regard. I also urge government agencies and non-governmental agencies to position themselves to propose project ideas to the NTRC.

Perhaps I should take the time here to explain that the Universal Service Fund will function under established guidelines and regulations. The NTRC shall be more than pleased to make these available to the public since stakeholder confidence in the operation of the fund is of utmost importance to us all.

The establishment of the fund at this time is very important. Telecommunications and Information Technology (ICT), after all, play a pivotal role in all modern economies including that of St Kitts and Nevis. And although this sector has been somewhat affected by the global economic crisis, it nonetheless continues to make a sizeable contribution to our GDP. The sector, for example, accounted for 10 per cent of GDP in 2008 with the dollar value of telecommunications revenues being EC$120 million. Also in 2008, there was growth in both mobile and internet penetration with the former reaching 148 per cent and the latter moving upwards to 25 per cent. Fixed line subscription on the other hand was practically unchanged compared to one year before with penetration remaining at 40 per cent year to year.

Let us compare telecoms sector indicators for St Kitts and Nevis with those of our OECS and Caribbean neighbours. According to ECTEL's review, St Kitts and Nevis' 40 per cent penetration level for fixed line services in 2008 was the highest in the ECTEL region, and compares favourably with other Caribbean countries as well. Jamaica, for example, is 12 per cent; Trinidad & Tobago, 23 per cent; the Bahamas, 40 per cent; and Barbados, 59 per cent. This trend also applies to mobile and internet penetration rates. At the same time, there are opportunities in the Federation for the USF in relation to the internet and broadband.

I must say that I was very pleased to learn that Universal Service Funds have either been established, or are in the process of being established, in the other ECTEL member states. This is yet another manifestation of the telecommunications harmonisation that has been made possible by ECTEL.

In 2010 ECTEL celebrates its tenth anniversary. And in 2010, we are noting the establishment of the USF in St Kitts and Nevis and other ECTEL member states. There is a neatness and a symmetry to that, a sense of progress and forward movement, and that is good.

ECTEL and regional governments have travelled the early stages of liberalisation together with a great deal to show for it. And the past ten years have brought us to a stage where we can look forward with confidence to the ongoing cooperation and collaboration in the field of telecommunications regulation that awaits. Our partnership is solid and this partnership will continue to serve the interests of this region's people. The implementation of telecommunications projects financed by the fund will represent a major advancement for many throughout the region. And anything that is a major advancement for many will also be a major advancement for us all.

Let us go forward then, recognising, welcoming, and celebrating the advances of modern technology. But let us also, as the wise and visionary thinkers and patriots that we are, always strive to ensure that all that we do, and all that we embrace, and acquire, and implement in the field of telecommunications advancements, will forever redound to the social upliftment and economic advancement of the people of these islands whose interests it is our distinct honour to protect.

RE-OPENING OF SCHOOLS AND LAPTOP ARRIVALS

Ask the Prime Minister Radio Programme
ZIZ Broadcasting Corporation, January 11, 2011

Good morning. And thank you for tuning in to this week's edition of *Ask the Prime Minister.*

Yesterday the nation's children returned to classes. Fifth formers and CFB students are facing the final stretch to CXC and CAPE. Students from grade one to fourth form are moving forward with habits and attitudes that will either strengthen their chances of leading independent, respectable lives, or lives of difficulty and frustration. I urge that parents do their part to rear God-fearing, decent, and hard-working children. I urge teachers to remember the tremendous impact they have on their students' self-image and performance. I urge society at large to give maximum moral and practical support to our nation's teachers. And I urge pupils and students to realise that they are living in a challenging and highly competitive global community that demands the highest standards of effort, decency, and behaviour from them all.

I urge us all to see the education of the nation's children – academic, spiritual, educational, moral – as the most important undertaking of this society, and I urge us all to act accordingly. And as we all do our part to equip the nation's children for the demands of the twenty-first century, I am pleased to report that the specially designed Hewlett Packard laptops earmarked for our fifth formers will arrive in port on January 15. These laptops, purchased by the government to strengthen our young people academically, and not to serve as further distractions, will have filters to block pornography and various social networks, and will be delivered to the Federation's fifth formers this month. And before our summer vacation begins, all other eligible students will also have received their laptops as well.

CAPISTERRE COMPUTER INITIATIVE
Parsons Community Centre, February 21, 2011

Access to Information Communications Technology (ICT) in communities and in schools is important in helping to produce graduates of the education system who are armed with ICT-related skills useful for further education as well as for employment.

It is crucial to understand that computers and their Internet connections are important tools in our hands for the facilitation of learning. Every effort is being made by my government to ensure that our ICT policy addresses core issues of integration at all levels of the education system, and with communities, if we are to achieve a real revolution between education and information technologies. Teachers, school management, and appropriate government ministries must work towards goals that facilitate the nexus.

It means they must be equipped with the crucial knowledge and skills to enable the effective use of technology. Training, at all levels, has to be a significant aspect of ICT implementation. Coordination is critical, as crucial as the financial resources that are required. It is important to understand that ICT in the education system has to include all areas of teaching and learning from subject registration, syllabus planning, coursework/homework assignment, to correspondence with parents, and assessment. Getting to such a point is a process that requires many resources so phased approaches will have to be the order of the day. Regardless of the resources at any given time, we must ensure that all our endeavours are aimed at producing quality output in terms of our students' education and skill sets, and the empowerment of our communities as well as the institutional strengthening that is required to sustain development and growth with regard to ICT, and education.

It is important to think about the future and the relationship between St Kitts and Nevis, the Caribbean region, and the world at large. Clearly, the world is more integrated today than ever before, and our most recent illustration – the global economic and financial crisis – should leave us in no doubt. As a consequence, Caribbean Community leaders mandated the CARICOM Secretariat to develop a CARICOM ICT strategy, given the fact that Information and Communication Technology is considered to be a vital facilitator of further integration, especially in relation to the success of the CARICOM Single Market and Economy, the CSME. The ultimate context relates to St Kitts and Nevis and the rest of the Caribbean Community being able to compete effectively on the global scene. Our economies must be sustainable and globally integrated as the ICT borders become more blurred. We prepare for the future, therefore, by preparing our human resources to function effectively in a highly competitive global environment. The process must begin in the early years of our children.

Silver Reef Resort construction site visit, 2009

Silver Reef Resort, 2009

*Unless otherwise indicated, photos are by Willet's Photo Studio, St Kitts

Reviewing the Honour Guard — Opening of National Assembly, March 2010

Opening of National Assembly, March 2010

National Assembly March, 2010

Commonwealth Games Federation Assembly, November 2011, St Kitts

*PM Douglas with Sir Cuthbert Sebastian, second Governor-General of
St Kitts and Nevis, November 2011*

Greeting Saddlers stalwart Brother Edward Bailey, 2010

25th Anniversary of Independence Freedom Concert, September 2008

Chi-Lites performance, 2009

*Official opening of the Embassy of St Kitts and Nevis
in Havana, Cuba, June 2014*
Photo by Emilio Herera

2015 Labour Election Team
Rear L to R: Dr Terrance Drew, Dr Vance Gilbert, Glen 'Ghost' Phillip, Konris Maynard, Dr Norgen Wilson
Front L to R: Nigel Carty (Senator), Dr Denzil Douglas, Dr Earl 'Asim' Martin, Marcella Liburd

Rt Hon. Dr Denzil Llewellyn Douglas, 2014

National Security

NATIONAL SECURITY

Of all the major policy files the Douglas government had to address during its twenty years in power, the most intractable was national security. Denzil Douglas had come into office in 1995 primarily on a pledge to reduce crime and provide law and order to a country that had only recently been referred to as 'Devil's Island' in the British media. By the start of his third term, some types of crimes had been reduced but serious crimes involving guns and gangs and homicides were still on the rise.

The Labour government knew that restoring law and order and maintaining a secure and orderly society was fundamental to the achievement of the social and economic development goals of the nation. Public disorder would restrict foreign investment, discourage tourism, and undermine all that had so far been accomplished. While it did not flinch from its original commitment to restoring and maintaining an orderly society, it was a continuing, frustrating uphill battle.

The government introduced a number of new measures to lessen crime in the Federation including the appointment of a new Commissioner of Police from outside the country with a strong US and UK training background; construction in SKN of a regional police and security personnel training centre to increase expertise and generally raise policing standards; and sourcing of increased European Development Fund (EDF) money for the purchase of much needed hardware and equipment including a mobile police station.

For their part, the police increased their effectiveness by stepped-up community policing including more street patrols, better public communication using social media, increased Neighbourhood Watch programmes, and improved forensic training and equipment. In the first half of 2009, major crime (wounding, house-breaking, larceny) was down 18 per cent year over year but murders, while confined to a particular sub-culture, increased by almost 12 per cent, despite the establishment of an anti-gang intelligence unit. Five years later, in 2014, the Federation had witnessed a 29 per cent drop in major crime over the past two years but the murder rate remained stubbornly high at twenty-four homicides, attributed primarily to gang violence.

The government also knew that fighting crime was not simply a matter of more, better trained police and substantial prison sentences. It had to be confronted and tackled early on by all areas of civil society including educators, church and village groups, social workers, government ministries, the business community, and parents and families. To this end, a coalition of police and civil society partners was created to advise the government and do their part to find workable and practical solutions to the crime situation.

Unemployed youth, especially males, were identified as a large component of the crime problem. In late 2012, the government introduced, as part of its crime fighting agenda, the People Employment Programme (PEP). With funding from the Sugar Industry Diversification Foundation (SIDF), PEP's aim was to provide jobs for youth and encourage them to take the path to responsible citizenship. There were some objections to this use of SIDF money but Douglas believed that crime was inter-linked with lack of opportunity in the post-sugar economy. PEP participants learned an array of new skills which made them more employable and their salaries had a major impact on local businesses.

Despite these efforts, violent crime continued to increase in the Federation and crime reduction, especially focused on guns and gangs, remained one of the government's biggest challenges in terms three and four.

FBI NATIONAL ACADEMY ASSOCIATES CONFERENCE
Multi-National Collaboration on Crime and Security
St Kitts Marriott Resort, June 12, 2007

I am delighted to join you here today as you embark on a programme of dialogue on issues that are acutely relevant to all of us given the highly global nature of your work. When one looks at many of the security issues affecting small and large countries around the world, we notice that there are several areas of common ground that include, for example, the challenges posed by narcotics traffickers, youth crime and violence, and global crimes like money laundering, terrorism, and the financing of a host of other crimes.

It is well understood that crime and violence affect every nation and society. It eats away at the social and economic fabrics of our countries and creates untold damage, particularly to the potential mainstream productivity of our young people. Needless to say, the battle against crime has to be intensive and for effective engagement, many human and physical resources are required. I believe it is safe to say that no law enforcement agency has all the resources it needs, or that most countries can provide all the financial resources required by their law enforcement agencies. It leaves the next most effective and some would argue more effective, alternative in the form of multi-national collaboration on crime and security.

In the Caribbean, crime and security have captured the sustained attention of the Heads of Governments of the Caribbean Community (CARICOM) for some years. Indeed, we recognised early that there was need for a vibrant and efficient approach in dealing with the security issues of the Caribbean, and it is especially critical for us today as we take on the challenges of globalisation and trade liberalisation. Beyond that is our urgent requirement to sustain anti-crime initiatives to enhance public safety and to maintain an environment that promotes investor confidence, and generally to enhance social proficiency and productive capacity.

As a result of these kinds of concerns, the Caribbean Community has been actively engaging in discussions with several countries with a view to strengthening law enforcement capability and capacity within the region. Significant to the enhancement of security in the region have been agreements reached between CARICOM and the UK and US governments on several specific components. These include, among others:

1. The training of law enforcement officials;

2. The establishment of a Regional Information and Intelligence Sharing Network;

3. The setting-up of Maritime Cooperation and Border Security mechanisms.

Just as important are the policy and management frameworks that will guide the enhancement of regional security. These have been produced through the establishment of the Security Policy Advisory Committee (SEPAC) and the Implementation Agency for Crime and Security (IMPACS). These arrangements were put to the test during the International Cricket Council World Cup in 2007.

Perhaps one of the key security features that emerged from this undertaking was the implementation of the Advanced Passenger Information System and the high level of collaboration between law enforcement agencies around the world. In addition, much focus has been given to the region-wide Mutual Assistance Agreement that provides the framework for mutual assistance in an agreed range of circumstances and especially for assistance from one country to another in emergency national security situations.

And there are other equally important developments taking place. Among these are discussion on the criminal deportee policy of the US government and initiatives being jointly taken through CARIFORUM especially as they relate to the issue of drug trafficking. Both are perceived as substantial threats to Caribbean security and require appropriate strategies. Some would argue that south-north narcotics trafficking throughout the region has been the single most destructive activity to reach the shores of the Caribbean. Some of our youth have fallen prey to this trafficking, and with it came the illegal firearms trade as well. This is a situation that we cannot allow to escalate any further. We must aggressively work to make the region an unprofitable route for the trade.

However, for the most part, the region will continue to enhance its policies and implementation frameworks and proceed with multi-national dialogue and agreements on the various issues.

Meanwhile, with the assistance of The University of the West Indies and various social agencies, work has been proceeding on obtaining a clearer picture of the underlying causes of crime and violence in our regional communities. For instance, we need to truly determine to what level poverty, unemployment, and social marginalisation play in the nature of crime and violence in the Caribbean region. Obviously, there will be implications for the social stability and morale of the people in the region as well as for law enforcement authorities.

Clearly, cyber crime has to become one of the newer crime-fighting fronts for the region. Some of it is connected to money laundering activities, but there are other significant illegal activities that will have to be monitored as part of the global fight against terrorism. This is not just a challenge for the Caribbean region, it is an even greater challenge for the most developed countries of the world. The concept of the 'global village' applies here.

Most needed, however, are more effective adjustments to the way law enforcement agencies fight crime in the region. This is where conferences such as this one are useful and it is my hope that the discussions that will take place here over the next few days will be extremely helpful to all involved. Indeed, I am encouraged by your packed agenda and I believe that this conference will be a tremendous success.

As possibly the most prestigious law enforcement school in the world, the FBI National Academy paves the way for improving standards of individuals and eventually institutions. As Associates of the Academy, you have a profound mandate to spearhead the quality of collaboration among agencies through your training and international conferences. This Federation has benefited from the academy through the training of our police superintendent, who, as you know, is the current chairman of the FBINAA Latin America and Caribbean chapter, and of course our assistant commissioner. Their achievements are very important to us as we continue to improve the standards and quality of our St Christopher and Nevis Police Force, always aiming of course to heighten the level of professionalism. Our objective is to create a police force that is highly competent, prominent for its courage and integrity, and one that forges close relationships with our communities.

In closing, ladies and gentlemen, I can only reaffirm that our Caribbean region, for the most part, is one whose police forces are governed by law and the constitutions of our nations, and in that context we uphold the values of human dignity, justice, and freedom of choice and expression. We believe strongly that our police forces will continue to serve the citizens and residents of Caribbean countries in such a manner that promotes social and economic viability. We must work diligently to ensure that our police forces receive the support of both citizens and policy-makers so that our region can continue to enjoy relative peace and tranquillity.

I wish this conference every success.

ROYAL ST KITTS AND NEVIS POLICE FORCE AND FIRE & RESCUE SERVICES

36th Passing-Out Parade / Graduation
Working Together to Combat Crime
Police Training School Complex, October 28, 2008

Today, I feel a sense of pride in joining with the rank and file of the Royal St Christopher and Nevis Police Force, and the Fire and Rescue Services, families, friends and our specially invited guests, to witness the official induction of the new recruits into the respective forces.

Let me make special mention of the Commissioner of Police and the Fire Chief who are the heads of both agencies represented here today, along with all the members of the security forces. I wish to recognise the contribution of the commandants and the hard-working staff at the training centres who have been diligent in the execution of their intensive programmes to ensure that the various work plans were effectively delivered with the level of satisfaction that resulted in the staging of today's event.

Today, I am pleased to welcome all to share this memorable and historic moment marking the first joint passing-out parade of recruits from two of the agencies that comprise the security forces in the Federation. Indeed, the level of collaboration that defines their collective efforts in the performance of their respective duties is demonstrated here today as the recruits stand proudly uniformed and united on the parade square. These are young, able-bodied men who have responded to the call to serve our proud country. Join me in commending them for a job well done!

In August of this year, I reassumed the portfolio of minister with responsibility for national security and I reaffirmed my commitment to the people of this country that the government will ensure that safety and security remain an area of priority, especially considering its paramount importance to all aspects of development in our small nation. As we transition into a service-oriented economy, we appreciate the importance and significance of sustaining the peaceful environment that will positively impact the prospects of economic growth and development in our beloved country.

I wish to commend the security forces for your collaborative efforts in confronting the scourge of crime and you, the members of the police force, in your capacity as the principal law enforcement agency in the Federation. There is strength and successes in unity. You have experienced that in a meaningful way as you continue to collaborate with your colleague agencies (Defence Force, Coast Guard, Fire and Rescue Service, and Customs) to ensure the safety of our citizens. In addressing the members of the police force earlier this month, I took the opportunity to highlight some of your successes that have made us all proud:

- 100 per cent court conviction in murder cases to date;

- Over five thousand marijuana plants have been uprooted as a result of the increased joint operations of the forces;

- Thirty firearm confiscations from our streets for the year to date. This is a significant achievement given the growing concerns with the increase in gun-related crimes that are unsettling our people in the Federation;

- We have seen the positive outcome of your town hall meetings which are the highlight of the community outreach programmes that have taken you into the various villages in our Federation. From all reports these interactive sessions have not only brought you closer to the residents but they provide a platform from which you can rebuild your image as professionals with a mandate to maintain law and order. It is from these community-based sessions that you will be able to glean critical feedback from the public on your own performance. The critics have been frank in their assessment of your performance. You now have the opportunity to make a fresh start.

With this new batch of recruits you can re-strategise. You can re-deploy your manpower to increase your visibility in our communities. You must be re-energised so that the negative perceptions can be dispelled.

There is no doubt that the current statistics reveal that certain categories of crime are on the decline. But you cannot become complacent. The rising level of certain other categories of crime is still cause for concern.

In the earlier part of this year, the fire chief and his team have been kept busy by the phenomenal increase in cane fires. As you will have heard from his report, there has now been a drastic decline in all fires, including cane fires, especially for the last quarter. In fact, the Fire and Rescue Services have attained their target having realised a 15 per cent reduction in overall reports of fire in the Federation to date.

Officers, you have to sustain the operations that will continue to impact crime reduction in St Kitts and Nevis and demonstrate that you are not overwhelmed by the criminal elements that have infiltrated our communities.

The members of the high command repeatedly assure the government and the people of the Federation that you possess the will and the ability to maintain law and order and demonstrate, over and over again, that you are not overwhelmed by the unscrupulous and criminal elements that seek to unsettle the peace in our communities. You committed to operate within the mandate of the solemn oath that you have all taken upon joining the Royal St Christopher and Nevis Police Force.

Let me reiterate that government is serious about the implementation of initiatives that will enable you, the security forces, to formulate strategic plans and programmes that are designed to reduce crime and violence in our communities. This is in keeping with the crime detection and crime prevention imperatives that will restore and sustain the peace and tranquillity of our nation. It is our commitment as a government to strengthen the platform from which the forces can be developed. In view of this, I have already put in place the National Security Advisory Group that will ensure the speedy implementation of recommendations, projects, and initiatives designed to improve the security infrastructure and mechanism in the Federation.

The upgrading of the National Security Plan will be ongoing to ensure that your crime-fighting strategies remain relevant. This will allow for continued input from all the agencies concerned. Policy directives include the implementation of approaches that are to bring about immediate and long-term positive results in the area of crime prevention.

Immediate focus will continue to be given to:

- The implementation of an interim plan to stem gun-related crimes. This includes the law enforcement agencies of St Maarten and St Eustatius.
- Continued increased vigilance at our ports of entry and joint operations by our officers and members of the K-9 units of the security forces.

- Stepped-up stops and searches in known hot spots to improve crime detection.

- Island-wide mobile patrols to enhance the visibility of officers. Government has committed the resources to purchase additional vehicles for the forces. By the end of this month, the police will receive an increase in its current fleet of vehicles.

- The strengthening of inter-sectoral collaboration among the forces.

- Community policing through greater community-based interactions.

- Strengthening of the Anti-Gun/Strike Force Unit. This agency is leading the illicit firearm eradication operations of the ministry and has been working closely with the security forces to ensure that they are equipped with the requisite tools and resources to carry out their duties.

- Increased regional and international cooperation. Crime transcends geographic boundaries and as such we cannot be insular in our approach to eradicate it from our communities. Safety and security has now become the fourth pillar for functional cooperation among CARICOM member states. The implementation of the new Regional Management Framework for Crime and Security is moving ahead with much success. This is the framework for functional cooperation and the increased regional initiatives which are of significant benefit to the regional security mechanism.

- Our operational plan will be intelligence-driven. The ministry has already solicited the involvement of the Regional Security System (RSS) to avail the services of the C26 Air Wing to assist in our crime eradication operations. The RSS aircraft will do frequent aerial reconnaissance (fly-overs) of selected areas to get first-hand information that will be useful for the agency.

- We have observed frequent cane fires that have been linked to certain related criminal activities that the Fire and Rescue Services are working with the police to investigate.

- Intervention programmes targeting youths are part of a proactive approach to crime prevention. The Our Men at School Programme with its thrust to reach out to youths and focus them in the right direction is one of the long-term strategies that will reap the desired behavior changes. I would like to take this opportunity to commend the force for the continued implementation of the Boys Club programme that is also a preventative approach to crime. I wish to recognise the officers who are spearheading this programme and commend you for your tenacity, dedication, and commitment to mentoring these youths and inspiring them to lead meaningful lives.

- We have sought professional assistance from renowned international agencies such as the Federal Bureau of Investigation in addressing gang violence and crime in general. The initial phase of this consultancy has begun with a fact-finding visit to the Federation of a high ranking official who is committed to working with the government and the police force to address crime in a holistic manner.

- It is our intention to take every opportunity to build the capacity of both police and fire and rescue service officers in our effort to ensure that they are adequately equipped with the requisite skills to perform their respective duties.

I must, at this point record my profound appreciation to our international and regional partners who have buttressed our own national efforts in combating crime through a battery of initiatives that involve officers from both agencies.

Many of these initiatives involve training and technical assistance as well as regional approaches to fighting crime. Officers of the police force continue to have the opportunity to be attached to regional institutions such as the CARICOM IMPACS, which is a regional organisation that has been established by CARICOM to address regional crime and security, and the Barbados-based Regional Security System (RSS), both of which provide officers with needed and relevant experience and exposure that will assist them in the training of other officers at the national level. Such an approach is further assisted by our international partners, especially the United Kingdom, Canada, the US, Japan, and the government of the Republic of China on Taiwan. All of these countries are providing assistance to the forces and are providing training opportunities for all levels of the police force.

This year in particular, under the Canadian Law Enforcement Training Assistance Project, officers were trained in Improving Performance Through Strategic Planning and Effective Leadership.

This latest training held in May and in August has resulted in over fifty security force officers trained under this project. It is also important to note that the ministry is facilitating training not only for police officers but also for the Defence Force, Customs, and the Port Authority as well as private security agencies in the Federation. In upcoming months, assistance from the RCMP (Royal Canadian Mounted Police) will specifically provide assistance in the areas of crime detection, analysis, prevention, leadership, management training, and succession planning...a holistic approach.

Furthermore, members of the police force are being trained in areas of money laundering, drug and cyber crime investigations and management, border security issues, and terrorism and disaster management. Just a few days ago, the Ministry of National Security, through the joint assistance of the United States Embassy in Bridgetown, the US Diplomatic Security Service, and the Office of Anti-Terrorism Assistance, conducted a regional executive seminar on digital investigations and security here in the Federation. This seminar emphasised, among other matters, the use and role of technology in fighting crime in the context of an evolving use of computers to commit crimes globally.

I have mentioned all of these things to demonstrate that the government has the issue of crime fighting on the 'front burner', and it is ensuring that our security forces obtain the kind of training required to effectively operate in a challenging environment. One should also take note of the wide range or training programmes that are being conducted because the threat of crime to our economy and social life not only comes from within our borders, but from international sources as well.

The matter of crime, safety, and security remains high on our agenda and the government will continue to provide focused attention to the upgrading of our security forces. Our intention, again, is to ensure effective crime-fighting capacity and capability within the security forces. Your safety and security come first and we shall engage a wide cross-section of avenues to effect appropriate strategies in the fight against crime and violence in the Federation. I assure you of this as we continue to develop St Kitts and Nevis socially and economically.

My government is committed, therefore, to realise a highly professionalised and effective security operation in the Federation and will continue to work on the local front in collaboration with regional and international agencies that are leading agencies and entities in the fight against a wide range of criminal activity.

These are the initiatives that will reap the desired outcome. The construction of the co-ed facility has begun and will be an avenue for the coordination of a more long-term programme designed to save our generation of young men and women who can carry our legacy of discipline and civic pride.

Government will continue to make available the requisite resources that will assist you in implementing its zero tolerance policy on crime. We have embraced a proactive approach to security and will be focused in our efforts to ensure that our people are safe and our streets are free of those who would wish to instill fear in the hearts of the law-abiding citizens of this country. The island-wide town hall meetings of the high command of the police force have allowed the police to engage the public and receive first-hand information from residents of the respective communities that they have visited.

Notwithstanding the successes, the increased incidence of certain categories of crime remains a concern for all of us. Notwithstanding our investment in building the resource capabilities of the security agencies to ensure the implementation of strategies and policies reflecting government's zero tolerance stance on crime, the onus is on all of you to raise the standard of service to your country.

I challenge you as leaders of the respective agencies to fulfil the solemn oath that you have taken in executing your role as officers of essential services in this country. Be exemplary in every sphere of your operation. Be effective managers and do not compromise your standards and the high ideals that built the institutions which you proudly represent here today. Yours is a call of service to humanity, while embracing and sustaining the values that give us all a purpose to live and enjoy the fruits of years of hard work and achievement.

I further challenge you to be consistent in the execution of your duties. Strive at all times to maintain the highest level of commitment, professionalism, and productivity as members of the principal law enforcement agency in the Federation. Be committed to the job! Get out into the communities! Be visible! Patrol the streets – there is where you are detailed to be. There is where we want to see you!

The members of the fire and rescue services are assisting with some of the VIP duties to ensure that police officers are available to be more involved in crime-fighting. Clerical duties are to be performed by civilians and officers must be deployed strictly to carry out police duties.

My government has never turned a blind eye to your conditions of work. However, discipline and due process must be the guiding principles of how we do business. As officers charged to ensure that law and order are upheld, you must ensure that you exercise your duty with responsibility and respect at all times. Policing is a business. Crime prevention and detection is your mission, safety and security is your watchword. The government, citizens, and residents of this country are your clients. Let us work together as a team. What matters most in this organisation is teamwork. The community is willing. You must take up the mantle and lead them back to embrace you and rebuild confidence and confidentiality as guiding principles for the way forward. You owe it to the people. You owe it to your families. You owe it to the nation of which you are a part.

I wish to take this opportunity to address you, the new recruits, who have just arrived at the first milestone on the career path that you have chosen. I want to commend you and extend heartfelt congratulations to all of you for your success during the course of training. You have a role to play in the effective operation of your respective agency, whether as first responders in Fire and Rescue Services where the focus is on safety and saving lives or as a law enforcement officer whose first line of duty is to maintain law and order. Stay your course. Avoid the distractions that will lead you away from your assigned duties. Go out into the communities with the same zeal that brought you through the weeks of training and bring the perpetrators of all forms of crimes to justice. Do not compromise your standards. Do not turn a blind eye to petty crimes. These are the inconsistencies that cause deviant behaviours to degenerate into lawlessness and heinous crimes. Be fearless, firm and respectful.

Finally, I wish to challenge you, the parents and guardians of this our beautiful land, to play your part in molding our young children. Bad habits are formed when not stamped out at an early age. You are the guardians of the cradle and the molders of their young minds. You are to instill in them sound principles and values that will fit them for life. Do not abdicate your responsibilities as parents to those who are reckless and ill-disciplined. Teachers will assist. The elders in the communities may assist, but the God-given duty is yours 'to train the child in the way it should go.' Adhering to this divine directive will ensure that the children who are our future are equipped with lifelong values that will strengthen the moral fabric of our society.

The emphasis on human resource development in our security forces is a priority because it is our men and women in the security forces who must inform the strategic focus and implement those strategies in a manner that brings results. I believe that with such intensive approaches as I have outlined, St Kitts and Nevis will continue to be an excellent place to do business as we bring greater focus on improving the safety and quality of life of citizens and residents of our beloved country. Let me also remind our communities that crime-fighting is not the sole responsibility of our security forces. It is the responsibility of law-abiding citizens and residents to play their part in assisting the police. By working together, much can be achieved.

Finally, let me once again commend all those persons who have assisted in the training of our police recruits and our fire and rescue trainees. I believe that you have done well. I again congratulate the graduating trainees for the Police Force, and for the Fire and Rescue Service. I wish you well and remind you to perform to the best of your abilities in your duties. I join your families in support of your conviction to follow careers in these critical institutions of our nation.

NATIONAL CONSULTATION ON CRIME
St Kitts Marriott Resort, December 12, 2008

On the surface, this session will be about crime – particularly gun and gang-related crime. At a deeper level, however, this session is really about who and what we have become as a people, who and what we want to be, and to what new standards we must now commit ourselves in order to get there. And so, much that we will discuss and think about today as we attempt to chart a course *away* from gun and gang violence, will have to do with what each of us is willing to contribute to this all-important battle.

If we want the kind of society where respect for self and others, compassion, and conscience are our defining characteristics, new attitudinal, behavioural, and relational standards will be required of us. Because, let there be no doubt, a society in which respect for self and others, compassion, and conscience predominate, will be a society in which there will be less rage, less pathology, less brutality, and less crime.

Focusing solely on the guns, the knives, and the gangs will miss the point. The far more difficult but the far more pressing challenge is for us to critically examine what about our society is causing young people to reach for the guns, reach for the knives, and reach for the gangs.

I know that hostility, brutality, and criminality are gripping much of the world. But that is of little comfort. The point is that these pathologies have reached our shores. However, whether these pathologies defeat us here in St Kitts and Nevis, or we defeat them, will have everything to do with whether we, as a people, can find the will and the courage to confront these pathologies at the level of the human psyche and soul, or whether, like far too many other societies, we will miss the boat entirely by focusing solely on the handcuffs and the jails and the squad cars.

Let there be no confusion about my essential point. Handcuffs and jails and squad cars are *key* to our battle against crime. Handcuffs and jails and squad cars most assuredly have their place and our speakers today will address the law enforcement aspects of my government's crime-fighting efforts. My government is relentless in identifying, apprehending, and prosecuting anyone who attempts to wreak havoc through wanton acts of violence. But the time has come for us, as a concerned and visionary people, to go far beyond that. And in a hurry. So I welcome hearing from all of you how you might help to usher in an era of new behavioural, attitudinal, and societal standards so that a more humane, a more self-respecting, and therefore a more stable and safe existence can be shared by all.

The words 'crime and violence' can sometimes leave the impression that crime is 'out there' somewhere, that it is something distant that needs to be fixed, somehow, preferably by someone else. And so many of us tell ourselves that crime really has nothing to do with us unless, of course, we become one of its victims.

I would like today to throw out the idea that gun and gang crime may indeed have everything to do with all of us. Because if we want to stop having to lament and wring our hands, if we want to begin making real headway, we are all going to have to bring keen powers of discernment to this problem. We are all going to have to insist on bold new behaviours and standards as to how we rear our children, what we instill in them, how we interact with each other, how we conduct ourselves, how we live together as a people, because crime does not exist in a vacuum – it grows out of the society in which it is found. And so, as a society, we are going to have to come at gang and gun crime backwards, sideways, and every other way that holds even the slightest promise of denting, cracking and eventually breaking whatever habits, behaviours, and practices, large or small, create first in little ways, then in larger ways, the wayward, don't-care attitudes and behaviours that later morph into the mindless brutality that we have all witnessed of late.

Albert Einstein once said that proof of insanity is doing the same thing repeatedly and expecting a different result. With this in mind therefore, we cannot come here, have a stimulating discussion, only to leave and continue thinking exactly as we have been thinking, behaving exactly as we have been behaving, and shrugging at exactly the same realities we've shrugged at for years, all the while expecting crime to abate on its own, for that would indeed be proof of our insanity.

And so, today, I beseech the church to take a long hard look at itself and to identify ways in which it must change if we are to have any chance of improving the way our young people regard themselves, the way they regard life, and the way they regard each other. Because it is, after all, their utter disregard and contempt for each other that allows them to wipe each other out without a second thought.

I urge everyone in government – civil servants and government ministers alike – to take a long hard look at ourselves and at existing government policies and practices with a view to identifying and changing those policies and practices that may inadvertently and unintentionally work against young people leading responsible, respectable, and respectful lives. I am thinking here of students being asked to leave school at very young ages because of poor performance; minor offenders being housed with hardened criminals; police doing nothing despite witnessing young people smoking ganja, manhandling each other, etc., etc.

Radio and television station managers, DJs, video producers and others in the media: You are uniquely and powerfully positioned to counter and dampen the appeal of thug culture, glamourised lawlessness, and crass carnality, all of which are major contributors to the problems we are facing today, and so much of which is promoted via the media, both here and abroad. Are there new standards to which you would be willing to commit yourselves, as an industry, as your contribution to battling this plague that has beset us?

To the business community: Are there ways in which your merchandising policies, the advertising images you use, the jingles you approve might be chosen so as to create a new mindset, a new atmosphere, a new ethos and frame of reference for your customers? Are there ways in which you might be even more assertive in the establishment of socially-stabilising, youth-based activities?

What I am really asking is whether we in St Kitts and Nevis are confident enough and visionary enough to seriously try to reshape and redirect our society for ourselves, to do what is right for us as a people, whether other countries are advocating these types of changes or not.

There are so many influences that shape a society. Carnival, for example, is around the corner. That is always a happy time. We are a free and joyous people, and for that I am truly grateful.

But it is also true that normal behavioural restraints sometimes elude us. Sometimes, especially during carnival, we fail to identify the boundaries between exuberant celebration and revolting excess. What will we see on the streets this carnival? What will we hear in the lyrics?

Can we afford to continue pretending that what we embrace as our celebratory 'culture' does not also seep into and shape who and what we are when the music stops? That it has no impact on how we see each other, and relate to each other throughout the rest of the year? I am referring here to beautiful women in beautiful costumes lying flat on their backs in the streets during carnival with their legs spread wide and gyrating for long periods, sometimes with no partner, sometimes with a male partner, in full view of old, young, and in-between. Several of these pictures were posted on SKNVibes last year for the entire world – literally – to see. Many of us were horrified and we had to fight with the manager of SKNVibes to get him to take the photos down. The point is that the police or other officials should have intervened when these types of 'performances' were taking place in broad public view. Calypsonians, songwriters, stage and street performers – how can you help?

The criminal justice system will continue to handle existing criminals. Society's challenge, however, is to create an environment that does not produce a never-ending stream of new criminals. And this requires us to promote those habits, both minor and major, that enhance our people's dignity, their humanity, their automatic differentiation between the appropriate and the inappropriate, from earliest childhood to very old age. And it requires us to recognise and reject those habits that speed a society's downward slide.

I ask that as we discuss gang and gun violence we look beyond the immediacy of the stabbing and shooting and killing to see that these acts are the final manifestations of lifetimes of no controls, no restraints, no standards. Lifetimes of waywardness and lawlessness. Lifetimes of human behaviour run amok. If we accept and understand that, then we can then begin to work backwards and identify those ways in which all of us may have been unthinkingly accepting, encouraging, or endorsing wayward, wild, and 'own-way' behaviours, not realising the power of these behaviours to take root, grow into a broader societal slackness and coarseness and then harden into unthinking brutality.

The physician in me asks that we not simply lament the obviousness of the disease. Instead, I ask that we get down to the more difficult work of identifying the far less obvious but truly deadly bacterium, virus, or pathogen that caused this disease. It is not the guns that are our problem. It is not the drugs that are our problem. It is the factors that damaged the minds and damaged the souls and damaged the psyches that now reach for the drugs and reach for the guns that are our problem. And in order to identify and eradicate these factors, each and every one of us must step forward to do our part.

Before closing I wish to thank the leader of the opposition for the time and energy he has invested in analysing the issue of crime and violence and for the insights and recommendations that he has been good enough to share with my government. I also wish to thank the premier of Nevis with whom my cabinet met as recently as last week, and who has given every indication of his commitment to be a steady and reliable partner on this path on which we are about to embark.

Again, I thank you all for being a part of this important national consultation. I await your insights and your plans of action with great interest.

ANTI-CRIME RALLY AND MARCH
Warner Park Stadium, Basseterre, April 2, 2009

We are here today because we are fed up with gang violence. We are here today because we want all neighbourhoods – not just some – to be places of peace. We are here today because you want and need to have an impact! You want and need to make a difference! You want and need to count – each and every one of you!

And so, when I look at you, I do not see just 'marchers.' I do not see just 'participants in a rally.' I see tens and hundreds and thousands of concerned individuals ready to serve. I see tens and hundreds and thousands of true patriots reporting for duty.

And so I say, 'Welcome Aboard!'

At a December consultation on crime, my government urged the churches, the NGOs, the schools, the business community, the youth groups, the political parties – everybody – to step up, to speak out, to take a stand, to do their part. And I want today to thank the Evangelical Association, the St Kitts Council of Churches, and the St Kitts-Nevis Chamber of Industry & Commerce for doing just that. And I thank each and every person here today who stepped right up with them.

I have two main messages today – one for the shooters and the stabbers, and the other for the rest of society.

To the shooters and the stabbers I say this: You are not a law unto yourselves. And you will not hold any segment of this society hostage. My government has joined forces with anti-gang and anti-crime units throughout this region and around the world and our police will identify you, our courts will try you, and the justice system will make sure that you feel the full force of the law.

To those who are not involved in either crime or violence but are being pulled in that direction, I say: Reach out. Reach out to a religious minister or a government minister. Reach out to a teacher, the police, or a business person. Reach out and seek guidance as to how you might resist that downward negative pull, how you might avoid the hell that gang life always ends up being – can't go here … can't go there … people trying to kill you … ducking and hiding like an animal … being lost in jail or eventually facing the hangman. Reach out.

And to every other national and every resident, whether you are inside the park, or outside the park, whether you are hard at work or relaxing on the beach, I say this: You have a responsibility, a burning and inescapable responsibility, to help to halt the creation of new criminals in St Kitts and Nevis.

Let us all remember that not one newborn, not one infant, anywhere in this federation, was born to be a gang member, a stabber, a shooter, or a killer. But something happens to these children.

They see things that young children should never see – adults smoking, using and selling drugs; adults brutalising each other physically; adults involved in intimacies that should be private; adults worshiping the material and ignoring the spiritual.

They hear things children should never hear – parents, teachers, neighbours calling them 'dumb' or 'stupid,' adults boasting about wicked or criminal acts, adults telling children how to be junior partners in crime.

They feel things young children should never feel – raw panic when mothers and fathers leave them by themselves all night and go off to party, depression and rage when, instead of so-called 'getting licks,' they are repeatedly brutalised.

Whether the child is in St Kitts and Nevis or in Switzerland, any child who sees and hears and feels, all of these things, all of the time, will be damaged. And the broader society will be made to pay.

At the same time, there are those children, both here and abroad, who never see what children need to see – parents and neighbours really trying to be good people, parents and neighbours valuing not only possessions, but character as well, parents and neighbours demanding that young people control themselves and control their behaviour.

There are children of the wealthy and children of the poor who have *never* heard –

'Don't do that. That is wrong.'

'Be thankful for what you have.'

'If something is not yours, leave it alone.'

'An "A" through cheating is a mark of shame.'

'Think of the other person's feelings.'

'Come, let us pray together.'

Let us not think that it is only negligent parents who need to do better with their own children. Every adult in this society needs to be more active and more instructive in our dealings with children we don't even know, because if we want the young people of St Kitts and Nevis to follow a certain path, we are going to have to clear the way.

If we see students strolling through Basseterre or Cayon or Dieppe Bay at 10:30 in the morning, we need to care enough to let them know that they need to be in school. If we see fifteen-year-olds at the strip at two in the morning, we need to care enough to let them know that they need to be at home. If we see bartenders selling alcohol to minors, we need to care enough to tell the bartender that that is not right. If we see our young girls emulating the vulgarity glamourised by the media and our young boys emulating the thug persona being peddled on television, we need to care enough to *convince* them that they are better than that. But if only one or two people do all of the caring, all of the intervening, all of the trying while the rest of us sit back, nothing will change. Young people must hear from their left and their right, from their front and their back, when they are running off the tracks.

We have to speak up. We have to instruct. Because whoever is not part of the solution is part of the problem. Everybody has to make a down payment on the type of future we want in this country. And so, everybody has to start investing either time, or money, or talent, or materiel – something – into efforts that show the nation's youth a different and better way.

And finally, to the young people: Those of you who are blessed enough to have some solid adult somewhere, guiding you, advising you, encouraging you, and keeping you on the straight and narrow, fall on your knees and thank God. You have no idea just how lucky you really are. To those who are not so lucky, I say: Turn to prayer as a source of comfort, strength, and encouragement. Turn to your school counsellors for guidance and advice. Turn to a church and its minister for stability. Turn to the Ministry of Education, or the Ministry of Community Affairs, or the Ministry of Sports to learn of programmes that can help.

If you have not behaved as you should have in the past, the past is the past. Today is a new day. You must now strive to create a new you.

Respect yourself.

Respect others.

Work hard.

Find your conscience, and be guided by it.

Believe that you can be better today than you were yesterday, and work hard to make it so.

May God bless us as we move forward as one people – united – to create the kind of country that we want.

NATIONAL SECURITY BROADCAST
New Policies to Fight Crime Escalation
ZIZ Broadcasting Corporation, August 31, 2011

The entire nation has expressed great shock and dismay over the recent escalation in crime as manifested in the senseless and ruthless murder of four of our young people in the course of four days just over a week ago. Indeed, the number of murders in the first eight months of this year has already exceeded the number reported in the entire twelve months of last year and has, in fact, reached record levels. This situation has been very distressing to me and has been dominating my attention and thought processes on an ongoing basis.

Notwithstanding the economic crisis that continues to haunt the entire globe, we have been making great progress in addressing our fiscal imbalances and we are on the verge of reducing our debt substantially through a debt restructuring programme that we are implementing with the assistance of the International Monetary Fund. Indeed, we believe that our efforts in this regard will lay a solid foundation for the attainment of sustained growth over the medium-term and long-term.

Unfortunately, the current levels of crime in our country, if continued for an extended period, could undermine our programme of debt reduction, growth, and development and bring all of our efforts to naught. We run the risk of shattering the confidence of our many foreign investors, scaring away potential tourists, and depleting our confidence in ourselves as a people and our willingness to engage in investment and other economic activities critical to the development of our nation.

I am aware that the Ministry of National Security under the leadership of the deputy prime minister has been working assiduously to combat crime and I am certain that many of the initiatives that have been introduced will bear fruit over time. However, I believe that crime in our country has reached the stage where the people of St Kitts and Nevis must be able to definitively and unequivocally hold its prime minister responsible for its resolution over a reasonable period of time.

We cannot continue to pass blame from one person to another and to randomly pick and choose the persons and entities on which we would wish to lay blame. The buck stops with the prime minister whom you elected to serve you and protect you with the help of the cabinet and the various organs and institutions of government. Indeed, I am convinced that crime represents such a huge risk to our society and to all of our achievements as a nation, that it must be addressed at the very highest level of our government.

Tomorrow, our newly recruited police commissioner, a proud and distinguished son of the soil, will formally assume the mantle of leadership of the St Christopher and Nevis Police Force and we expect that he will help to modernise the force, enhance discipline among the various ranks, and boost the effectiveness of the force in fighting crime, bringing criminals to justice, and carrying out the overall mandate of the police force. In addition, today in our parliamentary debates, we are passing the *Gang (Prohibition and Prevention) Act 2011*, which will dramatically enhance our capacity to undermine and counter dysfunctional gang activities and crimes. But these actions along with the many initiatives that we have been introducing in recent months to combat crime must be bolstered by even greater accountability through monitoring, general policy oversight, and regular reporting to the people by policy-makers occupying the highest levels of government.

It is in this context that I have decided to establish a Ministerial Task Force that will be comprised of the deputy prime minister, the attorney-general, the minister of works, and myself as chairman, to provide general oversight and policy guidance in relation to all crime-fighting activities in our Federation. This task force will ensure that the security forces are provided with the resources that they require to effectively fight crime and will monitor the implementation of a comprehensive crime reduction plan that we intend to publish shortly. We expect that the new commissioner will take the lead in formulating this plan which will consolidate all of the initiatives and plans that we have announced in recent times, take full account of the many views and opinions expressed by our people through various media, and bring on board many of the commissioner's own ideas and strategies based on his vast experience and outstanding credentials as a law enforcement officer in the United States of America.

This plan will identify clear and concrete objectives and targets, timelines for each planned activity, the person or entity responsible for the implementation of each activity, and critical milestones and indicators of success in the implementation of the plan. This will allow me, as chairman of the Ministerial Task Force, to report to the public at least quarterly in very clear and precise terms as to the progress being made in implementing the plan and in combating crime and violence generally.

This task force will also liaise with the Parliamentary Select Committee on Crime and Violence which was recently established by the minister of national security and will seek to ensure that all plans and initiatives in relation to crime are subjected to meaningful bipartisan consultations and supported by appropriate legislation in parliament. As chairman of the Ministerial Task Force on Crime, I will keep the Parliamentary Select Committee updated on a regular basis on the progress that we are making in respect to the fight against crime and violence and take full account of their views and comments.

To ensure that the fight against crime is given maximum support at the highest level of government, I also propose to establish a Special Anti-Crime Unit in the Office of the Prime Minister that will provide administrative and secretarial support to the Ministerial Task Force, monitor the implementation of the crime plan, coordinate the activities of the various law enforcement agencies, and provide an effective administrative interface between the policy-makers and the security forces. This unit will be headed by a permanent secretary who will be assigned specifically to the management of the Anti-Crime Unit and will be responsible for the discharge of administrative functions in relation to the police and the defence force.

To give effect to this new arrangement, His Excellency the Governor-General, acting on my advice and in keeping with our constitution, has assigned the subjects of police and defence force to me. This will enable me to effectively carry out my duties as chairman of the Ministerial Task Force and provide policy direction in relation to the fight against crime. It will also give the Anti-Crime Unit in the Office of the Prime Minister the necessary authority to discharge its administrative functions in relation to the police and defence force.

It is intended that the deputy prime minister will continue to hold all his other portfolios in a restructured ministry, restyled the Ministry of Homeland Security, Foreign Affairs, Labour, and Social Security. The department of homeland security will include immigration, passports, prisons, fire, and rescue services, and the National Emergency

Management Agency (NEMA). He will also continue to play a major role in the fight against crime through his involvement in the Ministerial Task Force, thereby enabling him to provide help in carrying forward many of the crime-fighting activities and programmes that he initiated. Indeed, the government and the entire nation owes the deputy prime minister a great debt of gratitude for his hard work in the fight against crime to date and for the devotion and commitment that he displays in the discharge of his mandate as minister of national security.

Fellow citizens, my government will do its part to eradicate this scourge of crime and violence in our beloved country. We take full responsibility for effective law enforcement in our country. Indeed, we have always identified law and order as well as the protection of our people and their property as a critical objective of this government. We are convinced that the initiatives we have introduced, and will continue to introduce, should reduce crime dramatically.

It is a fact that the criminals are responsible for the crimes they have committed. Those who have committed these heinous crimes, especially homicides, will not be allowed to rest easy. No option under the law will be excluded in tracking down these killers, in charging them, and punishing them. The tears, pain, and suffering of the families of the victims must not be in vain.

However, our law enforcement agencies require the full support of our community. We must continue to pursue our long-term initiatives aimed at crime prevention and remove the culture of fear from our communities. It is our homes and our schools that are the factories that produce criminals. My government will therefore continue to refine our education system and support our families through training in parenting and appropriate intervention where necessary. We are also pursuing an expansive social agenda aimed at getting to the root of crime and violence and countering deviant behaviour. I encourage our people, our families, our institutions, our non-governmental organisations, our churches, our schools, our political parties, and civil society in general to lend a helping hand. This is not the time for political haggling. It is the time for action on every front.

HIV/AIDS, NCDs
AND
HEALTH CARE

HIV/AIDS, NCDS
AND
HEALTH CARE

As a medical doctor and the lead head of government for Human Resources, Health and HIV/AIDS in the CARICOM quasi-cabinet, Denzil Douglas led the regional strategy to combat AIDS. While there were still many obstacles and challenges to this multi-faceted problem to overcome including access to adequate funding and technical and human resources, the work of the Pan Caribbean Partnership Against HIV/AIDS (PANCAP) was bearing fruit. Established in 2001 as a regional, multi-sectoral umbrella network of governments and NGOs, it was successfully assisting Caribbean countries to scale-up their HIV/AIDS programmes and lobbying for cheaper prevention and treatment drugs through the Clinton Foundation and UNAIDS. PANCAP became a recognized AIDS prevention and treatment best practice model and Dr Douglas was lauded by former US President Bill Clinton in international fora for his leadership role in the AIDS crisis in the Caribbean.

With AIDS now in a stabilisation mode, Douglas began to focus more aggressively on the creation of a regional approach to tackling another health issue that impacted the well-being and resources of Caribbean peoples and that was the growing number of victims of non-communicable diseases (NCDs) such as diabetes, hypertension, and heart disease. Collectively, these diseases caused far more deaths than AIDS but did not receive the attention they warranted. Dr Douglas had been pushing for years for more focus on SIDS and the UN had also come to the conclusion that a new worldwide thrust to combat and prevent NCDs was required. Douglas gave a well-received presentation on the alarming growth of NCDs to his fellow CARICOM Heads of Government as well as to Commonwealth members but it was a continuing challenge to get the attention and resources required. At the end of his fourth term in office, he was still actively advocating for more attention to NCDs.

On the national stage, the Douglas Labour government launched its National Strategic Health Plan in 2008 which would inform and guide critical health care decision-making in the Federation for five years. The plan stressed the connections between the health of its nation's citizens and productivity and nation-building with a focus on healthier lifestyles, prevention, and NCDs. During this period, the quality of health care services on St Kitts and Nevis rapidly advanced including the upgrading of Joseph N. France Hospital and the virtual rebuilding of Pogson Hospital in St Kitts, and the refurbishment of Alexandra Hospital in Nevis; creation of more local health centres around the island; increased cancer screening capability as well as CT scanning and MRI services; opening of a kidney dialysis centre; more mental health and substance abuse programmes; more training for health care professionals; reduction in infant and maternal mortality; and continuing development of a national health insurance programme.

Pan-Caribbean Partnership Against HIV/AIDS (PANCAP)
From Idea to Reality
4th Annual General Meeting
Barbados, October 21–22, 2004

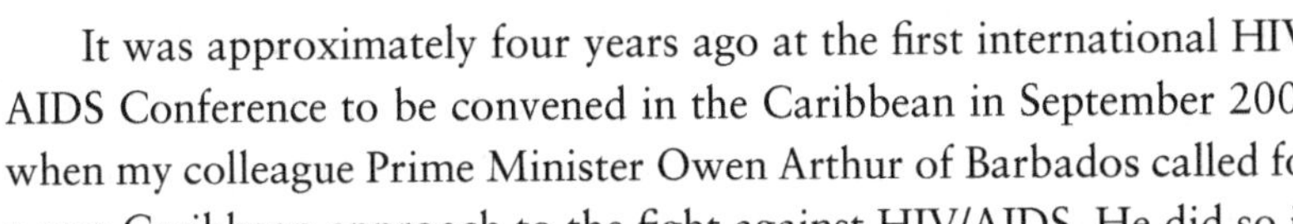

It was approximately four years ago at the first international HIV/AIDS Conference to be convened in the Caribbean in September 2000 when my colleague Prime Minister Owen Arthur of Barbados called for a pan Caribbean approach to the fight against HIV/AIDS. He did so in response to the obvious trends outlined in a plan of action undertaken by a regional group chaired by the CARICOM Secretariat and including representatives from CAREC, UNAIDS, UNDP, PAHO and The University of the West Indies.

The vision that emerged was one in which an accelerated response required the collective action of the countries in the Caribbean which include a vast array of small- and medium-sized states with varying economic fortunes and relatively high rates of poverty. The vision is also quite compatible with the current thrust of the Caribbean Community toward the establishment of a CARICOM Single Market and Economy (CSME) by 2005 which includes fifteen member states, Suriname and Haiti among them. The vision takes into consideration that the incidence of HIV/AIDS ignominiously ranks the Caribbean second only to sub-Saharan Africa. At the same time, a The University of the West Indies study graphically demonstrates that the price of inattention to this trend is likely to be irreparably high. It shows that the disease is likely to have a negative impact on the GDP growth of the Caribbean in the range of between 4 to 5 per cent and the cost treating the disease is likely to increase by 25 per cent to 35 per cent of GDP over a five-year period.

Despite the fact that the Caribbean Epidemiological Centre had for almost 10 years previously been advocating for the need for an affirmative policy, most states paid little attention and very little was done by way of preventive strategies until there was an obvious upsurge in this epidemic ranging from 1 per cent in a few countries like Cuba to as high as 8 per cent of the population in Haiti with a regional average of approximately 2 per cent. In fact, the burden of the disease is spiralling in the Caribbean in stark contrast to both Latin America and North America which have witnessed a downward trend.

The inauguration of the PAN Caribbean Partnership Against HIV/AIDS (PANCAP) as an idea in 2000 was institutionalised by a PANCAP Partnership agreement in 2001. Conceived as a 'network' of governmental, private sector, NGO, national AIDS programmes, institutions, and agencies, including faith-based organisations and international partners, PANCAP has blossomed into a vibrant mechanism. PANCAP has played an important role – and a successful one so far from the evidence – in coordinating resource mobilisation for the region's response to HIV/AIDS and shared responsibility among partners for the delivery of programmes and related activities. At the heart of this success story is committed leadership through a demonstration of political will at the highest levels.

In June 2001, six prime ministers and ten ministers of health from the Caribbean region – the highest level representation from any region – attended the United Nations General Assembly Special Session (UNGASS) in New York and contributed in no small measure to the UNGASS declaration which in fact drastically changed the global approach to HIV/AIDS. The Global Fund for HIV/AIDS, TB and Malaria, for example, is one major result. In addition, the CARICOM states were the first in any part of the world to follow-up on UNGASS at the CARICOM Heads of Government meeting in July 2001 when it fashioned the Nassau Declaration that *the health of the region is the wealth of the region* and charged PANCAP with the institutional responsibility for a coordinated regional response to HIV/AIDS and which established time-lines for achieving certain goals. So far, with the exception of universal access to ARVs, almost all the targets set have been met. Its advocacy campaign has paid dividends in changing the perspective of the funding institutions, among others, from scepticism toward acceptance of this regional network. This is attested to by the fact that PANCAP was the first regional coordinating mechanism to receive a grant from the global fund (2003). It was at Barcelona at the XIV HIV/AIDS Conference that PANCAP created history by negotiating a collective agreement with six pharmaceutical companies in a massive price reduction for anti-retroviral drugs from US$12,000 per person per annum to US$1,200. Through further collective action and the support of the Clinton Foundation, the price for generics is now at a level of approximately US$200 per annum. Bahamas is the first member country of PANCAP to benefit from this price deal and during the coming quarter other PANCAP countries will also benefit.

The CARICOM Secretariat, the administrative arm of the Caribbean Community, is the location of the PANCAP coordinating unit that deals with all the logistic arrangements for sustaining the network. This is given direction by a steering committee which oversees the operationalisation of the Caribbean Regional Strategic Framework linking the objectives and programme outcomes of all core partners that play key roles in implementing the various elements of the framework. The membership of PANCAP has an opportunity at its annual general meeting in October each year to review PANCAP's progress and be involved in shaping its future activities. In addition, the CARICOM Secretariat has lead responsibility for programmes in the area of human rights and stigma reduction as well as resource mobilisation. St Kitts and Nevis will have the honour of hosting the first PANCAP Regional Conference on changing attitudes toward stigma and discrimination against PLWA in November 2004 in collaboration with the UK's DFID. This is a direct result of a consultation between the UK prime minister and CARICOM prime ministers held in London in December 2003. The CARICOM Secretariat also presides over several grants including the Global Fund, the World Bank, the German Foundation for Development (GTZ), the European Union, CIDA, USAID, IDB and DFID. Funds from these sources over a five-year period amount to approximately US$50 million. Yet when measured against basic needs there still remains a major financial gap to stem the tide of HIV/AIDS in the region.

The implementation of programmes initiated through the coordinating role of CARICOM and other agencies depends on the capabilities of core partners each of which has responsibility for various components of the regional strategic framework. For example, the Caribbean Epidemiology Centre (CAREC), itself a major mobiliser of resources, has lead responsibility for surveillance; the Caribbean Health Research Centre (CHRC) has lead responsibility for M&E; the Caribbean Network for People Living with HIV/AIDS (CRN+) for care and treatment; UNAIDS for prevention and special programmes for vulnerable groups; The University of the West Indies (The UWI) for research and training; and CARICOM for human rights and stigma reduction and resource mobilisation.

These core partners are supported by a network of other partners such as the Red Cross, the Caribbean Council of Churches, CARICOM Youth Ambassadors, to name a few. Leadership through partnership is the basic tenet guiding the work of PANCAP and has to be carefully negotiated to ensure that through the sharing of resources the value of the partnership is manifested by maximising the impact of an accelerated response through the implementation of an integrated regional strategy.

Several key programmes have been facilitated by a number of partner groups:

1.   UNDP, IDB, USAID and DFID and The Clinton Foundation in developing the proposals to the GFATM.

2.   PAHO/WHO/UNAIDS in the early regional negotiations for cheaper anti-retroviral drugs resulting in the signing of agreements of principles with six pharmaceutical companies in Barcelona in July 2002 at the International HIV/AIDS Conference.

3.   The William Jefferson Clinton Presidential Foundation for its assistance in negotiating cheaper prices for generics which have so far benefited the Bahamas.

4.   CDC in collaborating with The UWI to develop and implement the Caribbean HIV/AIDS Research and Training Initiative (CHART).

5.   The Caribbean Commission on Health and Development, a think tank of leading experts chaired by Sir George Alleyne, responsible for advancing the research and policy dialogue on macroeconomics and health.

These are some illustrations of the dimensions of leadership that have driven the regional network from an idea to a reality. But sustainability requires other forms of leadership at the national level.

Hence, in the next rounds of implementation of the PANCAP strategic framework, emphasis is being given to building capacity at the national level and sub-regional levels through sharing of information and best practices, reducing the duplication of effort such that models for stigma reduction developed at the regional level may be adopted with special reference to specific country applications. The formula for sustaining the PANCAP model therefore revolves around leadership at all governmental levels including the Ministries of Health and Education and the national HIV/AIDS programmes. More and more emphasis is being placed on developing the capabilities of CRN+ and the Caribbean coordinators of national HIV/AIDS programmes.

The real test for PANCAP is to devolve leadership in the national HIV/AIDS programmes through institutional capacity and human resource development. The approach has to aim at reduction of stigma and discrimination, at greater universal access to ARVs, and more emphasis on the protection of our youth, especially young girls and women. In this venture the faith-based organisations have a critical role to play as well as the business community and the NGOs. In this context the idea that must now be translated into reality is a PANCAP process that is recognised as a pivotal mechanism for collective and visionary leadership and for fostering a coordinated regional response to the fight against HIV/AIDS. Already PANCAP is being hailed as an international best practice. Given the dynamics of the Caribbean – a proliferation of small- and medium-sized states – perfecting the core leadership values in PANCAP provides the best option in our fight against HIV/AIDS. A coordinated approach offers the best hope for the Caribbean and that must be the guiding principle of the Caribbean as we marshal all troops in the battle against HIV/AIDS, a battle that we must win.

HIV/AIDS in the Caribbean UN Update 2008

United Nations, New York, June 9, 2008

Thank you all for sharing your insights on the search for sustainable solutions as countries are accelerating efforts towards universal access. It has been widely acknowledged that access to affordable commodities for HIV diagnostics, prevention, and treatment is a fundamental requirement to achieving universal access and our health MDGs.

However, as we have heard from previous speakers who have shared country experiences as they move towards scaling up their national AIDS responses, notwithstanding some successes, most countries continue to face difficulties in gaining meaningful and sustainable access to fundamental commodities related to prevention, medicines, and diagnostics, all of which are crucial to a comprehensive response to AIDS. This is equally the case in my own country St Kitts and Nevis as well as all the other countries in the Caribbean region.

We heard that salient prevention efforts are affected by affordability issues which jeopardise programmes to scale-up implementation strategies to prevent mother-to-child transmission, ensure blood safety, and ensure wide access to preventive technologies and measures such as condoms, both female and male, as well as nutritional support to children and adults affected by AIDS. Given the growing feminisation of the epidemic and the scarcity of programmes to address it, expansion of the provision of female condoms and accelerating development of microbicides is obviously required.

It has been highlighted that as more persons with HIV and AIDS access ARVs, more persons will need to switch from first-line ARV to second- and third-line combinations. However, the costs of newer drugs and diagnostics still remain out of reach for most of the world including small island states like my own.

Brazil is widely recognised as a trailblazer country that has achieved more success than many other countries in the area of accessing basic AIDS commodities for its citizens. As the minister indicated, this has been largely due to a clearly defined multi-pronged strategy that has included national manufacturing of non-patented drugs, negotiating prices with drug companies, and playing a role internationally in changing regulations on intellectual property and access to drugs, all of which has resulted in reducing the average costs of ARVs by five times over a seven-year period. However, it too is now facing the cost of second-line and third-line treatments which remain high. As well, the increased drug resistance factor remains.

Global and regional collaboration is another recognised strategy in moving towards greater access to commodities. For example, in my region, the Caribbean, we have moved towards improving the availability of affordable commodities through the Clinton Foundation which has successfully negotiated price reductions that have benefited many small island states in the Caribbean.

Also in 2004, UNAIDS supported the regional mechanism CARICOM/ PANCAP to successfully bring together several pharmaceutical companies and effectively negotiate price reductions and procurement for Caribbean countries. Even today, we continue to reap the benefits of this global/ regional collaboration.

While these are all effective strategies to having affordable commodities, they remain only part of the solution. As articulated by the civil society representative, countries need continued support to address systemic obstacles and ensure that all persons, but especially the most at-risk populations, are not ignored and that they have equal access to services and commodities.

Other approaches that were mentioned by presenters include galvanising national leadership, political commitment, forging partnerships behind national HIV responses, and providing greater space for the meaningful engagement of civil society and persons with HIV in defining and operationalising solutions. It was also stressed that diverse political leadership can bring together all sectors to play a critical role in the HIV response.

These are some of the various ways to achieving universal access and MDGs and to addressing critical obstacles regarding affordable commodities.

Please allow me to summarise my remarks by bringing to your attention the six main areas where major systemic barriers have to be removed in order to speed up access to affordable, quality HIV prevention commodities, medicines, and diagnostics.

Let me note that the issues that are being discussed here and the major systemic barriers that I am going to outline now, all resonate with the outcomes of the regional consultations on universal access that were held by PANCAP about two years back. For those of you who may not be aware, PANCAP is the regional multi-sectoral umbrella network that was established in 2001 and brings together diverse stakeholders from across the Caribbean to respond to the AIDS issue.

The six areas where major systemic barriers should be removed are:

1. Governments, where needed, should remove regulatory and other legislative barriers that block access to effective HIV prevention interventions and commodities.

2. Multilateral organisations in collaboration with existing global and regional procurement facilities have to help lower prices for HIV prevention and treatment commodities including second- and third-line ARVs. They also have to promote informed demand forecasting and bulk procurement, differential pricing and, where appropriate, voluntary licensing.

3. Countries where needed should reform tax and tariff codes and legislation to exempt HIV prevention and treatment commodities, including HIV medicines, from taxes and tariffs.

4. National governments with support from international partners and multilateral organisations should employ where needed the flexibilities in the World Trade Organisation's Agreement on Trade-Related Aspects of TRIPs to secure access to a sustainable supply of affordable HIV medicines and essential health technologies including through local production where feasible.

5. Countries should reform their regulations as necessary to allow WHO pre-qualified medicines, or medicines approved by other widely recognised stringent drug regulatory bodies, to obtain provisional marketing approval to allow access to life-saving HIV medicines and diagnostics prior to full registration by national drug regulatory authorities.

6. Finally, the private sector must be actively engaged in public-private partnership with multilateral and other partners to promote quicker development of paediatric ARV formulations and other medicines and new HIV-related pharmaceutical products like vaccines and microbicides.

Clearly much remains to be done to remove barriers – in pricing, tariffs and trade, regulatory policy, and research and development – to speed up access to affordable quality HIV prevention commodities, medicines, and diagnostics. Until addressed, these obstacles will continue to impact on broader development to strengthen national health systems. Indeed, the availability of affordable commodities is critical to the achievement of the major development efforts of our time.

17TH INTERNATIONAL HIV/AIDS CONFERENCE

Mexico City, August 3, 2008

It is a profound honour and pleasure for me to be part of this momentous occasion here in Mexico City and to share this platform with such distinguished world leaders and, in particular, to associate myself with the hopes and aspirations of the members of the various delegations, especially persons living with HIV and AIDS. I hope that this 17th International AIDS Conference will be a significant landmark in charting the way forward in achieving its objective – *Universal Access Now*.

There is no better location to concentrate this attack on HIV/AIDS than Mexico, a country which emerged out of the political struggles for independence from Spain over 187 years ago and built on the foundations of the Mayas and Aztecs, highly developed civilisations and vibrant economic, social, and cultural systems so admired by the Caribbean region.

There is no country more fitting to host a meeting on *Universal Access Now* than Mexico, because Mexico has demonstrated to the world, through its health reform programme, the inextricable link between health and development. The current health system of Mexico is structured on a new formula of health financing designed to reduce the burden on poor and vulnerable groups. It is complemented by a health insurance scheme that provides for universal coverage for AIDS treatment, among others. It has created a separate fund for community health services and embarked upon unprecedented efforts to strengthen health-related public programmes such as epidemiological surveillance, environmental health, regulations to protect the public, and intersectoral interventions that define health policies capable of modifying the social determinants of diseases such as HIV and AIDS.

I take this opportunity to congratulate you, Mr President, for the model and leadership in health and HIV/AIDS that Mexico presents to the world by laying such a solid foundation on which to launch the imperatives of *Universal Access Now* for HIV/AIDS prevention, care, and treatment.

I wish also to acknowledge the bonds of friendship and goodwill established between Mexico and the Caribbean Community in trade, education, health, culture and, more recently, climate change, and for your leadership on behalf of Latin America and the Caribbean region on the board of the Global Fund for HIV/AIDS, Malaria and Tuberculosis.

I speak to you on behalf of a region that has taken extraordinary steps to establish a viable structure to fight HIV/AIDS. I speak to you as chairman of the Pan-Caribbean Partnership against HIV/AIDS (PANCAP), a unique multi-country network with membership stretching from Belize, The Bahamas, and Cuba in the north, through Haiti, the Dominican Republic, the Leeward and Windward Islands, and the Dutch, French and English territories, down to Guyana, and Suriname in the south. It is a network comprising governments, non-governmental organisations, the private sector, media broadcasters, faith-based organisations, and development partners. A network that has been acclaimed an international best practice by UNAIDS and which is leading the pan-Caribbean response by mobilising resources, advocating the placing of AIDS high on national and regional agendas, and forging synergies in strengthening the public health response. The Caribbean is inviting the world community to use PANCAP as a resource and a tool for the establishment of future regional partnerships to address the challenges posed by HIV/AIDS.

Many successes have been achieved in individual Caribbean countries in areas such as care, treatment, and the prevention of mother-to-child transmission of HIV. However, as a region, there is no certainty that we will achieve universal access goals if we continue to do business as usual. Understanding that fact, PANCAP is starting a major advocacy activity in close collaboration with UNAIDS and its co-sponsors. This will involve the use of available information to support countries using evidence-based research to implement action in a national context where human rights are respected and promoted, stigma and discrimination are dramatically reduced, and most-at-risk populations are the priority targets of HIV prevention programmes.

We fully recognise that one of the social determinants of health is the creation and diffusion of knowledge. We also recognise the critical involvement of people living with HIV in shaping and spearheading the response. Our experience in the Caribbean is adequate testimony to the need for building and sustaining partnerships to scale-up interventions and move towards universal access targets. We take the opportunity of this 17th International HIV/AIDS Conference to further reach out to the international community gathered here in Mexico in the refrain of that celebrated global chorus 'reach out and touch' or, as our own Bob Marley would say, 'Let's get together and be all right.' Universal access now requires global partnerships.

Global partnerships require us to appeal to you gathered here to join in our struggle to reform the philosophy and practice of our multilateral agencies and the Global Fund that impose unrealistic barriers on middle-income countries without taking into consideration the peculiar circumstances of a region like ours which is fashioning a CARICOM Single Market and Economy specifically to achieve a measure of competitiveness as a collective of fifteen states and a population of approximately sixteen million within the global community.

We publicly acknowledge the sensitivity displayed by the US Presidential Emergency Fund for HIV/AIDS Response in broadening its support to the entire Caribbean Community and to our PANCAP members. We know that the AIDS epidemic is far from over. It requires evidence-based interventions and sustained long-term commitment and support. Therefore, the Caribbean is asking the international community to commit itself to that long-term support which will consolidate gains made and broaden successes accomplished.

I also wish to take this opportunity to commend UNAIDS for its continued leadership, especially in the movement toward universal access, and generally for its guidance and direction which has sustained global partnerships around agreed principles. The recent production and launching of the very informative UNAIDS Report on the Global HIV/ AIDS Epidemic is one of many initiatives of UNAIDS. In this regard, permit me, on behalf of the Caribbean Community and the Pan-Caribbean Partnership, to pay tribute to a man whose outstanding leadership and commitment to the cause of HIV/AIDS is no doubt one of the reasons why, at this 17th International HIV/AIDS Conference, I can stand here and say with confidence that we are on our way to declaring victory through universal access. I refer to none other than Dr Peter Piot, executive director of UNAIDS.

I also wish to recognise the bonds of friendship that have been recently consolidated during the ongoing Trade and Cultural Exposition 2008 in Zaragoza, Spain and in particular the role played by Prime Minister Zapatero in honouring the Caribbean by dedicating August 14, 2008 as CARICOM Day in Spain, thereby highlighting the achievements of our emerging integration machinery – the CARICOM Single Market and Economy. That you are here along with Prime Minister Diogo of Mozambique who is a firm advocate for the reduction of stigma and discrimination against persons living with AIDS is further testimony that this 17th International HIV/AIDS Conference fully endorses the value of international partnerships in achieving *Universal Access Now*.

In July of last year, in Brazil, Dr Piot warned that 'The world must accept the exceptionalism of AIDS. There is simply no precedent in history for such a crisis. And please let's not have an illusion that in a few years, one fine day, the world will return to what it was before AIDS. No. AIDS has simply rewritten the rules. And to prevail, we too must rewrite these rules. An exceptional threat demands exceptional action'. We must adhere to this injunction and redouble our efforts.

Let us use this conference to remember and celebrate the role of our heroes in this struggle against HIV/AIDS. Let us too recognise our collective responsibility to build on the foundations of our heroes. In the words of Martin Luther King (1968):

> It really boils down to this: All life is interrelated. We are all caught in an inescapable network of mutuality, tied into a single garment of destiny. Whatever affects one directly, affects all indirectly.

Herein lies the essence of fostering and strengthening the global partnership which this conference offers. It is undoubtedly the most sustainable approach to achieving *Universal Access Now*.

NATIONAL HEALTH STRATEGIC PLAN 2008-2012

Royal St Kitts Hotel, November 6, 2008

This event marks an important milestone in our continued efforts to improve the quality of life of the citizens and residents of St Kitts and Nevis. Today marks the launch of the National Strategic Health Plan 2008–2012. It is a key document that will inform and guide critical health care decision-making as well as policy development over the next five years.

I am pleased that the plan includes the input of a wide cross-section of stakeholders, as well as the use of empirical data collected through a health situation analysis. Let me use this occasion to express sincere thanks and appreciation to the Pan American Health Organisation (PAHO) for its timely and substantial assistance that enabled the implementation and completion of the document. I believe that it is correct to say that the plan is practical in its recommendations as well as flexible enough to accommodate evolving situations. I extend commendation to all those persons who have worked diligently to complete the final document.

I cannot emphasise enough how important it is for our citizens and residents to have good health. Apart from the very obvious desires of the individual, it is well accepted that healthy populations translate into economic productivity, country growth, and development. It goes hand-in-hand with other prerequisites for development, such as education and training, but is a core element on matters of productivity.

It is for such reasons that a few years ago CARICOM ministers declared that, 'The health of the nation is the wealth of the nation', which placed emphasis on the linkages between human health, productivity, and nation-building. It gives impetus to accelerate health development in terms of infrastructure and human resources. In the Federation, millions have been spent on upgrading hospitals and clinics accompanied by additional training for nurses and increases in the number of medical doctors available for service. It is an ongoing, dynamic process and the health sector will continue to receive the attention required.

Through the adoption of the National Strategic Health Plan, greater attention will be placed on the achievement of several national, regional, and international goals and objectives. I speak, for example, on the need to achieve goals outlined under the Caribbean Health Promotion Charter and the United Nations Millennium Development Goals. What is important in the process is that greater attention is placed on influencing lifestyle behaviour in order to bring about reductions in the prevalence of some of the main health challenges of St Kitts and Nevis.

This country has a high prevalence of diabetes, heart disease, and hypertension and their related complications, and many of these disorders are related to obesity, inadequate diet, and insufficient exercise. Hypertension affects 50 per cent of the Caribbean population over forty years of age and diabetes affects over 20 per cent of the same group. There are additional issues as well such as mental health, visual impairment, and other disabilities. Into this mix we put the presence of HIV/AIDS and its tremendous challenges regarding treatment, stigma, and discrimination, as well as the challenge to achieve positive behaviour modification of people.

Much investment in time, expertise, finances and other support has been given to the improvement of health conditions in the region. Donor countries, institutions, and agencies and governments have all been engaged in the challenging task of building infrastructure, instituting systems, training, and education. Today, it is well recognised that greater emphasis needs to be placed on the matter of changing lifestyle behaviour. This of course requires media involvement and support, and it requires the development of penetrating themes and messages.

I believe that greater attention needs to be placed on preventative measures in order to reduce the substantial financial burden associated with health care. We have to be cognisant that the health sector must share financial resources with other areas of activity that are also important for our development. I believe that attention will have to be placed upon cost reductions by way of waste reduction and greater efficiency at all levels of operations.

As we launch this new National Strategic Health Plan, I wish to invite the citizens and residents of St Kitts and Nevis to become more conscious of the need to improve their health. Let's adopt correct dietary practices and increase physical fitness for ourselves and for our children. Let's modify our personal behaviour in such a manner as to improve our potential for longer and more productive lives, and let us commit to change in the interest of the growth and prosperity of the nation.

HEALTH CARE UPDATE

Ask the Prime Minister Radio Programme
ZIZ Broadcasting Corporation, January 27, 2009

This morning I would like to have a conversation with our listeners on health care. As you know, before I entered politics I was a medical doctor so anything pertaining to health care is near and dear to my heart. In addition to that, it is a fact that without good health, nothing else means very much.

When I was a child, the state of health care in St Kitts and Nevis was not at all good. And that's putting it mildly. Access to medical advice, access to medication, access to clinics and hospitals was available to very few people in this society. And the consequences were there for all to see. For far too many people, cuts, minor illnesses, and other day-to-day ailments simply had to go unattended. What should have been minor problems became far worse than they had to. And so, while training to be a doctor, I always told myself that if I ever attained a position of influence in this country, I would ensure that we in St Kitts and Nevis would have the best health care possible within the context of the resources available to us.

Today, I am pleased to say, St Kitts and Nevis is in a very strong position where health care is concerned. We have all, for the past several years, been benefiting from the rebuilt, expanded, and dramatically upgraded J. N. France Hospital. In addition, we have also built health centres throughout the Federation so as to save those who live in the countryside the stress, the time, and the expense of having to travel into town and back just to receive health care. This has been a major advance. In a few weeks we will have the official opening of the completely rebuilt and truly impressive Pogson Hospital in Sandy Point. Anyone just driving by would be quite impressed by the mere look of the facility. However, Pogson is far more than an attractive building. This new and improved Pogson Hospital will offer to the people it was built to serve a state-of-the-art labour and delivery suite, a radiology unit, a pharmacy, a dental unit, and a medical services unit. In addition, it will contain a fully equipped health centre with treatment, examination, and counselling rooms so that the people of Sandy Point and the surrounding areas have access to these services easily and conveniently without having to travel to Basseterre. In establishing these health care facilities, we are not just focusing on the buildings and the medicines or the staff, we are also trying our best to be increasingly sensitive to a range of issues. For example, the ill and the aged often have difficulty managing stairs and so we are making a point of retrofitting all our buildings with ramps and rails so that we will not just make quality health care available, we will also be making it easier for those who need it to access it.

In addition to expanding the country's health care infrastructure, we have taken a serious look at the needs clusters throughout the country and have ensured that needed services are available. As a result, we now have dramatically expanded screening for breast and cervical cancer, not just in our hospitals but at health centres throughout the Federation. Four years ago we established a dialysis unit at J. N. France. We have been working with the Republic of China on Taiwan and thanks to their generosity, we are now expanding that service to ensure that even higher-level dialysis diagnostic and treatment services will now be available in the Federation.

It was not so long ago that Kittitians and Nevisians had to find both airfare and accommodations abroad whenever they needed a CT scan. No more. The Ministry of Health stepped forward and partnered with the Pierrot Group out of Guadeloupe to make CT scans available right here on the island for anyone who needs these services. And, not willing to rest there, this year the government will be moving to provide MRI services as well.

All of these programs, activities, and services fall within the four-year Strategic Health Plan that my government launched last year. This plan identifies seven very clear priority areas:

1. We have to get incidences of <u>chronic, non-communicable diseases</u> like diabetes and hypertension down. These are serious killers, but they don't have to be. Our people have to understand this, fight these diseases, and win. And the truth is that simple changes like healthier food and more exercise are powerful, powerful weapons in the fight against these diseases. We just have to learn to use them. So, battling these non-communicable diseases is our number one priority.

2. <u>Family health.</u> We are beginning to look at the health of the whole family rather than just one individual family member,

and key for us is helping young people to better understand how to avoid becoming ill. For those who are ill, the aim is to teach them how to fight their way back to health, or at least to better manage their illness if there is no cure. And one of the examples of our commitment to the entire family, for example, is the dental sealant program that we continue to provide in order to preserve the dental health of the Federation's children.

3. <u>Health Systems Development.</u> I've already noted how we have upgraded and expanded the country's health care infrastructure in a physical context but beyond this, the government is also working to create a National Health Insurance programme. Such a programme is key if we are to provide ever-improving health care to as many Kittitians and Nevisians as possible, and to do so in a cost-effective manner.

4. <u>Mental health and substance abuse.</u> This has to rank highly in any comprehensive health care programme. New influences and new habits have caused too many Kittitians and Nevisians to experiment with illegal drugs. This can cause serious addiction plus mental health problems and we have to both educate as a means of prevention, as well as treat once there is actual addiction. We have to get rid of this dangerous belief that marijuana is not harmful to one's mental health. It is. Very much so. And then, of course, added to that, there is the issue of that legal intoxicant alcohol which, when used to excess, creates real havoc on the road, in the home, and in society at large. We have also completed the building plans for a mental health treatment centre, and have authorised the training of more personnel in child psychiatry, psychiatric nursing, psychiatric social work, occupational therapy, and counselling psychology.

5. <u>HIV/AIDS and other sexually transmitted diseases.</u> This is very serious and is all related to those issues of self-control and greater personal responsibility that I have been stressing week after week on our earlier shows. Wild and irresponsible behaviour has wild and deadly consequences and the Ministry of Health continues to stress this because of the implications that irresponsible sexual behaviour has for the spread of disease, unwanted children, juvenile delinquency and, eventually, criminal activity.

6. <u>Health and the environment.</u> Human health does not exist in a vacuum. Both the broader environment in which we live as well as the personal space in which we live and work affects our physical health. Pesticides, dust, chemicals, mould, all of these things affect our health and we have to understand this and act accordingly.

7. <u>Human resource development.</u> Over the thirteen years that my government has been in power, we have placed great emphasis on the ongoing training and development of our health care professionals and we intend to continue doing so.

All over the world, women live longer than men. Maybe that's because women are more comfortable going to the doctor than men are. Maybe women are less embarrassed to admit that they do not feel well. The Ministry of Health understands these psychological differences and they are very serious about working around them. As a matter of fact, the Ministry is implementing a special campaign to help our men to be more open and more careful where their health is concerned. This new model is being implemented in New Town, in Sandy Point, and in St Paul's, and we intend to do whatever is necessary to make certain that our men make it into the health centres. Many of them say that they cannot keep their appointments because they have to work. Okay, then we'll change the hours of the health centres so the men can come after work. Whatever it takes. Women need their husbands. Children need their fathers. And men deserve to live long and healthy lives. And this country needs its men. We're serious about helping them to live longer, but they must help us to help them too.

This, in a nutshell, is where we stand today in terms of health care. I look forward to talking with today's listeners.

Caribbean Public Health Agency (CARPHA) 2nd Partners Meeting
Charting the Future in Health and Development in the Caribbean
Pan American Health Organization, Washington, DC, June 13, 2011

Today we gather in the auditorium of one of the most enduring and respected organisations in the hemisphere of the Americas, the house of health of the Americas, to discuss and take forward the agenda for establishing the Caribbean Public Health Agency (CARPHA). I am sure that in time the delegates to this partners meeting will look back with pride to our individual and collective roles in the establishment of a landmark institution.

I am here today not only as prime minister of St Kitts and Nevis but on behalf of the chairman of CARICOM and all my colleague Heads of State or Heads of Government of CARICOM because we believe that this CARPHA initiative is for the regional public good and we are supportive of it.

We who have been involved in this process know the challenges that have been encountered. There was the issue of overcoming the sceptics across the region and the international community concerning the vision and viability of the Caribbean Public Health Agency. There was the need to convince others of the feasibility of consolidating five institutions into one agency. This despite the evidence from a range of objective studies by the most credible sources and the careful scrutiny of the recommendations from these studies by our technical officers and decision-makers. Evidence shows that the configuration of the public health response by the existing health institutions was not the most efficient. There were also lessons from around the world. There were debates within the World Health Organization (WHO) on the ideals of *health for all* and within PAHO on *equity in health*. The report of the Caribbean Commission on Health Development (2006) underscored the need for revamping the region's approach to public health and helped to shape the underlying philosophy of CARPHA. In addition, the experiences of Canada, the UK, USA and European Union have provided useful guidelines for public health approaches. In the European Union for example, notwithstanding the long-established health systems within most of the member states, mechanisms for cooperation in health are being promoted including the European Observatory in Health Systems and Policies, the Association of Schools of Public Health in Europe (ASHER), the European Health Management Association and the European Public Health Alliance. These models notwithstanding, our biggest challenge was developing a formula that best fits the needs and peculiar circumstances of the Caribbean Region.

In so doing, it is important for us to place CARPHA in context. The Caribbean Community is no longer an experiment. It is a reality. It was constructed on the basis of a treaty – The Treaty of Chaguaramas in 1973 – which has evolved through amendments over the past thirty-eight years. While the establishment of the Caribbean Single Market and Economy (CSME) is the acknowledged flagship of the integration movement, it is not the only yardstick by which to measure the progress made in regional integration. The Treaty of Chaguaramas has identified three pillars of integration including Trade an Economic Integration, Human and Social Development, and Functional Cooperation. More recently, a fourth pillar, Crime and Security, has been added.

Indeed, it must be recognised that long before trade and economic integration took root, it was in the areas of health, education and culture that the Caribbean Community made its greatest impact. The activities in these areas, singly and collectively, continue to connect the Caribbean people, including the Caribbean diaspora and to project distinctiveness about the Caribbean in the global arena. In particular, the area of health cooperation has been an outstanding illustration of what can be gained by acting collectively to achieve outcomes that benefit all the citizens across the region, minimising the inequities and maximising the efficiencies. There is no better modality, in principle, than the Caribbean Cooperation in Health (CCH) initiative. The weaknesses of the CCH identified in various studies have to do with a failure to consistently implement its priorities due to a lack of a consolidated system and in many cases because of a lack of resources.

The Caribbean Public Health Agency is conceived as a response and a remedy to this situation. It is seen as an example of functional cooperation, as a mechanism by which the health of the people of the Caribbean will be promoted and protected from disease, injury and disability, thereby fostering the wellness revolution enunciated in the Port of Spain Declaration, unifying to fight non-communicable diseases (2007). It is also intended to advance the realisation, embodied in the Nassau Declaration (2001), that *The Health of the Region is the Wealth of the Region*. In this regard, it is expected to highlight the opportunity costs of pursuing public health functions in a consolidated way, rather than as disparate entities that duplicate efforts and dilute the public health objectives for which they were designed.

This is by no means to suggest that our existing public health institutions have not served the region well. In many cases they have functioned under circumstances that challenged the creative imagination and management capability of their respective directors, which we celebrate and which I ask you to duly recognise.

As we move forward with implementation of the Caribbean Public Health Agency (CARPHA), we note that the surveillance and laboratory functions of the Caribbean Epidemiological Centre (CAREC), will constitute the core of the agency. In this regard, we are deeply grateful that the government of Trinidad and Tobago is committed to supporting the relocation of the CAREC facility and thereby providing a home for the agency's core activities. Over the years the Caribbean Food and Nutrition Institute(CFNI) has provided the essential regional guidelines and directions for member states. Its integration into CARPHA, for example, will foster greater synchronisation of the laboratory functions while enhancing its ability to contribute to programmes and policies including the training of public health specialists in the area of food and nutrition. In the area of environmental health, many of the Caribbean Environmental Health Institute's (CEHI) programmes that focus on water and sanitation as well as the links between climate change and health will be maintained, but integrated more specially to respond to public health requirements. The functions of the Regional Drug Testing Laboratory will remain intact but again will be more clearly aligned to the overall mandate of the integrated agency. In the case of the Caribbean Health Research Council, its research and development capabilities are likely to be enhanced and expanded under the consolidated agency. Its scientific committees and its annual conference can help to transform the ethic within CARPHA with an infusion of international cooperation, thereby stimulating dynamism of Caribbean public health through its linkages with regional research centres and experts in the international arena.

This is merely a schematic illustration of CARPHA functions and organisation which no doubt will be further elaborated on in the substantive presentations. But an essential feature of CARPHA is the rationalisation of resources which may yet provide a model of how the Caribbean Community shapes the future of over twenty-five regional institutions. These span the gamut of services ranging from meteorology, disaster management and climate change through to quality and standards, examinations and accreditation to fisheries, agriculture, and crime and security. A review of these institutions together with that of the Caribbean Community Secretariat is currently being undertaken as part of a comprehensive plan to increase the effectiveness and efficiency of the conduct of the community's business.

The leaders of our region are quite aware that the global economic crisis has engendered a new economic order and escalated a changed political landscape with deep structural barriers and access to overseas development assistance (ODA). Hence there is a need to revisit our approach to partnership and resource mobilisation.

This is why in convening this partners meeting, the community has called for a resource mobilisation and sustainability plan that illustrates the commitment of its member states to maintain their quota contributions. This, together with PAHO's pledge to maintain the level of support to the regional institutions, will no doubt guarantee the delivery of basic public health functions during CARPHA's transitional period between now and 2014, and set the stage for a solid foundation in the periods to follow.

CARPHA is being inaugurated at a time when global debates on the evolving trends in HIV as well as new approaches to NCDs are taking place. In both cases, the role of public health in reducing the impact of the communicable and non-communicable diseases is being identified as a critical component of sustaining economic development. The costs of adequately responding to each of these sets of diseases are enormous. CARPHA therefore provides the possibility of being that bridge for channelling scarce resources and fostering shared responsibility and institutionalising effective management.

This is therefore the context in which we invite partners to collaborate in accelerating CARPHA's implementation plan. The tasks before us are many but not insurmountable. The immediate ones revolve around building up the laboratory facilities, strengthening its surveillance capabilities, increasing the cadre of public health professionals, enhancing public health leadership, supporting research and development, and investing in social marketing techniques to broaden understanding of the public health mission and generally set the stage for enhanced public/ private sector partnership.

The CARPHA Steering Committee, together with the CARICOM Secretariat and PAHO groups, have worked tirelessly since the last partners meeting in June 2010 to move the implementation process forward. I wish to commend them. On behalf of the CARICOM Heads of Government, I also wish to express my gratitude to the Director of PAHO and her staff for their invaluable contribution to this process and for their gracious hospitality in hosting this meeting. We are also aware of the vital role being played by the government of Trinidad and Tobago which has undertaken to continue to host CAREC, the core of CARPHA. In addition, we wish to recognise the support and outstanding contributions to this process made by the Public Health Agency of Canada as well as the ongoing collaboration of the UK Department of Public Health and the National Social Marketing Company of the UK. I also must place on record the deep commitment made by the European Commissioner for Development to support CARPHA and we are glad that he has accepted our invitation to attend the Heads of Government Meeting on July 1, 2011 in St Kitts and Nevis at which the ceremonial signing of the intergovernmental agreement establishing CARPHA as a legal entity will be done.

Let this partnership meeting therefore provide a further impetus for us to say that we are gathered here today on June 13, 2011 during the period designated by President Obama as Caribbean American Heritage Month. Let us use this occasion to rewrite Caribbean public health history. Let us join in amplifying the aspiring sentiments of the American writer Sonia Jones:

> *We must remember that one determined person can make a significant difference, and that a small group of determined people can change the course of history.*

THE TRANSFORMATION OF HEALTH CARE

Windsor University School of Medicine
Inaugural Commencement
St Kitts Marriott Resort, September 25, 2011

Congratulations to all the bright young people who are here today, and who for so long have worked so hard to get to this point. Sincere congratulations to you, sincere thanks to your teachers, and a particularly warm round of applause to all of the parents, relatives, and friends whose support – emotional, spiritual, and material – made this day possible.

Today will forever be a red-letter day in your lives and it should be. However, today is a red-letter day in the history of Windsor University as well. And not only because such a fine group of students will be graduating today, but also because this is the inaugural commencement ceremony of the Windsor University School of Medicine. And so, in the months and years ahead, you, as today's graduates, will be able to remember that on this day, at Windsor University School of Medicine, you made history on two counts.

As someone who, not so long ago it seems, was sitting where you are today, thinking ahead to the medical career that awaited me, I can imagine the emotions that you young graduates have been experiencing all day: Hope. Some degree of uncertainty. But, most of all, a certain sense of excitement and zeal as you ready yourself to step out and make your personal contributions to the communities in which you will choose to live and work.

The author, Denis Waitley, once said, 'There are two primary choices in life: to accept conditions as they are, or accept the responsibility for changing them.'

It is clear that anyone who chooses a career in medicine decided long ago not to accept conditions as they are, but instead to actively strive to make things better. And this reminds you, then, of the importance of being forces for good in the transformation of health care in the world.

You have worked long and hard. The challenges abound. And now you must choose wisely as you embark on your individual journeys of personal meaning and fulfilment, guided by a desire to improve the health and well-being of the individuals and communities with which you will, in the years ahead, be associated.

As you may be aware, I have just returned from a high-level conference at the United Nations at which the subject at hand was a matter with which many of you will have to grapple in the years ahead – the shocking rise in the incidence of non-communicable diseases. Of course, we have to hope that as a result of the hard work of health care professionals, governments, international agencies, and a more enlightened public, non-communicable diseases will one day be far less of a menace. At this moment in time, however, and at least for the immediate future, non-communicable diseases will continue to pose a real menace to individuals, societies, governments, and medical practitioners alike the world over.

It is a real cause for concern, I think we can all agree, that of the estimated fifty-seven million deaths per annum globally, some thirty-six million are caused by cancer, diabetes, heart and lung diseases. And so we must now search for the correct mix of idealism and pragmatism as we grapple with this reality.

There are many variables involved and the international community must now rise to the challenge with workable, effective approaches. And this is what makes today's graduation so important, because the societies, hospitals, and institutions of higher learning that await you are counting on your training and energy to strengthen the efforts of so many who are already engaged in the challenge of transforming, expanding, and improving health care, the world over.

The need for ongoing monitoring and analysis of non-communicable diseases worldwide is more acute than ever because the international community must be able to measure the impact of the practices and policies that we, with your involvement, will implement in the years ahead. So you have chosen the perfect time to enter what I consider to be, and I know that I am biased, the most fascinating of all professional fields.

Deaths from cancer and heart, and lung disease have risen astronomically. Indeed, they exceed the deaths from all other diseases combined. This is the challenge with which you must grapple in the years ahead. And I know that it is a challenge and a battle that you are ready and willing to help mankind win.

Wherever in the world you may work, it will be important for you to understand the importance of coordination at all levels, and on all fronts, between nations as well as within nations, if we are to have any chance of altering current trend lines where non-communicable diseases are concerned. And wherever you may end up working, it will be important for you to work alongside those health care professionals who are demanding the adoption of healthier lifestyles at the level of the individual, tougher and wiser health-related policies on the part of governments, and the awareness that profit-maximisation can no longer be the sole preoccupation of pharmaceutical companies.

The career path that you have chosen, as you know, has many dimensions – medical intervention, clinical and administrative issues, education and awareness, nutrition, exercise, elder care. The world awaits your involvement, trusting that wherever you may be, you will become an advocate for reformed, transformed, improved health care delivery.

I urge you to hold fast to the concept of quality health care for all races, classes, ages, and ethnicities, since the spirit of our profession, no matter in which country we practice, should lead us to support the notion of all patients having equal access to standard diagnostic treatment and services.

There are, indeed, many difficulties associated with transforming knowledge to action, and there is also a world of difference between the dissemination of information and actual implementation. And, over the course of your career, financial constraints, technical considerations, and procedural matters and issues will, from time to time, frustrate you. That is only normal. You will be more than prepared as you face these issues by having clear goals, proper intervention plans, and appropriate training, data collection, and analysis. You will, however, be able to rely on the implementation of evidence-based practices to stimulate improvements as you strive to transform and improve health care delivery throughout your career.

Technological changes are redounding to the benefit of medical practitioners everywhere. Advances in telecommunications are causing patients to be better informed, more aware of their rights, and to have higher expectations, and this is good for the medical profession, in that it has caused medical practitioners to deliver at a higher standard. This benefits not only the patient, but the profession itself as well as society as a whole. Throughout the health care profession, across the globe, then, there is an increasing emphasis on training and the enhancement of knowledge.

Most important to our field, however, is the commitment to deliver health care no matter the impediments. MHealth – Mobile Health Care – has long been symptomatic of the commitment of health care professionals to the effective delivery of health care, even when age, geographic, or other factors threaten to compromise diagnostic, administrative, monitoring, aftercare, and health care-related education. And it is precisely this very positive attitude, the attitude that underlies MHealth, that sets the medical profession apart. And it is an attitude with which I am certain we are all proud to be associated.

Many of you will head to other countries now that your training at Windsor University has ended. We were pleased to have you here in St Kitts and Nevis and wish you the very best in all your future endeavours. As you head out, the mission of health care reform here in the Caribbean continues as it must everywhere in the world. The priorities in this region include improved management, improved quality standards, enhanced advocacy and public education, and infrastructure modernisation.

Wherever you may be from, and to whichever country you may be headed, I hope that as a member of the medical profession you will always be a part of the movement that is encouraging governments to demonstrate the type of political will demanded by the health care challenges of the twenty-first century.

I hope that you will value collaboration across and between various sectors as your medical career unfolds. I hope that you will support efforts in your various countries to encourage greater community awareness of and support for health-enhancing policies and practices, and that you will encourage and facilitate the sharing of best practices.

In closing then, permit me to point out that the many words used in this statement, and the many pointers offered, amount to one thing, really:

I hope that you will take all of the steps, and adopt all of the attitudes that will deliver to you an intriguing, challenging, and rewarding medical career.

The medical field offers a lifetime of deep meaning and unparalleled fulfilment. You truly could not have chosen better.

Your being here today is evidence that you have successfully taken the very important first step of this important journey. I urge you to take all others with confidence, competence, integrity, and humility. The rewards will be great.

And this day, and this place, you will always remember as having been the portal through which you entered.

I congratulate Windsor University School of Medicine's Class of 2011 once again, and I wish you every success.

XIV Barcelona AIDS Conference 10th Anniversary

Parliament of Barcelona, Spain, April 29, 2012

Señora Presidenta, on behalf of the Caribbean Community (CARICOM), and the Pan Caribbean Partnership Against HIV/AIDS (PANCAP), I express my profound gratitude to you and your colleagues for your gracious hospitality. I am also pleased to acknowledge the presence of the deputy executive director of the Joint United Nations Programme on HIV/AIDS (UNAIDS) which has been an outstanding partner and leader in the fight against HIV and AIDS.

The commemoration of the tenth anniversary of the XIV AIDS Conference is particularly significant for me and for the Caribbean. It was a landmark. I had the honour to sign the agreement with six pharmaceutical companies in this great city of Barcelona, thereby triggering a new era of affordable drugs for people in the Caribbean as well as in other regions that followed our example. So much so that after ten years and with the combination of scientific biomedical and behavioural research, passionate advocacy of civil society, and creative leadership, we can truly and optimistically pronounce the aspirational goal to achieve an AIDS-free generation.

We in the Caribbean Community are engaged with our colleagues in Latin America and indeed with partners in Europe and throughout the world to make the end of AIDS a reality. But we can only do so with a concerted effort to ensure that the HIV programmes are adequately funded. We can only do so, in this era of scarce resources, if we embark on a judicious process of shared responsibility, engaging the private sector, placing emphasis on accountability, and keeping our commitments to accelerate investments in treatment and prevention. We can do so by stepping up the demands for the elimination of stigma and discrimination in keeping with the fundamental principle of the Universal Declaration of Human Rights, 'equality for all.'

I am pleased to note that the 2012 UNAIDS Report identified the progress that has been made in the Caribbean in the ten years since the Barcelona AIDS Conference. AIDS-related deaths have decreased by some 50 per cent and more people living with AIDS have access to anti-retroviral drugs. There is greater awareness of the need to increase access to treatment for the most at-risk populations and to make special provision for the poor and vulnerable. In this regard the governments of the Caribbean in collaboration with UNAIDS are pursuing an investment strategy for financing of HIV. Such a strategy is essential for identifying priorities, measurable targets, and tangible results.

Our targets are clearly stated in the PANCAP Declaration issued at its 10th anniversary annual general meeting in November, 2010. The Partnership agreed to the following targets by 2015:

- The elimination of mother-to-child transmission;
- Increased access to care and treatment by 80 per cent;
- Reduction of new infections by 50 per cent;
- Acceleration of the agenda to achieve human rights for PLHIV including the elimination of travel restrictions for people living with HIV/AIDS.

As you can see, these targets are quite consistent with those in the Political Declaration of the UN High Level Meeting (June, 2011). Indeed we in the Caribbean Community entertain the hope of being the first region in the developing world to eliminate mother-to-child transmission by 2015. After all, we did achieve this feat for polio and smallpox in the 1980s. We can do it again for HIV.

Yet there can be slippage. While chronic non-communicable diseases (NCDs) have emerged as a priority, it is important to recognise that HIV is both an infectious disease and an NCD as the infected are living longer. HIV also remains in the top five causes of death for the Caribbean for the age group twenty to forty-nine years.

Other important facts:

- At least fifty new HIV infections take place in the Caribbean per day;
- At least thirty-three deaths per day in the region are a result of HIV;
- Infection rates, although stabilised and decreasing in some countries, still show increasing patterns in, for example, Trinidad and Tobago, Belize, and Barbados;
- Prevalence rates are exceptionally high in selected groups such as men who have sex with men (32 per cent), transgender sex workers (24 per cent), youth (4 per cent), and prisoners (5 per cent);

- ARV coverage is still at a regional average of 48 per cent with only Barbados, Cuba, and Guyana achieving universal coverage.

We are pleased to note the results of a breakthrough scientific study done by the Centres for Disease Control (CDC) released last week that shows that one in four persons in Barbados has completely suppressed the HIV virus, supporting the benefits of anti-retroviral treatment and indeed the growing awareness of treatment as prevention. We in the Caribbean are resolved to press forward with universal coverage and for this we are taking every opportunity to make this a reality and seek the support of our colleagues and friends in Barcelona.

As we celebrate in Barcelona, we must take the opportunity to check any reversal in the gains we have so far achieved and to plan for the difficult fight that still lies ahead. Among the lessons learned from the past thirty years is that success revolves around openness and innovation. On the one hand, sharing information has dispelled irrational fears, encouraged debate, and challenged stigma. On the other, the case for treatment as prevention was preceded by a shift from drug approval protocols to task-shifting among medical teams and from fixed dose drug combinations to hiring 'campagnatuers,' community practitioners, to deliver community-based services.

I am indeed very pleased that civil society has been integral in the planning of this celebration and that its members form such a vibrant presence in the parliament today. This is appropriate. Civil society is an essential ingredient for sustaining openness and innovation. From the start, the accelerated response was fuelled by the most ambitious AIDS activism. It was the activist pioneers that fought this epidemic from the start. They tackled the structural forces of prejudice, social exclusion, and economic injustice. Today let us draw on that energy of activism to rekindle the values that inspire global development. The World Bank President aptly illustrated that vision in a statement, during the spring meetings in Washington, DC, last week, when he said 'Real development is grounded in solidarity, courage, respect for the dignity of all people and the unrelenting demand for justice.'

It is heartening to see that the lessons from the AIDS movement are inspiring economic development. Let us unleash the power of these values in our campaign to bring an end to AIDS.

PANCAP HIV/AIDS Consultation
Justice for All
St Kitts Marriott Resort, November 27, 2013

It is my pleasure to address you this morning as we gather for this PANCAP Justice for All Consultation.

I wish to begin by thanking the UN secretary general's Special Envoy for HIV/AIDS in the Caribbean, Professor Edward Greene, for his special efforts with PANCAP and UNAIDS in response to my request that the programme, with its human rights agenda, be expedited and also for taking the lead to implement the series of national consultations which will culminate with our regional conference in 2014.

First, I must say that the timing of this consultation is most appropriate because it allows us to soberly assess, as a region, the progress that we have made toward the achievement of the Millennium Development Goals, the end date of which is almost exactly two years from now. With two years to go, we can look back at the past twelve years and know that we have indeed accomplished much: we have reduced death rates from the disease by some 80 per cent; we have, through the use of anti-retroviral drugs, greatly increased the number of people who are now living with HIV and leading meaningful lives; and, as has been publicised in recent times, we have brought about a dramatic reduction in the incidence of mother-to-child transmission of HIV. As a result, the Caribbean can now realistically aspire to being the first region in the world to eliminate mother-to-child transmission, hopefully by 2015. PANCAP, as we know, has been at the forefront of every regional plan and model in this regard and has contributed in no small measure to our region's outstanding performance. PANCAP is indeed a compelling illustration of the impact of functional cooperation within the regional integration process.

At the same time, life is an ongoing process of re-evaluation and refinement. And so, even as we note our past accomplishments, we must forever strive to continue building and moving forward despite the gradual withdrawal of support for treatment by various international agencies and the demands that this will continue to place on OECS countries in terms of our own budgetary allocations. As a region, therefore, we will have to devise investment strategies that are capable of providing affordable medicines and support not only for HIV/AIDS but for other health issues as well, in order to ensure long and healthy lives for all our citizens regardless of colour, class, or creed. Indeed, it is this broad and inclusive vision that gives the Justice for All programme its special appeal.

In the months and years ahead, regional governments will have to continue managing our relationships with the private sector so as to ensure that there is compliance with workplace policies against discrimination against people living with HIV (PLHIV). And we will also have to be vigilant in our commitment to ensure that health workers and members of the protective services remain faithful to the principles of nondiscriminatory actions, that they demonstrate strict compliance to confidentiality requirements, and that our every action brings us ever closer to erasing all vestiges of stigma and discrimination.

And then there is the issue of sex education. It is vital that our countries' stakeholders in the fields of health and education, community development, social work, and social security remain mindful of the need for this, not only in the classrooms, but throughout all our communities, urban and rural alike. People simply may neither know nor understand as we think they do and we can no longer afford to be uncomfortable with this topic when studies show that exposure and initiation are occurring at troublingly early ages. That is why compulsory, age-appropriate health and family life education from primary school onward is so important. Our society must be informed, our society must be aware, and our society must know how, on this crucial matter, to properly strengthen and defend itself.

And in all of this, there is the need for severe moral and legal sanctions in our societies in response to the alarming rates of sexual harassment and violence against women, girls, and children. Our societies are now exposed to influences, attitudes, and behaviours that were unknown in this region just one generation ago. Modern telecommunications now reach into every nook and cranny of the globe and these influences are found throughout this region as well.

These matters demand our attention. They will not go away.

256

We now know, for example, that there is a direct link between sexual abuse and aggression, including rape, and the spread of HIV. Our legislators and our judicial officers now have a responsibility, therefore, to re-examine the legislation on our books and to take the necessary steps to bring forward measures that will prevent discriminatory practices that contribute to stigma and discrimination.

There are so many questions being raised in the context of sex education, not only about AIDS, but about homosexuality, so-called sex workers, and others in the lesbian, gay, bisexual, and transgender community. I invite the church, civil society, and other leading voices in our communities to become involved in these important discussions and to ensure that their voices are heard. These are the types of issues that trigger, and deserve, in-depth discussion and analysis. And whenever our nations arrive at eventual positions on these matters, it will be essential that they reflect the collective wisdom and belief system of the societies in which we live. And in the course of engaging in this national conversation, we will find that we will deal not only with these specific issues themselves but also with the stigma and discrimination that often surrounds them.

It is important then for us to elevate the discussion to the principles of human rights to which we are all already committed, and which are reflected in both the UN Declaration on Human Rights as well as the various protocols pertaining to the rights of the child, the rights of women, the rights of the disabled, the rights of migrants, and so on. These not only exist to protect the individual regardless of race, class, gender, or sexual orientation, but they are also generally enshrined both in our constitutions as well as in our spiritual upbringing with regard to compassion and inclusion.

It has therefore been gratifying to learn of the active role that faith leaders and organisations throughout the region have been taking in national conversations on Justice for All. And I must make a point here of commending the religious institutions here in St Kitts and Nevis in particular for the role that they have been playing in offering care and support for those in need in general, and those living with HIV in particular. The churches in St Kitts and Nevis have helped to keep the spirit of family cohesion strong, and have been key to promoting the national and regional solidarity that is so key to the Justice For All agenda. The houses of worship bring to the table the spirit of compassion and tolerance that is encouraged in the scriptures and that has from time immemorial guided the Christian faith that is so deeply engrained in Caribbean culture and traditions.

As we commemorate World AIDS Day on December 1, a Sunday this year, it is my hope that all religions and denominations here in St Kitts and Nevis will join their counterparts throughout the region, who see the Justice For All spirit as an appropriate focus for worship and as a possible theme for sermons as we strive to keep society on the path toward true compassion and inclusion.

We have been on this path for several years now. Our efforts clearly did not just begin and this conversation is in no way new. And as a result, each year finds us stronger and more effective than we were the year before. PANCAP and other organisations throughout this region have been on this important and much-needed course for years now. Indeed, many of us can remember the vibrant 'Champions for Change Conference' right here in St Kitts and Nevis almost a decade ago. And we can remember the recommendations for a Caribbean Stigma and Discrimination Unit. Indeed, this event was then followed by consultations with stakeholders such as faith-based leaders in Guyana, the media in Barbados, and so on. Since that time, we have all come to a better understanding of the ways in which discrimination impedes our battle against this disease. And as a result, we are now fighting on two fronts: on the one hand against the disease and on the other against the associated discrimination.

In closing, we are all concerned about human rights and equality as a general principle. The challenge before us as a region is to find ever new and innovative ways of helping society at large to understand that the important values of human enlightenment and compassion must apply to those who are living with HIV as well. This national consultation will build, with substance and insight, on all that was achieved in Guyana, and it will set an important bar for the consultations that will follow. At the same time, this is an issue which, as everyone knows, has long been especially important to me. I therefore very much look forward to learning of the outcome of today's deliberations. My commitment and leadership on this issue have been unshakeable in the past and on this, the region can continue to depend. Our region's progress over the past twelve years has been gratifying indeed, and this is the type of momentum which, greatly aided by consultations like today's, we can and must, together, continue to maintain and build.

HIV and Small Island States 2014 AIDS Conference

Melbourne, Australia, September 20-25, 2014

It is my pleasure to join the discussion with this distinguished group of panellists to examine the trajectory of HIV and AIDS beyond 2015. Indeed, my fellow panellists have identified most of the elements in the topic allocated to me, i.e., key messages that need to be injected into the SIDS meeting in September. It is a focus on Small Island Developing States (SIDS), most of which experience the same socio-economic challenges of developing states but with greater intensity from global fallout ranging from global financial crises to climate change and with less resources and capacity. Whether in the far yonder Caribbean or in the Indian Ocean or the nearby Pacific, SIDS suffer special vulnerabilities that need to be specifically addressed.

This is aptly captured in the *Caribbean Human Development Report 2012:* Human Development and the Shift to Better Citizen Security published by UNDP for which we give special acknowledgement to Helen Clarke. The argument in that document is framed by a philosophical axiom by the late Sir Arthur Lewis, the renowned Caribbean scholar from St Lucia and Nobel Laureate in economics. In 1955, he wrote, 'the advantage of economic growth is not that wealth increases happiness but that it increases the range of choice.' Amartya Sen, the Indian development economist and Nobel Laureate was later to endorse this view of human development 'as the enlargement of people's freedom to lead the lives they value.' But he expanded even further by enunciating that the human development approach is motivationally committed to concentrating on what remains undone – what demands most attention in the contemporary world from poverty and deprivation to inequality and insecurity.

There is connectivity between the human development aspirations of these development economists and the refrain for ending AIDS pronounced by leading advocates. Of these I make reference to two: At the 2012 IAS in Washington, DC, Jim Yong Kim, President of the World Bank, called for harnessing the moral power and practical lessons that the AIDS movement produced to speed progress against another scourge, poverty. This view no doubt reflects the fact that the course of the AIDS epidemic was changed by the intervention of social and structural factors. At this conference, Michel Sidibe, UNAIDS Executive Director, in his presentation to the opening session under the theme Justice for All, emphasised that revolutionising the AIDS response means leaving no one behind. This can only happen if we conceptualise and implement programmes shifting from a short-run emergency response to a long-term sustainability response with an emphasis on social justice. This shift must address the key determinants of vulnerability in order to change the trajectory of AIDS.

In this regard, I am struck by the emerging work led by UNAIDS in collaboration with the World Bank and other partners to simultaneously address extreme poverty and AIDS. In so doing, it links poverty and HIV risks. Poverty expressed in terms of financial inability to meet daily needs and physical isolation from economic and social opportunities, manifests itself in the inability to meet educational expenses, food insecurity, lack of spending on and physical access to health care. The outcome from these causal pathways of poverty is lack of schooling, school girl and boy relationships with a 'sugar daddy,' parents engaging in transactional sex, other untreated diseases, higher viral load for HIV positives, and increasing transmissibility. All of these impact human development.

I believe that the blend between these comprehensive philosophical and policy prescriptions provides useful guidelines for the key messages for the Accelerated Modalities for Action (SAMOA) Pathway to emerge from the SIDS conference in September. But more so are the lessons learned from the AIDS response. At the same time we recognise that the UN process through the open working group on sustainable development goals has proposed a list of seventeen goals and targets to be attained by 2030. These developments will no doubt influence the outcomes from SIDS.

KEY MESSAGES

So what are some of these key messages that I propose?

1. **Consolidate the alliance to jointly eliminate poverty and HIV.**
    Emerging from this alliance are three complementary elements that SIDS must take into consideration. They include:

- Aligning health and development efforts around country-led, time-bound goals towards ending extreme poverty and AIDS;
- Including targets towards ending AIDS alongside the goal of universal health coverage is necessary for improving health services and health outcomes. A recent *Lancet* publication estimated that up to 24 per cent of economic growth in low- and middle-income countries was due to better health outcomes and at the same time, yield substantial returns on investments in health;
- Promoting national, regional, and global monitoring and implementation research is critical to sound policy-making.

2. **Create viable partnerships aimed at sustainable development.**

   Sustainable development of Small Island Developing States, SIDS, the theme of the conference, can be achieved through international cooperation and partnerships of various kinds. In the case of the Caribbean, this is not only limited to north-south relations but also to south-south cooperation. These are illustrated by Brazil's collaboration with the Organisation of Eastern Caribbean States (OECS) with the provision of ARVs for people living with HIV (PLHIV). In this regard, the current development of cooperation between CARICOM and the African Union on shared responsibility with the support of UNAIDS, is another example. In addition, the emerging roadmaps from both regions are intent on reducing dependency and thereby enhancing the viability of programmes designed to end AIDS. For the Caribbean, we have learnt the need for creating indigenous regional structures rooted in the integration process that link community efforts with leadership at the highest political level. In our case, the PAN Caribbean Partnership against HIV and AIDS (PANCAP) has demonstrated what SIDS networks can achieve through collective efforts.

3. **Sustain and reconfigure the unfinished MDGs within the post-2015 Sustainable Development Goals (SDGs).**

   Progress in attaining the international targets in the MDGs among SIDS shows marked improvements over the past decade. However, the recently released gap analysis undertaken by UNAIDS demonstrates, at least for the Caribbean, the need for more robust financing models based on shared responsibility, accelerated and affordable treatment regimens, and accenting the elimination of HIV-related stigma and discrimination to arrest the economic regression that will occur if the gains are not sustained and accelerated in the post-2015 era. The UN General Assembly special event, in September 2013, Toward Achieving the MDGs, in which I had an opportunity to participate, provided a clear consensus around the intrinsic links between poverty eradication and promotion of sustainable development.

4. **Move beyond the MDGs with resolve to end AIDS.**

The rapid scale-up of HIV treatment remains one of the most inspiring achievements in global health history. Since 2001, the number of people receiving HIV treatment in low- and middle-income countries has risen from a mere handful to more than twelve million in early 2014. These advances are saving lives, with the number of AIDS-related deaths falling by 30 per cent from 2005 to 2012 worldwide. They are also preventing new HIV infections, with anti-retroviral therapy demonstrating the greatest prevention benefit of any biomedical prevention tool studied to date in randomised controlled trials.

With anti-retroviral therapy as a key element of a strategic combination of prevention tools, the world now has the potential for ending the AIDS epidemic and making HIV transmission a rare event. However, to make this a reality, the transformative potential of anti-retroviral therapy has yet to be fully realised due to failure to bring HIV treatment to all those who need it. As of December 2012, only 34 per cent of people eligible for treatment under the 2013 World Health Organization consolidated anti-retroviral guidelines were receiving anti-retroviral therapy. Applying these new guidelines, the figure on access in the Caribbean hovers around 50 per cent. We therefore support the call from the UNDP Global Commission for Human Rights and HIV to make access to affordable treatment a human rights prerequisite which would apply equally to other communicable and non-communicable health emergencies.

5. **Adopt a holistic approach to post-2015 global health applying the lessons learned from the AIDS response.**

    My sense is that this conference rightly supports the UNAIDS call for ending the AIDS epidemic by 2030. And from my perspective and our experience in the Caribbean, this is not only possible but imperative for stimulating action. Indeed the Caribbean plans to be the first region in the world to eliminate AIDS. We did this for polio and smallpox in the late 1980s and can do so for AIDS. But the message for SIDS must ensure that HIV-sensitive targets and indicators are aligned with other goals in areas such as health, gender, youth. It must also ensure that there is convergence with joint action from the community to the global level with policies that focus on the social, economic, and environmental determinants of HIV – poor health, poverty and inequality.

    The range of topics at this conference such as HIV and ageing, development of an efficient early HIV infant diagnosis programme to ensure universal access to HIV and health systems, building safe and sustainable cities, among others, reflect concerns with human development.

6. **Making Justice for All a fundamental requirement for getting to zero discrimination.**

    I mention this partly because it formed the theme of Michel Sidibe's presentation and partly because we in the Caribbean have identified the elements of Justice for All as our overarching inclusive strategy. The programme coordinated by PANCAP in collaboration with national governments and UNAIDS involved parliamentarians, faith leaders, youth, civil society, and the private sector. While CARICOM Heads of Government deferred the declaration to make provision for more national consultations, it did approve the mechanism for creating the agenda designed to eliminate stigma and discrimination. We feel confident that opening the debates on sexual orientation, sexual and reproductive health and rights, and the abolition of laws that discriminate against homosexuals, will provide another opportunity to clarify misconceptions that erode the march toward achieving human rights. We recognise this intractable challenge of zero discrimination. But the issues must be dealt with if we are to leave no one behind.

CONCLUSION

These messages are by no means inclusive. They at least point in the direction of highlighting those issues of human development which the HIV movement has illustrated through the discussions at these biannual conferences. They have truly sensitised us to the phenomenal progress that has been made since these gatherings began in Atlanta in 1980. I join the expressions of sadness and sense of loss of our colleagues who perished in Malaysia Air 17. Let us immortalise their work and their commitment to the fight against HIV and AIDS by continuing their research, community outreach, advocacy, and activism around the themes and ideals that have reverberated through this meeting:

- Let us acknowledge that we have made much progress but AIDS is far from over;
- Let us advocate for AIDS to be retained in the 2015 development agenda;
- Let us harness resources and foster international solidarity to crack the intractable barriers;
- Let us resolve to end AIDS by 2030.

Housing and Land

Housing and Land

There is only one speech in the Housing and Land section. By Douglas's third term, housing and land reform was a mature, successful programme and the government was in a sustainability mode.

When it came to power in 1995, the Labour government made the provision of housing a top priority. Owning a piece of land, 'a piece of the rock,' was a fundamental tenet of self-improvement and national development. The former government had only built two hundred low-income houses during its fifteen years in office and they were poor quality and often unserviced. Labour's first two terms were spent providing new homes for hurricane victims (five hurricanes hit the island in Labour's first five-year term) and catching up with generally growing demand.

When the sugar industry closed down in 2005, part of the generous compensation package for former sugar workers was a special housing programme that helped those without a home to get one and those who already had a home to expand or upgrade at minimal cost.

When the economic recession began to hit harder in late 2007, the government found itself cash-strapped with a very high debt load. Looking for ways to stimulate the economy and at the same time further empower its citizens, the government decided to distribute the now mostly fallow former sugar cane lands to the people. It was time to break the back of landlessness. They reduced the price to below market value and set up a government programme to lend money to those who couldn't do so through a regular bank. Land became an asset which, once paid for, gave greater opportunity to families, especially the younger generation, to get ahead and better their lives.

The sugar industry in St Kitts had made most people landless. Now, in an ironic twist of fate, the vacant sugar lands were now making Kittitians into a nation of property owners on the very lands their predecessors once toiled on as enslaved workers.

By the time of the Special Land Distribution Initiative (SLDI) in 2007, the Douglas Labour government had already built and distributed two thousand low-income houses and created an impressive five thousand fully-serviced building lots.

SPECIAL LAND DISTRIBUTION INITIATIVE

The Circus, Basseterre, August 24, 2007

On July 30, 2005, the sugar industry, which had dominated the social, economic and political life of the people of St Kitts and Nevis for over 350 years, came to an end after long and careful thought. As the final sugar train rolled into the factory yard on July 2, two years ago, never to again embark on that long and winding journey through the lush cane fields of the countryside, and as that very familiar sound of the sugar factory horn rang out for the final time on July 30, signaling the end of the productive life of an ailing sugar-producing apparatus, there was suddenly a deep sense of loss, and at the same time, a thrill of hope and a moment of ease.

The people of this country, many years ago, had come to terms with the mounting challenges of sustaining a sugar industry that was imperiled by globalisation and trade liberalisation, reduced prices on the European market for our local sugar, poor economies of scale resulting in exponentially increasing losses in the industry, and the movement of our workforce away from the sugar fields towards more modern and more rewarding jobs in other sectors of the economy. However, no single occurrence was as impactful and as critical to the survivability or demise of the sugar industry in St Kitts and Nevis as the planned reduction of the price of sugar on the European market by a further 37 per cent. That in essence was the nail in the coffin of King Sugar.

This year, 2007, we are proudly celebrating as a people the abolition of the trans-Atlantic slave trade. On behalf of the government and people of this fair land of ours, I express our deepest gratitude to the organisers, all of the distinguished guest speakers, and government and non-government agencies for the important sensitisation sessions which were held at the ECCB over the last few weeks. I say thanks to those who lent their voices to the debate and sensitisation of our people through the media and I ask for your continued support as we continue our activities to celebrate an important part of our history. In particular, I invite us all to the 'Cry Freedom' fair and concert at Independence Square next Thursday.

Citizens of St Kitts and Nevis, without losing the lessons we have learnt as a people over centuries, we must now put our dark past behind us and look to those things which are before us. Certainly, our struggles have made us stronger and our history makes us more determined. The closure of the sugar industry equally must be seen as an opportunity for our people to progress from what has been to what can be. As I said in the foreword of our *Adaptation Strategy In Response To The New EU Sugar Regime* that my government created in April of last year:

> Although the emotional and historic significance of this event cannot be exaggerated, what is of greater concern to us today is how we can move on from that chequered past and forge an economically sustainable and socially secure future for our children and ourselves.

The launch of this *Land Distribution Initiative* is another significant strategy of development being pursued by the Labour government. When viewed in the context of people empowerment, this new initiative is of enormous importance, the benefits being experienced by new landowners for many years to come. Directly and indirectly, this initiative addresses issues of poverty alleviation, the pursuit of personal development, and the support of national economic and social goals.

What is also important in this *Land Distribution Initiative* is that it takes residential development to almost every part of the island, a demonstration, yet again, of the inclusive nature of the Labour government. What is equally relevant is the symbolism associated with sugar and its legacies, one of which was landlessness for the vast majority of our people, and now in a post-sugar era, there is the promise and expectation of better and more opportunities for the people of this country.

My government in assuming office in 1995 promised to create a land and home ownership class in this country. That policy objective was made good, in 1996, when my government passed the *Village Lands Freehold Purchase Act* and the *National Housing Corporation Act*. Under these acts many former sugar workers were given the land on which they had lived continuously from 1967, free of charge. Houses for the homeless were also provided.

This new initiative will open up twenty-five different locations around the island where some five thousand lots will be distributed. Of these twenty-five areas, the locations at Buckleys, Sandy Point,

Shadwell, Taylors, St Paul's, Verchilds, Cayon, and Molineux will become available immediately because we have already made preparation for the infrastructure such as roads, water, and electricity in these eight active areas. We have now improved our new land administration system to ensure that a successful application for land in any of the eight active areas will be satisfied in three short weeks. This means that if you make your application on day one and quickly finalise your financial arrangements with your bank or credit union, you will receive your land allocation in three weeks. However, an applicant will be given up to six full months to negotiate with his or her bankers.

To give our citizens a comprehensive package and to facilitate your dealings with the bank, we have partnered with several banks in the Federation on this special land distribution initiative. You will find further details about the banks on the brochure which is available for your information. I am advising that you immediately begin to negotiate with your credit institutions to stay ahead of the curve.

Apart from the eight locations that will become active immediately, there are seventeen other locations which will also become available over time. These areas are Tabernacle, Mansion, Stapleton, Keys, Parsons, Harris', Garveys, Stonefort, Old Road, Lamberts, Half Way Tree, Newton Ground, Dieppe Bay, Saddlers, Christ Church, and Phillips.' It has become necessary to approach the special land initiative in phases since the entire infrastructure could not be installed in all twenty-five areas at once. I ask for your patience in this regard.

Applications made for land in the seventeen areas that are not yet fully active will take longer than the three-week period established for the eight active areas. Some of these seventeen additional areas will become fully active over the next few months and at such time, applications made in respect of those areas will also be satisfied in three weeks. Our citizens are therefore asked to make application for any of the twenty-five areas while bearing in mind that some areas will take a longer time to be distributed than others. However, the number of applications received will guide the government in determining which new areas should be activated as soon as possible. Application forms and information brochures are available at the Department of Lands and Surveys at East Park Range or at the Ministry of Sustainable Development, Church Street, in Basseterre.

My dear people, this special land distribution initiative is just one of the land distribution and people empowerment programmes this government will use to continue to empower our people. My government has managed to implement a number of exciting programmes in land distribution and home ownership unmatched by any such programme under the former administration. This government under my leadership has built and distributed about two thousand low-income homes and has issued over five thousand house lots to first-time homeowners throughout the length and breadth of St Kitts. This is an enormous achievement for all of our people.

I wish to inform you that our ongoing land distribution programme at NHC will continue to be in operation but with improved service and efficiency to cater to those low-income persons who may not be able to service a regular bank loan. It is here that my government, firmly rooted in its basic philosophy, makes the very important distinction between those who can afford and those who cannot. This is the thrust and reason-for-existence of the St Kitts-Nevis Labour Party. I am therefore pleased to inform you that not only has my government improved the efficiency of the NHC to better meet the needs of our people, but effective immediately we have also reduced the price of land from $4 per square foot to $3 per square foot. I must stipulate, however, that the new NHC programme will be accessible only to low-income persons who through the appropriate means test will have demonstrated that they are not otherwise able to access the special land initiative that is now being launched.

But I dare to go further and say that not only will new applicants under the NHC land scheme have to pay just $3 per square foot, but any outstanding land payments to the NHC for land that cost more than $3 per square foot is now, effectively immediately, reduced to just $3 per square foot. That's empowerment! That's people empowerment! We are now giving an opportunity for persons having any outstanding payments with NHC to benefit tremendously by meeting those payments at as much as a 25 per cent discounted rate. This is your time. This is the people's time.

Today, as a token of appreciation for the patience and hope of our ordinary people, we will be distributing land under our new land initiative to ten deserving citizens. This must be an emblem for all persons aspiring to land ownership signifying that this government cares and that this government can deliver on its promise of empowerment. This is not a gift. It is what they deserve. The land that they receive today is a perpetual form of empowerment for themselves and their families. Their time has come and your time will come soon too.

But let me warn you, my dear people. I know that there are some who will come to you once you become a landowner offering you real dollars to buy your land. Some of them will offer you far, far more than you paid for the land. While I cannot tell you what to do, because the land will indeed be yours, I would like to advise, in the strongest possible terms, that you hold on to your land. Land is different from everything else that you could possibly possess. You can lose your jewelry. Your house, heaven forbid, can be burnt to the ground. Your money can be stolen. But land lasts forever. Be careful because the land is not infinite. It is limited and others would like a piece too. This is why this Labour government decided to do whatever has to be done to place land in your hands. Because land lasts forever! Hold on, I urge, to your land.

Fellow nationals, we all know that when we purchase a car, no matter how beautiful and shiny it seems at first, every single morning that we wake up that car is worth less. That is a fact. Every single morning that we wake up, our cars are worth less than the day before. That is true whether we bought our car for $100,000 or we bought it for $5,000. And the value will continue to drop and drop until one day we wake up and the car is worth nothing. On that day, we realise that the only place for the car is the dump. And on that day, after having paid month after month after month for your car for years, we have to go and find more money to buy another car. And we begin all over again, until that car too ends up as junk. But every single morning that you wake up, as a landowner, your land will be worth more than the day before. Every day. Every month. Every year.

That is why this Labour government decided to do whatever has to be done to place land in your hands. Because land is worth more today than yesterday. And it is worth less today than it will be tomorrow. Hold on to your land.

Then there is the matter of financial opportunity. In the years ahead, you will from time to time need money to start a business, to send your children to university, to do something that will improve your life and that of your children. When you have land, when you own land, it will be easier for you to go to the bank and get a loan to do the things you want to do. You will have this land and you will be able to use this land as collateral. Banks need you to show that you have something, that you own something, before they will give you a loan. This land will give you collateral. And that is why this Labour government decided to do whatever has to be done to place land in your hands. So you will be able to do what you need to do to move yourselves and your families forward. Hold on to your land.

I want to share this moment of excitement with you and all future landowners as we journey along the path of progress and prosperity. This important ceremony today epitomises the theme under which the St Kitts-Nevis Labour Party is celebrating its seventy-fifth anniversary this year: '*Struggle, progress, vision – the experience to lead.*' It has been seventy-five years of working to empower ordinary citizens of this country, seventy-five years of struggle against poverty and oppression, seventy-five years of attempting to change the condition of landlessness of our people, but finally the moment has arrived. Do not be fooled by the detractors who are promising what the Labour administration is already fulfilling.

I understand that some people have an issue with the price of land but let me remind you that the price includes a contribution to the putting in of infrastructure. The PAM administration on leaving office left behind a number of projects for which my government had to borrow money to put in infrastructure. We are trying to avoid that mistake.

The Labour Party government is working for you. We have tried to keep our promise of hope and prosperity for all. We have educated our people over the years. We have provided our people with improved health and social and physical infrastructure. We have provided low-income owners with affordable homes. It is now time to break the back of landlessness. Words cannot express the hope and elation that I feel at this moment as I brace myself to help you access even greater opportunity to advance yourselves. I am truly excited by the success and the challenges we have shared over the years.

I end with a quotation printed on the cover of the 2007 Budget Address as I seek your indulgence in partnership to move our great country forward:

> *This is a wonderful moment, an exciting moment when you can join with your government in creating a new future, and not simply be a hitch-hiker on the side of the road.*

NEVIS

NEVIS

By 2005, at the beginning of Labour's third term, the Douglas government thought it had moved beyond the earlier strains in the St Kitts/Nevis relationship including calls for secession. However, the cross-strait relationship was still one of general uneasiness and residual distrust which cast a shadow over the Federation's future. It became clear that if SKN was going to successfully transition into a mature, modern economic state, Nevis needed a larger presence in federal planning and decision-making. Considerable time was invested in determining what could be done to improve the relationship between the Nevis Island Administration (NIA) and the Labour administration.

When CCM (Concerned Citizens Movement) was replaced in 2006 by the NRP (Nevis Reformation Party) which did not support secession, a renewed working relationship with Nevis was established which resulted in the NIA having more autonomy within the SKN constitution. All areas of possible collaboration including a range of institutions and activities were reviewed in an atmosphere of cooperation and mutual respect. Perhaps one of the strongest symbols of this 'new' relationship was the appointment by Denzil Douglas at the beginning of his fourth term of a member of the Nevis National Assembly to the cabinet as the Federation's attorney-general and later foreign minister.

By the end of Labour's fourth term, a blueprint for moving forward collaboratively with the NIA was firmly in place and it was now standard practice to include Nevisians in the top levels of government through regular joint cabinet meetings, sectoral consultations, and cooperation in fiscal planning and debt management. St Kitts's outreach to Nevis was an economic proposition, not a constitutional one – Douglas was always respectful of Nevis's constitutional rights. Only a few days before the February 16, 2015 election, SKNLP and NRP issued a formal 'Contract for Progress' which outlined in detail their shared goals for the continued advancement of all the people of the twin-island Federation.

Nevis Division
Chamber of Industry and Commerce
Inaugural Meeting
Four Seasons Resort, Nevis, January 16, 2007

It is an honour for me to accept the invitation of the council of the Nevis division of the Chamber of Industry and Commerce to address you at your first luncheon meeting on the working relationship between the federal government and the Nevis Island Administration (NIA). I believe that it is quite apt and timely for us to engage in a discussion of this important issue that not only goes to the heart of governance and administration of the beloved islands of our Federation, but also bears great relevance to the ability of our country to compete and prosper in the shifting sands of regionalism and globalisation.

The world has become a treacherous place for small island states and there is a dog-eat-dog mentality that has pervaded international economic relations. The rich and powerful nations no longer feel obliged to assist small and vulnerable countries such as ours, except of course as such assistance advances their strategic interests.

But at the same time, our small islands are continually bombarded by a plethora of economic shocks of international origin. Indeed, one of the effects of globalisation is that very few economic, social, or political contingencies are localised. They reverberate throughout the entire global system and deal particularly devastating blows to small countries such as ours.

It is therefore critical that small states pool their very limited resources and draw upon their combined strengths and capabilities to confront the immense challenges that they face. Such pooling of resources will enable such states to mitigate some of the risks associated with small size and to take advantage of the opportunities that present themselves for social and economic advancement.

Indeed, a recent review of the Small States Agenda that was proposed by a Commonwealth/World Bank Joint Task Force in April, 2000, advanced the view that

> Given their small size, individual small states will inevitably be unable to deliver all the necessary government policy, regulatory and service functions required of a modern state to service the needs of a vibrant private sector ... Enhanced regional cooperation is needed not only to better provide for domestic needs, but also to increase engagement with a globalising world.

The countries to which this study was referring include countries such as Jamaica, Namibia, Botswana, Lesotho, and Estonia with more than thirty times the population of St Kitts. It seems to me therefore that if countries with populations of such magnitude find it necessary to cooperate with other countries to overcome the limitations of small size, it is even more critical that our tiny island state of St Kitts and Nevis pursue regional cooperation with great vigour and urgency.

However, even as we venture out into the Caribbean Sea to cooperate with our neighbours in the OECS and the Caribbean Community, we must ensure that as two small islands in a single sovereign nation, we explore every avenue for collaboration and cooperation between ourselves. Already the Federation has considerable experience that we can share with the rest of the Caribbean. We have a single economy in which capital and labour as well as goods and services move freely between our islands. We also share many common services including the police, army, and foreign service.

But we must do more. In particular, our enterprises must fully exploit the market in the Federation so that they may grow and prepare themselves to launch into regional and international markets. We need to see more Nevis firms establish themselves as truly national enterprises by offering their goods and services throughout the entire Federation, in St Kitts as well as in Nevis. Similarly, more St Kitts firms must become national in scope by venturing across the narrows to give the people of Nevis the benefits of their products and services.

The CSME arrangements give regional firms the right of establishment in our Federation. It would be ironic if non-national firms from throughout the region were to establish in both of our islands and exploit our market more fully than our own enterprises. I am therefore of the view that the federal government and the Nevis Island Administration need to consult and collaborate more on the issue of business licences so that when a licence is issued in either of the two islands, it gives the licensee the automatic right to operate in the entire Federation. This right, of course, must be subject to development and planning control at the island level in relation to the specific physical location of the enterprise.

I believe such an initiative will assist significantly in fostering the development of truly national enterprises and in fostering greater competition and lower consumer prices for the people of St Kitts and Nevis. This would also give our enterprises a significant advantage in relation to their participation in the proposed OECS Economic Union and the CSME because our enterprises would have had experience operating in a multi-island market.

Of course, efficient inter-island transportation must be a critical element of this strategy. In this regard, our private sector has responded admirably to the inter-island transportation needs of the people of St Kitts and Nevis and now offers a very efficient and reliable service. The proposed inter-island car ferry would also help to enhance the efficiency and availability of transportation between our two islands.

I am also persuaded that over time, the construction of a bridge between St Kitts and Nevis will become feasible and will accelerate the pace at which our enterprises become national in scope and develop the capacity to compete more effectively in regional and international markets. However, in view of our relatively high public sector debt, I do not believe that the federal government or the NIA should take up scarce resources or borrow money to build this bridge. It is my view that as soon as such a bridge becomes financially viable from a commercial standpoint, the private sector should be facilitated in undertaking this project, perhaps on a build, operate, lease, and transfer basis.

It is in the area of public sector debt management that there is perhaps the greatest need for collaboration between the federal government and the Nevis Island Administration. The national debt, which includes the debt of the federal government, the Nevis Island Administration, and the public corporations is higher than what my government deems acceptable. While this debt is more than covered by the aggregate saleable assets of the governmental entities, and while the federal government and the NIA have been meticulous in servicing the debt, it is still critical that we address it comprehensively to eliminate any possible risk to our excellent investment climate.

It must be noted that in assessing the performance of our country the international community engages with the federal government. They assess the country as a whole. Hence, it does not make sense for any island of the Federation to focus exclusively on its own fiscal position and neglect the performance of the other island or of the entire Federation. In other words, we must work together to overcome the very substantial public debt challenge that we face as a nation. It is my view therefore that in the area of fiscal and debt management, the federal government and the Nevis Island Administration must sit together and agree on fiscal and debt targets for the country as a whole as well as the contribution of each island to the attainment of national targets.

It is also necessary for the federal government and the NIA to collaborate in expenditure management. A few years ago the World Bank carried out a public expenditure review in the Eastern Caribbean and established that public expenditure per capita in St Kitts and Nevis was among the highest in the OECS. Of course, our tiny population relative to the populations of the other independent countries of the OECS was a major contributor to this situation. Indeed, the report on small states that I mentioned earlier made reference to the problems posed by expenditure indivisibilities of certain essential public services and it argued that 'in contrast to larger countries, the costs of providing these essential government services have to be a borne by a small population.'

By way of example it suggested that Malta has a population equivalent to one-one hundred and fiftieth (1/150) of that of the United Kingdom and if the Maltese government were organised proportionally, many departments would employ less than one person. I would venture to suggest that in the case of St Kitts and Nevis with a population that is about one-tenth of that of Malta, many departments would have to employ less than one-tenth of a person to achieve the efficiencies of the United Kingdom.

But the small size of our population is not the only contributor to our high cost of administration. We also have a constitutional arrangement that requires the duplication of many civil service positions in our Federation. Of course, I am of the view that if the people of Nevis are to assert their constitutional right of autonomy in administration then there must be separate ministries and departments in Nevis and they must be headed by ministers, permanent secretaries, and heads of department in a manner similar to arrangements in St Kitts. However, I still believe that in the engagement of relatively expensive technical personnel that may be underutilised in any one of our islands, there may be scope for joint recruitment and for the sharing of such services. For example, when my government recruited the Crown Agents to undertake the customs reform project, we were able to extend their terms of reference to include Nevis with only a slight elevation in the overall cost of the project. We need to diligently search for more opportunities like this one with a view to minimising the cost of public administration in our Federation. Of course, there is also scope for us to engage in joint negotiations and joint procurement of a range of goods and services with a view to obtaining the best deal for the people of the Federation.

As the saying goes, 'Rome was not built in a day,' but I am persuaded that we are moving in the right direction in relation to addressing the key issues that I have raised here today. The cabinets of the federal government and the Nevis Island Administration have met and have agreed to formalise a framework for greater collaboration and cooperation between the two governments. This framework provides for regular joint cabinet meetings, regular sectoral consultations between the ministries in St Kitts and Nevis involved in the same sectors of the economy, and greater collaboration in fiscal planning and debt management.

We believe that this comprehensive consultative and collaborative framework will yield significant benefits for our Federation. After all, it is taxpayers that must pay for the higher costs associated with administrative inefficiencies. Moreover, high tax burdens as a result of high administrative costs, could compromise the ability of our enterprises to compete effectively in domestic, regional, and international markets. We must, therefore, work together through this consultative and collaborative framework with a view to identifying and exploiting the synergies and cost-saving opportunities that will inevitably result from greater cooperation between our two administrations.

In fact, with the closure of the sugar industry and the adaptation strategy that has been developed to transform the national economy, there are additional opportunities for close collaboration between St Kitts and Nevis to develop a truly diversified economy led by services, in particular tourism, hospitality, investment, financial, and ICT services. I should point out that in promoting greater collaboration and cooperation between St Kitts and Nevis, I am not proposing to disrupt in any way the constitutional rights that the people of Nevis have fought so hard to obtain and secure. As prime minister, I respect those rights, which are duly entrenched in our constitution and which cannot be changed in any way without the consent of the people of Nevis. Of course, my government has embarked on a policy of constitutional reform but our aim is not to water down in any way the right to the high degree of autonomy that the people of Nevis currently enjoy. Indeed, if anything, our approach to constitutional reform will probably enhance those rights, but we also believe there should be greater balance in the constitution and that the people of St Kitts should enjoy similar rights.

The proposition I have set out here today is essentially an economic proposition and not a political or constitutional one. The global economic climate has changed and it has become critical that we collaborate to reduce the cost of doing business and to offer competitive goods and services to our people and to the world. The world is rapidly becoming a single global market place with no tolerance of economic inefficiencies. I believe that we can, in this beloved Federation of ours, show the world what it means to truly cooperate and thereby become the stimulus for even greater regional cooperation at the OECS and CARICOM levels.

I also believe that the spirit of cooperation must extend beyond inter-island relationships. It must permeate all aspects of life in our Federation and thereby root out all forms of tribalism to create a united country capable of holding its own in the new global economy.

St Kitts-Nevis Labour Party (SKNLP) Nevis Reformation Party (NRP) Joint Press Conference

Labour Party Annex, Basseterre, February 12, 2015

Five years ago, in January 2010, from positions of strength – not political necessity – the St Kitts-Nevis Labour Party (SKNLP) and the Nevis Reformation Party (NRP) came together to work closely and collaboratively for the ongoing progress and advancement of all the people of St Kitts and Nevis. Many of us have family members on both sides of the strait and we share the same principles of mutual respect, fairness, and justice or all. Our cooperation and good working relationship has already resulted in millions of dollars for Nevis for a variety of programmes including fisheries, energy, tourism, and water. The Hon. Patrice Nisbett has been a member of the federal cabinet for the past five years and he has provided extraordinary insights into the priorities and perspectives of the people of Nevis leading to the expansion and intensification of our collaboration last December with the introduction of the Labour/NRP Contract for Progress.

With a general election only a few days away, Premier Parry and I want to reiterate and strengthen the ties between the federal government and the Nevis Island Administration (NIA). We have consulted with our respective citizens and asked you what more we can do to improve and grow our relationship and bring even more progress to the Federation. You have asked for an even more expansive relationship and your demands have been incorporated into both the Labour/NRP Contract For Progress and the Labour manifesto for this election.

In summary, the Contract contents include:

- Equity in representation, appointments and distribution of resources;
- Exploring the possibility of extensive constitutional reform initiatives;
- Expanding the mandate of the Sugar Industry Diversification Foundation (SIDF) with a special focus on Nevis;

- Better education initiatives including expanding and upgrading the Clarence Fitzroy Bryant College (CFBC) campus in Charlestown and more scholarships;
- More and better health care including National Health Insurance Commission (NHIC) coverage for everyone and two new hospitals in St Kitts and one in Nevis;
- Improvements in the federal police with a focus on Charlestown and New Castle;
- Expansion of the youth rehabilitation programme with a facility in Nevis;
- More support for small- and medium-sized enterprises (SMEs) on both islands;
- More land to be made available for business, agriculture, and housing;
- Development of green energy – geothermal, solar, and wind;
- Improvements in tourism including better inter-island ferry service;
- More federal initiatives like the Nevis Federal Office and the proposed Nevis-based Federal Constituency Empowerment Office;
- Standardisation of government services for all citizens.

For more detail, copies of the Contract For Progress will be available following this press conference.

The two parties representing the people of the Federation, Labour and the NRP, are continuing to join forces following consultation with the people. The Labour Party and myself have worked tirelessly to improve lives on both islands and bring the nation of St Kitts and Nevis closer together, despite the obstacles created by the opposition, and we have established excellent communication and mutual trust through our years of cooperation. CCM has failed Nevis on all counts. The NRP deserves to continue to represent the proud people of Nevis and we look forward to positive and productive collaboration with the NIA for another five years.

Regional Affairs

Regional Affairs

—◇—

This section has more than doubled from *Coming Of Age* and reflects a growing awareness by Douglas and his regional colleagues that increased communication and cooperation was the most effective way of having their voices heard on the international stage.

CARICOM and the OECS had always had a two-pronged approach to their mandates – positive policy initiatives to move the region forward, and a coordinated regional response to international events over which the community had little influence although often impacted in major ways.

By the late-1990s, increasing numbers of geopolitical trends were affecting the Caribbean including rapid climate change and an increasing number of natural disasters, communicable diseases challenges, a worldwide financial crisis, the high cost of energy, escalating regional conflicts and terrorism threats, and erosion of preferential trade agreements with the region's traditional European partners.

A further reason for the greater prominence of this section is the increasing participation of Denzil Douglas in regional affairs, especially in the OECS. Having completed his first ten years in office, Douglas was the longest-serving leader in the sub-region, a valued, experienced agent of change, and was subsequently called upon to play a more active role in the community's external relations.

The two areas where Douglas and SKN probably had the most impact on the region and beyond was its HIV/AIDS amelioration programme that not only addressed SKN's own AIDS crisis but became a global best practices model, and the development of its Citizenship By Investment (CBI) programme which also became a Caribbean and international best practices model.

Throughout his entire premiership, Denzil Douglas's consistent, unwavering message delivered forcefully and often to the metropolitan world audience has been that small states, especially small island developing states (SIDS) like SKN, require special differential treatment by world bodies, especially financial entities such as the International Monetary Fund (IMF), World Bank (WB), Inter-American Development Bank (IADB). SIDS experience virtually all the negative events including climate change, disease, and security threats that larger, richer countries do without the technical resources and funds to tackle them.

During Douglas's second two terms many good initiatives and programmes were developed regionally including the Caribbean Basin Security Initiative (CBSI) which saw the US partner with CARICOM and the Dominican Republic on regional security issues; launch of the Caribbean Public Health Agency (CARPHA) when Douglas was the CARICOM Head of Government for Human Resources, Health and HIV/AIDS; signing of a revised Treaty of Basseterre establishing the OECS Economic Union; and the PetroCaribe deal with Venezuela to supply petroleum products to OECS members on favourable terms.

However, there were also a number of disappointments the greatest of which was the failure to launch of the Caribbean Single Market and Economy (CSME), the free movement of people and skills within CARICOM. A vocal proponent, Douglas regretted the missed opportunity to strengthen the region and perhaps develop another best practices model. In a similar vein, neither the OECS Economic Union nor the Eastern Caribbean Assembly (ECA) have lived up to their promise or potential.

Another area of disappointment, especially to Douglas, a medical doctor, was not being able to convince his colleagues to put non-communicable diseases such as hypertension, diabetes, and heart disease in the same context and priority as HIV/AIDS.

He also advocated for improvements to CARICOM and the European Union (EU) to make them more efficient and effective and sought a closer relationship with the Organisation of American States (OAS).

8TH WORLD CONGRESS OF CONSULS

Ritz Carlton Hotel, Montego Bay, Jamaica, November 7, 2006

I am delighted to bring you greetings and best wishes from the government and people of St Kitts and Nevis, as well as from member countries of the Caribbean Community (CARICOM). I wish to congratulate you on the hosting of this Congress of Consuls here in the Caribbean, particularly because it comes at a time when the Caribbean Community is accelerating its developmental strategies in response to, and in anticipation of, worldwide influences on our regional economies.

CARICOM countries have been dealing with a number of matters that impact our economies and societies including the erosion of preferential trade agreements with our traditional European trading partners, the devastating effects of natural disasters, the high cost of energy, cultural degradation resulting from external influences, and global medical challenges to our development like the HIV/AIDS pandemic and the increase in non-communicable chronic diseases. The environment within which we operate today is most challenging. We strive diligently to raise the standard of living of our Caribbean citizens by dealing with matters such as poverty alleviation and the empowerment of our people to take a larger slice of the economic pie and help shape their own destiny.

One cannot also divorce geopolitical trends that have had some negative impact on the Caribbean, from the emerging economies that are joining the European Union to the global impact of the war in Iraq and the threat of international terrorism. All combine to make the economic environment for development more challenging than ever before. Nevertheless, I believe that within the framework of the Caribbean Community, recently strengthened by the revised Treaty of Chaguaramas, as well as our own national developmental agendas, Caribbean countries are forging ahead with a positive spirit to ensure that our development is sustainable and that we can protect and maintain our natural environment which is so crucial to our overall well-being.

I am of the view that the future of the Caribbean has to be grounded in its ability to effectively integrate in such a manner as to effect workable strategies that inform our foreign affairs and trade policies and overall development strategies in an increasingly competitive world. The issue for us, as I have indicated, is one about sustainable development, especially in recognition of our size and limitations in natural and fiscal resources. Issues of market size, capacity weaknesses, shortcomings in institutional structures and systems, and productivity problems all play a role in shaping our development agenda.

Some of you may be well aware of CARICOM's newest economic-based initiative, the Caribbean Single Market and Economy (CSME), that involves several strategies aimed at advancing economic well-being with the private sector playing an important role in the process. Among the principal objectives, of course, are the thrust to improve our international competitiveness by providing an environment of internationally accepted standards, efficiencies, and productivity levels. It would seem to me, however, that the development of Caribbean companies as competitive entities within the region necessitates some essential elements.

These elements can be identified as follows:

1. The necessity to establish standards across the board;

2. The need to effectively utilise our human resources by way of free movement of labour;

3. The need to consistently engage in the training of our human resources;

4. The need to pay special attention to energy usage, sourcing, and conservation;

5. The effective free movement of capital as well as the availability of competitive financing;

6. The enhancement of leadership and management teams in all economic sectors;

7. The importance of maintaining and strengthening dialogue between the public sector and the private sector.

Caribbean Community countries have to deal with the complexities of global trade issues and, given our size and resource constraints, this is not an easy endeavour by any means. For example, for many of us here in the Caribbean, our ministries of trade are not in a position to engage significantly in trade negotiations or the implementation of trade agreements and commitments. The small ministries simply cannot cope with such large demands.

Further, there is the issue of having the relevant professional skills available to deal with many of the technical aspects of trade negotiations and the lack of research data upon which decisions can be based. Such circumstances have implications for our ability to develop highly functional and efficient trade institutions in the public sector. What is evident also is the acute need to enhance inter-ministerial co-ordination in all areas that facilitate trade and business activities – telecommunications, transportation, insurance, ports services, legal services, and sector regulation.

Part of the response to such a scenario has been the establishment of the regional negotiating machinery that has served to develop a co-ordinated regional response in global trade negotiations. So far, the system has served us well vis-à-vis our common front, but the fact remains that there exist significant structural weaknesses in the public sector that supports the RNM. These deficiencies will have to be addressed sooner rather than later as it is expected that the challenges of international trade negotiations will become even more demanding. It is imperative that the region protect its interests. Certainly, negotiations with the World Trade Organisation (WTO) are not easy, nor are the negotiations in the other trade arenas, namely the hemispheric FTAA and the European EPAs. Nevertheless, we maintain our view that development must be placed at the core of any trade arrangement and we will resist attempts to marginalise the quest for differential treatment of our small developing states.

As I indicated earlier, the CSME now provides the basis for the region's businesses to begin looking outwards in a more substantial manner. The legislative and legal frameworks have been established to make the prospects of intra- and extra-regional trade even more workable. While there have been mixed reactions to the establishment of the Caribbean Court of Justice, this institution is absolutely necessary if we are to forge ahead with the CSME to any meaningful extent. Obviously, this kind of integration still has to account for the need for differential treatment which, in my view, must apply within the region as we advocate extra-regionally. Finding the right mix, therefore, is an important challenge and it is one that needs to be addressed expeditiously.

For most Caribbean countries, the great challenge in stimulating economic growth and competitiveness of our industries and service providers is the parallel reduction or removal of port tariffs which for some time have been key sources of revenue for governments. The expected loss of revenue from import duties will have to be addressed elsewhere in our economies. Economic diversification will have to be a central theme throughout the region. Enhancing financial services and paying increased attention to information and telecommunications technology as well as research and development will be critical in any future approach.

When all factors are taken into account, one can only conclude that the way forward for countries of the Caribbean lies in the effectiveness of our integration, the efficiencies and relevance of our regional institutions, increased access to tertiary level education, greater exposure to specialised training, and effective implementation and operation of CSME. Having said all of this, we must acknowledge other important adversarial conditions that could grind away at every turn and every chance of success. I refer to the following:

1. Lifestyle changes now impact today's Caribbean person in negative ways for the most part, and non-communicable diseases such as hypertension and diabetes are significantly counter-productive to the ideal environment for nation-building;

2. Every effort has to be made to control the spread of HIV in the region. The implications of failure are well known – there are villages in Sub-Saharan Africa with 50 per cent of the child population orphaned;

3. Rising fuel costs will play a major role in our ability to move forward in a substantial manner. Just as important will be research into alternative sources of energy that can support regional growth and development. And how is the friendly gesture of the Bolivarian Republic of Venezuela through the Petro-Caribe agreements with CARICOM countries being interpreted by our great trading partners in the north?

4. The annual threat of hurricanes, along with other natural hazards, remind us persistently of how fragile are our island economies.

As I inferred earlier, the matters of cultural strengthening, community empowerment, and heritage preservation are all critical elements in developing sustainable economies. The Caribbean is at a point where we have to take serious stock of what I perceive as cultural degradation coming as a result of the penetration of external moral values through the influence primarily of television programming. Careful attention has to be paid to our young people, particularly the males in our society, many of whom slip through the cracks and engage in illicit activities in a life of crime. I believe that it is important to address the issue of moral values in our societies and to place emphasis on multi-disciplinary approaches that engage families, the church, community organisations, government, and private sector companies and institutions. I believe that we are still at a stage where positive change is possible.

Cultural and moral enhancement must be considered therefore as essential to sustainable development. Our societies must be engaged in such a manner that we can be justly proud and that we can stand out in a sustainable way as the best place to live and to do business. Such must be the destiny of Caribbean nations and Caribbean people. This must be the realisation of the billions of television viewers and the thousands of visitors and sport enthusiasts who we are inviting into the Caribbean to witness the ICC Cricket World Cup 2007 matches in nine host countries.

As professionals representing your countries and their interests, one has to be cognisant of the wide range of influences that impact your important work. I have used the Caribbean Community to point to this critical truth. What is certain is that country size is by no means relevant to the complexities that face our nations, and population size does not give the entire picture of a country's human capacity with today's new advanced technology at its full disposal. Each country, each region, has its own set of problems and of course, opportunities, and in each region the courses of action must be tailored to suit national and regional aspirations.

What is also certain is that the world is ever more interdependent and there is a critical need to promote international co-operation, reduce political, economic, and ethnic conflict, and reduce in significant ways the threat of terrorism. In short, we must work to secure world peace, economic and social justice, security of our borders, and security of the means of ensuring that the people of the world can prosper and can escape the scourge of human indignity.

In closing, I remind you that you play a particular and significant role. I encourage you to share your experiences and to continue to dialogue in your quest to enhance your own positive influences on the people and countries you serve.

ORGANISATION OF AMERICAN STATES PROTOCOLLARY MEETING

OAS Hall of the Americas, Washington, DC, December 17, 2006

My visit here today is to forge an even stronger connection between my government and this organisation which is so important to us. But more importantly, it is an opportunity to engage and to sensitise this organisation with regard to the role that we in St Kitts and Nevis and the Caribbean Community (CARICOM) – speaking as indeed I should in my capacity as the current chair of the CARICOM Heads of Government – envision this organisation playing as we of the Small Island Developing States (SIDS) of the Caribbean sub-region seek to advance our interests. The role of the Organisation of American States (OAS) is increasingly more critical as our nations act in the face of the evolving scheme of global factors that challenge our resourcefulness and our ingenuity. It is imperative that the OAS becomes our genuine partner as we strive to deliver on the promises of development, poverty alleviation, and equitable prosperity to our expectant and deserving peoples. I am delighted to have this opportunity therefore to reiterate some of the critical challenges that are before us as small island developing states of the Caribbean.

I am confident that we have made some measurable gains since those early days of dialogue on issues pertaining to development of small states, but undoubtedly there is very much still to be done and our message has to be consistent and persistent for the ears and for the consideration of those whom we believe should be concerned.

A CASE OF LOST PREFERENCE

Allow me, for a moment, to take my beloved country St Kitts and Nevis as an example: In August 2005, a little over a year ago, due to the negative impact of trade liberalisation on our small and fragile economy, we were forced to cease the production of sugar for export. St Kitts and Nevis is one of eighteen ACP countries that have been impacted by changes to the EU/ACP Sugar Protocol that will result in a 36 per cent fall in the intervention price of sugar in the EU market over a four-year period beginning in 2006. Sugar production for export therefore became economically unfeasible. It was costing us far more to produce it than we could demand for it. Its continued production would simply have strangled our economy. We are the first of the countries so affected to make this bold political decision. Our people were fully consulted on this action and they must be complimented for supporting our decision despite their realisation of its anticipated attendant hardships.

Sugar cane had hitherto been cultivated and processed in St Kitts for over three hundred and fifty years. This activity had constituted the mainstay of our economy, employing directly some 10 per cent of the island's workforce. But in addition, its cessation has indirectly impacted the livelihood of a much wider sector of our economy and consequently has been manifest also as a major shock to the emotional, social, and cultural landscape of our country.

My government took this bold decision with regard to the sugar industry against the backdrop of a contemporary global economic scene which presents St Kitts and Nevis with some extremely difficult challenges including decreasing preferential trade arrangements; changes brought about by advanced technological developments, particularly in the field of information and communications; the declining availability of concessionary aid; a widening and intensification of international linkages in trade, finance, and production; and increased competition in the wider global economy.

In addition to the changing external environment, there are mounting challenges inherent within the domestic context complicated by high levels of public sector indebtedness and fiscal imbalances aggravated by the closure of the sugar industry and a relative entrenchment of poverty. Economic restructuring and transformation in St Kitts and Nevis is therefore necessary in order to meet these challenges and ultimately to facilitate greater integration into the world economy.

But it needs to be said that the combination of monoculture and primary production together with diseconomies of scale in production and the openness of the economy resulting in economic vulnerability and a lack of sustained economic growth over time, are as applicable to St Vincent and the Grenadines and St Lucia in relation to bananas, to Antigua and Barbuda in relation to internet gaming barriers, and to other small and vulnerable states in other regards.

ADAPTATION STRATEGY

Consequent upon our bold decision to abandon sugar production for export, St Kitts and Nevis has put forward an adaptation strategy which attempts to chart a course of reconstruction and transformation over the next ten years. Fortunately, in anticipation of this move, we had begun some years earlier an economic diversification drive with particular emphasis on new industries such as tourism, financial services, and information and communication technology. These are growing and we endeavour to build further in this sector.

In anticipation of this move also, several re-training programmes have been implemented and are ongoing as we seek to equip our displaced workforce for self-employment and for assimilation into other areas of economic activity. The programmes which emanate from the adaptation strategy elaborated by my government require cooperation on multiple levels. It explicitly acknowledges that the public sector, the business community, and all elements of civil society must make their contribution towards the success of this national transformation initiative. It will require an upward shift from the way we have previously operated and it must of necessity result in a culture change. The government of St Kitts and Nevis is taking the lead, as we are duty-bound to do, in this critical national transformation initiative.

We are inviting the Organisation of American States as well as resourceful member states which are a part of this eminent body, to journey with us and partner with us on a path toward sustainable development. This is indeed a challenging undertaking but one that we cannot avoid.

The acceleration and sustainability of economic growth in St Kitts and Nevis is most important for social development, the reduction of unemployment and poverty, improved fiscal performance, and a more sustainable external position, all of which will depend significantly on the country's ability to improve competitiveness.

Our focus will be on five areas:

- Macro-economic policies to reduce vulnerability and facilitate investment;

- Improving competitiveness in the production and export of goods and services;

- Social policies to support economic development and support the most vulnerable;

- Ensuring an environmentally sustainable development agenda;
- Addressing cross-cutting issues that bring cohesion to these efforts.

DEVELOPING OUR HUMAN RESOURCES

The impact of economic fluctuations and shifts could be quite difficult and it is crucial that human resource development in the context of small island vulnerabilities is pursued. What this really means is that our education and training policies must be structured in such a manner that they reflect and anticipate the challenges that are peculiar to small island states. While there is general recognition of the relevance and importance of human resources as a response to such challenges, it is important that relevant international agencies and institutions continue to strengthen their programmes, funding, and technical assistance to ensure that desired outcomes can be achieved. Herein lies an opportunity for bilateral and multilateral donors to enhance rather than decrease assistance.

Obviously, when we speak to the issues of human resource development, we speak not only in terms of education and training but also in terms of health, poverty alleviation, housing, and the overall enhancement of human dignity. Addressing these areas of vulnerability is pertinent to long-term success in sustainable development. From our end, we have to create avenues to enhance functional cooperation, to establish and maintain regional bodies, systems and mechanisms, and to ensure that public sector reform is implemented to optimise levels of efficiency, promote savings, strengthen institutions, and build capacity.

And while on the one hand we must commend the OAS for the part it has played in assisting small island states to address their peculiar difficulties, it is critical that this momentum is not diminished. Rather, we must work towards accelerating programmes to address those needs lest we lose the ground that we have hitherto gained.

For example, we continue to call for the development of a Natural Disaster Fund and a Special Renewable Energy Resources Fund. We know that the Caribbean islands are vulnerable to natural disasters, especially to hurricanes. We know that the rising cost of fossil fuels is creating severe problems for the majority of Caribbean countries. These are two areas that are of tremendous challenge to the sustainable development of small island economies and we are yet hopeful that they will receive deserved attention within the inter-American system.

A RELEVANT OAS

I was pleased to learn that as recently as last year, the OAS embarked on a programme of restructuring. I shall continue to follow closely progress in this undertaking. I hasten to caution, however, that the organisation should not allow itself to become too introspective lest its own attempts at reform undermine its relevance. By this I mean that the OAS must learn to survey the landscape and plan its alteration while continuing to travel purposefully to desired goals. As we say in my vernacular – we need to 'walk and chew at the same time.'

No longer can the organisation afford to commit resources to projects that are inherently top-down in approach. If the national reality does not inform how programmes and projects are developed and executed then the OAS may very well continue to squander tremendous opportunities to create ownership in the member states and to make the organisation seem more like an asset to its membership than a drain on scarce national resources. I am aware that the OAS has done some invaluable work in member states. If, however, a culture of bureaucratic lethargy and pandering to narrow agendas is allowed to prevail, the organisation will become a peripheral player in this hemisphere where its track record of 'good years past' should rightfully give it pride-of-place in national psyches and priority attention on the agendas of the finance ministers of the hemisphere.

I believe that the OAS with its convening powers can be a viable partner and forum for the exchange of ideas, best practices, and expertise on issues of trade negotiation. I understand that the organisation cannot and should not be all things to all people, but when a significant number of its constituents suffer a common problem, the organisation has an obligation to demonstrate its relevance and to show that its reforms are essential to making it more responsive to its membership.

Likewise, the organisation should pay greater attention to the issue of development. I am pleased to understand that both the secretary-general and the assistant secretary-general appreciate the inherent linkages between democracy and human rights, good governance, security, and development. These issues are inextricably intertwined. I therefore commend the present leadership for their commitment in addressing this nexus and making it an integral part of the organisation's focus in the coming years.

OTHER CHALLENGING ISSUES

I believe we have to continue sending the message loud and clear that Caribbean trade under special preferences is no threat to global trade liberalisation. Neither for that matter is the granting of trade concessions to small island developing states in any way inimical to the interests of larger states. We must continue our call for special and differential treatment on trade and other relevant matters, and we must continue to lobby strongly for a refocus to include development issues as integral to the sustainability of small island states.

Alongside this it is worthy of mention that the security and consequently the governance and democratic integrity of small Caribbean societies is under considerable threat by the influx of some displaced/deported persons especially in cases where family or other support systems are non-existent and where acquired and well-practiced skills are incompatible with social order and good governance. This is creating a new security reality, that of violence, gangs, and related domestic and trans-national criminal activities. There may be a role for this organisation to play in addressing this problem. My government hopes that the organisation will provide value added to the Declaration on Security in the Americas. I urge this organisation to broaden its understanding and interpretation of the Bridgetown Declaration so that the work of the OAS might faithfully reflect the multi-dimensional character and diverse nature of security.

As the CARICOM prime minister with responsibility for health, I am acutely aware of the tremendous impact of the HIV/AIDS pandemic on our region and worldwide. I have come to appreciate how it undermines productive activities and destroys families and societies imposing financial burdens on governments, obligating them to dedicate scarce resources to prevention activities, treatment, and care to the exclusion of development activities. HIV/AIDS may appear at face value to be a health issue. I assure you that it is cross-cutting and as much a security matter as any other listed in the Declaration on Security. I therefore exhort this organisation, within its multi-dimensional security framework, to partner with agencies within and without the inter-American system to fight this scourge to our societies.

Also, in the context of good governance and the nurturance of democratic values, St Kitts and Nevis is now embarked on an electoral reform initiative and in this process my government has had widest possible consultation with nationals at home and abroad, with all political parties, and with private sector and civil society interest groups. We look forward to continuing our engagement with the secretariat for political affairs in the continuance and indeed in the expansion of this project to the overarching issue of constitutional reform.

IN CONCLUSON

On September 11, 2001, the very day that terrorists challenged our resolve to defend the values which we hold dear, there was signed in Lima, Peru by the General Assembly of the OAS, an Inter-American Democratic Charter which speaks to the promotion and consolidation of democracy in the Americas. Now, five years later, you are embarked on the framing of an Inter-American Social Charter which will give greater meaning and relevance to the principles espoused in the Democratic Charter. My government welcomes this initiative and sincerely hopes that the Inter-American Social Charter will be a bold and imaginative document which challenges us to bring a solution-focused mindset and rich aggregate to build the pillars of democracy with sustainable development, poverty alleviation, and equitable prosperity.

The Organisation of American States is one of our most treasured institutions. We praise its strength and fully acknowledge its limitations. I know that in the past we have asked it to do more with less and the time seems to have come for us to reconcile resources with expectations. Time has also come for the organisation to be true to its charter, its priorities, and its mandates. Governments have to act and the organisation has to act as well. The organisation must embrace and value the cultural and intellectual diversity of our hemisphere and the general secretariat must truly reflect that reality. It is time for a holistic re-thinking. I believe in democracy and I subscribe to the value of social equity, human rights, and all the important tenets of freedom and human dignity. These are important not only within and among states but also within regional and hemispheric organisations tasked with shepherding the interests and policies of our states. This is a philosophy that I know to be shared by my CARICOM colleagues. I commend this philosophy to the consideration of this organisation.

CARICOM Heads of Government 18th Intersessional Meeting
Outgoing Chairman's Remarks

Kingstown, St Vincent and the Grenadines, February 12–14, 2007

There is much that the Caribbean Community (CARICOM) can be proud of in respect of the advancement that we have been making in bringing the people of the region together as a community. I am sure you will recall that when I assumed the chair, I expressed concern about the situation in Haiti and the need for the region to be more proactive in embracing the Haitian people as brothers and sisters and as important members of the community. In pursuit of this objective, I led a prime ministerial delegation, including the secretary-general, to Haiti to gain a first-hand understanding of the needs of the Haitian people and to engage in a dialogue with the Haitian leadership in respect of the future development of Haiti and the integration of Haiti into the Caribbean Community. This visit set the stage for a number of technical missions to Haiti and for the operation of the CARICOM office in Haiti. I know that my successor in the chair is deeply committed to the alleviation of the plight of the Haitian people and will ensure that these initiatives move forward with even greater haste and focus so that they may bear fruit for the Haitian people over time.

The community can also take pride in the progress that we have made in advancing the agenda for the Caribbean Single Market and Economy (CSME). I am fully persuaded that the CSME is a critical tool that we must utilise to the fullest to bring meaningful benefits to the people of the region. It is important that all components of the Single Market and Economy are fully implemented within the time frames that we have set ourselves. I am particularly pleased with the framework outlined in the paper 'Single Vision for the Single Economy' which will be presented to this meeting. It is for me a signal achievement, which given the political will, ought to define the future development of our community. I congratulate Professor Norman Girvan for this comprehensive insight.

I am also pleased with the tremendous work that has gone into the establishment of the Regional Development Fund and with the serious attempts made through this mechanism to address the special needs of the OECS countries. The progress that we have made in this regard will undoubtedly help to accelerate the pace at which the CSME is implemented.

The OECS is embarking on a major new initiative that will give them the means of participating even more fully in the CSME and of providing a smooth and effective interface between the tiny islands that comprise the OECS and the wider Caribbean Single Market and Economy. I speak here of the proposed OECS Economic Union that we expect will deepen the integration process in the sub-region and empower OECS countries to overcome some of the limitations of size and play a more meaningful role in the Single Market and Economy. We do not view the OECS Economic Union as an alternative to the CSME. We view it as a critical element of the wider regional integration movement and we feel strongly that to the extent the OECS is able to break new ground in the integration process, the Caribbean Community as a whole will benefit significantly. We therefore encourage the Caribbean Community to continue to support the sub-regional integration movement and to be prepared to lend a helping hand when requested to do so.

The eyes of the world will be intensely focused on the region over the next few weeks as we invite the world to the region to participate in the ICC World Cup 2007. Just yesterday, at a meeting of the prime ministerial sub-committee on cricket we were reminded that the start of the World Cup cricket games is just four hundred hours away. In other words, we do not have much time to continue the preparation for this historic event.

This most challenging undertaking can provide the entire region the opportunity to shine and to demonstrate to the world the resourcefulness and immense capabilities of our people. But at the same time, any 'hiccup' of any kind can bring international embarrassment to our region. We must therefore work steadfastly to resolve all outstanding issues. In some cases it may be necessary to devote more resources to work full-time in addressing these issues. But the time for action is now. We have invested heavily in the preparation for the ICC World Cup. Let us not waste this investment. Let us, as a region, harness the talents and capabilities of our people and extract every ounce of benefit from the ICC World Cup.

In particular, we must maximise the legacy benefits of hosting the World Cup so that our people, including our young people in particular, will reap rewards from this momentous event for many decades to come.

The empowerment of young people is a challenge faced by all members of the community. As we develop the CSME, we must specifically prepare our young people to be active and dynamic participants in all aspects of the integration process. I believe firmly that the time has come for the region to enunciate a comprehensive regional strategy for the empowerment of young people. This strategy must be informed by extensive research aimed at establishing in a scientific way the real issues affecting young people. Hence, our institutions of higher learning as well as our social workers and our educational planners who deal specifically with youth issues must collaborate with the secretariat in developing such a strategy.

In a similar way, we must move forward urgently with our follow-up actions to realise the specific missions that have emerged from the Report of the Commission of Health and Development. In this regard, we have consolidated our initiatives in the fight against HIV/AIDS, but with similar urgency we should develop a comprehensive regional strategic plan to respond to chronic non-communicable diseases and the havoc they are wreaking on our Caribbean people.

In closing, I wish to call on the region's media to play an even greater role in educating our people and in fostering greater awareness of the many social and economic challenges that we face. We must change attitudes so that productivity and excellence will become important hallmarks of the way of life of Caribbean people. The media is a most powerful force that we need to engage and deploy even more meaningfully in the attainment of a just and progressive Caribbean society.

The entire integration process is about uniting and empowering the people of the region to enable them to realise even more fully their tremendous potential and capabilities to the benefit of the entire community. Let us over the next few days focus specifically on this important objective with a view to making even greater and faster strides in the advancement of the quality of life of the Caribbean people.

PETROCARIBE V SUMMIT
Maracaibo, Venezuela, July 13, 2008

St Kitts and Nevis features prominently among the countries of the region who are proud beneficiaries of PetroCaribe and the Bolivarian Alliance for the Americas (ALBA). It is imperative for me to emphasise that this intense desire to strengthen the bonds of integration and union by your esteemed government is reflective of the proud legacy of your forefathers who fought so valiantly to liberate your peoples thus transforming them into sovereign and free nations. Today, we can see the evidence of a clear path that will allow us to reach and further enhance the development of our people based upon a complementary solidarity premised on reciprocal cooperation.

The Venezuelan government under the leadership of President Hugo Rafael Chavez Frias has certainly revolutionised and transformed the energy matrix of our region with the resulting economic and social benefits. Between December 2007 and June 2008, St Kitts and Nevis received regular shipments of fuel amounting to over one hundred and fifty thousand barrels of diesel. The volumes required must be discharged over a period of time due to our lack of adequate storage facilities. This has caused the government to enter into contractual arrangements with Sol Petroleum for storage and throughput, an arrangement which is due to end in the not too distant future as the government of Venezuela through PDVSA (state-owned oil and natural gas company) has begun preparations for the construction of a US$24 million fuel tank farm in St Kitts which will consist of:

- 2 – 10,000 bbl tanks for diesel
- 1 – 5,000 bbl tank for jet fuel
- 1 – 5,000 bbl for gasoline
- 1 – 2,000 bbl tank LPG
- 1 – 5,000 bbl tank for water
- 1 – 5,000 bbl tank at the Power Station

Demolition and other site work began in earnest a month ago. The proposed construction of the tanks is scheduled to be completed within a twelve-month period. The joint venture company (JVC) has already been formed and now that the necessary fiscal arrangements have been put in place, operationalisation will commence shortly. This joint venture will be a model for the rest of the region and will enable the government to utilise its services as an intermediary between itself and PDVSA. The St Kitts and Nevis Energy Company, as it is officially called, is a statutory entity incorporated is St Kitts and Nevis with a board of directors comprising representatives from both countries. Through the JVC several requests have already been made and been processed.

We have now added two additional products to our supply contract, namely asphalt and fuel oil. Both of these products are to be delivered shortly.

My government has entered into an arrangement with MAN B&W of Houston, Texas to purchase two generators and to convert the existing generators from diesel to heavy fuel oil (HFO). This conversion however, was based on the availability of extra storage capacity and was heavily contingent upon the tank farm construction. Due to some delays experienced and the timetable for the conversion, the government must now enter into another contractual arrangement with Sol to store its HFO and have it transported to the power station. Failure to effect the conversion as set out in the schedule will cost government 10 per cent of the contract price of US$4.5 million.

Through the JVC we are now negotiating the 'lease to own' arrangement made with Antigua Barbuda Investment Bank (ABIB) in Antigua and I must inform that considerable progress is being made. Through ALBA the government has benefited from US$10 million to assist with the housing programme for former sugar estate workers. A total of two hundred homes will be constructed while others will be renovated with the appropriate infrastructural developments. The government applauds ALBA and wishes to place on record its gratitude and desire to continue to work with ALBA for the betterment of its people through social upliftment.

Mr President, I am happy to report that the $10 million received was approved at the III Summit of PetroCaribe held in Caracas in 2007. There were other projects also submitted, two of which were pre-approved by the relevant minister and have been awaiting your kind signature. I crave your indulgence, Mr President, in according to these projects the requisite consideration.

We realise that there are still some limitations but these limitations are compensated for through ALBA which goes beyond the framework of energy cooperation to support social development through economic contributions and new projects for infrastructure. Not only has the energy matrix of the region changed significantly but there is a totally new paradigm shift which has greatly reduced the geopolitical vulnerability of our region thanks to your valued efforts.

PetroCaribe embraces unity, solidarity, and endogenous development in a most realistic way. This path will enable us to rewrite our history as we contemplate with joy and hope the fruits of these new initiatives developed by your esteemed government. My government and the people of St Kitts and Nevis will continue to laud the praises of a country which has understood the struggles and plight of a region scarred by the marks of colonialism.

I thank you, Mr President.

NATIONAL NUTRITION COORDINATORS CONFERENCE – CARIBBEAN FOOD AND NUTRITION INSTITUTE

Food Price Inflation and Food Security in the Caribbean

St Kitts Marriott Resort, November 25–27, 2008

We have gathered here today to deliberate on the impact of rising food prices, to share best practices, and to advocate for sustainable practices that will achieve good nutrition for all.

'*The urgency of now*' are the famous words of Martin Luther King Jr., the US civil rights leader and anti-poverty advocate. It has been given new life and meaning with the advent of president-elect Obama and in the context of the crises in international finance, climate change, fuel production and consumption practices, and the impact on what, how, and how much, we eat.

The term can be applied, most succinctly, to the need to address food price inflation, the risk it poses to food and nutrition security in the Caribbean, and the implementation of action to avert and eradicate extreme hunger in the Caribbean.

I must congratulate the organisers, local and regional, for assembling such a wide range of stakeholders. The multi-faceted approach to food and nutrition security is indicative of the level of collaboration and inclusiveness required to find a solution to reducing the impact of the current crises on all of us, but targeted to relieve its effects on our more vulnerable populations in the Caribbean. We might even arrive at a solution that is applicable globally.

A Caribbean Food and Nutrition Institute (CFNI) document, presented at the May 2008 COTED meeting, showed record increases in the Consumer Price Index of staple foods across the Caribbean. The percentage increases ranged from 16 per cent to 18 per cent in Antigua, Bahamas and Dominica, to 133–230 per cent in Jamaica, Dominican Republic, and Haiti. The range for St Kitts and Nevis was in the region of 22–30 per cent.

The document's compelling argument is that there is a positive correlation between food and nutrition security policies and programmes, and sustaining a good quality of life. It also emphasised the deleterious consequences for our human development goals and the negative impact on targets for the development of our human resources, the Caribbean's most valuable asset, if we do not implement corrective measures urgently.

This challenge will take a combination of political will as well as personal and social responsibility. It will require interventions that will change attitudes towards agricultural production in the Caribbean. It will call attention to the inequities between the developed and developing countries. It requires partnerships, some traditional and others in the form of new and innovative coalitions, all directed to ensuring that our people survive this new century as productive citizens in optimal health.

We have theorised and shall continue to theorise. We have crunched the numbers and will continue to analyse the data. The discourse that reconciles or polarises energy security and food security must be ventilated. Ideas, however, must work in tandem with action-oriented research.

It is time to act. Each day that rising food prices remain a solely academic exercise for policy-makers, nutrition experts, and agriculturalists, more persons drift uncontrollably towards and below the poverty line.

Caribbean Association of Industry and Commerce 93rd Board Meeting

Ocean Terrace Inn, Basseterre, February 5, 2009

Almost every day now, the news is filled with stories of major companies undergoing significant employee cutbacks, temporary and permanent closures, as well as bailouts of corporations deemed too important to go under. These are the times the world finds itself in. As the tentacles of the global economic crisis reach the far corners of the earth, there is one inescapable fact and that is that no country can continue to do business as usual.

Countries around the world have felt the shocks of the high cost of food, excessively high fuel prices, and now, the fall-out from the financial crisis and economic downturn in the economy of the United States. The ripple effect has been astoundingly fast, a true testimony to the reality of globalisation. Everywhere there are reports of declining trade and growth rates. For poor and developing countries, the prevailing global conditions are serious threats to the economic and social gains that have been made over the years. A report of the Economic Commission for Latin America and the Caribbean (ECLAC) suggests there is a risk of reversing the achievements in poverty reduction.

For most such countries, there is little capacity and capability, if any at all, to engage in the kinds of stimulus packages being pursued by those in developed countries. Added to this is the potential for significant reductions in foreign aid which will have a debilitating impact on critical social programmes such as the fight against the spread of HIV/AIDS, and programmes aimed at reducing the levels of poverty in developing countries. Falling remittances, reductions in foreign investment, as well as a declining demand for exports from developing countries, will have a substantial negative impact on the economies of small island developing states such as those here in the Caribbean.

A World Bank review of developing countries reports that

> Investment is expected to bear much of the direct impact of the financial crisis. Investment was the main driving force for developing-country growth over the past five years, contributing almost half of the increase in domestic demand …. There is a risk that investment in developing countries may be headed for a perfect storm with the convergence of slowing world growth and withdrawal of equity and lending from the private sector.

If nothing else, such a proposition must awaken each one of us here in the Caribbean to the essential need to work together to ease the impact of the global crisis on our citizens.

The United Nations Secretary-General, Ban Ki-moon, told the Group of 77 that the cooperation of developing nations is critical to overcome the concurrent crises in finance, climate change, global health, and extreme poverty and warned that these global challenges threaten to undo the progress made towards the development goals of the last decade.

ECLAC projections for growth in Latin America and the Caribbean is 1.9 per cent, down from 4.6 per cent for 2008. Indeed, public financing will come under pressure as governments face the challenges of implementing measure to stabilise economic growth and of providing crucial assistance to the most vulnerable in our populations.

Perhaps now, more than ever, the challenge to regional integration through the instruments of CARICOM and the OECS will be most severe. Circumstances call for assertive action and a high degree of collaboration and coordination as global conditions will impact every sector of our economies including manufacturing, tourism, and agriculture. It must also be understood that national and regional private sector institutions have important roles to play and they must participate fully in the process. We are all in this together.

Meanwhile, we have to remind ourselves that the region's dependence on fossil fuels adds another dimension to our situation. While oil prices are currently low, it is almost certain they will rise again. It should be instructive to all of us that there is a need to explore potential development of alternative energy sources.

Here in St Kitts and Nevis, we have been moving in that direction – geothermal development on Nevis and creating a framework for wind and solar energy development on St Kitts. At the same time, it is critical to push energy conservation and to assist our populations in doing so on a sustainable basis. This has to be effected across the board, across the region, from residential properties to commercial properties, in every sector of our economies. We must not make the mistake of divorcing energy consumption from the prevailing global crisis we now face. This is an opportune time to act in our own interest in this regard.

I am pleased to say that the level of cooperation within CARICOM and the OECS is highly functional and likely to be very productive as we tackle the emerging challenges in our region. Most of you are aware that the recent meeting of the ECCB Monetary Council and the OECS Authority resulted in plans and strategies in response to the global financial and economic crises in the sub-region. Agreed to are mechanisms to coordinate regional and national responses inclusive of policy formulation and implementation, as well as the establishment of a task force, headed by the prime minister of St Vincent and the Grenadines, to provide overall guidance to the action plan.

Among the tasks to be undertaken are securing support from regional and international institutions, countries, and the private sector in an effort to stabilise and improve access to credit and to stimulate investment. All such efforts require strategic programmes in areas such as tourism, fisheries and agriculture, taxation, investment and construction, our social safety nets, energy matters, and of course, transitional arrangements to achieve economic union by the end of this year.

Tourism has been greatly impacted across the region and we must move now to reposition our product. Among other matters, we are particularly cognisant of the need to address critical tourism issues such as tax relief to the sector, helping to secure employment levels, and promoting operational efficiency and reduced operating costs. We have to strengthen partnership programmes, engage in product enhancement, and devise new marketing strategies particularly in preparation for economic recovery in the key marketplaces. Tourism, as a key element of our economic basket, must receive crucial attention along with those sectors that are linked to it.

There is no doubt that the road ahead will be difficult. It will test our creativity as a people, our capabilities and capacities, our willingness to work closely with each other, our commitment to regionalism, and our perseverance. We, as a people of the Caribbean region, have come a long way over the past decades. We must fight to sustain our gains. We must avoid the spectre of isolationism and protectionism. Instead, we must build economic confidence in the region and enhance our economic frameworks now to take advantage of the recovery when it comes.

I am confident that the region will ride through this storm and emerge stronger to face the future. Over the next few days, you will have the opportunity to further understand and explore how the region's private sector can and should be an integral part of the process. I am certain that you have substantial ideas of your own that will be of tremendous benefit to the region.

CARICOM CONFERENCE ON YOUTH CRIME AND VIOLENCE PREVENTION

St Kitts Marriott Resort, June 22, 2009

It is my pleasure to welcome you to this regional conference on youth crime and violence and to thank you for responding to this call to discuss the challenges and the solutions involved. This conference was motivated to a large extent by the high and sometimes increasing wave of crime and violence in our societies and in particular the involvement of our youth. I am glad that Prime Minister Patrick Manning who has lead responsibility for crime and security in the region has been able to grace us with his presence and that the secretary-general has been able to eke out time from his busy schedule to be part of the opening session of this conference. I regret that President Venetiaan and the Suriname delegation were unable to be with us as they advised that travel from Suriname had to be curtailed in view of the number of cases of swine flu that had been detected in that country. We pray for its control and speedy recovery of those affected.

I also wish to thank all those regional and international agencies and in particular the United Nations Office of Drug Control for their collaboration with the government of St Kitts and Nevis in trying to develop a viable programme to combat drugs linked to crime and to focus particularly on our youth

THE NATURE AND SCOPE OF THE PROBLEM

I am aware of the various initiatives that are ongoing in the region and internationally. These form very useful frameworks for the discussions on which we will embark at this meeting. The joint World Bank and United Nations Office for Drug Control 2007 report entitled *Crime, Violence and Development: Trends, Costs and Policy Options in the Caribbean*, fully illustrates the severity of the trends and the economic implications of non-attention to the growing wave of crime and violence in Latin America and the Caribbean. Specifically for the Caribbean, there is a high relationship between illegal arms, illegal drugs, and crime. In addition, the links between crime and security and the millennium development goals are manifested in the life-years lost through violent crime, the health risks associated with drug use, and the economic and social cost in combating the illicit drug trade. I have no doubt that the trends that link crime, security, health, and economic and social determinants in our societies are also reflective of the trends that are aptly portrayed in a study undertaken by The University of the West Indies Centre for Gender Studies on *Gender Differences in Education*, specifically the under-performance of males at all levels of the educational system in the region.

THE FOCUS OF THE RESPONSE

It is necessary for us to focus on the special problems of our youth especially in the case of a recent study by PAHO on health risk behaviours of youth thirteen to fifteen years in the Caribbean:

- As high as 40 per cent use alcohol;
- 30 per cent have used drugs;
- As high as 50 per cent of boys and 25 per cent girls have sexual intercourse;
- A range of 12–25 per cent have contemplated suicide.

It is clear that these problems can only be effectively tackled by the establishment and implementation of partnerships: partnerships involving the private sector, civil society, law enforcement and protective services, as well as international agencies through technical and programme support. It also requires an inter-sectoral approach involving education, health, youth, gender, and culture together with our ministries of planning and finance in implementing educational and promotional programmes to deal with behavioural change. It also requires more sustained research on the part of our higher education institutions to provide the basis of policies that could help to reverse the adverse effects of crime and violence in our societies. These adverse effects all translate into social costs that negate economic growth and our attempts to improve health status and reduce poverty.

The challenge here is enormous. This is the reason why in discussion with my colleagues, I thought it would be necessary for us to brainstorm on a framework for violence prevention in the Caribbean and to understand the reasons for the persistence of gang and youth violence as well as the determinants and risk factors for violence. We have entrusted the thinking on these issues to some of the leading researchers in the region as well as those associated with international agencies that focus on these matters. As a result, we are hoping that what will emerge are best practices for intervention and prevention and for the social safety net mechanisms that focus our attention on rehabilitation and reintegration of our youth into the mainstream of society so that they can utilise their creative talents in a meaningful way.

AN IMPLEMENTATION AGENDA

As we develop a constructive agenda, we must ensure that we incorporate the perspectives of youth in dealing with the challenges confronting them.

I am very pleased to learn that the CARICOM Commission for Youth Development has been involved in extensive discussions throughout the region intent on establishing the risks and challenges youth themselves identify and the dreams and aspirations in which they locate their futures. I am aware that President Venetiaan is very keen for the report of the commission to be discussed at the heads level as soon as it is completed later this year. In the meantime, at this conference, we will no doubt have a preview from our youth panel which will help us to understand much better how we frame solutions and how we incorporate youth as part of these solutions.

Our youth are highly aware of growing treachery and temptations they face on our streets, often by lurking terrorists and greedy criminals intent on expanding their ill-gotten economic gains by using and abusing our youth, women, and children. So how do we take back our streets so that they are safe for our children, our youth, and ourselves?

First, there is the need for a constructive plan of action that will bring together a cross-section of our stakeholders in the form of a national commission for the reduction of crime and violence. It will mean placing emphasis equally on providing our law enforcement services with the training and equipment they need to combat crime as well as promoting community policing. It will mean establishing a regional rapid response mechanism so as to foster greater functional cooperation in fighting crime and fostering crime prevention. In this regard, the establishment of a regional crime and security architecture under the Council of National Security and Law Enforcement and complemented by the Implementation Agency for Crime and Security (IMPACS) is a useful regional endeavour for functional cooperation. Nowhere is this better illustrated than in the events leading up to the Cricket World Cup in 2007 where security arrangements including common surveillance, mass emergency, health, and safety programmes, among others, remain as legacies on which the region can build sustained and sustainable policies on crime and security.

Another regional model that needs to be adopted more widely is the drug demand programme coordinated by the CARICOM secretariat which aims at a series of interventions geared towards youth as well as adults to prevent and reduce their involvement in drug use and abuse. In this context, the issue of substance abuse has also to be confronted with policies and programmes to mitigate its lasting effects and devastating consequences for individuals and our societies.

THE SPECIAL ISSUES IN DRUG DEMAND REDUCTION

There is a school of thought that emphasises harm reduction which postulates that substance abuse is a health malady and ought to be treated as such. An article in a recent book on sexuality, social exclusion and human rights edited by three UWI professors challenges our laws on drug abuse and argues that 'drug policy should shift focus from reducing the scale of the drug market to reducing the negative consequences of the drug war.' There is a common countervailing thought that people who abuse substances are weak and that they need only to get a grip on things, pull themselves up by their bootstraps, stop blaming others, their parents and society, and get on with life. We will not debate the theoretical underpinnings used to frame our perceptions and opinions of who or why people abuse drugs. Rather, I wish for us to ask ourselves the question: What are we doing to assist them, especially the youth?

CARICOM's regional drug demand reduction strategy and plan of action rolls out key elements and interventions for dealing with substance abuse and addiction. Key elements addressed in the strategy and plan of action include: prevention education, treatment and rehabilitation, institutional strengthening, policy development and research. The strategy, taken as a whole, makes perfect sense and provides a useful model that can be rolled out at the national level. The problem for us in St Kitts and for most countries in the OECS and perhaps elsewhere in CARICOM, is capacity, both human and financial, to execute this plan at a national level.

In this regard, I would like to speak for a brief moment on the issue of treatment and rehabilitation. Firstly, we need to know that there is evidence to show that treatment and rehabilitation works. The longer the exposure to interventions, the greater the positive response. Treatment and rehabilitation recognises the value of the lives of substance abusers and gives each another chance to recover and be re-integrated into his/ her community.

Secondly, there are many persons who need to access treatment and are denied because of the absence of programmes to meet their specific needs. This is the case for women and children. The other main reason access to treatment is denied is due to stigma and discrimination, especially against homeless addicts.

The final point I want to make in connection with demand reduction for drugs is that we can do something immediately about improving this situation. I say 'we' because the problem of drug abuse and addiction, like HIV/AIDS, is a development problem. I say 'we' because drug addiction is the 'Pied Piper' luring our most valued assets, our young people, to destruction. I say 'we' because paying the piper will necessitate a concerted effort from my fellow colleagues and you, our valued partners from the university, the business sector, civil society, and the international development community. I pause to acknowledge the critical role that the NGO community is playing in minimising the health and social consequences of substance abuse among street and homeless addicts. We need to strengthen our partnership with them.

Similarly, any effort to curb, control, and eradicate gang violence will also require partnership – partnership between and amongst governments, the NGO community, the church, the schools, and so on. Gang violence is not, as I have said repeatedly, solely a law enforcement problem. Instead, whether here, in the United States, or in Eastern Europe, gang violence is a societal problem, a societal malaise. And so we as a region and as a people are going to have to devise and commit to broad, multi-faceted, and innovative societal solutions.

Let me just share with you the fact that in keeping with this realisation, my government convened a national consultation on crime last December. And at this session, we sought the recommendations of the entire community – teachers, doctors, youth, the business community, politicians, everyone was involved. I am very pleased to say that out of that came a wealth of ideas as to how we, as a society, might join forces to curb and conquer this problem. Since then various churches have been taking their message of inclusion and new beginnings right into the heart of crime-ridden communities. Anti-crime peace marches have been organised. Our ministry of education has initiated a project that urges responsible members of society to go into the schools to volunteer in after-school programmes, thereby re-establishing those inter-generational bonds that were once so strong in Caribbean societies but which, to our great detriment, are now almost gone. And as a direct consequence of this consultation, my government has implemented a second-chance, skills-transfer programme to provide marketable job and life skills to youth in need of these assets. Over one thousand youth are now employed in this YES programme. And although, on the surface, it is a skills-training programme, in truth and in fact it is one of the most effective crime-prevention programmes that I can think of because it gives vulnerable youth hope and confidence, a way out and a way up.

PARTNERSHIPS IN SECURITY COOPERATION

But if these regional policies are to be meaningful, there needs to be a connection with national programmes and therefore building capacity at the national level is necessary to benefit from and implement the regional strategies. It means therefore, establishing or developing new patterns of governance that embrace the inter-sectoral approach and the multi-agency cooperation to which I have already referred.

The issues for security cooperation that were identified in the report of the CARICOM regional task force on crime and security presented to heads of government in 2002 and which have gone through several iterations, puts in context the variety of issues and related challenges for which we need a common regional approach. Among these are developing a regional security strategy, regional information and intelligence sharing, a regional rapid response mechanism, police reform and community policing, a concerted regional effort to stem the illicit drug trade, emphasis on mutual legal assistance, and anti-money laundering programmes in addition to adherence to a regional drug demand policy. The report also places emphasis on a national crime prevention programme and plan of action. It is clear that confronting the challenges of youth violence in this society is part and parcel of a wide array of actions that focus on the wider communities which form the environment and the culture of our youth. It is this environment and these cultural factors that shape the social, economic, and at times criminal, dispositions of our youth that must be tackled.

And while we do not seem to have the exact answers or solutions to the issues that I have raised during the course of this brief review of the situation, it is clear that we have to find them soon. I am hoping that the discourse at this conference will at least point the way forward. I have already alluded to the need for partnerships in confronting these challenges. Hopefully, this conference will more fully identify how to make these partnerships function effectively and commit to a region in which youth violence is minimised and obliterated.

OECS Economic Union
Launch of Public Consultations

Eastern Caribbean Central Bank, Basseterre, September 28, 2009

It is with pride and joy that I participate in this important ceremony to mark the launching in our Federation of public consultations on the proposed OECS Economic Union. I know that the integration movement in the Caribbean has had a somewhat chequered history and it would be tempting for sceptics to view the economic union initiative as just another grandiose economic and social experiment destined for the mounting debris of failed integration initiatives that have littered the history of the Caribbean people.

I am persuaded, however, that it is different this time. Indeed, I do not think that there has been a more propitious time in the history of the Eastern Caribbean for establishment of a truly meaningful economic union capable of ameliorating many of the risks faced by our countries, and of bringing real and tangible benefits to the people of the region. The proposed OECS Economic Union is timely for a number of reasons.

In the first place, the global economic climate dictates that we move rapidly to the next level of integration. The challenges that many of our countries have faced over the past months as a result of the global financial crisis have forced us to put our heads together to arrive at joint solutions to the problems that we face. We have had to develop a stabilisation plan that seeks to coordinate and harmonise a wide range of monetary, fiscal, regulatory, sectoral, and social policies. Many of these policies were considered to be outside the realms of regional decision-making, but in the context of mammoth global challenges, we found it advantageous to cooperate even more broadly and meaningfully for the benefit of the people of the region.

I am convinced that the great collaboration and cooperation demonstrated by our policy-makers during this period of global economic malaise must be continued and enhanced in an appropriate institutional setting. The global crisis will pass but the dynamic nature of global economic relations and the impact of globalisation are such that new challenges will emerge with even greater frequency in the years ahead. Hence, we must quickly put in place the economic union to provide the institutional framework that will foster united or coordinated responses to the challenges that will confront us from time to time.

Secondly, if the countries of the OECS are to achieve levels of growth consistent with continuous improvement in the quality of life of the people of the Eastern Caribbean, we cannot only react to global phenomena. We must also be proactive and actively search out opportunities in the global economy. The deputy managing director of the IMF correctly pointed out recently that 'seizing the opportunities presented by globalisation means by definition increasing integration with the world economy.'

Unfortunately, increasing integration with the global economy is a very treacherous and risky endeavour for a small island state, especially a nation with a population of forty-five thousand. It is therefore critical that the small island states of the OECS combine our resources with a view to realising the benefits of economies of scale and enhancing our bargaining power so that we may compete more effectively in the global marketplace. Similarly, a more tightly integrated OECS will be better equipped to take advantage of opportunities in the CARICOM Single Market and Economy (CSME).

Thirdly, the OECS economic union is timely because it seeks to build on a set of institutions that were facilitated and provided for by the Treaty of Basseterre in 1981 and that have grown from strength to strength over the years. In a sense then, the economic union is the natural next step in the historical evolution of OECS economic integration. Indeed, today's event is the culmination of a more than three-decades-old vision that set in motion one successful collaborative effort after another including the twenty-six-year-old Eastern Caribbean Central Bank, the forty-one-year-old Eastern Caribbean Supreme Court, the twenty-year-old OECS Pharmaceutical Procurement Unit, the nine-year-old Eastern Caribbean Telecommunications Regulatory Authority and, more recently, the Eastern Caribbean Civil Aviation Authority.

Fourthly, dramatic global geo-political shifts over recent decades have diminished the strategic importance of the Caribbean region and we run the risk of marginalisation in global political and economic decisions. Indeed, it is becoming increasingly clear that shared sovereignty through effective collaboration and coordination in a strong union may be an important avenue through which we may protect our national sovereignty and ensure that our voice is heard in international forums.

Finally, I am convinced that the OECS Economic Union is timely because the people of the region have seen the benefits of collaboration through the existing OECS institutions and they are now ready for the next step. I cannot help but detect a sense of frustration among our people over the relatively slow pace of regional integration. This is vastly different from the situation that existed when the West Indies Federation collapsed because integration is not being pushed upon us by outside forces. Instead, it is being recognised by our people as a potential force for significant social and economic transformation.

I am confident, therefore, that the consultation process that is being launched today will be fruitful and constructive and it will give our people the opportunity to play their part in shaping future Caribbean society.

As for me, I am proud to share in this momentous event that I believe will help to unite our people as we push the wheels of social and economic progress forward. The creation of a single economic space in the region will give our people more room to express and manifest their immense talents and capabilities and will prepare them to venture confidently into global waters in search of opportunities. The economic union will also provide the framework for the people of the Caribbean to pool their efforts to fight crime and other social ills and to build stronger and more effective institutions for the continued development and safeguarding of our society. This was the vision of the founders of the political party that I have the honour and privilege of leading today.

The integration of the Caribbean has been an important policy plank of every Labour administration that has held office in St Kitts and Nevis. Indeed, our First National Hero, the Right Excellent Sir Robert Bradshaw, played an important role in the West Indies Federation and actively supported the establishment of the Caribbean Free Trade Association (CARIFTA) and the Caribbean Community (CARICOM). When the Federation collapsed, he did not give up on the dream of political union in the Caribbean and he was one of the leading proponents of the Grenada Declaration of 1971 which sought to bring a number Eastern Caribbean countries into a political union with Guyana. Today, I believe that integration is the vision of our people as a whole and I urge each of you to participate fully in the consultation process and etch your mark in the continued evolution of the regional integration movement.

EXPO CAGUAS 2009
Puerto Rico, September 30, 2009

I am delighted to extend the best wishes and greetings of the government and people of St Kitts and Nevis as well as member countries of the Organisation of Eastern Caribbean States (OECS), to the mayor and the good citizens of the City of Caguas.

As chair of the Eastern Caribbean countries that are members of the OECS, I can tell you that we welcome your invitation to participate in this exposition as it represents new efforts to develop practical and mutual relations between Puerto Rico and the Eastern Caribbean countries. This is a very good thing, for I believe that in the short- to medium-terms such relations will facilitate enhanced trade, tourism, and general commerce between our countries and strengthen the Puerto Rico/Eastern Caribbean partnership.

Expo Caguas 2009 can be perceived as the latest spark in the new building processes between us. Moreover, it gives reality to earlier and significant initiatives that were undertaken between Puerto Rico and the OECS. Some of you may recall that in 2006 the OECS established an office, with consular attributes, here in Puerto Rico. It was a watershed achievement in relations between Puerto Rico and the OECS and a wonderful example of regionalism at work, an important illustration of cooperation and collaboration. Among the responsibilities of this office is the stimulation of trade, tourism, and investment promotions, all representative of the new outward looking approaches that are being adopted by the OECS. It is also indicative of the economic environment that points to the need for greater economic interaction for sustainable development. Therefore, we can expect that the office will grow in its capacity and capability and provide important commercial support to Puerto Rico and Eastern Caribbean businesses.

The other important point of collaboration took place earlier this year when an agreement was signed between the University of Puerto Rico and the OECS secretariat providing for nationals of OECS member countries who enroll at the university to be accorded the same status as Puerto Rican students with all of the attendant benefits and advantages.

This is a substantial achievement that allows for the pursuit of higher education that is affordable and education that is of excellent standard. Falling under a 2004 Memorandum of Understanding between the government of Puerto Rico and the OECS member countries to facilitate joint initiatives in functional cooperation in agriculture, education, trade, investment, environmental management, justice, air and seaports, security, and policy, the agreement with the University of Puerto Rico will ultimately result in beneficiary students being excellent ambassadors for the Commonwealth of Puerto Rico.

Also coming out of the 2004 MOU have been other important developments including the appointment of an Honourary Consul, official visits of Eastern Caribbean OECS prime ministers to Puerto Rico, the attendance of a former Puerto Rico secretary of state to an OECS authority meeting, and of course, the hosting of an OECS ministers of tourism meeting in this lovely city of Caguas. Let me take this opportunity to express the appreciation of OECS member states to our Honourary Consul for his diligent representation of our interests to the government and people of Puerto Rico.

All of this, in my view, places the context of Expo Caguas 2009 as one that signifies a new level of interaction between our countries. Caguas and its many industries and services is an ideal point of contact for Eastern Caribbean business interests. It is potentially a point of contact for the mutual exploration of a wide array of products, services, tourism, and investment. Through events such as Expo Caguas and other initiatives, we can safely say that we have begun a process that can only lead to further improvement in the quality of life for the people in our countries.

Our Caribbean islands have had a common historical background that was anchored in agricultural commodities such as sugar, bananas, coffee, cotton, and rum. Our trading relations in the late twentieth century reflected those bonds between the Caribbean, Europe, and the United States.

Today, traditional economic ties are being broken in an environment of trade liberalisation and globalisation. For small island economies, it is both a potential benefit as well as a real challenge. The Caribbean can no longer afford to be inward looking but must solidly become an effective player on the global stage by maximising advantages and effectively presenting them to the world. As an example, in my own country we have had to face the challenge of rebuilding an economy which is now based on trade in services rather than on the export of sugar, which was our main industry for many years. As a result, many areas of land that were formally under sugar cultivation have been made available to investors for the development of hotel resorts, golf courses, universities, marinas, and other mixed uses and we have been reaping benefits from this initiative. The St Kitts Investment Promotion Agency (SKIPA) which was established in December 2007 to facilitate investment into St Kitts, has been receiving requests from many interested persons and corporations wishing to establish businesses or to develop properties and resorts on the island. The Park Hyatt has just recently signed a deal to develop its first 5-star Caribbean hotel in St Kitts which is a significant achievement for such a young tourist destination.

OECS members are now embarking upon a new journey through the currently proposed OECS Economic Union. The 'experiment' with the OECS functional cooperation framework has worked exceedingly well for us. Now it is time to move to a new level. This kind of cooperation and collaboration is of immense importance to the survival of small states in the Eastern Caribbean. After all, strong and stable countries create the basic foundation for health, wealth, and opportunities. When we think about repositioning the Caribbean region therefore, let us think about these five points in the process.

We must dig deep within ourselves and determine what are our advantages and know how to package ourselves in an ever-changing economic environment.

We must diligently work to harness our God-given natural resources that can be a source of renewable energy – green energy. Our university-trained engineers must think along those lines and become innovators in their own right.

For many of us, tourism has become a major engine of growth and development. Yet, we know how challenging it can be. Visitors' perceptions, wants, and needs are influenced by socio-economic factors that translate into a variety of trends. I believe that in recent decades, the Caribbean has surfed the waves of tourism in a manner that will no longer be most effective. As a region responding to the current global environment, we still struggle to create a highly effective brand. We must accelerate our efforts in anticipation of the future rebound of world financial and economic conditions. At the core of our strategies, however, must be attention to our environment, respect for and use of our culture and heritage, a re-think of the ways we use energy, the effective development of our human resources in a diversity of areas, and making the cross-linkages between tourism and other areas of the economy work. We must, of course, present the region with distinctiveness in look, feel, and experience. Excellence and value must also be our watchwords.

Future development and investment in infrastructure will of necessity have to be modern, competitive, creative, and marketable on global standards. ICT will have to be integral to developmental processes. Policy and legal frameworks must facilitate Caribbean modernisation in both the public and private sectors. The challenge is about anticipating future needs in the marketplace and it is also about meeting the aspirations of the Caribbean people.

Isolationism and individualism have their place in future socio-economic environments but make no mistake, sustainable results will have to be predicated upon new and different levels of regional cooperation and collaboration. This is the reality today, the necessary ingredients to function in an international arena.

I leave you with these thoughts. Expo Caguas 2009 is a special event of regional significance. The work that is done long after the doors of the exposition have closed will determine longer-term areas of success for all participants. It is a wonderful tool, and I am pleased that member states of the OECS have had an opportunity to be a part of it. I believe that the Caribbean has a unique opportunity to shine. In all the gloom that prevails globally, we as people of the Caribbean must rise to the occasion. Let us not be stymied by our size. It is our chance to be inventive and creative with the resources at our disposal. Let us together strive for a new vision for tomorrow by working together today.

Revised Treaty of Basseterre
Address by the OECS Chairman

Sandals Beach Resort, Gros Islet, St Lucia, June 18, 2010

The eighteenth day of June 2010 is a particularly proud day for the citizens of the OECS. On this day, while we celebrate the story of twenty-nine successful years, we also make history, for it is today that we chart the course for a truly bright future. Today, as we toast the past, we defy the skeptics and the cynics and confirm and live up to the expectations of those who have shown faith in our region, its leaders, and its people. Today is the beginning of a continuation, another turn in our OECS journey towards self-fulfillment and achievement. And I, just a citizen tasked with leadership, feel exceptionally proud, yet humbled, to be associated with the proceedings to be conducted today.

A Proud Record of Success

Since 1981, June 18 has held special significance for us, for it was on that day twenty-nine years ago that the founding fathers of our organisation affixed their signatures to the Treaty Establishing the Organisation of Eastern Caribbean States, commonly referred to as the Treaty of Basseterre after the city in which it was signed. And what a legacy they have left us!

As it marks the beginning of the thirtieth year of its existence, the OECS stands as the leading integration grouping of micro-states in the world. With a total land area of approximately 1,000 square miles and a population of just under six hundred thousand, it boasts a record of success in integration far greater than its physical size and resource capacity would lead one to expect. This success can be measured by the high quality and international reputation of its flagship institutions.

For the last forty years, long before the formal establishment of the organisation, the people of the OECS have benefitted from the operation of a single, fully functional regional judiciary, the OECS Supreme Court. This institution finds no parallel in the world except perhaps with the European Court of Justice.

Since 1965, long before it was ever contemplated by our friends in Europe, OECS member states have enjoyed a single currency, the Eastern Caribbean Dollar, which stands today as one of the most stable currencies in the world. It must be noted that our EC dollar has maintained a fixed rate of exchange to the US dollar for the past thirty-four years. And of course, this currency and the entire banking system within the OECS is managed and regulated by a single authority of the highest repute, the Eastern Caribbean Central Bank.

Another institution of long standing is the Eastern Caribbean Civil Aviation Authority, which boasts a successful record in the management and regulation of airspace and civil aviation within the OECS.

The region's success at integration is also evident in the establishment and successful operation of other institutions of more recent vintage but of equally high international standing, such as the Eastern Caribbean Stock Exchange, established upon a platform that is one of the most technologically advanced; the Eastern Caribbean Telecommunications Authority, the single authority for oversight of a fully liberalised telecommunications sector; and the OECS Pharmaceutical Procurement Service which has realised tremendous benefits for the regional health sector through the joint procurement of pharmaceuticals. Indeed, the OECS approach to the procurement of pharmaceuticals has attracted much interest in various parts of the developing world.

And there are numerous other successes which the OECS has achieved through pursuits such as joint diplomatic representation in major international capitals and institutions and policy harmonisation and coordination in various spheres of human endeavour including critical areas such as energy, tourism, air transportation, health, education, judicial reform, and foreign policy and trade negotiations.

These successes have resulted in a dramatic increase in the international profile and stature of the OECS with its development model and success story being promoted internationally to other Small Island Developing States. Additionally, the organisation's success has attracted the attention of many countries and institutions with a significant number of them seeking to develop and enter into various forms of closer relationship. Within the last seventeen months alone, six countries, including four from the European Union, have established diplomatic relations with the OECS.

The successes of the OECS are truly amazing when viewed against the backdrop of an international environment that is so hostile to Small Island Developing States. Those of us who are now charged with the responsibility of leadership of this great organisation owe it to the founding fathers and to future generations to guard jealously the legacy which has been bequeathed to us. We have as an imperative to consolidate the gains that have been made thus far and undertake the engineering which will place the organisation on a stronger footing and at a higher institutional level, in order that it can withstand the persistent threats and the new and emerging challenges that are a hallmark of our times.

THE MAKING OF HISTORY

While we celebrate the past, we have come together in the main to herald the future, to witness and to engage in a symbolic re-enactment of that aforementioned historic event, by affixing our own signatures to the successor treaty, the Revised Treaty of Basseterre Establishing the Organisation of Eastern Caribbean States Economic Union. This seminal and far-reaching document will stand through history as testimony to our maturity as a people and a testament of our faith in each other and in our collective future.

But we are not here engaged in mere symbolism. We are engaged truly in the making of history by meeting frontally the demands that history has made of us. And even as it makes its demands, history is generous in its offering of lessons and precedent. In 1981 the founding fathers of our organisation were seeking to consolidate the achievements which had been made up to that point through joint action in respect of the governance of the region, and to formalise related institutional arrangements to guide such action into the future.

They were also reacting out of sheer necessity to the reality of new and emerging circumstances. In 1962, the Caribbean experimental ship, the *S.S. West Indies Federation,* foundered on the rocks of apparently irreconcilable differences when the plug was pulled in Dr Eric Williams's now famous mathematical aphorism, 'one from ten leaves nothing!' Those who appeared better able and equipped swam each to the safety of their own independence, leaving the most vulnerable of those on that ship to face the turbulent waters that threatened to overwhelm them. But they picked up the pieces of the wrecked ship, banded themselves together, and fashioned their own survival craft which they would use and continue to reshape to take them ever forward, notwithstanding what they were to encounter on that journey. This was the foundation of what we are observing today. This was the genesis of the OECS.

Following the experiences of the 1960s, the world of the 1970s and beyond had become even more challenging, dangerous, and uncertain. By the early 1980s, as newly independent micro-states, vulnerable, on their own for the first time, no longer assured of the protection of the so-called 'mother country,' but fiercely determined to prove their maturity, they had seen the wisdom and value of joint action and had found great comfort in it.

In this regard, the leadership of the day saw the necessity of formalising the existing institutional arrangements and relationships between their countries at the highest level, via treaty. They were making a statement not merely to themselves but to the wider world as well that they were taking the relationship among their countries to a higher level. It was as if history had made a particular demand of them, that the existing global realities required a new political construct if there was to be a chance for survival. Thus they had to move on with what had been put in place in the 1960s.

LEST WE FORGET

History has shown that our founding fathers stood up to the challenge and responded well to the demands made of them. As I have done on previous occasions, I again wish to acknowledge, publicly, the contribution which they have made to the history of our organisation and our region. As we prepare to advance on and to re-shape that most historically defining act, I am moved, lest we forget, to make special mention of those individuals who laid the foundation from the 1960s, or who brought the OECS into being through the Treaty of Basseterre in 1981, some of whom are still with us – persons like Dr Kennedy Simmonds of St Kitts and Nevis, Lester Bird of Antigua and Barbuda, Austin Bramble, John Osborne and Franklyn Margetson of Montserrat, and Allan Louisy of St Lucia. There are those who have passed on – persons such as Robert Llewellyn Bradshaw of St Kitts and Nevis, Vere Cornwall Bird of Antigua and Barbuda, Dame Mary Eugenia Charles of Dominica, Eric Matthew Gairy, Herbert Blaize, and Maurice Bishop of Grenada, Sir John Compton and Winston Cenac of St Lucia, and Milton Cato and Hudson Tannis of St Vincent and the Grenadines. Their very names resound through the corridors of time as the titans who shaped the collective destiny of the OECS through their will and foresight.

A Challenge Historically Similar

The world has undergone a profound and dramatic transformation since that time in 1981, from the end of the cold war and the attendant loss of strategic value by the Caribbean to the new reality of a unipolar world in terms of the projection of military power; globalisation and the emergence of new economic blocs, and the promotion, spread, and enforcement of trade liberalisation via the authority of the WTO; the emergence of the Asian Tigers, and now the BRICs (Brazil, Russia, India and China) as potential new global economic powerhouses, in particular the transformation of China and Brazil and their emergence as major forces in the world economy with a commensurate growing political weight; the dramatic re-design of the criteria for superpower status; the geometric improvements in computer engineering and ICT; genetic engineering and its implications for agriculture and health. I could go on and on.

What has become crystal clear however, is that we, the current generation of the leadership of the OECS, are faced with a challenge historically similar to that faced by the founding fathers in 1981, and that is: How to ensure in the face of a dramatically, continually changing global reality, that the member states and the organisation of which they are constituent parts, will be able to maintain relevance and the capacity to deliver on the goals and aspirations of their citizens well into the future. This is the essence of the challenge which history has placed before us. So how are we to respond?

Seizing the Moment

Some five years ago, it became clear to the leadership of our organisation that the member states and the organisation itself were at a particular historical juncture where decisions needed to be made which would determine whether we move forward in keeping with the demands of our time, or whether we remain at rest, in a state of stasis.

As in 1981, the leaders of our organisation had come to the conclusion that there was a necessity for the design of a totally new construct if the organisation was to remain relevant and capable of responding to new and emerging challenges at the national, regional, and international levels.

As with their forbears twenty-four years before, they became convinced that there remained no other meaningful or realistic option available to them but to further deepen the level of integration among the member states. This deepening pointed in only one direction, to the logical next step in the integration process, that of economic union. And so, on the occasion of the 25th anniversary of the organisation, the OECS authority decided with great resolve to seize the moment and agreed formally to proceed toward the establishment of an economic union of the OECS, through the signing of an agreement of intent.

LESSONS FROM A CRISIS

Events since then at the national, regional, and international levels have proven not only the timeliness of that decision, but its correctness as well. Within the last two to three years for example, our region has had to endure the devastating effects of the global financial and economic crisis. During that period, we witnessed an already complex international financial landscape being rendered even more complicated and dangerous by a financial and economic crisis of a kind never experienced since the Great Depression. Our experience of the collapse of international capital markets, including on the home front the triple trauma of the CLICO, Stanford, and British American failures, confirmed very forcefully the role of the OECS and its institutional machinery in securing the fortunes of member states.

One shudders to contemplate what would have become of Antigua and Barbuda after the Stanford debacle had there been no OECS. And even then, mere membership of an integration grouping would have been insufficient. In the final analysis, what saved the day was the quality of the institutional machinery and arrangements which are at the heart of the OECS enterprise, and the speed with which they were mobilised in response to the crisis. One recalls the resolve and decisiveness with which the monetary council through the ECCB intervened to restore stability, credibility, and respectability to the OECS financial sector in the wake of these failures. That resolve was also matched by the OECS secretariat who for the past four years or so, at the behest of the authority had embarked on a process of representing the region's strategic interests through the development of relationships at the regional level, with non-traditional partners in different parts of the world, a move which has brought dividends by way of mobilisation of unprecedented levels of developmental resources. Today it is absolutely clear that in the absence of the OECS and its associated institutional arrangements, the fate of the countries which make up the organisation would have already been sealed in a negative and most deleterious manner.

DESIGNING THE ECONOMIC UNION – LESSONS FROM A PROCESS

The process of designing the mechanisms for the OECS Economic Union is one which holds important lessons for us. A major lesson speaks to the wisdom of ensuring that popular consultation and engagement was a central feature of the process. Throughout the length and breadth of each of the member states of the OECS, organisational structures were established across sectors, demographic groups, and other relevant categories. These structures facilitated consultations of various kinds including interactive town hall meetings, formal and informal lectures, seminars, and workshops to explain the meaning and significance of the economic union concept and the benefits to be derived. Most importantly however, the consultations sought to obtain from members of the public their own views on the economic union concept, its desirability and applicability in their current circumstances, and in particular, ideas for incorporation into the design of the institutions and arrangements to underpin them.

The process has allowed not only a greater understanding of the economic union by the people of the OECS, but also a popular identification with it. A feature of the economic union arrangements which has fired the popular imagination relates to the provisions for the movement of persons. Unlike the free movement provisions of the CARICOM Single Market and Economy, the provisions for the movement of persons in the OECS Economic Union protocol make no distinction. Instead, it secures the free movement of citizens of protocol member states within the economic union area, and requires that such movement 'entail the abolition of any discrimination based on nationality between citizens of the Protocol Member States as regards employment, remuneration, and other conditions of work and employment.' While these are certainly bold provisions, they are a necessary element of the new construct, and their popular appeal facilitates acceptance at the political level. This reflects the well-entrenched sense of community that is so evident among OECS citizens.

The process also provided us with a lesson which points to the value and power of compromise and accommodation. Over the last four years, representatives of OECS member states have been engaged in negotiations at a number of levels. At the political level of heads of government in particular, we have been meeting, working long and hard, quietly and without fanfare, to iron out problems and to work around or to remove obstacles to progress. Inspired by the goal of economic union and guided by the objectives established in relation to the process, many compromises were made. Indeed, the OECS could not have arrived at this juncture were it not for the tremendous spirit of compromise which prevailed and which was exhibited by all. We were all motivated by that sense of a common purpose, the continued integration of our people and our efforts to improve welfare. We allowed nothing to distract our eyes from that ball, and we were always prepared to do what was needed to be done to move the process forever forward.

ACKNOWLEDGEMENTS

The journey has been long and hard, but never once have we questioned the goal. Our confidence and our resolve are resolute.

There are many who deserve our thanks and our commendations for their contribution to the success of our enterprise thus far. I must thank my colleague heads of government, past and present, for staying the course through all the difficult moments and providing inspiration to all those others toiling in the vineyard. I trust that Sir James Mitchell, former prime minister of St Vincent and the Grenadines will see this generation of leaders as those providing an answer to the question he posed in Tortola, Virgin Islands in 1987, 'To be, or not to be...?'

But I wish to single out for special mention two of my colleagues who have given so much to this venture. Dr Ralph Gonsalves, prime minister of St Vincent and the Grenadines, is one of those persons who has played a leading role throughout this process. From the earliest days he served with distinction as prime ministerial spokesperson and he has been providing intellectual and political direction to the process down to the very end. In similar manner, at the start of this exercise, Dr Kenny Anthony, former prime minister of St Lucia, had been a tower of strength. It was under his chairmanship that this project started in earnest. He too provided intellectual and political guidance to the process ensuring that it was charted through the complexities of constitutional consistency.

These two gentlemen have been true champions of this cause and are truly deserving of our recognition and our thanks.

I must also thank the members of the OECS Economic Union Task Force under the chairmanship of Sir Dwight Venner for their tireless efforts in support of this process, particularly in respect of the design of the Revised Treaty. The secretariat of our organisation, soon to be transformed into a commission, itself also a member of the task force, under the leadership of its indefatigable Director-General Dr Len Ishmael, has been most faithful to the process providing every necessary logistical and technical support to ensure that we attained our goal by the deadline which we had set ourselves. As chairman of the OECS, I convey to all of these persons and bodies the authority's deepest appreciation.

Finally, the people of this OECS region, they are the most deserving. They are the ones who have been clamouring over the years for closer union. They are the ones who have provided the inspiration and the motivation. They are the ones who deserve and should receive our greatest praise. On behalf of my colleague heads of government I say thank you, over and over again.

STEPPING FORWARD, BOLDLY

Certain simple truths are learnt from the circumstances which life throws upon us. Some, the old fables and stock of folk wisdom taught to us in our youth by our parents and teachers, never leave us, such truths as, for example, 'time and tide waits for no man.' I am also reminded of a famous quote from Shakespeare's political classic *Julius Caesar* which speaks so eloquently to our current circumstances, and which I beg you to ponder. It goes thus:

> *There is a tide in the affairs of men,*
> *Which, taken at the flood leads on to fortune;*
> *Omitted, all the voyage of their life*
> *Is bound in shallows and in miseries.*
> *On such a full sea are we now afloat;*
> *And we must take the current when it serves,*
> *Or lose our ventures.*

I leave you these simple, yet profound lines from the master of the word, whose vast reservoir holds for us so many of the lessons of life.

History has taught us that we, as Caribbean people, have the capacity for greatness. Indeed, in this land of two Nobel laureates I can assert with the greatest confidence that we can accomplish anything once we set our minds to it. It befalls us therefore, to prove to the world, which is watching and waiting, that we are indeed capable of meeting the demands that history is making of us. In meeting that great responsibility we can also provide leadership to those among us in the wider region who hesitate, unsure of the course, being not yet convinced that the demands of history are non-negotiable, and that '… we must take the current when it serves, or lose our ventures.'

I see our achievement here today as one in keeping with Divine guidance – 'Behold, how good it is for brethren to dwell together in Unity.' In this vein, the inspiring words of a son of the OECS, Patrick Prescod of St Vincent and the Grenadines come to mind:

> *The Right Hand of God, is pointing in our land,*
> *Pointing the way we must go…*
> *In these many-peopled lands*
> *Let his Children all join hands,*
> *And be one with the Right Hand of God.*

And so, in the full knowledge that I speak to the converted, I say 'Come, let us step forward boldly, to meet the demands of history.'

Pan Caribbean Partnership Against HIV/AIDS (PANCAP)
and the
US President's Plan for AIDS Relief (PEPFAR)
Inaugural Meeting
Hilton Hotel, Barbados, January 12–13, 2011

It is my pleasure to have been invited to speak to you at this very important session convened by the United States government. I wish to convey special thanks to the PEPFAR Regional Coordinator and his staff for your kind invitation to address this first annual meeting of the Caribbean Regional Framework for HIV/AIDS. This initiative has been one of the outstanding examples of the technical assistance of the US to the world as it grapples with this pernicious disease of HIV and AIDS.

It has to be noted that since the US President's Emergency Plan for AIDS Relief (PEPFAR) was launched in 2003 to combat global HIV/AIDS, the financial commitment of up to US$48 billion for an accelerated approach to global HIV/AIDS, tuberculosis, and malaria, has been the largest commitment by any nation in history to combat a single disease. While in the earlier dispensations of bilateral arrangements, the Caribbean beneficiaries were limited to the highly indebted poor countries (HIPC) including the Dominican Republic, Guyana, and Haiti from this region, the United States *Global Leadership Against HIV/AIDS, Tuberculosis, and Malaria Reauthorisation Act* of 2008 expanded the US commitment to all CARICOM countries.

This act is very significant. It accords with the spirit of CARICOM's response to these diseases and to the position which the CARICOM heads of government articulated to the then Bush administration during the celebrated US-Caribbean dialogue held in Washington, DC in June 2007. This legislation expands the US government's commitment to a programme of activities for five additional years, from 2009 through

2013. It is an example to our other partners in the developed world. Nowhere is this better illustrated than in the consistently high level of contributions of the United States to the Global Fund for HIV/AIDS, TB, and Malaria at a time when other developed countries are wavering in their support. Reductions in support could immeasurably reverse the gains of the past decade that have resulted in the modest but steady decline in prevalence rates, reductions in mother-to-child transmission (MTCT), increased access to anti-retroviral treatment (ART), and increased emphasis on human rights.

In the case of the collaboration between the US and the Caribbean, we are deeply appreciative of the enlightened approach that has been taken to link the support from PEPFAR to the Caribbean Regional Strategic Framework 2008–2013. This framework is the flagship of the Pan-Caribbean Partnership against HIV/AIDS to which all CARICOM member states and other partners of the French, Dutch, and English-speaking Caribbean, including the Dominican Republic and Cuba, subscribe. This investment by the US through PEPFAR fully endorses the philosophy of the CARICOM heads of government that strengthening regional capabilities to combat HIV, especially for small countries like those in the Caribbean, is one way to maximise resources and foster a collective and viable response.

While there is no need to repeat the statistics in a gathering such as this one, it is necessary to reflect on the fact that this region has demonstrated to the world what can be achieved through acting collectively in the face of adversity. The *Nassau Declaration; The health of the Region is the wealth of the Region,* resulting from the conference of heads of government in the Bahamas in July 2001, was the very first activity anywhere in the world that followed up on the bold call at the UN Special Assembly in June 2001 by then Secretary-General Kofi Annan for establishing a global fund for HIV/AIDS. Stimulated by the outcome of that conference, the CARICOM Heads of Government meeting in Nassau resolved that the Pan-Caribbean Partnership against HIV and AIDS would be one of its two pillars, with Caribbean Cooperation in Health as the other.

History has since revealed the prescience of the Nassau Declaration. First PANCAP, with its unique network and composition of governmental, private sector, non-governmental, and development partners has attracted over US$80 million in ten years for its strategic framework and in the process has been designated an international best practice. Caribbean cooperation in health, on the other hand, is about to take on new meaning with the establishment of the Caribbean Public Health Agency (CARPHA) in another couple of months which will consolidate five regional health institutions into one agency.

While others will speak to the technical details of the regional and country programmes that fall under the framework that is being discussed, I wish to deal with the parameters that define the tasks that confront us. In this regard the conjuncture of PANCAP and CARPHA is indeed consistent with the prevailing regional discussion resulting from the seminal report of the *Caribbean Commission on Health and Development* (2006) chaired by Sir George Alleyne, and *Port of Spain Declaration: Unifying to fight the non Communicable Diseases* (2007). It is also consistent with global discussions on the achievement of the Millennium Development Goals on health and HIV and the health sector response to HIV that featured in the discussions at the international HIV/AIDS conference in Vienna in 2010. It is moreover consistent with the initiatives of the current US administration for a coalition of global health advocacy organisations to consider how US development assistance for health should be structured in the future.

It seems to me that the celebration of the 10th anniversary of the Nassau Declaration in July 2011 provides the Caribbean with a golden opportunity to provide another regional best practice to the world by bringing together organisations focused on HIV/AIDS and infectious diseases, child health, maternal health, sexual and reproductive health and rights, the health workforce, neglected diseases, and comprehensive primary healthcare. This would no doubt help in breaking down silos that too often prevent coordinated advocacy efforts and a progressive vision of what the next phase of global health and development could look like. Maybe that discussion can begin right here at this consultation.

In this regard, UNAIDS ten priority areas in the *Joint Action for Results: UNAIDS Outcome Framework 2009–2011*, seem most appropriate to the objectives of the PEPFAR programme for 2010–2015. The ten areas are:

- reduce sexual transmission of HIV;
- prevent mothers from dying and babies from becoming infected with HIV;
- ensure that people living with HIV receive treatment;

- prevent people living with HIV from dying of tuberculosis;
- protect drug users from becoming infected with HIV;
- empower men who have sex with men, sex workers, and transgender people to protect themselves from HIV infection and to fully access anti-retroviral therapy;
- remove punitive laws, policies, practices, stigma, and discrimination that block effective responses to AIDS;
- meet the HIV needs of women and girls and stop sexual and gender-based violence;
- empower young people to protect themselves from HIV;
- enhance social protection for people affected by HIV.

The UNAIDS Outcome Framework therefore covers all the priority areas in the Caribbean Regional Strategic Framework. What, however, is critical for the discussions at this PEPFAR forum is how the priority areas are identified and how they can be implemented so that they directly contribute simultaneously toward achieving the country-set universal access targets for HIV/AIDS prevention, care, and treatment and the Millennium Development Goals by 2015. This is possible only if we see our priorities as interlinked, and hence, progress in one area contributing to progress in others.

The significance of this forum is that it launches a year in which we have an opportunity to benchmark a series of successes in activities that will mark the 10th anniversary of the signing of the PANCAP Agreement which took place right here in Barbados on February 14, 2001; the establishment of CARPHA possibly in Grenada in March; the tenth anniversary of the Nassau Declaration in July 2001; and the UN Special Assembly on Non-Communicable Diseases that is intricately linked to the Port of Spain Declaration (2007).

Let us therefore use this occasion well and let us continue the proud tradition of health and development in the Caribbean.

CARICOM COUNCIL FOR FOREIGN AND COMMUNITY RELATIONS (COFCOR)

St Kitts Marriott Resort, May 4, 2011

We meet at a time of unprecedented global tumult. Before we are able to fully absorb the scope and implications of one social, economic, or natural disaster, another emerges, as if to test mankind's ability to absorb and respond.

From the devastation inflicted on Haiti one year ago to the socio-political tumult sweeping North Africa. From the earthquakes that have rocked Chile, New Zealand, and elsewhere, to the financial crisis that almost toppled Wall Street, the rest of the United States, and the rest of the world. From the strife throughout the Middle East, to the 'tsunami of zero-mercy' that tore across Japan, change – and rapid change – is now the order of the day. And the warp-speed technological capabilities of the twenty-first century, combined with galloping globalisation, bring these global crises almost instantaneously right to the Caribbean's doors, whether in the form of economic, environmental, diplomatic, climactic, or other consequences.

Whatever CARICOM's efforts in the past, and whatever our successes of yesteryear, this moment in world history, and this moment in Caribbean history, demands a special marshalling of our manpower, financial, diplomatic, and other resources to skillfully analyse, predict, plan, pre-empt, and respond – or not respond – to these respective and rapidly evolving international scenarios.

In Lewis Carroll's *Alice in Wonderland*, we are reminded that if one does not know where one wishes to go, any road will get you there. In this era of global economic, cultural, environmental, and other uncertainties, we in CARICOM must maintain a clear vision of exactly where it is that we are trying to go socially, economically, and politically. And we must have the structures, the communications systems, and the built-in flexibility to enable us to adjust and adapt our strategies – not our principles, but our strategies – as the world around us changes. And it is this clarity of vision that will enable us in the pursuit, in the forging, and in the nurturing of relations with third countries, to protect the social, economic, environmental, and other interests of our region.

We have spoken before within CARICOM of the principles that should shape and instruct our foreign policy conduct, among them:

i. development and preservation of our identity, way of life, democratic systems, and economic space;

ii. ensuring the sustainability of small states within the international community;

iii. adherence to the principles of good governance;

iv. maintenance of the peace, security, and territorial integrity of the community;

v. adherence to the purposes and principles of the United Nations;

vi. adherence to treaty commitments.

What are our strengths as a region as we face this sometimes daunting global scenario?

First of all, CARICOM is not an entity held together by contrived linkages. Instead, the histories of our individual states are almost identical. Therein lies our strength, our commonality. And it is this commonality, along with our reputation as stable democracies, our highly literate populations, our respect for political freedoms, and so on, that will be key to our ability to forge foreign policies that redound to the benefit both of our component national parts as well as to the broader region as a whole.

It is not only history and these other attributes that we share, however. And while they may be positive, another shared feature is the size of our respective nations. To many, we are, indeed, 'micro-states.' And in the world of geo-strategic wrangling, being small is not always an advantage. Indeed, it rarely is. As a region, then, we must continue to put countervailing strategies in place in order to compensate for any natural disadvantages associated with our size as we pursue mutually beneficial relations with third countries. And it is my view that in the context of current world conditions, the constant strengthening of our region's negotiating capabilities must be recognised as a crucial component of our region's efforts to skillfully advance its interests. And this must be undergirded by rigorous training, because the challenges that we face demand it. And in addition to our heightened capabilities, well-coordinated approaches to foreign policy formulation must be considered sacrosanct.

The failure of the World Trade Organisation to agree on a new category of small vulnerable economies constitutes a major threat to the region's socio-economic and political well-being. The erosion of preferential market access in trading relations has caused many of us to take drastic steps. We certainly have in St Kitts and Nevis. As you know, we were forced several years ago to rapidly restructure our entire economy in order to avert social and economic disaster.

In addition, there are the challenges that countries like ours face as a result of the premature denial of concessional funding at the World Bank, the International Monetary Fund, and the Inter-American Development Bank. This constitutes a *de facto* penalty for our attempts to move our nations steadily forward and this too must be addressed.

And then, there are the new resource burdens that we all must now bear due to the heightened security standards necessitated by the rise of global terrorism beyond our shores.

You, esteemed colleagues, are perfectly familiar with these issues. Our task then is to forge the type of relations with third countries that will enable us to leverage mutually respectful, mutually beneficial relations into articulated support of, and advocacy for, these matters which are so important to our region and which will have such a powerful bearing on the lives of those who elected and sent us here.

We have acknowledged in the past the normal inclination of nations in times of economic vulnerability to focus more intently on their own social and economic well-being, as opposed to the broader interests of the regions to which they may belong. Even as we strive to enhance the socio-economic prospects of our own nations during this period of global turbulence however, let us as a region also strive to identify and seize those opportunities that lead to meaningful advances at the regional level as well. Because, as we have been saying with increasing urgency, we in this region must renew and enhance our efforts in the area of foreign policy coordination. And in this, the input and recommendations of COFCOR are key.

There must be an ongoing examination of the principles, practices, and mechanisms by which we coordinate our approach to foreign policy, in the same way that there needs to be a review of the mechanisms by which we engage third countries and groups of countries. As we do so, we must pay particular attention to our bilateral relations and framework agreements including memoranda of understanding and co-operation agreements, the regular scheduling of high-level meetings, the joint commission of similar mechanisms, and the accreditation of plenipotentiary representatives.

The challenges that our region face are real. In addition to the list already enumerated, there is the reality of increasing xenophobia. There is the matter of global corporate attempts, not always obvious or openly admitted, to secure and place in private hands fresh water sources from every continent, the 'oil' of the twenty-first century. There is the issue of illegal drugs and weapons. There is global warming.

All of these challenges demand exactly what we have already committed ourselves to – serious introspection and self-analysis as a region so that we will be able to effectively chart the type of course that we must in order to preserve the environmental, socio-political, and economic integrity of both our individual member states and our broader Caribbean community.

Co-ordination will assume an increasingly important role in the months and years ahead, co-ordination in the form of joint representation, co-ordination in order to continue the adoption of joint positions on matters of regional and international import, and co-ordination within the context of non-Caribbean inter-governmental organisations. We are fortunate to already have in place a number of foreign policy coordinating mechanisms and structures: the Bureau of the Conference of Heads of Government; the Bureau of COFCOR; the regular and informal meetings of COFCOR; consultations among senior officials of CARICOM member states and the secretariat; caucuses of CARICOM ambassadors in Washington, New York, Ottawa, Geneva, and Brussels. These we must continue to utilise and build upon while also striving to strengthen existing ties with members of the Caribbean diaspora whose numerical, financial, political, or other strengths beyond the Caribbean, when strategically applied, could redound to the benefit of the region from which they, our nationals, originated.

The advantages of our establishing mutually beneficial, mutually respectful relations with like-minded nations in both the industrialised and the non-industrialised world can be significant as we strive to develop our resources, preserve the security of the community, and expand our economic space. In this era of rapid technological change, our relations with nations with which we can partner as we strive to develop our own technological capabilities can also be significantly advanced by the coordinated regional foreign policy orientation of which we often speak, the objectives, positions, and initiatives that we, as a region, have already identified as being key to our prosperity, stability, human resource development, and national security.

Let the pursuit of these goals then, shape and guide both our bilateral as well as our multilateral relations. And let us within this region find ways via collaboration, coordination, and ongoing communication amongst ourselves, to advance precisely those national and regional interests that we have identified as key and which, properly pursued, will provide the type of momentum that we as policy-makers desire to see not only in terms of the process, but far more importantly, in terms of the results.

CARICOM 23RD HEADS OF GOVERNMENT MEETING
Paramaribo, Suriname, March 8–9, 2012

We are acutely cognisant of the fact that these are, indeed, trying times, and our region is being called upon to defend itself and to chart a way forward in the murkiest of global waters. This meeting is being convened at a critical juncture in our integration movement when we appreciate the need to move from the crossroads where we stood at the beginning of this century and reiterate firmly from the title of the Report of the West India Commission to enunciate our own expectation that 'The time for action is now.' If the thrust of that seminal report on the way forward with the CARICOM community held relevance then, our deliberations today on the current report submitted by the consultants engaged in the restructuring of the CARICOM Secretariat is of even greater significance almost two decades later.

As outgoing chair, I wish to underscore the need for optimism. In light of our goals for efficiency and a strengthened governance mechanism, this meeting will see us more steadfast in our resolve to move beyond the enunciation of our priority in this regard and to see the realisation of our vision. This requires all hands on deck if the ship of this community is to sail safely through the turbulent waters.

The world in which CARICOM was born is no more. Geo-political, socio-economic, and other global stresses have caused our operational landscape to be ever-changing and our problem-solving challenges to be ever more complex. CARICOM therefore, must continue to adapt and re-invent itself – never in terms of our undergirding values, purpose, and principles, of course – but certainly in terms of how we function, how we operate, the extent to which we are or are not efficient, effective, and relevant with a sharper focus on being more results-oriented.

The goal, form, and practical thrust of regional integration, for example, is still being debated and examined in the streets of Kingston and Kingstown, Bridgetown and Basseterre, and will be discussed this week in Paramaribo. And so, in light of ever-changing global and regional conditions, it remains CARICOM's essential responsibility, along with all of us gathered here today, to provide greater clarity and form regarding the ideals of integration so that we inspire hope and confidence for the people of our region who are questioning our resolve to truly transform their lives. These are not easy times. Global uncertainties, the genesis of which for the most part is external, still pose significant challenges to our region.

At first, the EU, which is one of the major donors of development aid to our region, looked anxiously westward, deeply concerned about a possible contagion effect. Now, not only do they know that the crisis was indeed 'contagious,' but they themselves are now fully in its grasp. Similarly, due to the interconnected nature of the world economy and our own economic linkages with both North America and Europe, we too have found ourselves over the past two or three years anxiously looking both eastward and northward because uncertainty there means uncertainty here. I reiterate that 'The time for action is now' and it requires a demonstration of political will to engender real and sustainable transformation.

As outgoing chair, I want to underscore the need for optimism and to highlight some of our achievements over the past months. These include but are by no means limited to our ongoing efforts to inject new vigour into the advancement of the process to set the region on a path of renewed focus. Being fully cognisant of the need to be strategic, CARICOM must position itself to become more meaningfully engaged, though not subsumed, in other regional groupings. We must continue to forge strategic alliances recognising that their respective strengths and resources can assist our community in propelling itself towards a platform of strengthened functional cooperation. We must purposefully pursue our goals as a region focusing on acquiring enhanced risk-management capabilities and sharpening our negotiating capabilities.

Expanded intra-regional economic activity is a priority for us all. And intra-regional sea and air links are key to both expanded economic activity on the one hand, and the undergirding of a truly 'Caribbean' frame of mind on the other. Unpredictable fuel costs and unreliable fuel supplies however, are a twenty-first century reality. The challenge therefore, is for us to meet the need of the Caribbean to know that there are reliable air links that cannot and will not disappear overnight simply because some businessperson thinks they should, as well as the imperative that any such service under the region's control be truly competitive.

Then there remains the challenge of climate change, our region's contribution to which is utterly miniscule, probably not even measurable. We should nonetheless consider adopting specific, region-wide lifestyle changes as a means of raising awareness of this phenomenon and its implications. And we must, at the same time, take very seriously our need to convince the world of the responsibility of those who have caused this climatic shift to bear the financial burden of the associated disasters that do not merely 'befall,' but indeed pound, states like ours.

The issues that challenge us to take collective and decisive actions are indeed profound. Whether the issue at hand is security, crime, or protecting our region's reputation globally, we must be resolute in our responses. And the people of the community expect from us not only technical proficiency but indeed visionary leadership. On the issue of security, we understand the importance of regional and international co-operation, both as a matter of law-enforcement, and as a matter of crime prevention. We have worked together on this important issue and I have every expectation that we shall continue to do so.

Our security apparatus and the mechanism that in large measure accounted for our successful hosting of world-class cricket must continue to evolve and be the vanguard of our defence against the new and emerging threats to global peace and security. While we build strong collaborative ties with our traditional and non-traditional partners in strengthening our capabilities to address the real threats associated with 21st century criminalities, let us continue to commit the necessary resources and to devise creative means for the sustainment of our crime and security framework and the management and delivery of our agencies that have been established to maintain an enabling environment for growth and development in our respective countries.

Caribbean nations have traditionally been respected across the globe as bastions of peace, justice, and democracy. We have been able to enter any chamber and assume any role without anyone ever raising even the slightest question about our individual nation's – or indeed our region's – honour. This is of incalculable value. Let us strive, with all our might, to keep it this way. Most importantly, let us commit ourselves to remaining alert, vigilant, and resistant to anything within the region that might taint this reputation that our forebears worked so very hard to build and in a spirit of utmost faith and trust, bequeathed to us.

EASTERN CARIBBEAN ASSEMBLY INAUGURAL SESSION

St John's, Antigua and Barbuda, August 10, 2012

When one considers our fractured and traumatic past as a subject and restricted people, the infinitesimally brief period that the majority of OECS member-states have been sovereign nations, and our very real constraints in terms of population, land mass, and natural resources, the accomplishments of the Eastern Caribbean in such areas as democratic governance, respect for the rule of law, and responsible management in this period of global volatility and turbulence causes one to quickly recognise that the defining feature of this region is the unique attributes indeed, the unique strengths, of the people that our history has produced.

Divided by water but connected by blood, the visionaries of this region long ago understood the promise that was within our reach if only we would take those first, path-altering steps in our quest for greater effectiveness and self-mastery. And so, from the establishment of the Eastern Caribbean Common Market almost fifty years ago, we in this region have been moving with resolve and purpose to this special time and place that now has us witnessing the realisation of yet another objective in our multi-faceted thrust toward greater effectiveness, the establishment of the Eastern Caribbean Assembly (ECA).

Decades ago, Antigua and Barbuda, the Commonwealth of Dominica, Grenada, Montserrat, St Kitts and Nevis, and St Vincent and the Grenadines set out to undo centuries of psycho-social separation and the myriad consequences that that separation left in its wake. And they did so by bringing into being the Organisation of Eastern Caribbean States in 1981, thereby giving form and substance to a long-held dream of greater cooperation, collaboration, and effectiveness.

And today, some thirty years later, we establish this new legislative body through which the people's representatives from throughout the region will now be able to confer and deliberate on matters pertaining to the peoples' business as legislators, mindful of constitutional constraints, while as always, committed to the common good.

June 15, 2012 will prove to be a historic day in the social, economic, and political evolution of the Eastern Caribbean. Often difficult to find on a world map, we have nonetheless repeatedly demonstrated our desire for, and our commitment to the ideal of, self-mastery. In the process, we have repeatedly demonstrated, to our people and the world, the concrete and quantifiable benefits of greater cooperation. And today, characteristic of our region and the people it has produced, we once again position ourselves to further advance the interests of our region, for generations to come.

ECCB Monetary Council
Remarks by the Incoming Chairman
Eastern Caribbean Central Bank, Basseterre, June 29, 2012

Firstly, let me applaud the Honourable Reuben Meade, premier and minister of finance of Montserrat, on his excellent stewardship as chair of the Monetary Council during what can be considered one of the most challenging periods for the currency union. As I reflect on the challenges and accomplishments during the 2011/2012 financial year, I consider it an honour to accept the chair of the Monetary Council for 2012/2013. In doing so, I am conscious of the unfavourable situation which confronts us and the dedication that will be required for us to achieve our goal of maintaining financial stability as the basis for sustained growth in the currency union. However, I am confident that with the collective approach of the council, we will achieve our goals.

As we are aware, the economic performance in the ECCU is linked with the performance of the international economy. Global economic recovery during 2011 can be described as only moderate in an environment of uncertainty and income volatility.

Although the global economy is estimated to have expanded by 3.9 per cent in 2011, growth performance continued to be led by developments in the emerging economies and in particular China and India. The performance of the US, the main trading partner of the currency union, continued to lag behind the global growth rate and is estimated to have expanded by only 1.6 per cent in 2011. Growth remained subdued in most of the other advanced economies. The forecast for economic growth is not very optimistic. The global economy is projected to grow by 3.5 per cent in 2012 and 4.1 per cent in 2013. In the advanced economies, the US is projected to grow by 2.1 per cent in 2012 and by 2.4 per cent in 2013, while the United Kingdom and Canada are projected to grow, on average, by 1.9 per cent and 2.1 per cent respectively between 2012 and 2013.

The ECCU economies will continue to feel the lingering effects of slow growth in the advanced economies as these are transmitted through our dependence on tourism, remittances, and foreign direct investment. In this context, the currency union experienced three consecutive years of contraction in economic activity – national output declined by 5.4 per cent in 2009, a further 1.8 per cent in 2010, and is estimated to have contracted by 1.0 per cent in 2011. The domestic economy is expected to emerge from the recession in 2012 when it is projected to grow by 2.0 per cent.

In response, the heads of government of the currency union and the ministers of finance have created two instruments to address the challenges of the global crisis, namely the Revised Treaty of Basseterre establishing the OECS Economic Union, and the ECCU Eight-Point Stabilisation and Growth Programme. In particular, the OECS Economic Union has provided a platform for the development of the region and has created a new paradigm in terms of governance structures and policy coordination for the region.

During my tenure as chair of the Monetary Council, financial stability will remain paramount. The bank will be guided by its mandate as outlined in Article 4 of the ECCB Agreement as follows:

1.   to regulate the availability of money and credit;

2.   to promote and maintain monetary stability;

3.   to promote credit and exchange conditions and a sound financial structure conducive to the balanced growth and development of the economies of the territories of the participating governments;

4.   to actively promote through means consistent with its other objectives the economic development of the territories of the participating governments.

Within this mandate, the operations of the Central Bank will continue to be informed by the ECCU Eight-Point Stabilisation and Growth Programme. In this regard, during the 2012/2013 financial year, the bank will focus on four main policy priorities, namely financial sector stability, fiscal and debt sustainability, money and credit, and growth and development.

The financial sector issues will be addressed in keeping with Point 6 – Financial Safety Net Programmes, Point 7 – Amalgamation of the Indigenous Commercial Banks, and point 8 – The Rationalisation, Regulation and Development of the Insurance Sector of the Eight-Point Stabilisation and Growth Programme. In particular, the Bank will continue to implement the following:

1. the single financial space;

2. an integrated regulatory framework that covers all financial institutions, markets, and instruments in the currency union;

3. a consolidated supervisory framework which can deal effectively with the increasingly complex nature of financial institutions;

4. the rationalisation of liquidity facility arrangements across the currency union involving the interbank market (IBM), Regional Government Securities Market (RGSM), Eastern Caribbean Home Mortgage Bank (ECHMB), and the Eastern Caribbean Central Bank (ECCB);

5. an appropriate deposit insurance scheme.

While taking into consideration the recommendations of the ECCU Financial System Task Force, the bank will continue to closely monitor threats to financial sector stability and special attention will be placed on addressing structural deficiencies and legal impediments in the financial sector in the context of the movement towards a single financial space. In this regard, the Resolution Trust Corporation, which was established to restructure, recapitalise, and manage troubled assets in financial institutions, will be deployed where necessary to provide technical assistance to financial institutions.

As advisor to the member governments, the bank will continue to collaborate with the member governments on the implementation of Point I – Financial Programmes, Point 2 – Fiscal Reform Programmes, Point 3 – Debt Management, and Point 4 – Public Sector Investment Programme of the ECCU Eight-Point Stabilisation and Growth Programme.

With regard to financial programming, and as agreed by the Monetary Council, member governments will continue to publish their fiscal targets. Member governments have now benefitted from the recommendations of the Commission on Tax and Tax Administrative Reform and the Commission on Pension and Pension Administration Reform. The Monetary Council has also established the Public Expenditure Review Commission to investigate and make recommendations on appropriate ways of rationalising the form and functions of public sector expenditure. The commission has submitted its report to the Monetary Council for consideration at this meeting. These reports will form the basis for the fiscal reform programmes of the member countries of the currency union.

During my tenure as chair, the Monetary Council will give active consideration to the debt situation of the member countries and will implement the decision of the special meeting of the Monetary Council to adopt a joint approach to addressing the debt issues and to strengthen collaboration and coordination among the member countries of the currency union. CIDA-sponsored Debt Management Advisory Services at the ECCB and the debt units in member countries have put forward proposals for addressing the debt situation and the ministerial subcommittee on debt will continue to perform its advisory role to the Monetary Council.

The issue of growth will be at the forefront. The Monetary Council will consider the report of the Task Force on Debt, Growth and Development which will give some practical recommendations for spurring sustainable growth in the currency union. We also plan to hold discussions between the OECS Authority and the Monetary Council to re-examine the growth and development targets established in 2002 and to set new ones if necessary. We have already put in place arrangements for financial support for growth initiatives through the Eastern Caribbean Enterprise Fund which is now being operationalised.

The 2012/2013 financial year will be challenging but I am confident that the Monetary Council will rise above these challenges and the exchange rate arrangement and the stability of the financial system will be maintained.

Caribbean Basin Security Initiative (CBSI)
St Kitts Marriott Resort, October 3, 2012

Today, we continue our pressing, collaborative efforts in order to insightfully anticipate and effectively counter the myriad threats being posed to this region's peace and security. Threats which become increasingly complex with each passing day, but threats which we most assuredly will confront, and which with vision, insight, and fidelity, we are determined to subdue.

Permit me to begin, of course, by once again expressing the region's deep and collective appreciation to President Barack Obama and his administration for the clear, forward-thinking, and resolute manner in which the United States has partnered with CARICOM on the matter of law enforcement and national security. This has resulted in our being able to, together, sharpen and intensify our battle against the multi-faceted national security challenges bedeviling our region. And this is making a world of difference.

This modern age, with its advances in travel, technology, and other phenomena, has forced our region to confront head-on many threats not of our making. Threats that are alien to our socio-cultural and historic evolution and which, as a result, on our own we were often experientially and materially not used to fighting. The Caribbean Basin Security Initiative however, has greatly enhanced our capabilities in this regard. We in the Caribbean did not get to nationhood by being faint of heart and so, with the involvement of our key international partners, we shall continue pursuing a resolute course in defence of our national security interests. We know that we have to both anticipate and effectively battle these threats as they arise.

We know that criminal elements are now using, with great efficiency, highly advanced technological and organisational tactics in order to make inroads in this region. Complicating matters is the fact that the resultant threats with which we must now contend are no longer either exclusively from or of this region. Indeed, those who create these threats are emboldened and networked by the best in twenty-first century technology and the worst in twenty-first century pathology.

What I also know, however, is that this hemisphere possesses extraordinarily visionary, technologically advanced, and determined interests, determined to not only meet but indeed anticipate and pre-empt the types of challenges that criminal networks pose. Indeed, some of these outstanding minds, to which I just referred, are right here in this room this morning. We understand the task that is before us, we understand the demands that have been made of us, and we move forward, thanks to your extraordinary expertise and your commitment to the challenges at hand.

Illegal trafficking, in its myriad forms, is indeed the scourge and the bane of the twenty-first century. The enormous amount of time, energy, resources and expertise that go into the production, acquisition, storage, and transfer of illegal narcotics, into the illegal trafficking in weapons of various types, and, most depraved of all, into the trafficking of human beings, demand a multi-dimensional and incisive counter-attack from the forces of law, the forces of order, and the forces of good governance. And that is what makes the work of the CBSI so very important.

Indeed, it is the organisation and technological advances of those against whom we battle that make our projected thrust in the area of expanded regional coordination so key. The ability to share information in a time-effective manner always has a pivotal impact on the types of operations that entities like the CBSI undertake. Because not only must there be enhanced access to data traditionally controlled by individual countries, but there is also, in our case, the complicating factor posed by the fact that in our region linguistic differences abound.

No one would ever question the depth of our commitment but the peak effectiveness that we all seek also demands that we be able to communicate quickly and clearly, with the necessary arrangements in place to ensure that the time-consuming and sometimes inaccurate translations that have long plagued multilingual collaborations all over the world, neither hinder nor compromise the CBSI mission in this region.

In addition, even after the linguistic hurdles have been adequately addressed, there still remains the challenge of the technological infrastructure between and amongst member states not always being compatible thereby posing yet another challenge when there is a need for the timely dissemination of crucial intelligence.

British politician and military strategist Winston Churchill during the Second World War publicly, resolutely, and famously proclaimed that Britain would fight its enemies on the beaches, fight them on land, and fight them at sea. It should be clear to all that our determination to fight local, regional, and international criminal elements within the framework of the Caribbean Basin Security Initiative is no less steely as can be seen in our shared commitment to maritime and aerial dominance. Indeed, our working with US and partner nations to detect, monitor, and interdict illicit trafficking moving in and out of the Caribbean by air, sea, and ground makes this quite clear.

The countries of CARICOM, like countries all over the world, are now grappling with the unpredictability of the global economy. In addition, the geographical profile of Caribbean nations is such that hundreds of miles of water separates nation A from nation B, making quick, easy, and cheap movement between nations problematic. And as a minister of finance, and as one who is understandably concerned about the prudent allocation of resources region-wide, I therefore especially applaud our acknowledgment of the importance of modern technology in the form of virtual training, video-conferencing, and so on as we strive to secure all of the benefits of 'almost-in person' collaboration while avoiding the traditionally burdensome costs.

It has been almost two and a half years since our first annual Caribbean-United States Security Cooperation Dialogue in Washington DC and we have covered considerable ground since then.

Let us resolve, as we go forward, to maintain strong bonds between our development partners and CBSI governments. Whatever other relationships may exist between donor partners and various segments of our regional community, there is no denying the shared interests, common focus, and special synergies that emanate from government-to-government collaboration. There is a validity, a credibility, and indeed a sense of responsibility that go along with being the elected voice of the people on all sides – the US, the Dominican Republic, CARICOM – that only exists if one is functioning within the context of collaborating democracies.

And then, there is that universal priority of governments everywhere – insulating at-risk youth from the machinations of criminal elements. Not only is the sharing of best practices in this area particularly vital, but we must also recognise that best practices will change and evolve over time.

Ongoing exchange and collaboration *vis-à-vis* at-risk youth is therefore of particular importance as are exchanges pertaining to prison reform.

As we all know, the Education Committee of the Regional Security System met in St Kitts and Nevis at the beginning of this week in order to advance a goal that we all support, the establishment of uniform training throughout the region. Uniform skill sets, uniform philosophies, uniform training, as we have agreed, will be key to our efforts as a region since, to revert to an old adage, a chain is as strong as its weakest link. And we as a region, with all our twenty-first century national security and law enforcement challenges, produce forces region-wide that represent uniformly strong links.

The very fact that most CARICOM nations are islands poses very clear challenges in terms of border security. And, once again, the United States has been instrumental in enhancing our capabilities in that area. However, understandably, the challenges of border security are still enormous and the threats ongoing and real. By definition, border security poses the supreme challenge for us affecting as it does our ability to fight the flow of illegal narcotics into our international waters and onto our shores, our ability to fight the flow of illegal weapons into our jurisdiction, and our ability to identify human traffickers who may decide, as they move from one country to another, to in some way use our territory.

This partnership that has been forged among the United States, the Dominican Republic, and CARICOM in the form of the Caribbean Basin Security Initiative, reflects the spirit of friendship and collaboration that exists among our member states. Most importantly, it reflects the inescapable reality that the production of drugs, the consumption of drugs, and the flow of weapons that always follow the drug trade, has embroiled our hemisphere in a predicament from which we would all wish to be extricated. This, however, will not happen because we wish it. It will happen only as a result of the type of focused work that has taken place under the auspices of the CBSI, and that will continue to happen.

The social, economic, and overall stability of our CBSI member states stand to benefit greatly from the type of deliberations that have been occurring, and will occur here today. The CBSI serves as a key defender of this region and its people. You know and I know that that is no exaggeration. Let us go forward then, always alert to ways in which we might strengthen our levels of strategic collaboration and practical effectiveness, always alert to ways in which we can protect our nations from those who wish to create mayhem and despair.

CARICOM 40TH ANNIVERSARY

CARICOM *View* Magazine, 40th Anniversary Edition, July 2013

Even the most far-reaching accomplishments have their genesis in man's capacity to imagine what has never been. All advances begin as a spark within the human mind and this, too, explains the evolution of the abstract *idea* that has since become the Caribbean Community (CARICOM).

For eighteen years, I have had the honour of joining forces with the leaders whom the people of the Caribbean have elected to advance the interests of their respective nations. And I have always understood that with the assumption of our national responsibilities as Caribbean prime ministers, we were simultaneously assuming a shared responsibility to protect and advance the interests of the wider CARICOM as well.

We are clearly farther along the road to integration today than we were forty years ago. The Caribbean Court of Justice, for example, being just one manifestation of our movement away from traditional dependencies. However, we must continue to work hard to ensure that member states' reconciling of their national and regional responsibilities keeps pace with the guiding ethos of the community. CARICOM has no room for insularity or a 'they' versus 'us' bias based on size and resources. These are the stumbling blocks that CARICOM was designed to confront and overcome. And it is on the Caribbean Single Market and Economy (CSME), with its ability to deepen and strengthen regional integration, that the region must rely if we are to completely dismantle all such stumbling blocks and continue to move forward.

CARICOM is a work in progress. And so should it be. All beings and entities, as long as they are alive and dynamic, are by definition works in progress. The raison d'être of the Caribbean Community however, remains incontestable. And the global crises of the past four decades have underscored the wisdom of the region having formulated and embraced a framework for a shared vision through integration.

There is broad-based agreement at the policy level that functional cooperation in such critical areas as health, security, trade, and human resource development is essential. However, the pace of regional integration would be accelerated by a more broadly-based realisation and acceptance of this by the millions of Caribbean nationals whose life prospects have been, and will continue to be, enhanced due to the existence of CARICOM. It is the people's full embrace of the idea of integration that will determine the actual pace and process of implementation in the months and years ahead. As regional governments therefore, we must continue to collaborate with the secretariat with a view to intensifying the communications and public education processes. And we must ensure that the thrust and apparatus chosen for the dissemination of the integration message reach beyond the capitals of member states and the technocrats of our respective societies and touch the hearts and minds of every Caribbean man and woman.

Some twenty years ago, Sir Shridath Ramphal and the West Indian Commission declared that it was 'Time for Action.' Twenty years later, in this era of increasing globalisation, ever-intensifying competition, and unprecedented global instability, that call is as urgent as ever. The task of designating change managers in each member state to ensure that decisions made by regional heads are implemented in a timely and effective manner is therefore key. And on this there can be no equivocation because we must have a re-energised institution ready to cope with emerging social and economic challenges through the organs of the community.

Agriculture, tourism, and manufacturing have long been seen as the main drivers of economic growth for our region. Heightened global tensions and the rise of terrorism over the past decade however, have added a new dimension to our priorities making it impossible for us to ignore these distant tensions. We now recognise the inextricable link between regional security and our prospects for continued stability and growth. The community's emphasis on security to date has redounded to our benefit in such areas as trade flows, foreign investment, and socio-political cohesion. This underscores the importance of security remaining the 'fourth pillar' of our union.

Increasing globalisation, intense international competition, and the economic difficulties being experienced by many traditional donor-nations demand that the region pursue foreign policies that emphasise insight and self-reliance, even as we maintain relations with traditional partners. The Economic Partnership of the Americas and the Free Trade

Area of the Americas, for example, have been important manifestations of our strong links in this regard, and the EU in particular has contributed substantially to the strength of the secretariat and the region. South-south co-operation, however, in this rapidly changing global landscape, must assume increasing importance if our priorities are to be the determining factors in the shape and direction of the region's development efforts. Limited economic bases and large debts must not define CARICOM island-states. Strengthened relations with emerging economies that recognise in us the potential for mutually beneficial relations will be key.

Caribbean nations are members of myriad multilateral organisations where our voices and votes matter. Foreign policy coordination within the community therefore, must be seen as an essential leveraging mechanism if we are to advance our interests within these organisations, and inform international discourse on the issues of global import.

A particular strength of the community is its quasi-cabinet dimension, a powerful manifestation of the integration ideal at work. Indeed, as the prime minister with lead CARICOM responsibility for human resource development and health, it was extraordinarily gratifying to have CARICOM approve the establishment of the Caribbean Public Health Agency in 2010, something I had long advocated. Within one year, the board and chairman had been named, paving the way for tremendous advances in health care delivery that will benefit the people of the Caribbean for generations to come. It is worth mentioning here as well, as a tribute to the value of CARICOM's quasi-cabinet structure, that as a result of the extraordinary efforts we undertook, AIDS-related deaths in the Caribbean have fallen by 50 per cent, a fact duly noted in the UNAIDS Report for 2012. And CARICOM's efforts resulted in the United Nations holding its first ever Summit on Non-Communicable Diseases in 2011.

Were our journey to integration to be represented by a trend line, fluctuations would without question be apparent. At the same time, there would be no denying of that line's definite upward trajectory over the past forty years. This we must continue because the global challenges of the twenty-first century await, becoming ever more complex with each passing year. The community has articulated its vision. The CSME has been identified as the way forward. What is required of us now as we look forty years into the future, is continued forward movement looking both within and beyond the hemisphere in order to expand our horizons, even as we embrace and ensure greater region-wide understanding of the benefits of integration.

Caribbean Public Health Agency (CARPHA) Launch

National Academy of Performing Arts, Port of Spain, Trinidad
July 2, 2013

Today, we are gathered in this splendid environment of the National Academy of Performing Arts in Port of Spain to celebrate an extraordinary achievement, the official launching of the Caribbean Public Health Agency. This is indeed a timely gift to the people of the Caribbean Community which marks its fortieth anniversary at the Conference of Heads of Government, beginning tomorrow. I am indeed pleased as CARICOM lead head for human resources, health and HIV/AIDS to be part of this celebration today and to bring you warm greetings on behalf of my colleague heads of government. We all recognise that CARPHA is indeed a triumph of the spirit of regionalism.

This launch is taking place at a time when CARICOM is groping for initiatives that build on the foundations laid down by the founding fathers, among them Errol Barrow, Forbes Burnham, and Vere Bird, who dared to inspire the re-engagement of a Caribbean nation out of the ashes of a failed federal experiment. It is taking place at a time when we are seeking to identify landmarks that build on the institutional arrangements so clearly enunciated in the Treaty of Chaguaramas that made bold provisions for knitting the economic, social, and political fabric of our individual nation states into a dynamic, competitive, and cohesive regional collective. Most of all, CARPHA is a fitting response to the challenge of our time to demonstrate that the Caribbean is capable of redefining and redesigning its institutions to better serve the people of the region and at the same time take its place as a centre of excellence in the international arena. This is what we are here to celebrate this afternoon.

We have heard from speakers before me of the evolution, challenges, vision, and aspirations of CARPHA. From the perspective of the CARICOM heads of government, we approved its establishment based on the overwhelming burden of evidence and the recommendations resulting from discussions and debates by our ministers, CMOs, and other experts that the consolidation of five institutions into one agency was the most feasible option. There were also lessons from around the world. These included the debates within the World Health Organisation on the ideals of health for all and within PAHO on equity in health. The seminal report of the Caribbean Commission on Health and Development (2007) chaired by Sir George Alleyne, also underscored the need for revamping the region's approach to public health and helped to shape the underlying philosophy of CARPHA. In addition, the experiences of Canada, the UK, the US and the European Union have provided useful guidelines for public health approaches. In the European Union for example, notwithstanding the long-established health systems within most of its member states, mechanisms for cooperation in health are being promoted including the European Observatory in Health Systems and Policies, the Association of Schools of Public Health in Europe (ASHER), the European Health Management Association and the European Public Health Alliance. These studies, models, and policies notwithstanding, our biggest challenge was coming up with a formula that best fitted the needs and peculiar circumstances of the Caribbean region.

It is therefore important to place CARPHA in context. The Caribbean Community is no longer an experiment. It is a reality. It was constructed on the basis of a treaty, The Treaty of Chaguaramas, in 1973. This treaty has evolved through amendments over the past forty years. While the establishment of the Caribbean Single Market and Economy is the acknowledged flagship of the integration movement, it is not the only yardstick by which to measure the progress made in regional integration. The Treaty of Chaguaramas identified three pillars of integration including trade and economic integration, foreign policy and community relations, and functional cooperation. More recently a fourth pillar, crime and security, has been added. Indeed it must be recognised that long before the trade and economic integration component took root, it was in the areas of health, education, and culture that the Caribbean Community made its greatest impact. The activities in these areas, singly and collectively, continue to connect the Caribbean people, including the Caribbean diaspora, and to project distinctiveness about the Caribbean in the global arena. In particular in the area of health, co-operation has been an outstanding illustration of what can be gained by acting collectively to achieve outcomes that benefit all citizens across the region, minimising the inequities and maximising the efficiencies. There is no better modality in principle than Caribbean Cooperation in Health (CCH). The challenges with the CCH, identified in various studies, have to do with a failure to implement its priorities due to a lack of a consolidated system and in many cases because of a lack of resources .

The Caribbean Public Health Agency is conceived as a response and a remedy to this situation. It is seen as an example of functional cooperation, as a mechanism by which the health of the people of the Caribbean will be promoted and they will be protected from disease, injury, and disability, thereby fostering the wellness revolution enunciated in the Port of Spain declaration (2007) to unify to fight non-communicable diseases. It is also intended to advance the realisation, embodied in the Nassau Declaration (2001) that 'The Health of the Region is the Wealth of the Region.' In this regard it is expected to highlight the opportunity costs of pursuing public health functions in a consolidated way rather than as disparate entities that duplicate efforts and dilute the public health objectives for which they were designed. This is by no means to suggest that our existing public health institutions that are now embodied in CARPHA did not serve the region well. In many cases they have functioned under circumstances that challenged the creative imagination and management capability of the directors of the respective institutions over the years.

As we move forward with the implementation of CARPHA, I am pleased to note the vision of the executive director for promoting centres of innovation in its business plan and highlighting its laboratory and surveillance functions, quality control and drug regulations, research and environmental health. The alignment of CARPHA's business with the tourism sector, climate change, and public health leadership training is a further demonstration of the creative culture that is being nurtured. Its mode of operation is indeed consistent with the notion of the vital contribution of health to economic and human development. This could only augur well for the future of the region.

I particularly expect CARPHA to build on and promote the scientific work that can help to transform the way health policy is influenced by research, and to accelerate the infusion of international cooperation, connecting with regional and global health priorities and simultaneously stimulating the dynamism of Caribbean public health. These are expectations to be fulfilled.

The global stage is ready-made for CARPHA, especially at this time when there is fermentation of activity around the post-2015 development agenda. In fashioning CARPHA's exciting work programme, it is essential to recognise that the world is increasingly characterised by massive shifts in wealth and resource flows while inequalities in wealth and access to health are increasing within and across countries. CARPHA must therefore be part of the conversation that articulates for global health in the post-2015 agenda to ensure that increased wealth actually leads to improved health, especially among the poor, that health expenditure is recognised as an investment in human well-being, increased productivity, and national wealth and that attention must be equally paid to the social determinants of health which include lifestyle behaviours.

These are the overarching values that will ensure that meaningful results are achieved from the rationalisation and harnessing of resources to which CARPHA is committed. In this way, CARPHA may yet provide a model of how the Caribbean Community shapes the future of over twenty-five regional institutions so that they make a difference in the gamut of services from meteorology, disaster management and climate change through to quality and standards, examinations council and accreditation, fisheries, agriculture, and crime and security. A review of these institutions together with that of the Caribbean Community secretariat is currently being undertaken as part of a comprehensive plan to increase the effectiveness and efficiency of how the community does business.

The leaders of this region are quite aware that the global economic crisis has engendered a new economic order and escalated a changed political landscape with deep structural barriers and access to overseas development assistance (ODA). CARPHA offers an opportunity for the region to revisit its approach to partnership and resource mobilisation. I therefore wish to offer profound gratitude to all those development partners that have contributed toward shaping this new landscape of partnership in global health, chief among which are the European Union, the Public Health Agency of Canada, the UK Department of Health, and the UK Social Marketing Company. We are especially grateful to the Pan American Health Agency that has nurtured the process of transition and continues to collaborate in charting the sustainability of CARPHA, and to the CARICOM secretariat for anchoring the process. No doubt as we move ahead we can expect the consolidation of support from the governments of Brazil and Argentina and many other partners including the World Bank, IDB, CDC and the Caribbean Development Bank.

I am sure I speak on behalf of my fellow heads of government in expressing appreciation to the government of Trinidad and Tobago for agreeing to host CARPHA and for its role in this official launching of CARPHA on the auspicious occasion of the region's fortieth anniversary. I am confident that a prosperous future beckons CARPHA.

COMMUNITY OF LATIN AMERICAN AND CARIBBEAN STATES
II SUMMIT

Havana, Cuba, January 28–29, 2014

Four years ago, in the beautiful Mexican city of Playa del Carmen, the idea was conceived to institutionalise a new organisation to deal specifically with Latin American and Caribbean challenges, deepen regional integration, and address issues which can advance our strategic development. Today, as we convene for the II Summit of the Community of Latin American and Caribbean States, it is evident that a tremendous amount of work has been executed to strengthen cooperation between our states and to achieve a greater level of integration.

St Kitts and Nevis looks forward to the continued collaboration of member states to fulfill the dream of the late President Chavez who worked assiduously to inaugurate and bring to fruition this new institution. As a people who share similar values and cultures and as a people who grapple with the challenges of development, it is essential that we take the necessary steps to ensure that CELAC develops into an organisation that can effectively resolve regional disputes and promote the interests of all its member states in international fora.

This brings me to the point of a very contentious matter that concerns the recent ruling on nationality that was handed down by the Constitutional Court of the Dominican Republic. We simply cannot continue to be discreet on this subject when basic fundamental rights are being violated. To do this would be to go against the very fabric of our society. It is therefore imperative that within the context of CELAC and in a spirit of unity, that we urgently attempt to address this issue and find amicable solutions that will redound to the benefit of all parties involved.

In a world where international developments continue to shape the global agenda, multilateralism continues to play a key role in charting the way forward. Although nascent, CELAC can be used as an instrument for effective multilateralism, finding possible solutions to the myriad challenges that we face individually as CELAC member states. It is for this reason that CELAC ought to suitably coordinate a regional policy responding to the needs of its member states with a view to advancing the socio-economic development of our peoples.

The participation of so many heads at this summit is a serious indication of the political will and commitment by our countries to continue to inject the desired energy into the development of CELAC. It is only through collaborative efforts and dedication of all that we will succeed in making this institution a force to be reckoned with.

It would be remiss of me not to highlight the work of the President and thank the Cuban government and people for the warm welcome and detailed planning that ensured the successful hosting of this event. On behalf of my delegation, I convey heartfelt gratitude to our Cuban colleagues for the warm expressions of hospitality and love bestowed upon us. We would also like to salute the collective efforts of the extended troika on preparations made to host this event and we look forward to the III Summit which will be held in Costa Rica in 2015.

International Affairs

International Affairs

St Kitts and Nevis's role on the international stage is minimal. However, as the smallest nation in the western hemisphere, it is important to the pride of both the Federation's leaders and its citizens that it has a voice and a vote in the world's leading international fora, especially at the United Nations (UN).

In virtually all international meetings and conferences, Douglas continued to make the case for special concessions, both financial and otherwise, for Small Island Developing States (SIDS). Globalisation and trade liberalisation put SIDS at a distinct disadvantage while the gap between rich and poor nations continued to grow. Climate change and security threats were especially challenging for SIDS and put the attainment of their UN Millennium Development Goals (MDGs) in jeopardy.

Although a consistent voice advocating for reform and revitalisation of the UN, the Commonwealth, and the Organisation of American States (OAS), Douglas and his government remained optimistic about these groupings and their ability to build strategic partnerships and devise sustainable solutions to the world's crises in today's infinitely more complicated and interconnected world.

WORLD FOOD SECURITY
FAO HIGH-LEVEL CONFERENCE
The Challenge of Climate Change and Bioenergy
Rome, Italy, June 3–5, 2008

The government of St Kitts and Nevis is pleased to participate in this high-level conference on World Food Security: The Challenge of Climate Change and Bioenergy. I would like to express my sincere appreciation to the Food and Agriculture Organization (FAO) and in particular the director-general for his kind invitation to participate in such an important meeting. The positive response from several heads of state and government as well as numerous ministers of agriculture, forestry, fisheries, water, energy, and the environment who are participating in this meeting is a strong indication of the relevance and timeliness of this conference. The purpose of this high-level conference is to address food security issues that have been exacerbated by soaring food prices and the challenges of climate change and energy security. This is of critical importance to all of us, especially the world's poor. The objective of this conference is to assist countries and the international community in devising sustainable solutions to the food crisis by identifying the policies, strategies, and programmes required to safeguard world food security in the immediate-, short-, and longer-term.

Climate change affects all of us but small island developing states (SIDS) and the world's poor are particularly vulnerable to such changes. It can be expected that the hundreds of millions of small-scale farmers, fishers, and persons who depend on the forests who are already vulnerable as well as food insecure, will be the worst affected by changes in the climate. Such changes are expected to affect the suitability of land for different types of crops, livestock, and pasture development as well as the marine environment. It will also affect the health and productivity of forests, the incidence of pests and diseases, as well as biodiversity and ecosystems. The effect of such changes is likely to be the loss of farmland due to increased aridity, ground water depletion, salinity, and the rise in sea level. Many of the world's small-scale farmers are the people who are most food insecure and are least equipped to adapt to climate change. These small-scale farmers are therefore the most vulnerable to climate change phenomena such as more frequent and intense drought as well as hurricanes and cyclones. As you are aware, the livelihoods of persons of small island developing states will also be severely challenged by such changes.

There is no doubt that the escalating price of fossil fuel has impacted negatively on food security, while there is continued debate about the effects of bioenergy. Bioenergy has been defined as energy produced from biomass such as energy crops, forestry residues, and organic wastes. Currently much attention is being paid to the production of liquid biofuels, mainly ethanol and biodiesel. Biofuels are mainly produced from food crops and are used for transport. Ethanol is mainly produced from sugar cane and maize while the production of biodiesel is from rapeseed but also palm oil and soya bean oil. The growing biofuel market is driving up commodity and food prices and represents a new source of demand for agricultural commodities. This growth can provide new economic opportunities for the many millions of people who depend on agriculture for their livelihoods. On the other hand, soaring food prices are bad news for poor consumers and are dramatically worsening their living conditions. We now have a situation in many parts of the world where food and energy crops are competing for land, water, and other resources. As policy-makers, we have the difficult task of determining how best to respond to the new opportunities while ensuring that our people can grow and buy adequate food.

There is clearly a strong need to better understand the nexus between food security, climate change, and bioenergy. It is important to note that the degree to which the rapid rise in demand for biofuel feedstocks has contributed to the current rise in food prices varies across countries and that the impact on livelihood is also variable. However, poor countries that are both food and energy importers are facing tremendous balance of payment pressures that can result in an erosion of economic and social gains. The four dimensions of food security which are availability, access, stability, and utilisation, can also be expected to be affected in varying ways. The diversion of land, water, and other productive resources from food to biofuel production can threaten the availability of food at both the national and international levels. Higher food prices can further erode the ability of poor persons to access food due to their low-income levels. However, farmers who are net producers can benefit from higher prices and investments in bioenergy growth can revitalise agriculture and provide employment opportunities. Food security can therefore be expected to improve for some persons while others are experiencing deterioration. A challenge for us is therefore to develop and agree on steps that will have to be taken towards developing sustainable bioenergy policies and programmes taking into account food security and rural development.

The dramatic increases in food prices within recent months are worsening the living conditions of millions of poor people, many of whom live on less than a dollar a day. Poor people generally spend more than half of their income on food and the rapid increases in food prices that we are currently experiencing make their ability to consume nutritious foods even more challenging. We have seen that in January 2008, the FAO Food Price Index jumped by 47 per cent from the previous year which included increases in cereals by 62 per cent, dairy by 69 per cent, and vegetable oils by 85 per cent. We have also seen that the prices of staple foods such as maize, wheat, rice, and beans have in some cases risen by more than 100 per cent. Not only have world food prices risen sharply but there have also been serious shortages of rice, wheat, and maize. This has created the worst food crisis in recent years for the entire world including Latin America and the Caribbean. Current high food prices make it even more challenging for us to achieve the first of the Millennium Development Goals which is to reduce by half extreme poverty and hunger in the world by 2015.

In the Caribbean, the current food crisis has resulted in dramatic food price increases as well as shortages of staples. This has resulted in food riots and even deaths and has threatened the survival of food insecure people and vulnerable communities. The Caribbean, though a significant producer, is a net importer of food. In many ways this has been influenced by our eating habits that have moved away from the consumption of local to imported foods. There is therefore an urgent need for product transformation of locally grown foods into forms that are more easily acceptable by our people. Simultaneously there is also a need to adjust our eating habits and consume more locally-grown food.

The development of bioenergy and other alternative forms are of critical importance to St Kitts and Nevis. As a result, we have developed an energy strategy that is intended to help promote and contribute to the sustainable development of the country. We are seeking to develop indigenous sources of energy and fuel substitution in the generation of electricity and transportation fuels. The use of biomass for energy generation is one area that is under active consideration. However, our aim is to ensure that such biomass use is sustainable and does not adversely effect domestic food production. In pursuit of this aim, we have recently given approval in principle for a biomass cane grass project as well as the establishment of a wind farm. Much attention is currently being paid to the development of a geothermal project for electricity generation while the use of solar energy is also under active consideration.

We urgently need to develop measures to ensure that the adverse effects of higher food prices on the poor are minimised and that sustainable measures are developed and implemented to reduce poverty. As policy-makers, we have a critical role in ensuring that bioenergy is developed in a sustainable manner thereby safeguarding food security and ensuring that the benefits reach the poor and those who are food insecure. Policy priorities should include safety nets to mitigate impacts of higher food prices on the poor and food insecure and the promotion of bioenergy policies that are environmentally sustainable and which will foster market opportunities for small holders and other vulnerable groups. Climate change is expected to impose new challenges to arable land areas, livestock rearing, and fisheries. We therefore need to agree on the actions that are necessary to achieve climate-responsive food security policies and programmes. There is need for greater investment in agriculture and rural development so that the world's poor can develop their potential to improve their nutrition and incomes.

I hope that this summit on world food security will be able to effectively address the many food security issues that have arisen as a result of soaring food prices and food shortages as well as the several new challenges of climate change and energy security.

The high cost of oil prices has certainly affected food prices and has resulted in calls for special and differential measures for the small island states of the Caribbean. It is therefore proposed that:

> the protocol with the World Trade Organization (WTO) be suspended to allow member countries to produce more local agricultural products, and the FAO assist member countries with seeds, fertiliser, and other inputs to assist farmers to carry out the rapid production of agricultural products.

We need help and we need it immediately.

UN GENERAL ASSEMBLY
63RD SESSION
United Nations, New York, September 25, 2008

Twenty-five years ago, almost to the day, two Caribbean peoples who had always been separated by water but had long been united by history, culture, and circumstance, joined forces to embark upon a bold experiment. Having between them a land mass of just over one hundred square miles and a population of approximately fifty thousand, the people of St Kitts and the people of Nevis decided to step forward as one nation to join the world community of sovereign states. It is an honour and a pleasure for me to be here to represent this nation at the United Nations, a potent symbol of freedom and sovereignty. That symbolism means all the more to my people at this particular time as this 63rd Regular Session of the United Nations General Assembly (UNGA) coincides with the celebration my nation's twenty-fifth anniversary of political independence.

Building and reinforcing the pillars of nationhood has not been easy, but we have always considered it an essential task and a challenge worth facing. And so, as chief servant of my people and my cherished land, I stand before you today emboldened by the pride of a nation which has taken its full and rightful place among the community of independent nations, a vibrant democracy with a thriving economy and a deep commitment to justice and human rights, and an abiding faith in social equity.

Mine is a pride which comes not only from realising the benefits of the practical policies and programmes created over the years to improve the standard of living and uplift our people, but from the sense of community, and partnership, and civic and personal responsibility that have shaped the destiny of my nation. It is also a pride which comes from witnessing first-hand the true value of freedom, a freedom which has enabled us to share in the triumphs of democracy and to mould the creative genius and the industrious, enterprising spirit of our people into a single community of goodwill and commitment which moves our people and country forward. It is a pride born of weathering storms of external economic shocks, including fluctuating commodity prices and the withdrawal of preferential market access, while being able to successfully transform three centuries of a mono-cultural, sugar-based economy into a vibrant and competitive services-driven economy without the typical social and economic shocks that so often accompany so drastic an economic transformation.

Many other small states have not been as fortunate however. This is evident in our sister Caribbean nation of Haiti where the devastating effects of four consecutive hurricanes in the space of one month and the consequence of high commodity prices and rising energy costs continue to undermine the government's efforts to build strong institutions as well as to invest in the productive enterprises and infrastructure that generate employment and improved living conditions.

The progress witnessed in St Kitts and Nevis was not achieved by chance. Since the birth of our nation twenty-five years ago, we have faced a multitude of problems, some of which are fortunately behind us, but several others have emerged and grown in intensity and scope. Our experience in St Kitts and Nevis demonstrates that good governance and prudent management of one's resources, appropriate investment in people and systems, protecting people's freedom of association, religion, and speech, the support and facilitation of a free and vibrant press, success at advancing the socio-economic well-being of one's people, and the upholding of democratic ideals, are determined not by land mass but by national character and political commitment. They are the result not of demographic or geographic size, but of long-standing socio-cultural traditions. They are a function not of GDP, but of an entrenched ethos of striving and determination. Our faith has steadied our resolve and belief in ourselves and our future.

And of course, along the way, we have relied understandably on institutions such as our beloved United Nations. Through membership in the UN, St Kitts and Nevis has built important and strategic partnerships and stood shoulder to shoulder with other member states to protect our individual rights and collective freedoms, and has fought battles far bigger than the expectation for a country of its size. We have also been witnesses to the positives and negatives, the strengths and failings, of our world but have soldiered on together in common cause.

And that is why, twenty-five years later, I remain optimistic about the progress of the United Nations and its ability to defend the poor and needy despite the pull of competing powerful national agendas that has occasionally risked undermining the ethos of the institution and indeed the common good. From where I stand today, I have come to appreciate these achievements and to appreciate that even at this juncture, providence affords us still new opportunities to renew our cherished institution. It is very easy to take side with the cynics when the Security Council becomes frozen in stalemate or when the need for action falls victim to political posturing. But the history, particularly of the past two decades, instructs me that the United Nations is far more than the sum of its weakness. For millions of people around the world, this organisation is their only hope, a bridge between life and death, a bastion of freedom and a beacon of hope.

It is my hope, therefore, that in this 'Assembly of Frankness' there will be a sober and unrelenting analysis of the human consequences of sweeping and globally-enforced trade and economic regimes on small states all across the globe. And it is also my hope that the economic uncertainties now being experienced in some of the world's larger economies will sensitise us all to the breadth of the uncertainty, the depth of the anxiety, and the real psychological trauma that often grips small states when policies that are formulated far beyond their shores and are utterly unresponsive to their entreaties are nonetheless thrust unflinchingly upon them.

Recent events have called into focus the issue of the stability of the world financial systems and financial institutions. The circumstances that have led to collapsing financial institutions and rising prices for food and energy were not created by small states such as St Kitts and Nevis. But yet again, as in the case of climate change, we are victims of the acts of others with no resources to combat the consequences.

Earlier this year I participated in a high-level conference on World Food Security. The upbeat response from several heads of state and government and from the numerous ministers of agriculture, forestry, fisheries, water, energy, and environment who participated in that meeting was, for me, a strong indication of the relevance and timeliness of the conference for nations seeking to take positive action on the issue of food security. The current trend continues to have a lopsided impact on the increasing numbers of extremely poor and vulnerable people who are least able to counter the impact of economic dislocations facing our countries. Mindful of our personal responsibility as leaders and of the heightened expectations of our citizenry, the government of St Kitts and

Nevis has been taking practical measures to alleviate the suffering on our resilient people.

We have addressed the important dimensions of availability and access to certain food staples such as rice, flour, and sugar. We have looked at how best to stabilise prices to inject predictability into the system without prejudice to free market economics. We have also begun to rationalise and promote proper utilisation of agricultural lands through land use diversion and diversification by providing financial and seedling support to farmers, and by recommending water rationalisation and enhanced irrigation techniques.

These problems to which I have alluded are not unique to St Kitts and Nevis. You will recall popular riots in some countries, including Haiti, which led to the resignation of national governments. This is evidence of the impact of the rising cost of food and the despair visited upon whole communities and how it can easily undermine peoples' faith in their governments to deliver on promises of democracy, free market economics, and globalisation benefits.

In January 2008, the FAO Food Price Index jumped by 47 per cent over the previous year which included increases in cereals by 62 per cent, dairy by 69 per cent and vegetable oils by 85 per cent. In some instances, prices of staple foods such as maize, wheat, rice, and beans have risen by more than 100 per cent. This global economic downturn coupled with the dramatic upsurge in commodity prices has created the worst food crisis in recent years. This new phenomenon will make it more difficult for us to address the growing incidence of poverty in and among our nations and our ability to achieve the Millennium Development Goal of halving extreme poverty and hunger throughout the world by 2015.

Against this backdrop and the need for urgent action, we also urge that the issue of reform, a recurrent United Nations agenda for some fifteen years, be re-visited with renewed vigour and commitment. Far too much time has passed. Far too little has been done. And far too much now hangs in the balance. Let us equip the United Nations with the tools necessary to fulfil its mandates, especially in the areas of protecting individual freedoms and human rights, as well as promoting economic development as an integral element of human security around the world. As Clarence Darrow said: 'You can only protect your liberties in the world by protecting the other man's freedom. You can only be free if I also am free.'

The continuous suppression of freedom – overt or disguised – under the cloak of civil order or territorial integrity, must be tackled openly. Freedom and personal responsibility go hand in hand. How can we encourage people to take personal responsibility but deprive them of their personal freedom?

Our presence here today is both a demonstration and an acknowledgement of the increasingly interconnected nature of our world. Much of what St Kitts and Nevis has achieved over the past twenty-five years has been the result of our peoples' hard work and discipline, combined with the benefits that have accrued from both our multilateral as well as our bilateral relations. In this regard, the UNDP has been a vibrant partner in advancing the programmatic goals of our twin-island Federation, as have UNESCO and other UN agencies. Our relationship with this organisation is one that we cherish dearly.

We have worked with and through sub-regional entities such as the Organisation of Eastern Caribbean States (OECS); regional mechanisms such as the Caribbean Community (CARICOM); and hemispheric institutions like the Organisation of American States. Through regional mechanisms we have been able to map a course for functional cooperation on issues such as trade, security, and health. Within a Pan-Caribbean Partnership (PANCAP) we have developed a regional response to tackle the epidemic of HIV/AIDS. In the area of environmental protection, we continue to collaborate on and work towards disaster reduction and mitigation, and we are assiduously exploring renewable energy sources including geothermal energy on which we have made encouraging progress.

On the subject of bilateral relations, I am pleased to say that we have built many deeply valued relationships over the years and we continue to further strengthen these relations. In light of this, we urge that a way be found to facilitate the participation of the Republic of China on Taiwan in the specialised agencies of the United Nations. As world challenges have expanded, the Republic of China on Taiwan has stepped forward to provide technical assistance in the areas of social and agricultural development as well as disaster relief in many countries, bringing enormous benefits to both public and private sectors.

Whatever the tone and tenor of the ongoing debate, climate change is a factor of our modern experiences. Because of our activities and assault on the earth's atmosphere, many processes have negatively impacted rivers, lakes, and oceans, resulting in fast-melting polar ice caps, rising sea levels, and have exposed us to greater risk of harmful solar radiation and greenhouse gas emissions. Wherever culpability may reside, these processes all have serious implications for, and consequences on, small island states. These changes impact, in varying degrees and at different levels, hundreds of thousands of small-scale farmers, fishers and other people who depend heavily on the natural environment for their livelihood but who are already witnessing lower crop yields and smaller catches.

It is no longer sufficient simply to lay blame at the feet of countries, businesses, and people who pollute. We need effective strategies based on scientific consensus and solution-focused approaches which address such issues as the suitability of land for different types of crops, areas for livestock, pasture development, marine environment, the impact on health and health care, productivity of forests, the increased incidence of pests, and diseases as well as the implications for biodiversity and ecosystems. We must collaborate in addressing these effects and take necessary corrective action in order to build a safer environment for ourselves and future generations.

Our destinies and our freedoms are all interwoven. It was Franklin D. Roosevelt who said, '...true individual freedom cannot exist without economic security and independence.' As St Kitts and Nevis commemorates its jubilee year of independence, we therefore feel compelled to call on the United Nations and the members of the Security Council to work together to put an end to genocide in parts of Africa. I also call on the United Nations to take firm action in the lead-up to the 'Follow-up Conference on Financing for Development' so that this event brings real relief and development even to the far corners of Africa.

For much too long, we have perhaps unwittingly separated human security from representative democracy, and economic development from human rights. These are inextricably linked. When we fight for the freedom of our brothers to vote, but ignore their inalienable right to food security, this is a skewed principle, a half measure of selective morality in which our fight will always be only partially won. We cannot simply tell our citizens they are free to vote but fail to help them transform freedoms into practical systems which support and advance personal dreams. Democracy is the best vehicle through which humankind can realise its dreams and aspirations. I firmly believe that 'true independence, like freedom, can only come from doing what is right.'

I continue to believe in the United Nations. But beyond that I have faith in the people of St Kitts and Nevis whose confidence in themselves as a nation and their commitment to the future have made possible the successes and positive growth and development as well as the international partnerships established over the last twenty-five years. Therefore, I say to the member states of this United Nations, let us commit to doing the right things. Let us continue the important work to reform and revitalise the United Nations. Let us tackle food security by recognising that globalisation was meant to improve our lives, not to worsen them. It was meant to facilitate free movement of goods and services, not as an opportunity for artificial and unilateral barriers that punish poor and less competitive countries. Let us do the right thing about climate change together, one step at a time. Let us use the 'Follow-up Conference on Financing for Development' to address the fundamental challenges facing developing countries in Africa and around the world. All this and far more is within the power and capacity of a re-ordered United Nations and member states who are willing to take personal responsibility.

UN Millennium Development Goals Review Summit

United Nations, New York, September 22, 2010

It is indeed a pleasure for me to represent the government and people of St Kitts and Nevis as we undertake this very necessary and important collective review of progress made toward achieving the 2015 Millennium Development Goals (MDGs) to which we agreed a decade ago, to free our peoples from want. In this regard, I would like to take this opportunity to share with you the extent of my government's work and its ongoing commitment to human security and the dignity of all people; reiterate our call for structured and meaningful global partnerships and cooperation to tackle the many challenges confronting our peoples; and remind countries to fulfil their pledges.

I need not remind this assembly that St Kitts and Nevis is the smallest independent nation in the western hemisphere with a population just under fifty thousand and land mass of one hundred and four square miles. Yet smallness has never been a deterrent to progress nor an excuse not to adhere to the highest standards of democratic governance, strict observance of human rights, sound economic principles, and commitment to a high standard of living.

I am pleased to say that since the late 1990s, we have implemented internal mechanisms and policies which, coupled with citizenship engagement, have allowed us, on an ongoing basis, to be able to make progress in fulfilling our own development needs which coincide with the MDGs:

1. According to the latest Country Poverty Assessment, extreme poverty in St Kitts and Nevis fell from 11 per cent in 2000 to 1.4 per cent in 2009;

2. Since 1972, St Kitts and Nevis has enjoyed compulsory universal access to primary and secondary education;

3. St Kitts and Nevis was among the first countries in the Western Hemisphere to establish a Ministry of Women's Affairs. Even before political independence twenty-seven years ago, women

were occupying high offices and decision-making roles. Today, women empowerment and participation in all levels of policy-making and governance is the norm and gender is not a limiting factor in assigning persons to key posts in St Kitts and Nevis;

4.   The infant mortality rate in the last decade has shown a positive downward trend;

5.   Maternal mortality has been negligible during the period under review due to my government's steady investment in the health sector, including capacity-building consistent with its commitment to improve the quality of life of its citizens;

6.   In terms of environmental sustainability, determined policies have resulted in implementation of geothermal and wind energy projects;

7.   PANCAP, the Pan-Caribbean partnership on HIV/AIDS of which St Kitts and Nevis is a member, is regarded as a WHO best practice centre in combating HIV/AIDS. It is also renowned for its practices in prevention, treatment, and care and also as an advocate for the elimination of all forms of discrimination against people affected by the disease;

8.   On the issue of global partnerships, due to diminishing Official Development Assistance (ODA), St Kitts and Nevis has had to fund and sustain MDG programmes mainly from the scarce resources of the state. Therefore, we welcome the contribution of the government and people of Taiwan to our national efforts to meet the MDGs through their investment in agriculture, food security, and technology. Such a partnership can be a model for developed countries some of whom have failed to live up to their commitments.

I assure you that our progress towards achieving the 2015 MDGs is the result of careful planning and prudent management. However, we live in complex times with myriad challenges where despite our very carefully calibrated macro-economic policies, fiscal prudence, and financial programmes, our best efforts and best practices are often undermined by external forces as we have witnessed since the onset in 2008 of the global financial crisis and economic meltdown.

Likewise, progress made through costly investments can be blown away in a matter of minutes leaving our small vulnerable economy to the mercy of an already tight financial market and the unavailability of grants or concessional loans. This has been exacerbated by the unfair calculation of our GDP per capita which places St Kitts and Nevis in a higher bracket that reality justifiably supports. Like other nations, despite our careful efforts to craft and implement our own stimulus packages, this issue of the GDP per capita remains a major handicap, one that predates the global financial and economic crises. It is unfair, arbitrary, indefensible, and economically destabilising. For while we manage our affairs responsibly, efficiently, and competently, we are still denied access to crucial concessional loans.

In the case of St Kitts and Nevis, the crushing burden of the high costs of borrowing, economic and social dislocation resulting from the closure of the sugar industry five years ago, the downturn in the global economy and the drying-up of investment capital, the assault on our service sector, and the rising level of commercial indebtedness, all threaten to undermine our progress in fulfilling the MDGs and to unravel the success of our small yet vulnerable country.

In addition to this and the impact of the economic downturn, hurricanes swirl throughout this hemisphere as I speak. The regularity and ferocity of floods, hurricanes, the incidence of sea level rise, and other catastrophic events are bold reminders that the consequences of climate change are real.

However, the fact that we are this concerned about the unravelling of the progress made at this point in our review, just five years before the target date for the achievement of the MDGs, is not consistent with the spirit of the Millennium Development Goals. I am not convinced that this is in any way indicative of the constructive multilateral collaboration we have spoken about so boldly for the last ten years. I encourage the nations assembled for this review summit to take action, whether in their legislative bodies or in multilateral agencies, to promote the kind of collaborative efforts which advance the common good and place partnerships above parochialism and move our peoples further along the path to personal growth and the fulfilment of their individual potential.

THE COMMONWEALTH: A NETWORK OF PARTNERS

FIRST Magazine, Diamond Jubilee Issue, London, Spring 2012

—⮚◆⮛—

The historic adoption on the Charter of the Commonwealth was a seminal moment in the necessary evolution of the Commonwealth. This Charter is the embodiment of the core values and principles of the organisation. It also simplifies, for its beneficiary citizens, the essence of the Commonwealth – ideals to which St Kitts and Nevis subscribes and supports. St Kitts and Nevis attaches great premium to membership. We value the Commonwealth's political pedigree, socio-economic partnership instruments, and work in promoting representative democracy and development as well as the currency of its international advocacy work. Therefore, the Commonwealth remains a partner of choice.

Understandably, there is an important and vigorous discourse happening within the Commonwealth which goes to the heart of the organisation's future. Although member states recently hammered out a strategic plan for the next few years, disquiet about the future of the Commonwealth simmers. That is not unusual given the differing priorities of member states. Unfortunately however, there is the misperception that some countries are democracy, rule of law, and human rights advocates while others are development supporters. This artificial dichotomy only serves to feed and perpetuate mistrust between developed and developing countries and suggests counter-intuitively that their priorities are diametrically opposed.

I very much look forward to the upcoming Commonwealth Heads of Government Meeting (CHOGM) in Sri Lanka. It is another important opportunity for us to initiate the required dialogue which leaders must have in order to correct such fundamental misunderstandings. Democracy and development are sides of the same coin. History has shown that democracy flourishes where development is advanced and vice versa. Thanks to the Commonwealth, seeds of democracy, planted years earlier, are bearing fruit and nourishing generations across the world. Still, as member states we cannot afford to relax our resolve and efforts to further entrench democracy and its institutions. It demands dedication and renewal. Consequently, developed countries must recognise that supporting developing country partners in their development goals is not a call for a Marshall Plan. It is simply about marshalling policies, action, and plans to support mutual prosperity. Likewise, advocacy for development assistance does not make developing countries any less committed to democracy.

Those developing countries whose populations are in dire need can be forgiven for their unconcealed insistence on 'bread and butter' issues but they also must balance this preoccupation with obligations to strengthen democratic institutions and safeguard the rights of citizens. Developed countries must reconcile that requests for technical assistance and capacity-building is as much about ensuring the advancement of poorer countries as it is about consolidating democracy. Developing countries too must demonstrate that democracy is a *sine qua non* for development.

The world is changing. Our individual nations are changing. The expectations and demands of our citizens are changing. Therefore, the Commonwealth must change. However, in shepherding that change we must ensure that this organisation is perceived and understood to be the unbiased partner and advocate of all. Therefore, whilst we mount the scaffolding to renew the structures and layers of the Commonwealth, we must be even more vigilant in preserving its core competencies, substantive components, its soft power, and the 'value for money' premium it brings to the citizens of the Commonwealth.

The CHOGM 2013 theme 'Growth with equity – inclusive development,' underpins the importance and role of democratic governments in advancing development. Inclusive development embraces the ideals of democracy and it encourages and signals a need for greater collaboration in addressing those areas of development that affect the rate at which Commonwealth member states advance. Strong democracies are built on the core strategies of networking and collaboration through every stage of the challenging development process. Our countries must therefore focus on new approaches that minimise and further remove barriers to our collective growth.

Commonwealth member states, irrespective of their levels of development, should see themselves as advocates of democracy and development. To guarantee the future viability and relevance of the Commonwealth, we must look at each other as partners. Although we may be competitors in some areas, the maturity of our democracies and the strategic significance of our collective development as Commonwealth nations should be such as to encourage us to engage in ways that continue to build up our peoples and nations.

We belong to a network of partners in which we help our fellow nations when needed and hold them and ourselves accountable for the collective good. It is a partnership which says we accept national responsibility, respect our international obligations, commit to the Commonwealth ideals, and rally around a common cause. Our strength lies in our shared values and principles and this will be essential to making sure that our citizens are the beneficiaries of a prosperous, democratic, and equitable future with inclusive development.

SMALL ISLAND DEVELOPING STATES THIRD INTERNATIONAL CONFERENCE

Samoa, September 2, 2014

Mr President, it is indeed a signal honour for me to address this august body at the Third International Conference of Small Island Developing States in this tranquil environment, the independent state of Samoa.

St Kitts and Nevis is pleased to lend its voice to the call for a concerted effort by the international community to recognise the special circumstances of Small Island Developing States (SIDS) as we continue to forge ahead with our thrust to achieve sustainable development in its three dimensions.

Indeed, my delegation is highly optimistic that this conference will provide the appropriate environment for the strengthening of existing partnerships and the establishment of new meaningful ones to assist small states which I have the honour to lead to achieve their sustainable development goals and objectives.

We recognise that on the sustained economic development front, it is necessary for SIDS to do all in their power to build their resilience to external economic shocks. We also recognise the importance of our development partners to conduct their macroeconomic and trade policies in a manner that will facilitate opportunities for SIDS to promote economic growth, reduce income gaps, reduce levels of poverty, and achieve our development aspirations.

St Kitts and Nevis, in spite of its small size, has a lesson to share with the international community of our experience in engaging international financial institutions to arrive at a position of debt sustainability. We will be happy to share these experiences at the appropriate forum facilitated by this conference.

Our tiny proud nation also has important experience to share in youth engagement and employment through our national People Employment Programme initiative which focuses on skills training through job placement. This initiative has touched the lives of thousands of young persons, offering them life-long experiences. We have been able to mobilise funding through a national foundation which stimulates economic growth and development. Lessons from this experience we shall also be delighted to share with the international community.

It would be remiss of me if I do not use this opportunity to call upon our development partners to assist SIDS to develop strategies to fight the scourge of non-communicable diseases (NCDs) throughout our regions. It is widely accepted that the wealth of a nation lies in large measure on its health. It is therefore necessary for SIDS to focus on this important aspect in order to achieve sustainable development. We therefore call for meaningful partnerships in achieving this objective.

Climate change for my country and region remains an existential challenge. Sea level rise in particular is of great concern to us given the historical pattern of settlement characterised by coastal communities. Such communities are most vulnerable to natural disaster and the more gradual yet real threat of sea level rise.

In this regard, I wish to reiterate the call for a stronger level of support from the international community for the development of climate change models which are appropriate to SIDS and for strengthening the region's capacity to conduct economic and social assessments for climate-proofing our development plans and programmes.

It is also critical that SIDS underscore the importance of the implementation of the Loss and Damage Framework under the meetings of the United Nations Framework Convention on Climate Change (UNFCCC). This important mechanism will play a critical role in mitigating the impacts on loss and damage associated with climate change.

The threats to us are real. They include loss of livelihood, loss of territory, waves of migration, forced or voluntary displacement, planned relocation, and catastrophic impacts on food supplies and national food security. We therefore cannot afford to sit by idly and discuss these threats without putting in place the required mechanisms to ensure minimal disruption to the livelihoods of our people.

We look forward to meetings that will seek to strengthen existing partnerships for sustainable development and the forging of new, meaningful partnerships.

Politics:
St Kitts-Nevis Labour Party (SKNLP)

St Kitts-Nevis Labour Party

In the run-up to the 2010 election, a number of events occurred which threatened SKN's hard-earned reputation for good government and peaceful, orderly elections. In January 2008, the Basseterre home of the manager of the SKN electoral office was set on fire by those opposed to the Labour government who wanted to provoke a crisis to distract the government from execution of its mandate and further their own political ambitions. Douglas was emphatic that political violence was not acceptable and that an attack on the electoral office was an attack on all Kittitians and Nevisians.

Part of the electoral process reform in 2009 involved adjusting the boundaries of constituencies to make them fairer and more equal. A constitutional requirement, constituency boundaries had last been modified twenty-five years earlier in 1984. Despite the fact that the boundary realignment was facilitated through a third-party Commonwealth assessment mission, the opposition spread rumours that the government was disregarding and trampling on the constitution, creating resentment and anger in some parts of the electorate. The charge was simply not true. That same year PAM also took two members of the Douglas cabinet to court on charges of contempt and further used the courts for political ends by also challenging the new boundaries.

By the second half of Douglas's third term in 2008, two members of the cabinet and a former cabinet member were speculating publicly as to how long Douglas would remain as political leader and what the succession process would look like. Timothy Harris, Sam Condor, and Dwyer Astaphan wanted him to set a firm date for his departure before the 2010 election. Douglas was always willing to go when the party wanted him to but he reminded the cabinet and party members that there was an established process for leadership renewal that involved all stakeholders including the cabinet, the SKNLP national executive, the leader's constituency branch, and rank and file party members. Increasing criticism of his leadership from the sidelines by the three dissidents was damaging the Labour brand and Douglas warned them that their behaviour could self-defeat the party in the coming election.

By Douglas's fourth term in late 2012, just before the 2013 budget presentation and encouraged by the dissidents, the opposition began questioning the legitimacy of the elected Labour government by sending to the clerk of the National Assembly a Motion of No Confidence. This was antithetical to the need for stability so that the country could continue to thrive and prosper. Douglas said voters expected cabinet members to be loyal to Labour. A Motion of No Confidence was a serious constitutional tool, he charged, being used in a 'very flippant and frivolous manner' for political gain.

In a meeting of the cabinet, all ministers except the two estranged members stated their full support for the 2013 budget. Harris and Condor walked out of the meeting and the budget was delayed awaiting sign-off of their sections although their cooperation was not needed to pass the budget through parliament. The cabinet crisis escalated from there with Timothy Harris undermining the government's programmes and initiatives and refusing to confirm that he would vote against a Motion of No Confidence in a government in which, ironically, he was senior minister. With no choice, Douglas had Harris's ministerial appointment revoked by the Governor-General on January 25, 2013. On January 30, 2013, long-time Douglas comrade and Deputy Prime Minister Sam Condor resigned from cabinet in support of Harris. Harris clearly wanted to be prime minister and was quite prepared to seriously damage the Labour Party in his quest.

Throughout 2013 and 2014, SKNLP ministers, candidates and senior party officials continued to defend what they believed to be the primacy of the ballot and warn of the danger of thoughtless parliamentary manoeuvres by the opposition designed for personal gain being sold to the electorate as acts of principle. Concurrently, there was a belief among PAM supporters that their party was virtually dead and that if they did not defeat Labour in the next election, Labour would become the 'permanent' government of St Kitts and Nevis.

The increasing desperation and tension were forcefully driven home early in the new year of 2014 when the Venezuelan embassy in Basseterre was torched and arson was attempted at the OAS building. Douglas condemned these acts of wanton violence as attempts to undermine the confidence of the people in the leadership of the government and destabilise the country. It was, he said, taking political opposition 'far too far.'

Douglas's and his cabinet's refusal to put the opposition Motion of No Confidence to a vote in the National Assembly gave his critics and detractors a cudgel to beat him with constantly for many months and, some say, was a major contributor to his defeat in the 2015 election. There was no law defining the time period in which a Motion of No Confidence had to be voted on although parliamentary tradition suggested that a No Confidence Motion should be dealt with in a timely fashion. To many, Douglas seemed autocratic and dictatorial and while Douglas accepted some responsibility for pushing the boundaries of democratic tradition, the Motion of No Confidence timing matter was before the court and he firmly believed that his stance was more about preserving the path to progress and development and ensuring that internal party strife, greed, and hunger for power did not stall progress. While the confidence of the National Assembly may have been in question, he had, Douglas said, the 'full confidence' of the vast majority of voters and the investment community.

CONSTITUENCY SPEECH PRE-2010 ELECTION
Sporting Complex, St Paul's, Capisterre, January 2010

I was conceived, born and raised in the bowels of LABOUR country. My secondary education was made possible through a scholarship that was personally sponsored by the late Robert Llewellyn Bradshaw, the first leader of a movement that came to be called the LABOUR PARTY. In other words, I am a natural-born LABOUR. Nothing can change that.

I have been very fortunate to live and serve among the people that I love and who love the LABOUR PARTY. My loyalty has been to them, as firm as it has been to our country. I have asked them to support each other. They responded by creating the Golden Age Club for seniors. They revitalised and re-energised YOUNG LABOUR ... see dem deh! They formed themselves into a support group for teen mothers.

Saddle Fiesta and Festivale de Capisterre have captured the hearts of all who love the culture. Two National Carnival Queens from Constituency 6, my constituency, were crowned between 2004 and the present. The resurgence of cultural currency is an indication that my people, the people of Constituency 6, have regained their dignity and self-worth.

After fifteen years of being treated as outcasts, denied access to some of the most basic social amenities, and existing in social and economic drought, my people have regained a sense of hope. Health centres have been renovated and refurbished in St Paul's and Saddlers. Sometimes two doctors are seeing patients at the same time in the Health Centre.

All the schools in the constituency have been expanded, upgraded and fenced to keep our children safe during my term in office. A major sporting complex and improved sporting facilities were opened in St Paul's, Saddlers and Newton Ground to serve the sports-loving people of the constituency. In Saddlers, a modern secondary education facility, the first of its kind on St Kitts and Nevis, is equipped to offer an expanded curriculum with equal emphasis on skills and academics.

I have yet to deliver on the day care centre for St Paul's as I delivered for Newton Ground and Saddlers. But it will be completed in my next term. A modern sporting complex which serves youth and adults alike in Newton Ground will also be completed during my next term. The construction of sporting facilities for Dieppe Bay and Parsons which have already been approved and started will be completed within the first few months of my next term.

I have promised to create in our midst, in the heart of back-a-de-lan, an economic centre, a hive of new job opportunities for the young, not so young, and the soon-to-be-born. We are training employees and entrepreneurs for the jobs that will emerge from the developments at Kittitian Hill, Black Rocks, Beaumont Park, and La Vallee. Developments which will transform the lives of the hard-working people of my constituency. I know my people need more opportunities for employment closer to home and we have begun the process to make that change. That's why thriving businesses in the construction sector have emerged such as Rock&Dirt, Roland's Construction, Thomas Richards, James Pinney and Lesroy French, and others in the retail trade like Maxine's Mega Bucks, Bevis Superette, Sunrise Bakery, Eugene 'Hearty' Thomas Restaurant, Avril's Catering Services, and Island Purified Water.

I have learned during my years in government that development comes at a slower pace than I would like for the people of my constituency and the country at large. I have asked my people to wait in the interest of the country and they have done so. My constituency has been patient with me.

Our youth population continues to challenge us with their demands for more higher education, a wider range of job opportunities, and secure family lives. They are less patient and they must be, for that is characteristic of healthy, educated, and ambitious young people, such as those who live in Constituency 6. It is for them and for those who have been supportive of me that I owe a depth of gratitude and the obligation to make our lives better.

The majority of our young people have accepted education as a vehicle to prosperity. Many have passed CXC with flying colours. Hundreds have passed though CFBC with associate degrees and other higher-level qualifications. Our people have studied at home and abroad and have returned fully qualified as engineers, agriculturalists, chemists, accountants, and chefs. They have been trained in landscaping, computer science, information technology, computer analysis, and engineering. There has been an influx of qualified men and women in the villages that I serve.

During the last two elections, over 90 per cent of you voted for me. You have given me an overwhelming mandate to represent you. I will soon return with a formal request for you to give me another opportunity to serve you. I will continue to do my best to ensure that I serve you with humility knowing that you are the ones who have given me this opportunity to serve. I will serve you with the conviction, dedication, and love that you have shared with me. We have shared moments of joy and pain together. We have laughed and cried together. You have encouraged me and come to my defence. You have been my ears and my conscience. You have kept me grounded in reality and reminded me that I have an obligation to stay true to the people who moulded me.

I have sought to practice integrity in my public lie. I have sought to serve with fairness and good intentions. I have held clinics and sought to meet your requests. I have listened and acted always with your interest in mind. I may not have met all your expectations, but I am human and I crave your understanding in ways and on occasions that I have erred.

I still believe in giving a hand up. I never lose the opportunity to ensure that doors are left open to those who come after me. I have been a beneficiary of a scholarship that changed my fortunes from a cane-cutter, cattle herder, or misguided youth. For as long as I serve you, most of you will have the positive, life-changing opportunities that you have come to expect from a hand-up. I will continue to serve you faithfully and ensure that your lives are improved by each decision that is made and every policy and programme implemented.

I am here to give you a second chance in life.

I owe a debt of gratitude to the people of my constituency. They have made me who I am and have given me the opportunity to serve them and this country for many years. Their overwhelming vote of confidence at the polls, time and time again suggest that I am serving them well. There is much more that I have to offer them although I can never repay them for the life experiences that they have afforded me from the office of an elected servant of the people.

Firebombing at the Home of the Electoral Office Manager

Basseterre, January 11, 2008

At 2:15 am on Thursday January 10, 2008, while most people in St Kitts and Nevis were asleep, and when most people were in what they consider to be the safest place for them, their homes, a terrifying explosion shattered the silence at the home of this country's Electoral Office manager. Flames filled his garage which is not separate from his home, but is attached to his home. Propane gas canisters, capable of inflicting untold harm on both the Knight family and others in Bird Rock, stood terrifyingly close to the flames. The family vehicle, inside their garage, was on fire.

Some ask whether the car could have spontaneously 'burst into flames.' Others question whether this could have been the result of an 'electrical malfunction.' Reasonable people would naturally explore these explanations. And that is, indeed, exactly what was done. As a matter of fact, those are the explanations that I was hoping to hear. Any other conclusions were going to be too troubling to me, as prime minister, and to you as well. It pains me to report, however, that my government has been informed by Acting Commissioner Williams of the Royal St Kitts and Nevis Police Force that all signs point to arson, that this was a deliberate act planned and executed with wicked and criminal intent.

Oliver Knight is a loyal servant of this nation. He serves as this country's Electoral Office manager. And he has, in recent weeks, been subjected to a barrage of verbal attacks and almost unending disruptions in the execution of his duties. Persons have attempted to force their way into his office demanding meetings for which there were no appointments. They have aggressively questioned nationals attempting to register to vote. They have tried in every way to disrupt the smooth functioning of the Electoral Office.

It is clear to me, and to my government, that there are those who are attempting to create confusion in this country, to spark a political crisis, to get grassroots activists from various political parties at each others' throats so as to advance their own political ambitions.

Let me be perfectly clear.

This is *not* Lebanon.

This is *not* Pakistan.

This is *not* the West Bank.

And my government and the security forces of this country utterly and completely refuse to allow any individual, any organisation, or any gathering of evil souls to turn it into such.

This country is the gem of the Eastern Caribbean. And this government will allow neither the plans of a few, nor the actions of their willing pawns, to cause our country to be viewed by the international community, and to be talked about by the international community, the way they talk about our dear CARICOM sister, Haiti, the way they talk about our beloved CARICOM partner, Jamaica, the way they look on with horror at the tumult, the confusion, the bedlam, in other countries far from our shores. That is not for us!

The ordinary people in Haiti and Jamaica are not naturally violent. But there are persons in Jamaica and persons in Haiti who have, over the years, revved up ordinary people, paid ordinary people, manipulated ordinary people, into creating confusion, spreading terror, creating panic and fear on command. Not here! And the people of St Kitts and Nevis must say – Not here!

It is because of the plans of a wicked few that everyone in those countries have had to pay such a tremendous price, and their countries' reputations have taken such a savage beating. We in St Kitts and Nevis have worked too long and too hard to get where we are for us to allow these types of acts and the associated panic and fear to take root here.

Let there be no doubt, the attack on Oliver Knight was an attack on the people of this country. It was an attack on the people of this country because Mr Knight has been tasked with the responsibility to manage the office through which Kittitians and Nevisians establish their right to choose their government in elections that are free and fair, and free from fear.

Those persons who entered Oliver Knight's property in the dead of night endangering the lives of Oliver Knight, Mrs Knight, and their neighbours in Bird Rock, are attempting to inject fear into the electoral process by bringing possible death and certain danger to the very doorsteps of those tasked with managing the electoral process. One newspaper in St Kitts predicted months ago that blood would flow during the upcoming elections. Another newspaper a few weeks ago wondered in an editorial how many would die during the elections that will be held this year or next. Everyone needs to get a grip. These are not thoughts that one should idly toss around. We must stop playing with fire.

I am calling on the people of St Kitts and Nevis to understand that a threat to one of us is a threat to all of us. The largest political conflagrations often begin with single, seemingly isolated acts. And countries that allow themselves to spiral out of control, with senseless outbursts of political violence, end up destroying themselves. In the end, everyone loses.

The rest of the world looks on and no-one really cares. It is up to us in St Kitts & Nevis to learn from the mistakes of other countries. It is up to us in St Kitts & Nevis to protect this country that we have built through our sweat and our vision. It is up to us all, young and old, black and white, rich and poor, to condemn in the strongest possible terms all acts of political violence, whether large or small, whether conducted in the glare of day or the dead of night. Because if we fail to condemn these acts when they first begin, they will, in time, spread and multiply and consume us all.

My government pledges to the people of St Kitts and Nevis to establish exactly who it was who planned this frightening act. We pledge to establish exactly who it was who executed this frightening act. And we pledge that they will be dealt with to the full extent of the law. Not only because of the danger this act posed to Oliver Knight and his neighbours, but, equally importantly, because of the dangers that this type of act, left unpunished, holds for us all.

ELECTORAL REFORM

National Assembly, June 12, 2008

Mr Speaker, it is with an elevated sense of pride that I rise to make a statement to bring members of this honourable house and the wider public up-to-date with our progress with the electoral reform process in general but more specifically, with the voter confirmation process. Without taking too much time to retrace where we have travelled over the past two years, since the entire public has been involved in this process, I will simply highlight some of the important milestones achieved over the past three years.

In August of 2005, in keeping with our commitment to improve our system of democracy, my government invited a Commonwealth assessment mission to St Kitts and Nevis to consult with a series of stakeholders including political parties, the supervisor of elections, the Electoral Commission, members of the media, and civil society organisations. The objective of the mission was to glean information on the electoral process in our Federation with a view to making recommendations for improvement.

Upon the receipt of the report from the Commonwealth assessment mission, my government set about to critically examine the report and to take onboard and implement its recommendations. As a result of this work, in August 2006, a white paper outlining a mechanism to achieve electoral reform was compiled and, shortly thereafter, the formal launch of the electoral reform process ensued.

The framework outlined by the white paper, and which was approved by three of our four major political parties, had at its core a number of committees whose role it was to assume responsibility for major aspects of the reform process. The Electoral Reform Consultative Committee was charged with harnessing the ideas of our people at home and abroad, by engaging them in public consultations and providing a report thereon. The National Advisory Electoral Reform and Boundaries Committee was charged with making concrete suggestions for electoral reform, having studied the report on the consultations conducted by the earlier group. Another committee created was the Boundaries Technical Committee.

The recommendations advanced by the advisory committee were submitted to the parliamentary constitutional and electoral reform and boundaries committee for its consideration so that it could advise the attorney-general as to how our electoral laws should be amended.

Mr Speaker, as a consequence of the work done by the appointed committees and the input made by the wider public and all political parties, on December 7, 2007, the *National Assembly Elections Act* was amended by this parliament, bringing into being a new order. Specifically for the purposes of the present discourse, it brought into being a national identification card which will assist persons in voting in national elections, and a new confirmation process. While I do not have more specific useful details to date on the issuance of the national identification card, I wish to inform that card printing and distribution, saving any circumstance yet unforeseen, shall have been commenced by the first week of July.

It is to the matter of voter confirmation that I now turn my attention. The aspect of our new electoral laws relating to voter confirmation represents the best compromise to satisfy the recommendation that our overseas nationals not be disenfranchised as we seek to reform the system and construct a new voters list. This fact has been well articulated time and time again. Voter confirmation, upon the declaration of the appropriate order, commenced on December 27 and it is presently scheduled to end on September 30, 2008.

In responding to the needs of the electorate, mobile confirmation was instituted giving every registered voter an enhanced opportunity to confirm his or her registration before September 30. In St Kitts specifically, the mobile confirmation began on April 14 and should conclude this coming Saturday June 14. This fact has been part of the motivation for my update today. I believe that people all across this fair land will concur that the mobile confirmation has indeed been successful. I make this conclusion for two reasons, as follows:

What we have undertaken over the past nine weeks is an exercise of mobilising people and hardware; working with telecommunication providers to install high bandwidth secure network connections on a makeshift basis; ensuring that the public is properly informed about confirmation schedules in a timely manner; and coordinating and synchronising the operations of the mobile stations and the operations at the central electoral office in Basseterre. The success of this exercise has been due to the diligent work of staff at the electoral office, many of whom came onboard as a result of the confirmation exercise. Their operations were technically supported by operatives in the Ministry of Technology. The support from the security forces was highly disciplined and commendable. What did us most proud, however, was the participation of the electorate by taking their valuable time out to make use of the mobile confirmation facilities. People of all ages and all levels of physical ability came and confirmed their registration to vote in the next general elections. That was truly amazing and I want to publicly and officially thank all who participated to make our efforts the success they have been.

The other area of success relates to the fact that our new electoral system was put to the test by a number of unscrupulous people over the past few months and it passed that test. This is an indication of the measure of the integrity of our new computerised voter registration management system. This new system has been able to detect attempts by persons to register multiple times and in multiple places. Such was the case when, very early in the process, two individuals confirmed in St Kitts and then attempted to register for a second time in Nevis. Such was the most recent case when a lady from Half Way Tree who had confirmed her own registration in Basseterre early in the process, turned up in Half Way Tree in the company of a well-known politician to confirm her registration for a second time in her daughter's name. These examples are evidence of the capability of the system that my government has implemented and of which my government is justly proud.

Never again will those who have sought to exploit the loopholes in the old system find comfort in this new electoral environment. The electoral office has over the last several months adhered to procedures requiring the very highest standard for registration and confirmation. Electoral officials were required to extract all the pertinent details and they sought all the necessary documentation to ascertain the identity of an applicant for confirmation or registration. It was difficult for some to understand and accept that a new era had come, and that no longer was the electoral system going to tolerate mere word of mouth or unverified claims. I want to thank members of the public who willingly complied with the new requirements because it is these requirements that have helped to bolster the integrity of the system and make it one that we can all be proud of. I am extremely proud of the new electoral system we have created.

Mr Speaker, we still have some work to do. The overseas confirmation of our registered voters is still very much on the agenda and we shall soon make the relevant announcements to facilitate those of our registered nationals who are living abroad. The groundwork is being done and we expect the overseas confirmation to be as successful as our mobile confirmation exercise has been.

Silver Jubilee
St Kitts and Nevis Independence
Warner Park Stadium, Basseterre, September 19, 2008

By the grace of God, we are gathered here today to celebrate twenty-five years as an independent member of the world community of nations, and for this we are truly grateful.

St Kitts and Nevis is the tiniest country in the western hemisphere. Indeed, we are one of the tiniest nations in the entire world. In light of this, we should all take special pride in the fact that during the twenty-five years in which we have been a sovereign nation, during the twenty-five years in which we have been fully responsible for steering our ship of state, during the twenty-five years in which it has been up to us to establish our own priorities and adhere to them, during these twenty-five years in a world so often torn apart by division and strife, pestilence and hardship, we the people of St Kitts and Nevis have together, all of us, built a nation that is both politically stable and economically sound.

It has been a long journey to this moment, and a difficult one. But it has been a heroic one as well, for we as a people have persevered over these many centuries and, with the help of a merciful God, we have triumphed. I say that our journey to this moment has been long, and I assert that we have triumphed because our story stretches back to a time few of us can even imagine. Ours was a journey that began with the extreme horrors of slavery and the sharp confines of colonialism. But through the assertion of our humanity, ours also became a journey of resistance and courage and mobilisation until our own efforts caused our journey to quicken with hope and lighten with possibility. It quickened with the hope presented by statehood and it lightened with the possibilities promised by independence. All because of our efforts. All because of our strivings. All because of our focus and sacrifice and determination.

And so, after almost four hundred years on these two islands, here we are. After twenty-five years in control of our own affairs on these islands, here we stand. In many ways, our strivings and accomplishments up until this point can be viewed as phase one of our evolution as a people. And because for hundreds of years our history had been one of deprivation and exclusion for much of the twentieth century, almost as a matter of necessity we were required to focus almost exclusively on the pressing need for material security, for economic advancement, for doors unfairly bolted to be opened at last.

These are the tasks that have preoccupied us thus far. Our coming of age as a people was marked by the determination and the success of the Rt Excellent Sir Robert Llewellyn Bradshaw, the Rt Excellent Sir Caleb Azariah Paul Southwell, and the Rt Excellent Sir Joseph N. France at winning for every Kittitian and Nevisian the right to vote, despite others' determination to keep us voteless. It was marked by their determination and success at winning for every Kittitian and Nevisian the right to a secondary education despite others' determination to keep us locked out, uneducated and uninformed. It was marked by their determination and success at winning for every Kittitian and Nevisian social security during old age despite others' indifference to the shame and destitution that gripped our forebears by the thousands when they became too old to earn their daily bread.

Messrs Bradshaw, France, and Southwell, national heroes all, started a movement that not only won for us the right to vote. More importantly, their efforts changed the way we saw ourselves, and the way others saw us. And their efforts stirred within us, and within the hearts of Caribbean people everywhere, the dream, the desire, and the demand for independence from Britain. And so it was with pride that we saw men like the Rt Honourable Dr Sir Alphonse Kennedy Simmonds complete the task that Bradshaw, Southwell and France had begun, when at the stroke of midnight on September 18, 1983, the union jack was lowered, our own flag was raised, and Sir Kennedy became the first Prime Minister of St Kitts and Nevis. We stood at the door of the great unknown, for the first time an independent people, vindicating the centuries-old struggles of our enslaved ancestors like Marcus of the Woods, to be truly free.

And so we gather here not only to celebrate, but also to reflect. Not only to look back, but also to look forward as we continue our journey as a people along an unknown and unknowable path, each step taken, each turn avoided, each choice that we do and do not make combining to shape and determine our destiny.

We have done very well over these twenty-five years. So well that our students in creating the theme for our independence celebrations have described the period thus: 'Pride, Development, Progress, 25 Years of Success.' The United Nations attests that the quality of life in St Kitts and Nevis is far superior to that of the vast majority of countries in the world today. Our macro-economic indicators have advanced us to the classification of a middle-income country. Indeed, judged by the United Nations Development Index, we are the leading nation in the Eastern Caribbean sub-region and we rank among the top third of all nations in the world.

Our future, with the help of God, is ours to shape. People of St Kitts and Nevis – what does the future demand of us? The future demands of us vision and determination. The future demands of us self-awareness and self-mastery. The future demands of us courage, conviction, competence, and compassion. Nothing less will do.

At this stage of our development, we must now – all of us – place as much emphasis on developing our intangible assets as we have on developing our very important tangible assets, our physical infrastructure. We must do so because it is the powerful intangible assets like discipline and determination, initiative and perseverance, fair play and integrity, respect for self and for others, that determine the fate of a nation. It is these powerful intangibles that determine which societies realise their potential, which people truly become masters of their own destiny.

Almost seventy years ago, Maslow noted that human beings in all cultures concern themselves first and foremost with survival, with physical safety, with their material well-being. He further noted that once these needs have been generally met, we begin to have higher order needs – the need for community, the need to have one's skills, competencies, and character recognised, the need to be thought of highly by one's fellow man. These are the needs of psychologically healthy individuals and these are the needs of psychologically healthy nations. And this is where St Kitts and Nevis now stands. We are at that point in our history where focusing only on physical, material, and economic advances will not do. We must now also stress and develop the powerful intangibles that define a people as well. And so, we must now, like all responsible peoples, begin to look inward to assess not only who we are as a people, but who and what we want to be, and what it will take for us to get there.

We have been very successful at building schools across the length and breadth of the Federation. Together we must now promote the intangible assets of dedication and discipline on the part of parents, teachers, and students, to stimulate innovative young minds so they will be equipped to seize the new opportunities being created by our evolving and expanding economy.

We have been very successful at establishing hospitals and health centres throughout St Kitts and Nevis to serve as oases of preventive and curative care. Together we must now promote the intangible asset of adults becoming very, very serious about shaping young people's characters so as to prevent our health care facilities and communities throughout the Federation from becoming embroiled in youth-based conflict, hostility, and rage.

We have been very successful at distributing hundreds of acres of land to the Federation's farmers. Together we must now promote the intangible assets of self-knowledge and self-awareness that will cause our people to avoid hypertension, diabetes, and other deadly diseases by choosing healthy, natural, life-preserving local foods over attractively packaged, but chemically-laden, unhealthy imports.

We have been very successful at establishing important educational facilities like the Clarence Fitzroy Bryant College and the Information Technology Centre. Together, we must now promote the intangible assets of vision and initiative so that our people will continue to gravitate toward these facilities, keenly aware that these institutions were established to ensure that the people of St Kitts and Nevis will be equipped to compete with anyone, whether as employees or as entrepreneurs, in the Federation's progressive post-sugar services economy.

Fellow citizens, I stated earlier that our history in St Kitts and Nevis began with the horrors of slavery. That was our history here. However, the origins of our ancestors were quite different. Long before the blow of transatlantic slavery, indeed as early as the thirteenth century, West Africans were smelting high quality iron, copper and steel, inventing musical instruments for their cultural and spiritual entertainment and upliftment, weaving and wearing fine cotton and linen, constructing fast-moving, sleek canoes to facilitate trade and commerce. Livestock and crop production was not merely for subsistence, but also for trade. Their goldsmithery was legendary. May the example of our ancestor's energy, competence, and self-mastery inspire us.

The late Errol Barrow, former prime minister of Barbados, said of the Caribbean, 'We are a people with an identity and a culture and a history ... We are viable, functioning societies with ... intellectual and institutional resources …We have a heritage of exquisite natural beauty entrusted to us. The Caribbean is, after all, a civilisation.' May his words empower us.

Finally, as together we prepare to build a future that is good, the second epistle of Peter, 1:5-8, seems to be speaking directly to us, for whom faith is the rock on which we stand:

'… add to your faith, virtue'

we are told, 'and to virtue, knowledge.

To knowledge, self-control,

and to self-control, perseverance.

To perseverance, godliness,

and to godliness, brotherly kindness.

And to brotherly kindness, love.'

If these things are ours, we are promised, and if they abound, we will be neither barren nor unfruitful.

May we ever be guided and inspired by these words. May we always do what is best for this land, this land of infinite beauty that has been placed in our care. May we forever consider and protect generations yet unborn.

ELECTORAL BOUNDARY CHANGES

Ask the Prime Minister Radio Programme
ZIZ Broadcasting Corporation, March 3, 2009

I want to talk today about electoral boundary changes. More accurately, I want to make sure that the people of St Kitts and Nevis understand the facts and hear the truth about boundary changes – what our constitution says, when the government is allowed to change boundaries, and when the government is not allowed to change the boundaries.

All around the world, people talk about how dangerous it is to shout 'Fire!' in a crowded room. This is discouraged, it is frowned upon, and it is the height of irresponsibility because it makes people panic. It causes people to stampede. It creates chaos and disorder. Well, I think that there are some in this country who have been doing the political equivalent of crying 'Fire!' in a crowded room where electoral boundary changes are concerned, because they have been deliberately misleading and revving up the public into thinking that this government is trampling the constitution and doing what we want where electoral boundaries are concerned. Nothing could be further from the truth.

I understand that in order to win political power, those in opposition first have to convince voters that those in government no longer deserve their support. That's fine. No problem there. What those in opposition must not do in their quest for power, however, is to deliberately upset, mislead, and fool the people. It *is* like shouting 'Fire!' in a crowded room when politicians try to sell the people of St Kitts and Nevis on the idea that their government is disregarding the constitution, changing the rules, and doing what they want with no regard for the law. Supporters of the former government have to cut this out because when they manipulate people's emotions in this way, they create resentment and anger, and this could lead to bedlam.

I want to turn now to the specifics of changing the electoral boundaries. There has been a lot of talk for months now about the government planning to change the boundaries although the constitution says that boundaries cannot be changed less than two years before an election. This charge has been raised during my monthly press conference by someone with legal training who is aligned with the opposition. It has been raised on talk shows by mouthpieces of the former government and, as a result, even their ordinary supporters have been misled into running around warning people about this.

But let us look at the facts:

The government of St Kitts and Nevis functions within the confines and constraints established by the constitution of this country. This constitution was drafted, crafted, and created by the former government. The leaders of that party, therefore, know everything that is in this constitution. Their party wrote it. And Section 50 of the constitution, subsection one, says that the Constituency Boundaries Commission is responsible for reviewing the number and boundaries of the constituencies into which Saint Christopher and Nevis is divided. It also says that the commission is to submit these reports to the governor-general. And it says that the commission can recommend that the boundaries be changed, or it can recommend that the boundaries not be changed. The important point here, however, is that the constitution says that boundary changes must be submitted to the governor-general anywhere between two and five years since the last report. Let me repeat that: The constitution says that boundary recommendations must be submitted to the governor-general by the Boundaries Commission anywhere between two and five years since the last boundary report.

Why on God's green earth then, have these people been trying to convince the public that the constitution says that electoral boundaries cannot be changed less than two years before an election? Do they want the people to become angry? Do they want them to feel wronged? Do they want them to feel disrespected by the government? This lie about the constitution prohibiting the changing of boundaries under two years before an election is huge enough to choke a horse. And let me tell you what is the best evidence of that. In March 1984, the then-supervisor of elections announced that there would be new boundaries in the upcoming elections. But he also announced that the people of St Kitts and Nevis would not know what these new boundaries would be until after parliament had already been dissolved. That is, when elections were right on the people's doorstep. And that is exactly what happened.

The citizens of St Kitts and Nevis need to get the facts on boundary changes because they need to know that, as we move toward elections, this government is acting in accordance with the constitution.

St Kitts-Nevis Labour Party Annual Conference

St Kitts Marriott Resort, May 17, 2009

We are gathered here today because we belong to the St Kitts-Nevis Labour Party. And we belong to a country, a tradition, a system in which we, the people, choose the government that we want. Governments are not imposed on us in St Kitts and Nevis. We choose our governments.

And at this time in our history, at this important crossroads in the fate of this nation, we understand very well the choices that stand before us. We know how far-reaching the consequences of our choices will be. And we know, now more than ever, that the future, yes, the very future of this precious land of ours, truly is in our hands.

Way back at the dawn of the Labour Party, before most of us in this room were even born, there was government in St Kitts and Nevis, yes. But back then, we the people had nothing to do with either the composition, the priorities, or the focus of the government. We the people had no impact, no relevance, no significance as far as those governments were concerned. Colonial governments existed simply and solely to protect the powerful, to protect those who clearly needed no protection.

The vast majority of people living in St Kitts and Nevis at that time though, in the '30s, and the '40s, and right up through the '50s, were in desperate, urgent, heart-breaking need of protection. And it was out of this urge to protect, it was out of this need to be more than we had been, it was out of this determination to bring about real change, constructive change, sweeping change, that the St Kitts-Nevis Labour Party was born. Our parents and grandparents needed change in the worst way. Change from sickness. Change from hunger. Change from poverty. Change from exclusion. Change from illiteracy. Change from powerlessness. Change from shame.

Those were the changes our people needed and those were the changes that Labour, through Bradshaw and Challenger and Sebastian and Manchester and France and Southwell and Bryant and St John Payne and all those who came before us, delivered.

Comrades! Labour brought about such sweeping changes in this land of ours that you and I have never had to sit and watch as others decide who will lead the government. Labour brought about such sweeping changes in this land of ours that you and I, today, do not have to feel helpless, unable to determine for ourselves in which direction this country will go. Labour brought about such sweeping changes that, today, every single man and woman, young or old, weak or strong, wicked or good, rich or poor has the right, the inalienable, sacred, forever-and-a-day right to determine who will lead this land of ours.

We may take the right to vote for granted today, but never let it be forgotten how truly phenomenal a change this was. Never let it be forgotten exactly how this sweeping change came about. Never let it be forgotten who brought this about, literally through blood, sweat, and tears. In that one, single, momentous act, Labour caused our hearts and our minds and our souls to matter for the first time. In ways we never mattered before. Because Labour gave us, every single Kittitian and Nevisian, the right to choose, the power to choose, the pressing and urgent and sacred responsibility to choose.

And so today, Comrades, as we gather once again, we know that St Kitts and Nevis is moving ever closer to that day when we will be called upon for that important ritual on which the very essence of our democracy rests. Yes, Comrades, before too long every able-bodied, registered voter in this country will be asked to step out, to step up, and to choose.

Before we talk about whom and what and why we will choose though, I want to talk about past choices. Choices made by you over the years. And in this regard, I want to thank you, the members of Labour, for choosing Labour. For believing in Labour. And for standing by Labour all these years.

And I want to thank parliamentary representatives Martin and Astaphan and Condor and Herbert and Harris and Liburd whose words and actions and perseverance and dedication caused you, dear comrades, to vote for Labour in 2004, and in the election before that, and in the election before that!

Let us all thank the Honourable Sam Terrence Condor, deputy prime minister of this country, for being the standard-bearer for Labour in constituency three. Sam is a man of commitment, and compassion, and decency who is the personification of our motto 'For the good that we can do.' At a time when the training and education of our young people is more important than ever before, Sam has been responsible for some of the most revolutionary and far-reaching education proposals our country has ever seen, and we thank him for his dedication and service to this party and this country. Sam and his wife, Jean, are stalwarts in this Labour Party. They are two of the pillars on which this party stands. And we, the St Kitts-Nevis Labour Party, thank them for all that they have done for this nation for all these years.

Let us thank the Honourable Asim Martin, parliamentary representative for constituency one. In recent years, Asim has held one of the most important and one of the most trying portfolios in this government. It is no secret that I am referring to the difficulties we were at one time facing with regard to electricity. The challenges were enormous, the trials seemingly unending. But Asim grappled with these challenges and demonstrated a determination and a tirelessness that was nothing short of extraordinary. And today, what was once a source of such frustration, is now, thank heavens, clearly and certainly a thing of the past. Thank you, Asim, for your steadfastness, for your effectiveness, for your dedication.

Let us thank the Honourable G. A. Dwyer Astaphan, parliamentary representative for constituency two, Central Basseterre, a constituency that has always held a special significance to all political parties in this country. Dwyer's rapport with the people of Central Basseterre and the impact that he has had on their lives, are significant. Indeed, his deep commitment to our country and our people represents, at its best, what makes Labour, Labour. Dwyer's vision and his passion have been an asset to this party and this nation and for this we thank him.

Let us thank The Honourable Rupert Herbert of Constituency 4 who, with his quiet strength, and his calm and understated manner, has served his constituency and this nation so well. As a result, Minister Rupert Herbert has been able to keep Old Road, Challengers, Verchilds, Middle Island, Lamberts, Conyers, Godwin Ghaut and Halfway Tree standing firm with Labour. The respect for Herbie, the affection for Herbie, and the regard for Herbie throughout the length and breadth of his constituency has ensured that the beliefs of Labour, the values of Labour, and the interests of this country, are honourably reflected in the man that constituency four has sent to parliament.

Let us thank The Honourable Dr Timothy Harris, chairman of this St Kitts-Nevis Labour Party. Tim is a man of keen intellect and powerful oratory. He is a man of great political passion who cares deeply about the progress and the advancement of every man, woman, and child in this country, and he works hard and effectively to protect the nation's interests at all times. At this time of swirling economic crises, his stewardship of the ministry of finance is key to the stability of this nation. Constituency seven, this party, and this country have been superbly served by the quality of Tim's efforts and the quality of Tim's mind and to him we are most indebted.

And I want to thank The Honourable Cedric Liburd for the thoroughness with which he approaches his responsibilities to the people of Cayon and Ottleys, Shadwell and New Road, St Peters and Keys and Conaree. At a time when food security is more important than ever, at a time when the availability of life-sustaining food is becoming a matter of national security in nations large and small, Cedric is at the helm of a key and crucial ministry, the Ministry of Agriculture, and with his keen management of this ministry he is securing our very health and survival way beyond today. For this, and so much more, we thank him.

I ask the parliamentary representatives to join me in applauding the members of the Labour Party who have entrusted with us the responsibility to lead this nation.

I ask the members of the St Kitts-Nevis Labour Party to join me in applauding the parliamentary representatives who have worked so hard and served this nation so well.

And I now ask everyone, parliamentary reps and all party members, to now welcome the new faces, the new energy, the new standard-bearers of this party, Marcella Liburd, constituency two! Glenn Phillip, constituency four! Dr Norgen Wilson, constituency five!

Marcella, daughter of the late Ann Liburd. Sister of the late Fitzroy Bryant. Sportswoman. Teacher. Lawyer. This country's first female speaker. But most importantly a good and decent, concerned and committed, dependable and visionary public servant. We thank Marcella for stepping forward at this time in our nation's history. You know and I know just how much Central Basseterre needs her commitment to creating the stronger families and the safer communities. Labour is stronger because of her.

Glenn Ghost Phillip. Humble beginnings. No connections. No special advantages. Just hard work. Followed by real success. Exactly the type of example that the young people of this country need to see more of. If anybody thinks that being born poor means that you can never escape, I say look at Glenn Phillip. If anybody thinks that hard work does not pay off, I say look at Glenn Phillip. The people of constituency four know that Glen has spent his life working with, playing with, sharing with them, as a star athlete, as an active member of the community, as an executive in a major corporation who, after attending university in the United States, came right back to constituency four. Glenn Phillip is connected to the people of constituency four. Glenn Phillip is of constituency four. And Labour is stronger because of him.

Dr Norgen Wilson. Hard-working student. Accomplished doctor. High-ranking member of the St Kitts-Nevis Defence Force. Staunch advocate of community pride. Firm believer in community initiative. A man who knows the power of community action. A man whose middle name is empowerment. Norgen Wilson is the man for constituency five. He has the confidence they need. He has the character they need. He has that human touch and that solid persona that they need. And Labour is stronger because of him.

Marcella!

Glenn!

Norgen!

New energy!

New vision!

New ideas for Labour!

And so, Comrades, we stand ready for the race ahead. Not only the electoral race, but the race for the future and the destiny of this land that we call home.

What is it that is at stake here, Comrades?

Let us look at the facts:

The Peoples Action Movement had fifteen years in which to turn our people into homeowners. In fifteen years, they created two hundred and fifty new homeowners.

In fourteen years, Labour created two thousand five hundred.

The Peoples Action Movement had fifteen years in which to give the young people of this country a chance for a university education. In fifteen years, they approved twenty-one student loans.

In fourteen years, Labour approved 1,776.

The Peoples Action Movement had fifteen years in which to help students finance their education beyond high school when their parents could not afford to. In fifteen years, PAM approved $965,000 in Development Bank student loans.

In fourteen years Labour approved $84.2 million.

The Peoples Action Movement used their time, their energy, and taxpayers' money to build that multi-million-dollar highway on the south-east peninsula through private lands, thereby sending the value of that land sky-high for its private owners and turning them into multi-millionaires.

We, in Labour, used our time, our energy, and taxpayers' money to build roads for new housing developments for the people of Keys, and Boyds, and St Peters, and Cayon, and St Paul's, so that the ordinary people of this country could be given a chance to move up economically. Move up socially. Move up, and up, and up.

Labour increased the minimum wage time and time again so that today, at $320 per week, the workers in St Kitts and Nevis earn more than workers in any other country in the OECS.

Labour wants and values freedom of expression and so we made a deliberate point of issuing more radio licences than any other government in the Federation. We issued more newspaper licences than any other government in the Federation. And we did this so that everybody can talk, so that everybody can say what they want to. So that this will be a free country. Think about that when you listen to the talk shows. Labour made this possible because Labour believes in democracy.

Comrades, the world is undergoing financial and economic crises the likes of which we have never seen. Who ever thought that the mighty General Motors could ever go bankrupt? Just the other day, General Motors had sales of $193 billion. That is $193 million, one thousand times. In 2004, General Motors employed three hundred and forty thousand people. Now GM could be filing for bankruptcy within a matter of weeks. As a matter of fact, they have just announced that, in addition to everything else, they will be closing one thousand, one hundred more car dealerships. Not letting off one thousand, one hundred workers, but closing one thousand, one hundred car dealerships. Just this week, Chrysler closed down 789 dealerships and even the US government itself is being economically tossed and financially turned by one crisis after the other. But the entire world is interconnected. And so what happens in America does not stay in America. It seeps, and it leaks, and it spreads until it reaches way beyond America. Now more than ever then, this blessed little country of ours needs a government made up of people with a proven track record of skilled and responsible management. Now more than ever, this country of ours needs a government in control that understands, backward and forward, the workings of the International Monetary Fund, the World Bank, and the international financial system. And we need a government in control that has proven time and again that it knows how to protect the interests of this country.

Labour has been able, thank God, to ensure that major foreign investment projects are still moving forward – Silver Reef, Ocean's Edge, Christophe Harbour, the Marriott Condomium project, with our people working, at a time when similar projects are being closed all across the region. Labour has been able to ensure that direct flights to and from London, New York, Miami, Charlotte, and Atlanta – with all the economic activity that these flights generate, and all the jobs that are tied to them – continue at a time when airlines are cutting flights to our friends and neighbours throughout the region.

Comrades, your government has cut our country's overdraft by 50 per cent. Your government has cut our country's Debt: GDP ratio by 20 per cent. Your government has slashed poverty in this country dramatically as attested to by the Caribbean Development Bank. Your government has created the type of environment that has enabled the workers of this country to produce more in exports to the United States than Dominica, St Lucia, Grenada, other OECS countries and Barbados combined! Your government has established health centres in Molyneux, Dieppe Bay, Saddlers, St Peters, Cayon, St Pauls, and Newtown and completely transformed the J. N. France and the Pogson Hospitals. Your government has joined forces with the Regional Security System, the premiere Caribbean national security entity, the Royal Canadian Mounted Police, and the FBI to undercut, and undermine, and defeat gang violence and criminality. Your government has invested millions of dollars in a second-chances programme for our youth called the YES programme so as to enable those who did not make the best use of their opportunities the first time around, to have a second chance. A second chance to acquire skills. A second chance to win and hold employment. A second chance to start small businesses. A second chance to resist the gangs. A second chance to resist criminality. A second chance to become constructive citizens in the land of their birth.

Your government is working to ensure that once any Kittitian or Nevisian has worked anywhere for ten years, they will be entitled to a gratuity when they resign. Your government is making land available to low-income wage earners at $2.95 per square foot, and giving concessions and exemptions to the banks to encourage them to make it easier for persons to get loans and mortgages who do not make high salaries, and therefore usually do not qualify. But if the banks still turn these people back, your government is putting a $10 million facility at the Development Bank to help people to purchase the land they need anyway. And your government is moving to ensure that once these first-time landowners have begun making payments on land, they will be given title to that land, so they can start building the homes that they and their families need.

Comrades, Labour has delivered in the past and, with your help, we will continue to deliver in the future. The time has come for us to move forward energised as a party. United as a party, mindful of what life was like during those fifteen years that the other party was in power. Fifteen years is a long time. Just think about it – fifteen years from now would take us to the year 2024. That is how long Labour and its supporters were in the wilderness. That is how long the people of St Kitts and Nevis had to deal with the unjust policies of an unjust government.

How did 1980 happen? Well, the 1970s were a rough time for our party. We lost Bradshaw. We lost Southwell. Pain and uncertainty were everywhere.

Is it possible that these traumas caused us to lose our way? Is it possible that the associated uncertainties caused our party to splinter and weaken? Most important of all, is it not now clear that those who care nothing about you, me, anyone in this room, or most people in the country, quickly and skilfully jumped on our splintering, capitalised on our splintering, and rode our splintering to victory in 1980? In retrospect, it is now clear that Labour at that time failed to realise the horrors of the wilderness that their splintering would bring.

Comrades, we are gathered here today because we belong to the oldest, the strongest, and the most capable political party in the country. And we can be proud to state that we belong to a country, a tradition, a system in which we, the people, choose the government that we want. Governments are not imposed on us in St Kitts and Nevis. We choose our governments.

And so, as the country gets ready to choose the next government, Labour's delegates need to be mobilised. Our party has undertaken a historic task, the task of transforming this country from a one-crop, sugar-based economy into one that is modern and diversified, with a multi-pronged focus on agriculture, hospitality, information technology, and services, an economy with expanded opportunities for employment and entrepreneurship, for social mobility and political stability.

Let us go forth from this 77th Annual Conference then, united and determined to ensure that the next government of St Kitts and Nevis will be a Labour government. Let us step forward from this day united – all for one, and one for all – energised not only by our horrific memories of those fifteen years in the wilderness, but more importantly, by our shared knowledge that Labour has changed St Kitts and Nevis for the better.

Let us step forward energised, strengthened, and determined to ensure an electoral victory because, separate and apart from politics, and focusing now solely on the interests of the country, we all know that Labour does, indeed, represent safe hands for serious times.

Comrades, Labour has started this task of transformation and we have won high marks from the International Monetary Fund. We have won high marks from the Caribbean Development Bank. We have won high marks from the United Nations and a host of impartial observers, analysts, and prognosticators. Most importantly, we have won high marks from you. This race that is now underway, the race to transform St Kitts and Nevis for the better, is a race that Labour was born to run. And this is a race that Labour was born to win!

Comrades! Let us run it – mobilised!

Let us run it – energised!

Let us run it, and complete it, and win it for generations yet unborn!

ALLEGATION OF CONTEMPT
Given at the Court, Basseterre, July 29, 2009

I'm here to lend support to my honourable attorney-general, Hon. Dr Dennis Merchant, and the member of parliament for constituency number eight, Hon. Cedric Roy Liburd. I have come to support them in their defence against an allegation of contempt brought against them by the Peoples Action Movement (PAM). They have provided me with support and so if they are to go to prison I will go with them.

I have sat in this court and I have noticed what PAM tactics are. This is a political trial brought by PAM against my government and the people to delay the general elections because PAM is not ready as neither Lindsay Grant nor Shawn Richards can provide a Certificate of Renunciation of their United States citizenship as required by law.

They are using the court to launch a political attack. They cannot do it themselves. It is interesting to note that their attack is not led by even a single lawyer from the Federation. They hide behind others from outside. They have brought into the country, among others, two politicians in the persons of Ms Mia Mottley, political leader of the opposition in Barbados, and Mrs Kamla Persad-Bissessar, deputy political leader of the opposition of Trinidad and Tobago, to lead the attack against the government of St Kitts and Nevis and its people.

I wish for these politicians from outside to be advised that they should not allow themselves unwittingly to be used by PAM to destabilise the country St Kitts and Nevis. In pursuit of their use of the court to pursue a political agenda, I have now been advised by the lawyers representing His Excellency the Governor-General, the Constituency Boundaries Commission, the Electoral Commission, the supervisor of Elections, and the Hon. Attorney General, that they have been served with affidavits of Mr Richard Caines, a former member of the PAM administration, and also from the former prime minister in the PAM administration, Sir Kennedy Simmonds.

Finally, I have been advised that yesterday in the court one of the counsels for the PAM legal team told the court that they were going to seek a subpoena to summon me to court. I hope that by my presence here in court today, they will be aware that so long as I'm advised by my lawyers to attend court, I will have no difficulty in so doing.

Electoral Reform and Court Challenges

National Broadcast, ZIZ Broadcasting Corporation, October 14, 2009

Fellow citizens, nationals, residents:

St Kitts and Nevis has been moving forward on two tracks for several months now. On one track, the track on which the duly elected government moves, there has been the same high level of assessment, planning, and activity that there has always been. There has been the drafting of laws and the signing of agreements. There has been our presence at historic international fora, and the beginning and completion of projects. Your government continues to assiduously address itself to matters pertaining to the management of the economy, the provision of vitally needed social services, and the protection of the nation's interests. In other words, the government that you elected has continued to govern as we have with energy and tenacity, and we have met the myriad and consequential responsibilities associated with the running, the protecting, and the shaping of the nation.

On the other track have been the cases that have been brought before the court by members of an opposing political party, supposedly as a means of signalling displeasure with the boundaries that were established by proclamation on July 3, 2009, with both the national assembly and the governor-general, respectively, properly and thoroughly assuming their constitutionally-mandated roles.

Let us remember as we review the events of the past few months that our constitution establishes and asserts the concept of separation of powers. And so, of necessity, the deliberations of the court have had to proceed on a track that is completely separate and distinct from the governance-related responsibilities of my government. That having been said, however, I must admit that I, as someone with special responsibilities toward this country, had hoped that by this time the nation would have received a ruling from the court, at the very least in order for the people of St Kitts and Nevis to have greater clarity *vis-à-vis* the thinking and analysis of the court, and secondly, because this ruling will have some bearing on how, as prime minister, and with strict adherence to the constitution, I assess the various timing scenarios regarding the people of St Kitts and Nevis exercising their sacred and most important right to vote.

Before discussing much further the importance to us all of the court issuing a ruling before too much longer, I want us to reflect, for a moment, on what an important and indeed, what an essential undertaking our recently concluded electoral reform process was. Commonwealth analysts had strongly recommended it. My own government had long seen need for it. And even opposing politicians themselves had repeatedly and stridently demanded it. And so, as a part of our sweeping and sorely needed electoral reform package, we consulted widely, both at home and abroad. Inter alia, we established a new national ID card system to avoid electoral fraud. We cleaned up the electoral lists. New electoral boundaries were established in order to ensure greater numerical equivalency amongst and between electoral constituencies. All of this was done, not simply by my government or my party, but by the duly empowered electoral authorities.

So, let me say now how fortunate we in St Kitts and Nevis are, and indeed how fortunate our brothers and sisters throughout the Caribbean are, that we live in constitutional democracies. Constitutions represent solidity because what happens and what does not happen, even in the face of unusual circumstances, is clarified by the constitution. When there is disagreement as to the way forward, there is the constitution illuminating the path, the cornerstone of stability.

Let me also say, however, that it is very important that those seeking political power, whether in St Kitts and Nevis or elsewhere, respect and adhere to the time-proven means of achieving such power. That is, they must be willing to put in the long hours, to make the extraordinary effort, and to invest the tremendous energy that is required in order to win the trust and support of the electorate. While the courts are a revered and essential component of our democracy, and while it speaks to the strength of our democracy that every national, citizen, and resident has inviolable access to our court system, our courts should, nonetheless, not be used as a means of settling legitimate disputes between dissenting political parties. While, as a matter of right, any political party is free to do whatever it wishes as far as the courts are concerned, as a matter of basic political maturity, one would expect political parties to understand how very inappropriate it is to use the courts as a means of getting attention that would otherwise not be forthcoming. There should be an instinctual awareness that the courts should never be used in an attempt to create a crisis where no crisis theretofore existed. And one would expect from such parties a natural shying away from even a suggestion that the courts be used to frustrate the electorate, test the limits of the constitution, or confuse the lives and minds of ordinary men and women. Yet there is the filing of one court case after another, after another.

Because of the unusual circumstances that the above-mentioned court cases have created, I thought that we should, together, have a clear understanding of what we should expect, and when. As you know, we are now in the fifth year since our last election. Because the constitution anticipated that, by this time, the country would be in election mode, it has made provisions for the automatic dissolution of parliament on December 16th of this year. All that this means, however, is that parliament will no longer meet on a routine basis for the passing of laws. Instead, parliament will meet on matters of national importance, in keeping with the constitution, if and when the governor-general authorises them to do so, at the request of the prime minister.

Let me say here, also, that although many fail to make the distinction, the parliament and the government are not one and the same. And so, under the constitution, even after the dissolution of parliament, the government still continues to ensure that the interests of the nation are protected and the public's business attended to, until the holding of elections, just as it has when parliaments have been dissolved before. Ministers of government will continue meeting their ministerial responsibilities. And government departments and agencies will continue functioning, just as before, because the constitution fully expects and indeed requires, that the nation's business continues to be taken care of.

My government accepts, and indeed honours, the independence of our judiciary. An independent judiciary is, after all, an important cornerstone of all modern democracies. However, it is also a fact that the cases brought before the court are quite different from the average case before the courts where two or more private entities are in conflict. The bringing of these cases has a direct bearing on a number of constitutional matters which will affect not me, as a private individual, and not the plaintiffs in their personal and individual capacities. Instead, these cases have a direct bearing, as I have said, on the procedures via which parliament sits, the deadline by which, under ordinary circumstances, elections must be called, and a range of other constitutionally relevant issues.

In light of this, while I understand the care with which these cases must be reviewed by the courts, as the democratically elected prime minister of this country, I hereby call on all parties to this process to respectfully join in giving voice to the very real importance of the courts being mindful of, and sensitive to, the fact that an entire nation, and not private entities, has been respectfully awaiting its ruling.

In the interim, the work of my government goes on. Our responsibilities to the people are being met and will continue to be met, and the growth and stability of our beloved country remains my government's most sacred priority.

May God continue to bless and guide us all through the period.

CIVILITY IN PUBLIC LIFE:
THE LESSONS OF ARIZONA

Ask the Prime Minister Radio Programme
ZIZ Broadcasting Corporation, January 11, 2011

Good morning.

And thank you for tuning into this week's edition of *Ask the Prime Minister.*

An entire year stretches before us, a year in which, like governments and people throughout the Caribbean, in the United States, in Europe, and across the globe, a heightened sense of discipline, a heightened degree of self-control, and a heightened sense of responsibility will be called for.

We have talked about this before, many times, but these discussions have often revolved around the growing need, globally, for discipline where economic or financial matters are concerned. The last few days in Arizona,[1] however, have caused people from Mumbai to Miami, and from Britain to Belarus to stop and think about those things that promote – and those things that undermine – social and political stability in *any* state. And the last few days should have caused us all, right here in St Kitts and Nevis, to stop and think about the civic responsibilities that every member of every society must assume in order to create the kind of society that all normal human beings want.

We are all aware of the divisive and militaristic direction that politics in some quarters in the United States has been assuming, and I raise this topic because even though St Kitts and Nevis is an independent and sovereign state, even though we have never been a US territory, even though it is important for us as a Caribbean people not to be obsessed with and preoccupied by everything that happens in the United States, globalisation in general and modern communications in particular, bring every cultural, political, and environmental crisis that occurs in the United States instantly to our door step.

---

1. A gunman opened fire on an outdoor political meeting with a US congress-woman, killing six people and injuring thirteen.

You will remember that during the BP oil disaster last year, the Caribbean, in general, and the Bahamas in particular, were forced to begin thinking very quickly about the implications of this environmental disaster for our region.

When the H1N1 virus was declared a major threat to the United States by the US Centers for Disease Control, governments throughout the Caribbean, with the rapid flow of American visitors into and out of our region, had to begin thinking very quickly about what these forecasts meant for us, and what we would have to do to protect ourselves.

What did Caribbean governments and people have to do with Wall Street's manipulation of the derivatives market, and the manipulation of sub-prime loans, in recent years? Nothing. Yet our awareness of that financial crisis begun far beyond our shores, caused Caribbean economists, financial analysts, and governments to begin thinking and working very quickly to assess the implications of this foreign crisis for our region, and it caused us to put in place clear plans and policies to insulate ourselves – to the best of our ability – from the ravages of a crisis begun very far from this region.

So, too, do we in the Caribbean find ourselves in a similar situation today, as a result of the violence unleashed just a few days ago in Arizona.

Why, you might ask, is what happens thousands of miles away in Arizona relevant to anyone in the Caribbean? More specifically, why is it relevant to us here in St Kitts and Nevis?

It is relevant because of what it has to teach us. And just as some elements in our society unfortunately seem to gravitate toward the worst aspects of popular culture in some large countries with their emphasis on gangsta rap and thug culture, so too have some political interests in St Kitts and Nevis been gravitating toward the worst practices of some political parties in large countries far away. But we must remember that the same political gimmicks and visuals that are dangerous and unhealthy in large countries are dangerous and unhealthy here as well. Many Kittitians and Nevisians have objected to the political use of the visuals of which I speak, and I want to make a point of objecting to them again.

I refer here to the unsettling uses of gun graphics, often on the front pages of a certain newspaper, in an attempt, I assume, to score some type of political advantage. It is not a very pleasant experience for Kittitians and Nevisians to pick up a newspaper and see the close-up of the barrel of a gun staring right back at them. And it does not help to create the

436

type of psychological calm and stability that we all need to healthily exist. It is also highly irresponsible, at a time of extreme global hardship for political types in St Kitts and Nevis to place on the front page of their newspaper a photograph of a cruise ship with a weapon pointed at, or in a position to suggest a threat to, that cruise ship.

Why? Because just as any act that has the potential to sabotage our agricultural sector would sabotage us all, and just as any act that has the potential to sabotage the work of, say, our security forces, would sabotage us all, so too does any act with the potential to sabotage and undermine the tourism sector with the multitude of ancillary workers and entrepreneurs attached to this industry. Most importantly, at a time when the Caribbean and the world are keenly aware of the destabilising impact of violence, it is essential that none of us do anything that would promote, normalise, or visually heighten in any way the role of weapons in our society. Here in St Kitts and Nevis, as you know, we have strict licensing requirements where firearms are concerned because we wish to send a message that their ownership and usage are not to be taken lightly. Regardless of political affiliation, therefore, we all have a special obligation to be extremely circumspect in our usage of weapons as a visual symbol to make a political point or gain some type of political advantage.

That is a path it really is best that none of us take.

I recognise, of course, that we cannot undo the fact that some have already begun walking down that path of using these unsettling symbols, but what we can do, and what we must do, is turn back, leave that path, and never go there again.

I am unbending where this is concerned because I very much want all of us to understand that democracy is about more than simply voting every five years. Voting is, of course, an essential and sacred democratic ritual, to be sure, but how citizens live and behave *between* elections is also very important. And so, we in St Kitts and Nevis must be wise enough and mature enough to understand and respect the sanctity of the ballot. We must understand that our overall security and stability are only possible when there are free and fair elections, and when the results of these elections are honoured until the next election when the people, once again, determine for themselves in whose hands they wish to place the leadership of their country.

Between elections is where the hard work lies. It is here that persons of all political stripes must have the self-control to place the good of the nation ahead of personal political advantage. And the raging debate in the United States now reminds us that regardless of political persuasion, we must never allow political opportunism to contaminate our thinking to such an extent that we recklessly begin to use weapon visuals and symbols in our mass communication efforts, whether to intimidate psychologically, or to undermine economically, because that is a slippery slope from which it is not always easy to return.

All of us in St Kitts and Nevis were, first, born in a country of exquisite beauty, a country of natural lushness and fertility. And as a result of all our combined efforts as a people, we have created a social and economic environment to which people from nations large and small are flocking. We clearly have created something of value then, something that is precious not only to us but to others all over the world as well. This places on us a special responsibility to understand the pillars on which social stability and political security – anywhere in the world – rest. And this places on us an even greater responsibility to ensure that in St Kitts and Nevis we keep these pillars strong.

Impassioned political debate? Strong disagreement? Yes.

Personal animus and hatred? No.

Concern for the long-term consequences of our decisions? Yes.

Concern for 'the moment' only? No.

Embracing the approaches of our national heroes? Yes.

Accepting the dangerous tactics of political parties far away? No.

America's debate over the Arizona tragedy reminds us that we in St Kitts and Nevis have something of great value here. We are a Caribbean people, with Caribbean approaches, traditions, and sensibilities. Let us cherish what we have. And let us band together to keep it this way. And, on the subject of undergirding democratic practices, let us once again thank Sugar City Roc, KYSS-FM, Freedom Radio, Radio One, Choice FM, and ZIZ-Radio for always having stepped forth, without reservation, to make these conversations possible. We thank these radio stations for their commitment, and I thank you.

ADDRESS TO THE
NATIONAL DEMOCRATIC CONGRESS
Preparing for Victory

St George's, Grenada, July 17, 2011

Good evening. Greetings from the St Kitts-Nevis Labour Party. Greetings from the government of St Kitts and Nevis. Greetings from the people of St Kitts and Nevis. And greetings from CARICOM.

It is great to be in Grenada today. It is great to be here among the people of Grenada and the friends and supporters of the National Democratic Congress (NDC). It is great to be with the elders/stalwarts, leadership, and executive of the National Democratic Congress.

And it is great to once again be with Tillman Thomas, leader of your great party – the National Democratic Congress. It was only a few weeks ago in St Kitts and Nevis that I succeeded your prime minister as the chairman of the conference of Heads of Government (HOG) of CARICOM. And it was just yesterday that we spent a few hours together with President Bouterse of Surinam as members of the bureau of the conference of HOG and, assisted by Prime Minister Freundel Stuart of Barbados, we interviewed our short list of candidates for the position of secretary-general of CARICOM. It was an enormously important and painstaking exercise which at the end identified the best candidate who, after deliberations with the HOG, will be publicly named and eventually appointed as the new secretary-general of CARICOM. Prime Minister Tillman has played a very important leadership and supportive role throughout. He deserves our applause.

This is a very busy and demanding time for the government and people of St Kitts and Nevis. Indeed, this is a very busy and demanding time for all of us throughout the region with all of the challenges that crises in the wider world have been causing for the rest of us. However, the moment I was asked to come to Grenada, to be with you on this important day, I knew I had to come. The moment I was asked to come here, to let you know what your country, and your government, look like from the rest of the region, I knew I had to come. The moment I was asked to come here, to be a part of your rousing and unstoppable determination to review and take stock of your party and its achievements in government, and to plan for the return of the New Democratic Congress to power, I knew I had to come. The moment I was asked to come here and point out and underscore and make plain for all to see the successes, and the accomplishments, of this National Democratic Congress, your National Democratic Congress, the one and only National Democratic Congress, I knew I had to come. But not at all to interfere in the party politics of Grenada but to share some thoughts and observations with the people of Grenada and express congratulations on the third anniversary of your party in power. Three cheers for the NDC!

Members and friends of the NDC, let me begin with the toughest, hardest part of any discussion anywhere in the world today, where politics and governance are concerned – the economy. I know that everybody here knows what is happening in America. You know what is happening in Greece. You know what is happening in England, and France. And in countries rich and poor all over the world.

Fears of bankruptcy.

Massive layoffs.

Pleas for bailouts.

Home foreclosures.

Frightening unemployment.

Social unrest.

Fighting. Tumult. War.

And yet, here we are in the Caribbean, so small you can't even find us on a world map. It is not that we have not been affected. It is not that other countries' problems have not spilled into our own countries. But we live under God's mercy. And we have, so far, been spared the most awful manifestations of the crisis, the horror stories that we see in the foreign media day after day, and night after night.

We in the Caribbean understand the importance of being humble and grateful at times like this, but nonetheless we use our God-given abilities fully to think, and to plan, and to protect ourselves to the best of our ability. We work like there is no tomorrow. And, even as we seek

Divine guidance we jokingly say, as they do in Jamaica, 'We likkle, but we tallawah.'

At this time of real and seemingly uncontrollable economic instability all around the world, your National Democratic Congress government has worked extremely hard to earn the respect and positive regard of institutions like the World Bank, the IMF, the Caribbean Development Bank, Standard & Poor's, and so on.

I see the work that has been done to your bridges, your retaining walls, your drains, your roads. Because the NDC understands the importance of solid infrastructure to Grenada's ability to attract direct investment whether from local or foreign investors, provide jobs, and generate revenues. And I commend the NDC for their accomplishments in that area.

And, as I was saying earlier, this NDC government has not only worked for the respect of the international community. They have actually earned that respect. As a matter of fact, I have been advised just last week when the monetary council of the ECCB met in Montserrat, that under this government, Grenada signed fifteen tax exchange agreements with several European countries as a means of demonstrating Grenada's determination to cooperate with the international community where financial criminality is concerned. Where money laundering is concerned. Where financial terrorism is concerned.

Because you live here, you are aware of the millions that this NDC government has attracted from a range of international financial institutions. And we all know how important the confidence of these institutions in any government, is. Grenada has earned that confidence. But let there be no doubt, the NDC has worked hard, not only to win the respect and regard of those outside of Grenada, this NDC government has worked hard to win the respect and regard of the people of Grenada. And in order to win your respect, they have used the power that you gave them in the last election to make life better for the people of Grenada.

You, as Grenadians, heard this government make clear the five areas that are absolute priorities for them and therefore for the future of this country, your country:

1. Agriculture

2. Tourism and Hospitality

3. Energy

4. Health and Education

5. Information & Communications Technology

Let us look, for example, at agriculture. You know there has been a significant increase in the agro-processing industry in Grenada. You see it, you hear about it, and feel the benefits of it every day. Because you live here. And you know how important these developments are to the economic growth and stability of this country. All over the world, Grenada is known for its nutmeg and cocoa. And the farm supports provided by your government have enabled Grenada's nutmeg and cocoa farmers to increase production of these important national exports.

But there are so many other ways in which this NDC government has demonstrated the importance it attaches to agriculture:

1. Subsidised fertilizer;

2. Cooperative irrigation programs with the Japanese;

3. The provision of equipment to your farmers, schools, and 4H Clubs;

4. The strengthening of the Farm Labour Support Programme;

5. The employment of one thousand persons in this programme;

6. Increased plant propagation;

7. The promotion of public-private agro-partnerships;

8. The donation of animals and feeds to vulnerable households;

9. Collaboration with Japan *vis-à-vis* the Gouyave Fisheries Development Facility;

The list grows on. Agriculture is important to the NDC. Agriculture is important to the small farmers, agriculture is important to Grenada. And it shows.

Most importantly, for those very few Grenadians who love to reap but hate to sow, the National Democratic Congress government and the Royal Grenada Police Force are moving forward with focus and determination with the 'Praedial Larceny Unit' of the Police Force. And there will be a new day in Grenada. Those who steal what Grenada's farmers have toiled to produce, before the farmers can even take their crops to market, will soon find out that this is no laughing matter. And this point will be made most clearly when they are made to feel the full force of the law. And you remember what our older folks used to say to us when we were younger, 'those who can't hear will feel.'

All of these accomplishments have taken me just a few seconds to mention but they require and demand a great deal of planning, follow-through, oversight, and leadership. They require a committed government, a committed leader and a committed prime minister.

And the reason that these initiatives were conceptualised and implemented in the first place is that food security matters to this government. The health of the Grenadian people, made possible via reliance on local foods, matters to this government. And increased employment and economic advancement, again made possible by a vibrant agricultural sector, matters to the government. To your government. Let us give the leadership of the National Democratic Congress the kind of rousing show of support that they so richly deserve. For all that they have done. And continue to do.

And now let us look for a moment at the NDC's social safety net programme. There are so many ways in which this government has moved to help the ordinary man and woman in Grenada, as those ordinary men and women have striven to help themselves. Public assistance in this country has been increased from EC$150 to EC$200. Persons in Grenada, Carriacou, and Petite Martinique who heretofore relied on wood and coals for cooking have been assisted via the distribution of stoves and ovens. There is a light and fuel bill assistance programme. An automatic pricing mechanism has been put in place. And this is very important. Because everybody knows that for far too long, whenever international prices have gone up, local prices have gone right up behind them. However, when international prices have gone down you know what happens, ... no reduction in prices. The NDC has fixed that.

For the people of Grenada.

Let's look at another example – the Christmas barrel. A Caribbean tradition. A very important and sociologically powerful Caribbean tradition. The Christmas barrel is supposed to provide emotional and financial relief to the recipient, not create greater financial stresses. And so this NDC government has removed all duties and all taxes on this important, longstanding, and sociologically significant cultural and family tradition.

In addition, they have made certain – and there were those who fought them on this – that there would be no increase in the price of the small cylinders of cooking gas.

The National Reconstruction Levy – gone. The duties on solar panels –gone. The duties on hurricane straps – gone. Clear evidence of the seriousness with which this government approaches governance. They not only want the people of Grenada to reduce their reliance on oil imports, but they have implemented policies to make it easier to use other forms of energy. They want the people of Grenada to be able to withstand the ravages of hurricanes and they have implemented policies to help.

This kind of government does not come along every day. The NDC government been very good for Grenada and Grenada has stood with the NDC.

In order to help those who are building homes or undertaking needed repairs, the NDC has reduced VAT on selected construction materials. For those who, for whatever reason, fell behind on their taxes, there was a successful programme of tax amnesty. And the Minimum Wage Law is about to be passed. This is extremely important. The NDC has reduced taxes on new vehicles. And they have protected hotel worker jobs by providing 50 per cent relief on general consumption tax in exchange for the maintenance of those jobs.

Flexibility. That is what is needed in a government. When times change and new challenges emerge, a government must be able to figure out how to change and shift, not in terms of principles, but in terms of tactics, in order to protect the people they were elected to protect. And this the NDC has done.

I want, before closing, to state that I am, as you may know, the CARICOM prime minister with lead responsibility on matters of health. And I am aware, as are you all, that without good health at the personal and the national level, we strive in vain. It is significant, therefore, and something in which you should take great pride, that in fifteen minutes flat, cataracts can now be removed right here in Grenada. How many can remember when this required the stress and financial burden of an overseas trip? It is also significant that Grenada is now acquiring advanced surgical equipment such as that used in the removal of kidney stones, in the implantation of screws for hip replacement, and so on. The increased presence of doctors at Princess Alice Hospital is also an important indication of the importance that the government attaches to expanded and improved health care in this country. But the provision of free cancer treatments in Grenada, treatments that often are worth over US$200,000, speaks for itself. And it does indeed demonstrate the

NDC's determination to do all in its power, even as a tiny nation, to relieve suffering where it exists and to deliver healing whenever that is possible. And that is health care policy at its best.

But nowhere are the efforts of government and society more important in this day and age than in the social development of our nation's youth. All over the region and in fact the world, too many of our youth are restless, not focussed on their personal development, and distracted with antisocial behaviour. Too many of them are attracted to a non-Caribbean culture of gang groups. And where there are gangs there will be drugs; and where there are drugs, there will be illegal firearms; and where there are gangs, drugs, and illegal firearms, there will be violent crimes and homicides. Our Caribbean youth need to be distracted away from this destructive culture. They need alternatives. Hence, the reconstitution of your cadet corps in 2009 will yield benefits for years to come. The government's drive to re-define and create a more uplifting definition of patriotism in the shaping of our young peoples' psyches is key. And the commitment of $12 million to promote youth employment is a measure of the NDC's commitment in this vital area.

I have the honour of being the longest-serving prime minister in the Caribbean. Permit me to say, in all humility, that I know responsible government when I see it. This is what you have in Grenada. This is what you have in the National Democratic Congress. This party has worked hard for you. Grenada now needs you to work hard for it. I urge you to leave this place re-energised, re-vitalised, ready to work harder for the National Democratic Congress and deliver victory for the people of Grenada.

ST KITTS-NEVIS LABOUR PARTY 80TH ANNIVERSARY CONFERENCE
St Kitts Marriott Resort, May 20, 2012

Comrades! This is the day that the Lord hath made. Let us rejoice and be glad in it. Good morning!

We have come a long way this Labour Party of ours. We've come a long, long way. Let us rejoice indeed. And let us be glad. For there is a great deal to rejoice about, a great deal to be glad about, especially when you are Labour!

Comrades and friends, we meet here today some eighty years after our people decided to combine their efforts through the Workers League to confront the immense social and economic challenges they faced and lift themselves from the pits of poverty and deprivation to which they had been consigned by a colonial economic system that was without compassion, was based on wanton discrimination against the poor, and was fuelled by the sweat and tears of our people. Our forebears understood that their individual efforts would not be sufficient to combat the colonial 'leviathan'. They therefore set about the task of liberation and empowerment as a single united force.

They put into action the adage 'unity is strength,' through the establishment of the Workers League in 1932. Indeed, their decision to unite and fight was a defining moment in the history of our people. It is that decision and the actions that followed which set us on the path to freedom, dignity, social and economic advancement, independence, and sovereignty. It is that decision that resulted in the creation of our proud political party, the St Kitts-Nevis Labour Party (SKNLP), which consistently champions the cause of the poor and vulnerable and which has brought to our people adult suffrage and the subsequent revolution in the political, social, and economic life of our nation.

This revolution has given our people the reins of power in our country and has secured for us political independence, comprehensive and accessible education, easy access to high quality primary and secondary health care, thousands of low-income houses, first-class infrastructure, and a progressive small island state that occupies a prominent position in the United Nations Human Development Index and which stands proudly among the nations of the world, notwithstanding its small size.

This revolution is what has given the people of this county control over the sugar lands and allowed us to distribute thousands of land lots to the nationals of this fair land of ours, and thereby bring an end to the scourge of landlessness that kept our people in subjugation throughout our colonial history. Indeed, we can be proud of our achievements as a nation.

Moreover, as the lead architects of our progress through the decades following that grand moment in 1932, the St Kitts-Nevis Labour Party can truly be proud of its achievement. It stands as a towering symbol of what the poor and downtrodden can do when they unite and stick together through thick and thin, in good times and in bad times, in the twentieth century and in the twenty-first century, indeed, at all times.

We have come a long way this Labour Party of ours. We have come a long, long way. Let us rejoice. And let us be glad. For there is a great deal to rejoice about, a great deal to be glad about, when you are Labour!

Who would have guessed? Who could have guessed? Who could have imagined back in 1932 at a time when we were being locked out, pushed around, and disregarded, that we would, at the end of the day, triumph despite all those who fought us?

Who could have known the countless ways in which we would continue going from strength to strength, year after year, that our hard work and determination would end up changing, dramatically, for the better, and forever, the politics, the economics, and the aesthetics of this land of our birth?

Who could have guessed, way back in 1932 that eighty years later, in 2012, the St Kitts-Nevis Labour Party, the party we honour today, would be, without question, the most experienced, the longest serving, and the most successful political party in the history of St Kitts and Nevis and in the history of the entire Commonwealth Caribbean?

Let us rejoice, I say. And let us be glad. Let us rejoice for the team of the past and the Labour team of the present – Cde Dr Asim Martin in number one; Cde Marcella Althea Liburd in number two; Cde Sam Condor in number three; Cde Glen Phillip in number four; Cde Dr Norgen Wilson in number five; Comrades of number six; Cde Dr Timothy Harris in number seven; and Cde Cedric Liburd in number eight.

Comrades and friends, we can be truly proud of the St Kitts-Nevis Labour Party, of Bradshaw's Labour Party, of Southwell's Labour Party, of France's Labour Party, of Moore's Labour Party, of our Labour Party, of your Labour Party. Our proud party continues to be the dominant party in St Kitts and Nevis. Our proud party continues to look after our people and to pull them into the mainstream of development through our creative social and economic initiatives.

Comrades, nations spin out of control all the time. When this happens, as we see on our televisions night after night, the rest of the world simply leaves them alone to paddle their own canoe. I am, therefore, quite amazed that there are those who lament the fact that we, here, have not been plunged into chaos. They are angry that this country has not plunged into chaos. It is disturbing to think that there are those who are genuinely angry that our nation is not yet in turmoil. It is incredible to watch them growing impatient with Kittitians and Nevisians because we have not yet shouted to the world that we are amongst the world's most broke people as a result of the global recession. It is disturbing to think that there are those who are genuinely angry that our nation is not yet in turmoil – those who tried to march on Friday afternoon and could not even attract a handful of people.

Who knows, Comrades, what lurks in the hearts of men? What I do know is that it is a rough world out there. And that is why we in Labour must be clear of mind, focused, and strong in defence of this democracy that we, the people, built from scratch. And we must be equally clear of mind, focused, and strong, in defending, protecting, and honouring this St Kitts-Nevis Labour Party that has done so much for so many for so very long. And we did build this democracy from scratch because it was Labour who single-handedly transformed St Kitts and Nevis from being a place in which by law – by law – only the rich could vote. It was our party, Comrades, the people of Labour, who turned St Kitts and Nevis into a place where every man and woman, regardless of class or status, is now equal at the ballot box. This is the legacy of Labour, Comrades. That is our shining badge of honour, a badge that will shine throughout the centuries, as bright as the morning sunshine, undimmed and undimmable, forever.

Our proud party has remained true to its philosophical foundation by demonstrating compassion, acting in accordance with its strong social conscience, and by remaining in the vanguard of the fight against poverty, against injustice and unfairness of every form, and of the fight to empower our own people by the creation of employment, entrepreneurial, and wealth creation opportunities. Our proud party has won election after election because we deserve to win. After all, we are Labour.

Comrades and friends, this proud party continues to carry our great country forward and to deliver on our commitments and make sure there is progress and not simply promises for our people. I want you to recall that on February 7, 2010 when the cabinet was sworn into office after handsomely winning the 2010 general election, I said in my address to the mammoth crowd witnessing the event:

> The size of the debt is an issue that must from time to time capture the attention of every national of St Kitts and Nevis. Hence, although our people can see and feel the enormous positive impact of the many projects funded by the debt, and we are satisfied with the progress that we have been making in dealing with this issue in the context of numerous challenges of global origin, we will not let down our guard.

We have not let down our guard. On assuming office in 2010 we studied the issue of national debt very carefully and thoroughly, paying particular attention to the risk it presented in view of the great recession that has plagued the global economy from 2008 onwards. We came to the conclusion that with the national debt approaching 200 per cent of GDP and with the global economy in turmoil, there was no easy way to avoid a crisis, especially because of the impact of the contagion that seemed to be spreading to capital markets all over the globe. We therefore, decided to restructure our debt and implement a home-grown economic programme with the assistance of the International Monetary Fund.

Today, just about mid-way through our current term in office, we have reached agreement with our creditors and our debt has been reduced dramatically. Indeed, we are confident within a relatively short period we will be able to announce that the national debt is below 100 per cent of GDP. In other words, in a period when debt is increasing dramatically across the globe, we have been able to go against the trend and to bring down our debt substantially. I am especially grateful to our creditors who demonstrated such goodwill and understanding in our negotiations. I would also like to place on the record of this conference our profound appreciation to the financial secretary and staff of the Ministry of Finance and to our debt advisers for their hard work and tireless effort in carrying forward our programme of debt reduction.

At the ceremony to mark the swearing-in of the cabinet in 2010, I also promised to give concerted attention to crime reduction. My precise statement was as follows:

> ... early in this new term of office, we will carry out a comprehensive
> review of all of the various crime fighting initiatives with a view to
> evaluating their effectiveness, committing more resources to the
> initiatives that are achieving results and developing new community-
> based approaches in the fight against crime.

We cannot yet begin to 'beat our chests' in relation to crime reduction.
In fact, our aim must be the total and complete eradication of violent
crimes because we must mourn the loss of every citizen that succumbs to
violence and criminal activity. But we must certainly give thanks for the
great progress that we have made in taking control of our streets, reducing
crime, and bringing criminals to justice. Our security forces, under the
outstanding leadership of commissioner Walwyn, must be applauded for
their excellent work in protecting our communities.

Comrades and friends, my government also made a commitment to
corporatising the electricity department and bringing a reliable supply
of electricity to our homes, offices, and businesses. We are pleased that
each month the number of outages has been decreasing significantly.
Moreover, we are given adequate notice of even the few outages that
we now experience. We are satisfied therefore that our corporatisation
initiative in respect of the electricity services is working.

Of course, we remain concerned about the high cost of electricity.
The price of oil has been moving erratically and has put upward pressure
on the cost of generating electricity. But I must put the St Kitts Electricity
Company (SKELEC) on notice. For us, corporatisation is not simply
about changing the form of the enterprise. SKELEC is a company
registered under the Companies Act and although its shares are owned
by the government, we do not intend to let it operate like a government
department. The electricity charge represents a large portion of the budget
of households and businesses in our Federation. We therefore intend to
realise increased efficiencies that must be passed on to consumers. My
government will be vigilant in protecting the interests of our consumers.
As a corporate entity, SKELEC has a duly empowered board of directors
and a professional management team so we do not intend to interfere
in the management and operations of that enterprise but we reserve the
right, as a Labour government, to take whatever action we deem necessary
to protect the interests of consumers.

Comrades, it is the price of oil on the world market that determines
the cost of energy in those countries that rely on fossil fuels. No
government, no president, and no prime minister has the power to reduce

the world price of oil. Not President Obama of the United States, not Prime Minister Cameron of Britain, not President Zuma of South Africa, not President Putin of Russia, not Prime Minister Noda of Japan, and certainly not Prime Minister Douglas of St Kitts and Nevis. What my government does have the power to do, however, what we have been doing, and what we will continue to do, is find ways to escape the fossil fuel dependency in which nations across the globe are now trapped. We know that families need relief in order to manage their finances. We know that businesses wish to keep operating costs down. We have relatives and friends who are directly affected. Most of all, we know better than any just how much our country needs a lighter energy load than it now bears.

Spiralling energy costs may be a global problem, Comrades, but your government is not waiting for the world to find a solution. We are moving ahead to identify practical, viable, workable ways out, and we are pursuing them aggressively. To those private individuals and companies that have been switching from oil-based to renewable energy sources, my government commends you. And in order to further encourage you and others like you, the Ministry of Finance and the customs department are now working as a matter of priority to come before our cabinet with a number of initiatives to cut and reduce tariffs on imports that will reduce home and business reliance on fossil fuels.

And with reference to those who cannot afford the up-front costs associated with renewable energy, the National Housing Corporation will begin building affordable homes with solar panels already installed as a part of the overall construction process. This will spare families the need to bear the up-front cost of the solar panels and it will also deliver to them, on an ongoing basis, the far lower costs associated with solar, as opposed to diesel-based, energy.

Comrades, together with you, and with the support and faith of the electorate, Labour has done great things, Labour is doing great things, and Labour will continue to do great things for the rich, the poor, the young, and the old of this country.

If you were listening to parliament last week, you would have heard there was a joint meeting between the Ministry of Finance and the board and management of the St Kitts Electricity Company. We have said that all persons who have been disconnected must immediately be reconnected so that they can receive electricity services. There must be a fair way of dealing with the existing arrears so that over the next few years those arrears will disappear and will no longer confront our citizens here in St Kitts and Nevis.

We will be forever grateful to the thousands upon thousands of men and women throughout our Federation whose faith in our party has given us the opportunity not once, not twice, not three times, but four times, to work and to struggle and to achieve on behalf of this St Kitts and Nevis that we all so dearly love.

Comrades and friends, when the workers of this country met eighty years ago to form the Workers' League, they were pushed to take this step by global economic circumstances. The Great Depression was in full swing, sugar prices were very low, and the workers in our country suffered severe social and economic consequences. They responded by uniting and facing their challenges together.

Today, we have been feeling the effects of a global recession that started in 2008 and has been 'on and off' since then. Indeed, of the countries in the European Union, only Germany seems to be growing in any significant way. The UK has been experiencing double dip recession and just a few days ago Spain announced that it had fallen back into recession. Even in the United States where there were early signs of recovery, such recovery seems to be faltering. In St Kitts and Nevis, we are projecting growth for 2012 but if the global economy loses momentum or contracts, we will undoubtedly be adversely affected.

If the Labour government is to continue to confront these challenges as successfully as it has done in the past, the Labour Party must be united and it must be strong. In other words, we must adopt the same strategy that our forebears adopted in 1932. We must vigorously pursue party unity. We must unite. The entire Labour team in office and the entire Labour executive must support and defend the policies decided upon by the Labour government and the cabinet if they are to succeed. Of course, we will not agree on everything, but the forum for disagreement among cabinet members and party executives must be within the confines of our great party.

I emphasise that on this special occasion that celebrates the eightieth anniversary of our great party that the party that we serve is bigger than any one of us in the party and in the government. The advantage enjoyed by the Labour Party over the years has been its level of organisation and discipline. We squander these critical attributes at our peril and risk the demise of our great party, the St Kitts-Nevis Labour Party. The party that we serve is bigger than any single one of us. It certainly is bigger than Denzil Douglas and if it is bigger than me, the leader, it is bigger than any one of us in this country and in this government. I have no doubt about that. It is a party that has a long tradition. It is a party that was formed and took root in the blood and sweat of our forefathers. It is a party that still must play a critical role in the protection of our people. Many of them have toiled hard and long with dedication and with commitment to secure this great party and the principles to which it adheres. Many of them understand that their ability to eke out a decent existence from the advancement of our nation is wrapped up in the future success of Labour.

That is why our people are so concerned with the slightest threat of disunity in our great party because disunity will divide us and if we are divided we will fall. Many of them do understand that very, very well and so we cannot give away their government based on some personal considerations. We shall not have it. We will not give away our government to any other party or to any other group in this country on the promise of some national unity.

Comrades, we have all made sacrifices in our different ways to bring this great party to where it is now. Whenever we are tempted to lose focus, we must remember the hardships unleashed on our party, on the union, and on our people when we were in opposition. I recall when I took over this party that we were totally 'brokes.' The government of the day was using every instrument – the police, the law, the National Bank – every single instrument at its disposal to wipe out our party and the St Kitts-Nevis Trades and Labour Union. We were in no position to fight any elections. I was fortunate to be running a successful medical practice. I had four offices around the island and I made it clear that whatever resources I had I was going to use them to help our party honour its commitment and prepare us for general elections and I did just that.

It was very difficult but it was a great experience for me because Labour people really pull together and they made their own individual sacrifices in their own way.

Some had money, but those who did not have money gave whatever they could. They gave generously of their time, of their skill, of their talent. That's why we are in power today. In fact, every true Labour man and Labour woman made sacrifices so that the sacrifices of any single person or group of persons does not entitle that person or group to any special privilege. This party was founded on the principles of equality and fairness so that the level of contribution made by each of us is not a measure of our worth in this party. It is the combined effort of the people of Labour that saw us through. It is our unity, organisation, discipline, and willingness to make sacrifices that brought us into government. It is these selfsame attributes that will guarantee us future success.

Let us keep our heads on. Let us remain alert. Do you hear me, Comrades? Remain alert! Be careful of 'the wolves in sheep's clothing' approaching from afar. Be wise as serpents and strong like lions, my Comrades, yet as innocent as doves.

There was an eighteenth-century strategist in what was then Prussia who observed that politics is war by other means, war without weapons. And he may have been right because there have been those who seem to have been committed to Labour's defeat from the moment of our birth. A goal that has lasted for eighty years because people wage wars to win. And so, the times may have changed, their faces may have changed, and their tactics may be new, but their goal remains the same. What also remains the same though, Comrades, is the fact that those who oppose us have never ever been able to gain the political upper hand without our own co-operation in the Labour Party. Just think about it for a moment. Those who oppose us have never been able to gain the political upper hand without our own cooperation, without our own help, without our own carelessness. There was only one time in our history – one time, Comrades – that Labour lost its focus. Only one time that we lost our way. And you must remember that one time lasted for fifteen long, hard, and terrible years. We must never, never, ever get back there. They must remain where they are. We must keep our party for Labour and for St Kitts and Nevis.

Only one strange, inexplicable period, when we played right into the hands of those whose ideas, whose philosophy, whose approach to life and living was not 'for the good that we can do!' Don't be fooled of the wolves in sheep's clothing. Labour is strong and it can form its own government. We paid dearly for that indiscipline, but we learned our lesson, and have been moving on ever since. And that we shall continue to do. Comrades, the St Kitts-Nevis Labour Party is the rock on which this nation was built. And whatever Labour has achieved for this country has come as a result of hard, unrelenting work. We are in government today because of the years, the decades, the century almost of extraordinary effort and historic accomplishments on behalf of the people of St Kitts and

454

Nevis. Ours, Comrades, is the party that led the most bold and historic movements in our nation's history: Labour got everyone the right to vote, social security, a high school education for the poor, and Labour started the push for independence despite vocal opposition.

Because of Labour, yesterday's downtrodden are today's professors and engineers, scientists and lawyers, doctors and managers, pilots and agriculturalists. Because of Labour, yesterday's people who were locked-out are in parliament today. They are your ministers of government and they are the members of your cabinet because yesterday's locked-out are today masters of their own destinies. Ours is the party that turned thousands of ordinary citizens into landowners and homeowners. It was Labour who provided millions in university loans and scholarships, something the previous government never did in fifteen years. Labour brought thousands of families into the digital age because we know that when you give a child a computer, you give a family a computer. Let us give three cheers for the Government of Taiwan.

We have protected civil service jobs when civil servants around the world are being let go. We have provided concessions to businesses large and small in our commitment to see business in this country thrive. We have distributed thousands of rich, fertile acres to established and aspiring farmers. Our YES and STEP programmes are evidence of our commitment to second chances for those who faltered the first time. And time and again, Labour has stepped onto the world stage in defence of our country and returned with the buffers, protections, and concessions that have been so key to us as a people.

Of course, if we are to survive as a party, we must put in place mechanisms for younger persons to carry on the torch of leadership when this becomes necessary. Specifically, we must address the issue of succession in a comprehensive and focused way. It was as early as 2008 that I called a special meeting among cabinet members and party executives to put in place a succession plan. Unfortunately, it seemed that a few of the persons attending the meeting saw it as an opportunity to set a deadline for me to leave the government. But I refused to be pushed out of office through such a devious, deceitful and undemocratic manoeuvre orchestrated by a man whose father ran against the esteemed National Hero, the Right Excellent Sir Robert Bradshaw, and who, even now, has taken up where his father left off and is trying to destroy the Labour Party by spreading lies, rumours, and propaganda.

I serve at the pleasure of the people of St Kitts and Nevis and of the St Kitts-Nevis Labour Party so my strong conviction is that any change in the prime minister must involve a change in the leadership of Labour which, in turn, must involve a decision by the Labour Party conference and ultimately a decision by the people of St Kitts and Nevis. Even now, at this half-way mark in our current term in office, I am busy trying to prepare the party for elections for whomsoever is chosen to represent this great party but I am also prepared to step down today or at any time that the party chooses for me to step down. Indeed, I can only go forward with the monumental challenge of nation-building if I have your full and unswerving support.

Comrades and friends, with your permission I will again initiate a process to agree on a succession plan. I cannot, nor do I intend to, hold on to the mantle of leadership forever. Neither do I think any of my colleagues would wish to hold on forever. The process for agreeing on a succession plan will be objective, transparent, equitable, and comprehensive and it will cover all leadership functions in this great party and in the government that I currently lead. You can be assured that the process itself will be rooted in the party mechanisms and will conform to the democratic traditions of our great party. There has to be a structure and a framework put in place because no political party in the Caribbean region has handled succession and transition successfully. In every single case where the current leader bowed out, they went into opposition. We don't want that here and it will not happen here. And that is why whenever it comes, it will be a framework that will be transparent, it will be scientific, and it will be a model for the entire Caribbean region because we are leaders and we have always been leaders in that regard.

There is no room for disloyalty, strife and division in this party. The challenge before us as a nation and as a party in government is monumental, especially at this time when the global economy is in turmoil. If the Labour government is to continue to provide effective leadership, the party from which this government is derived must solidly stand behind its government and must have in place processes to generate views and ideas consistent with our philosophy that will filter into government and bring benefits to our people.

If our nation is to adapt to the new global environment in which we find ourselves then the Labour Party, which forms the government, must also be adaptable and responsive to changing circumstances. This will only happen if the persons who hold leadership positions in the party give of their time and effort to support and advance the party. They ought not to occupy leadership positions in this party and give lukewarm support or stay on the periphery and criticise the party, the government, or its leaders. This would constitute a breach of trust that this conference places in such persons. Their duty is to work within the party to fix whatever they deem is wrong within it.

Comrades and friends, this party has a tremendous reservoir of energy we must tap to respond to our environment and carry our party and our country. This energy resides in our young people who valiantly support the party each time they are called upon to do so. We must make room for them in the party's leadership structure. The party must become like a school to them. We must train and nurture them so that they can help to carry our party and our country forward.

Comrades, I virtually grew up in this party. I attribute much of my personal development to my participation in Young Labour and other party activities. We must give our young people the same opportunity. This is the only way that we will continue to build this great institution that was handed down to us by our forebears. Let us pay tribute to our forebears by following their outstanding example and overcoming our problems and challenges through unity. Let us put the interest of our party above our personal interest. Let us put the nation above self.

We are only caretakers. This Labour government does not belong to us. We do not have the right to give it away. It is the legacy of the Rt Excellent Sir Robert Llewellyn Bradshaw. We do not have the right to give this party away. This party is also the legacy of the Rt Excellent Sir Joseph Nathaniel France. We do not have the right to give this party away to anybody. It is the legacy of the Rt Excellent Sir C. A. Paul Southwell who, as you heard, died in St Lucia on the May 18, 1979 while in service of the people of the Caribbean. It is the legacy of Sir Lee Llewellyn Moore. It is the people's party. You cannot give away the people's party. I understand this very well. That is why I have never sought to publicly attack any person who holds office in the Labour government or in the Labour Party even when provoked to the maximum. I have held a silent and still tongue. It is not that I am weak, because you all know Douglas not weak. It is not that I am weak, but I am not going to attack my own Comrades in the leadership. I will not do that. That is why, if those who cannot be part of the support of the leadership then they can be supportive from outside. I am not afraid, I am not weak, but I understand that I owe a duty of loyalty for the founding fathers of this movement and the people of Labour who I serve. I consider every Labour man a brother and every Labour woman a sister.

Comrades, I want to end by saying that we cannot be easily defeated. We can't be defeated by any opposing party in general elections but we can, I warn you, defeat ourselves.

We are now nearing the half-way mark of our term in office and so we must begin to put the machinery in place for the next general elections. We must be mobilised, comrades, for the next general elections because we do not know what can happen. We don't know if people are going to give away the Labour government. We will resist it, but we don't know and that is why I say we must be mobilised. We must mobilise our people and ensure oneness in purpose and dedication. We must unite our efforts. We must unite our resources in advancing our great Labour Party to another term in office.

Long Live Labour! Long Live St Kitts and Nevis! Long Live the St Kitts-Nevis Labour Party! Long Live the Labour Movement! Long Live the St Kitts-Nevis Trades and Labour Union!

POSSIBLE MOTION OF NO CONFIDENCE

National Broadcast, ZIZ Broadcasting Corporation
December 6, 2012

My Fellow Nationals –

On January 25, 2010, in free and fair internationally observed elections, the St Kitts-Nevis Labour Party was democratically chosen by the voters of St Kitts and Nevis to lead this nation for the next five years. Indeed, voters on that day entrusted to Labour an overwhelming 75 per cent of the seats here on St Kitts. They placed their trust in Labour and they voted for each of the Labour candidates on the basis that they would each become part of a Labour government and would stand solidly behind Labour throughout the term for which they were elected. By this support, we were both honoured and humbled. And for this opportunity we were most grateful, as reflected in the determination and skill with which we moved to confront and control the modern-day challenge of crime, to reduce the debt that is the unavoidable consequence of infrastructural development and natural disasters, to guard the stability of our tiny Federation in this era of worldwide uncertainty and volatility.

Impartial international financial institutions have repeatedly affirmed the competence with which my government has managed the economic affairs of our nation. Indeed, the massive reduction in debt and impressive turnaround in our fiscal performance appear miraculous to many and have drawn commendation worldwide. We are now poised to move forward with a progressive agenda for growth and development that will allow us to reap the rewards of the fiscal responsibility that we have displayed in these challenging times. This, at a time when even a casual glance across our region or around the world provides frightening reminders of the ravages that the global crisis has been inflicting beyond our shores.

And it is at this moment, my fellow nationals, it is in these conditions of global fragility and volatility, that the leader of the opposition has chosen to advocate a Motion of No Confidence in the government of St Kitts and Nevis.

Let me state at the outset that it is his right, as a member of the St Kitts and Nevis National Assembly, so to do, just as it is the right of most parliamentarians in most legislative bodies anywhere in the world. However, it is also an established fact that the government of St Kitts and Nevis has been resolute in our determination to shield our tiny Federation from the economic unravelling that we have observed in so many countries beyond our shores, and this we have been able to do. In light of this, therefore, I question the judgment of the Honourable Member's proposed motion at this particular moment in world affairs. I cannot help but ask whether he is concerned about the implications in this interdependent global economy of questioning the legitimacy of the duly elected government of St Kitts and Nevis. Countless Kittitians' and Nevisians' economic well-being depends so greatly on the stability of St Kitts and Nevis in the eyes of the international community, stability that this Labour government has worked so hard to create.

My fellow nationals, the St Kitts-Nevis Labour Party is the oldest, largest, and most competent political party in the history of St Kitts and Nevis. Indeed, 2012 marks the eightieth year of our existence. And we are proud of this achievement. And over the years, Labour has developed a tremendous store of goodwill, a goodwill born of Labour having delivered the right to vote for all. The right to free secondary education for all. The right to dignity in our advanced years via the protections of social security. Dramatically expanded access to university via the unprecedented provision of scholarships and loans. The transformation of thousands of traditionally landless Kittitians into first-time landowners. Thousands of young people and their households empowered via technology to facilitate both academic research as well as access to the e-commerce opportunities around which so much of the world economy now revolves. The rapid expansion of media outlets. The direct and regular questioning of public officials. The quantifiable and extraordinary expansion of homeownership at historic and utterly unprecedented levels all across this island.

This is the legacy of Labour. A legacy of social and economic transformation. A legacy of competence and dependability achieved through the support of a professional, committed, and hard-working public service. And it is for the vision, ethos, and competence of Labour that the people of St Kitts and Nevis voted so overwhelmingly in 2010.

Politicians who were unable, and remain unable, to form the government because of their inability to win the broad-based trust and confidence of the people at the ballot box, are pursuing alternate paths in their quest to lead St Kitts and Nevis. However, in our 2010 elections, the people of St Kitts and Nevis being of sound mind and clear vision, affirmed their desire to entrust the affairs of state to a Labour administration. And to this they remain entitled. There are many in our Federation who long to control the reins of government. They are not prepared, however, to undertake the difficult work that is required in order to win the broad-based trust of the people as reflected at the ballot box. This hard work Labour has always undertaken and this hard work Labour shall continue to embrace both today and in the years ahead.

St Kitts and Nevis is a democracy. And an overwhelming majority of voters in 2010 made clear their desire for St Kitts and Nevis to be led by a Labour administration. I wish to make clear today that not only did the voters choose Labour, they also decided *not* to choose other parties that wished to form the government. Hence, they do not expect that some of this country's Labour representatives will betray their trust by embracing combinations and permutations of persons the voters did not wish to lead the government. They expect that their Labour representatives will ensure that in keeping with the democratically expressed will of the people, the important responsibilities of governance will continue to be undertaken and managed in a spirit of humility and dedication by Labour.

I believe that this no confidence motion is designed to undermine the confidence and the stimulation that now exist in the economy of St Kitts and Nevis because the motion has the effect of eroding investor confidence in St Kitts and Nevis. As such the leader of the opposition has sought to employ a serious constitutional tool in a very flippant and frivolous manner in order to achieve a narrow political gain.

I wish to assure our many investors and potential investors, locally and internationally, that we have a long tradition of parliamentary democracy and that every action taken to date is in accordance with the constitutional rights enjoyed by our people and their representatives. I am also confident that, whatever the outcome of the proposed motion, our people will hold tightly to our cherished traditions of peace, stability, respect for the law, and democracy. Be assured, therefore, that your investment is safe and secure in our progressive country.

I also wish to assure our people that I will do everything in my power to ensure that the Labour government remains true to the mandate you have given us and that we do not betray your trust. I stand ready to move forward with the expansive programme of growth and development we have unfolded here in our beloved Federation and to discharge my obligation to complete the mandate that you so overwhelmingly and graciously gave us in 2010.

POSTPONEMENT OF PRESENTATION OF 2013 BUDGET

National Assembly, December 10, 2012

Over the past year, the Ministry of Finance has monitored prevailing economic conditions worldwide and worked within these parameters, in conjunction with other ministries, to prepare our nation's fiscal year 2013 budget. We have identified those policies, priorities, and funding levels most capable of enhancing the general stability that our nation has been able to maintain despite the socio-economic turbulence whirling all around us, and we are confident that this is a budget with which the people of this country will be pleased.

Indeed, I am able at this time to report that after several months of in-depth analysis and circumspection, the Ministry of Finance was able to prepare for presentation to the nation a budget for fiscal year 2013 that is completely tax-free. I stress and repeat – my government's proposed 2013 budget will be completely tax-free. My government is keenly aware that nations large and small are under tremendous pressure to increase public revenues via the levying of additional taxes. However, although St Kitts and Nevis has not been one of those nations that has been crushed by the global economic crisis, Kittitians and Nevisians have nonetheless borne their share of sacrifice in order to keep our nation on an even keel. And so my government feels a special obligation not to raise taxes in this budget.

The presentation of the fiscal year 2013 budget had long been scheduled for tomorrow, December 11, 2012. Indeed, this morning, cabinet met in order to affirm and solidify our support, as a cabinet, for this important budget, the mechanism via which our hospitals are funded, our energy imports made possible, our old-age pensioners and social safety net programmes supported, and our civil servants and auxiliary workers paid. However, there are two members who never arrived at this morning's cabinet meeting. Nor did they attend at an earlier December 5, 2012 cabinet meeting at which the budget was also discussed.

The 2013 budget is of utmost importance to the well-being of this nation. So is the unanimous participation of all members of cabinet in our pre-budget sessions so as to ensure that this vital legislative initiative, on which so much and so many in our nation depend, does indeed become law.

Up to 7:30 p.m. this evening, the members have not arrived to cabinet. As a consequence, we have taken a decision to postpone the budget presentation originally scheduled for Tuesday December 11, 2012. I wish to stress that all cabinet members, save two, were present at today's pre-budget cabinet meeting. And all who attended have made clear their complete support for the government's 2013 budget. Please be advised that once all cabinet members are able to meet as one body, without any absences, in order to clarify each member's position on our government's 2013 budget, a new date will be announced without delay for my presentation.

Fellow citizens and residents, the budget is one of the most critical components of the array of development tools that are employed by governments all over the world to advance the welfare of the people they serve. Be assured that I am determined to protect our investment climate by ensuring that we do not go through a prolonged period of uncertainty in relation to the budget for 2013. The budget address originally scheduled for Tuesday would have demonstrated clearly that the economy of St Kitts and Nevis is well managed. It would have projected an early return to economic growth, it would have reported a reduction in debt to GDP to well under 100 per cent, surpluses in all categories of the fiscal account, and the elucidation of a comprehensive development strategy that will dramatically enhance the capacity of our economy to achieve sustainable growth over the medium-term. It would also have created a multiplicity of employment and entrepreneurial opportunities, taking us closer to the realisation of a more advanced society replete with opportunities for our citizens and residents to achieve even their most ambitious goals through continued creativity and commitment.

Unfortunately, the world is not waiting on us, and the opportunities before us will not exist indefinitely. We must therefore move expeditiously to remove all uncertainties that could impede our progress and thereby ensure that our society continues to act as a magnet for inflows of investment through our reputation for peace and stability.

Fellow citizens and residents, be assured that in dealing with the critical matters before us the overriding factor that will determine the response of my government is our unswerving commitment to the motto of our nation, 'Country Above Self.'

Cabinet Restructuring and Expulsion of Timothy Harris

National Broadcast, ZIZ Broadcasting Corporation
January 25, 2013

Just three years ago, the people of this country endorsed the comprehensive development strategy that the Labour government had been pursuing since we assumed office in 1995 and gave us another overwhelming mandate to continue on the path of nation-building, human development, and economic expansion. It was clear that, based on our impressive track record, our people had placed considerable confidence in our ability to address the issues in respect to crime and the national debt which dominated the political debate during the 2010 election campaign.

Their confidence in us was well placed. Through enhanced management and strategic investment in the systems, equipment, and infrastructure of the security forces, we have made significant progress in the fight against crime. We appreciate the need for continued diligence and vigilance in combating crime and we will continue to intensify our efforts in law enforcement, in crime detection, in the prosecution of criminals, and in tackling the social issues that give rise to criminal activity.

Moreover, after just three years in office the national debt has dropped dramatically from nearly 200 per cent of GDP to some 130 per cent of GDP and is projected to fall even further to well under 100 per cent during the course of this year. At the same time our fiscal accounts have been improving at a rapid pace. During the last fiscal year we achieved a surplus on the current account, a surplus in respect of our primary balance, and an overall surplus from the fiscal operations of the government. Indeed, at a time when developed and underdeveloped nations around the world have been staggering under the weight of huge fiscal imbalances and cash flow difficulties, we now have money in the bank instead of an overdraft.

These dramatic achievements which now set the stage for the launch of a new era of growth in income, employment, and entrepreneurial activities were achieved notwithstanding strong and vocal opposition by a minority in the cabinet. Indeed, the opposition by senior minister

Harris, in particular, has become more and more vocal and intense and it is accompanied by political activity in the wider community aimed at undermining the programmes and initiatives of the government. It seems quite clear that senior minister Harris does not regard himself as being bound by the collective responsibility of the cabinet and this could become disruptive to the smooth flow of government business. Specifically, senior minister Harris has refused to support the government-sponsored 'St Kitts-Nevis-Anguilla National Bank Limited (Vesting of Certain Land) Act;' he has indicated to the cabinet and to the entire country that he will not support the government-sponsored senators (Increase of Number) Bill 2012; he has consistently refused to confirm to the cabinet that he will support the budget when it comes before parliament for approval; and he has refused to confirm to cabinet that he will vote against a Motion of No Confidence in the government of which he is a senior minister. Even more critically, he has clearly expressed his unwillingness to work with the leadership of the government and of the Labour Party to advocate and implement critical policies of the government.

In fact, based on my interaction with senior minister Harris in recent months, I have formed the view that the senior minister will not participate meaningfully in the government unless he is appointed prime minister. However, the Labour Party is a long-standing institution with strong democratic traditions that outline the processes by which one moves into a position of leadership in the party. It is not within my power to grant party leadership to anyone. It is the members of the party who must do so. Similarly, it is not in my power to leave the position of prime minister in my will or to give it to whomsoever I wish. The prime ministership is not a dynasty or monarchy. The choice of prime minister rests in the hands of the people of this country.

Of course, it is completely within the right of senior minister Harris or any member of parliament to hold and express views contrary to the government or the party of which he is a part. The constitution provides for freedom of speech and it is not my intention to muzzle anyone. However, when differences between a party or government and one of its members are of such a fundamental nature that it could undermine the ability of that government to discharge its obligations to the people it serves, then the leadership of the government has a duty to take action in the interest of the government and the people. The need for action in the case of senior minister Harris is even more acute in view of his activities and statements aimed at undermining the programmes and initiatives of the government.

It is in this context that I have today asked His Excellency the Governor-General to revoke the appointment of the Hon. Timothy Harris as a minister of government and he has acted accordingly in keeping with the provisions of the constitution.

This action became necessary because of the need to ensure that the government continues to function smoothly and that the investment climate is not unduly affected by the political manoeuvring that has become evident in recent months.

Whatever the outcome of such political manoeuvring, it is my duty to ensure that the government continues to carry out its mandate with a view towards advancing the quality of life of our people until the next general election, whenever such elections are held. Hence, to ensure that all functions of the government are effectively performed. I have also asked the governor-general to issue new instruments to effect the following appointments:

The Honourable Patrice Nisbett has been appointed minister of justice, legal affairs, international trade, industry, commerce and consumer affairs. Hence, he has been assigned some of the portfolios previously held by the Hon. Timothy Harris.

The Honourable Nigel Carty has been appointed minister of education, information, agriculture, marine resources and cooperatives.

I have also advised the governor-general that the appointment of a new senator to be assigned the portfolio of attorney-general will be necessary.

I will assume responsibility for the portfolio of constituency empowerment that was previously held by the Hon. Timothy Harris.

Fellow citizens and residents, I can assure you that I will do everything possible to ensure that my government continues to honour and respect the trust and confidence that you have placed in us. I intend to get on the with job of building homes for low-and middle-income families, eradicating poverty, providing jobs for our people including our school-leavers and other young people, and building infrastructure that provides modern conveniences to our people and enterprises and supports industry and commerce. The processes initiated in our parliament must run their course within the framework of our constitution but we cannot put our economy on hold. The world is moving at a rapid pace and we could easily be left behind if we allow ourselves to be distracted by the political gymnastics that are now evident in our Federation. Let us go forward together and build a new society for the benefit of all.

RESIGNATION OF SAM CONDOR

February 4, 2013

On Thursday, January 31, 2013, a letter dated January 30, 2013 was hand-delivered to the Office of the Prime Minister. This was a letter of resignation from the St Kitts and Nevis federal cabinet, signed by the Honourable Sam Condor.

Out of respect for Mr Condor, and in light of the great distance that we had travelled together as members and leaders of the St Kitts-Nevis Labour Party, I immediately attempted to reach Mr Condor by telephone to thank him for his many years of service, to state once again that I still, to this day, am unable to comprehend the cause of this breach, and to extend my very best wishes to him in his future endeavours. I deemed it essential that I speak to the former minister prior to addressing the nation in response to his resignation, and made several additional attempts to do so, to no avail. I therefore once again thank Mr Condor for his many years of service and hereby make official my acceptance of his resignation.

I wish at this time to advise the public that I have requested His Excellency Governor-General Sir Edmund Lawrence to make the following ministerial appointments:

To the current portfolio of the Honourable Marcella Liburd will be added the Ministry of Social Security.

To the current portfolio of the Honourable Patrice Nisbett will be added the Ministries of Foreign Affairs, Homeland Security, and Labour.

To the current portfolio of the Honourable Ricky Skerritt will be added the Ministries of International Trade, Industry, Commerce, and Consumer Affairs.

And the Honourable Asim Martin has been named deputy prime minister.

My fellow nationals, St Kitts and Nevis is on a solid social, economic, and political path. Crime has been reduced to levels we could never have anticipated a few short years ago. The dramatic reduction of our debt has freed up millions of dollars formerly used for debt servicing that can now be used to meet the needs of Kittitians and Nevisians. The IMF consistently declares our performance targets as having been met. And despite the sometimes frenzied political propaganda, this democratically-elected government has always been guided by the dictates of our constitution and this we shall continue to do.

There is a great deal of work to be done. There is our constitution that must be upheld. You can be assured that this government, your government, is completely committed to both.

Thank you, and may God bless and protect St Kitts and Nevis.

Court Ruling on the Appointment of the Attorney-General

February 28, 2013

My Fellow Nationals –

Our parliament is currently comprised of four senators, one of whom is Attorney-General Jason Hamilton. It is important to note that having four senators, one of whom is attorney-general, is completely legal under our constitution. Today, however, the court ruled that – procedurally, and I stress, procedurally – Mr Hamilton should have first been named a senator and then be appointed attorney-general.

My government aims at all times to adhere to the rules and guidelines of the constitution and so, following the court's ruling, moved without delay to ensure that the process via which Mr Hamilton was named senator and attorney-general was corrected. Under our constitution, the Federation of St Kitts and Nevis must have an attorney-general. In order for Mr Hamilton to properly serve in this capacity, therefore, he was today named a senator in the National Assembly of St Kitts and Nevis, the Honourable Nigel Carty having resigned as senator in order to make this possible. In response to the points raised in today's court ruling, Senator Hamilton was then appointed our nation's fifth post-independence attorney-general.

This procedural requirement having been respected and in full compliance with the constitution, the Honourable Nigel Carty will then be reappointed as a senator in the National Assembly of St Kitts and Nevis, thereby making it possible for him to resume his responsibilities to the state in his capacity as minister of education and information, agriculture, marine resources and cooperatives.

Today's court ruling gave our government the opportunity to ensure full compliance with the procedural requirements of our constitution. This we welcomed, and on this, we have acted.

We have decided to appeal the court's ruling based on the interpretation of Section 26 (2) of the constitution which does not speak to a procedure, and given that there has been another interpretation of the section in the past when there were the appointments of His Excellency Delano Bart, QC and Dr Dennis Merchant as senators and attorneys-general. On the present court ruling, it is now being suggested that when Delano Bart resigned as senator and attorney-general in 2006, in order to have appointed Dr Dennis Merchant as a senator and attorney-general, another senator/minister would have had to resign at the same time, in order to make the appointment. And obviously, this was not done.

As at this moment we are still awaiting clarification on the *Senators (Increase of Number) Act* 2013 as there appears to be some confusion in whether the judgment declared that the act is unconstitutional and/or invalid as being in contradiction of Sections 26 and 41 of the constitution.

We want to reiterate that the priority of my government at this moment is the pursuance of the government's parliamentary agenda in support of the improved quality of life of the citizens of St Kitts and Nevis and the consolidation of the principles of good governance on which our democracy is grounded.

CABINET / CANDIDATES RETREAT
St Kitts Marriott Resort, August 24, 2013

Comrades, good morning. And thank you for being here.

We've been talking about having this retreat for several weeks now, and so I am very pleased that we are now all here together this morning. In one room. Away from everything and everyone else. Focused on what we, as a party, have to offer this country. And focused on making absolutely certain that in the days, weeks, and months ahead, we – individually and collectively – recognise, build on, and convey all of the positives that set the St Kitts-Nevis Labour Party apart from every other political party in this Federation. And those positives are many.

As I look around this room this morning, I am immensely proud to be a member of this team, separate and apart from being party leader, and I am uplifted by the knowledge that of all of the options open to us, each of us individually chose to align our talents, our energies, our skills, our hearts and our minds with the extraordinary historical and political phenomenon known throughout this country as Labour. Our party's legacy in unparalleled. Our potential, unmatched.

And so, today we gather for an accounting of sorts, a stock-taking, as we ready ourselves for an election that will be more fiercely fought than ever before. Because, unlike previous elections, where the issue was simply one of whether party A will win or party B, this time around there is so much more in the mix. Most importantly, there is the matter of the real, immense, and personal humiliation for the other side if, after all the supposedly grand parliamentary and other manoeuvres, their gamble fails. Everything will be done by them, therefore, to avoid that searing public humiliation.

And so everything must be done by us, individually and collectively, to reinforce and energise the bond between Labour and the people of this country. And everything must be done by us, individually and collectively, to sharpen and project Labour's reputation for competence, compassion, cohesion, and real, quantifiable progress.

In order to do this, we have to be informed and conversant about the structure and role of government. Each and every one of us. We have to be more aware than ever before that what we say, how we say it, and indeed how we conduct our daily lives will have as great an impact on the electorate as anything we may or may not say from the platform. It is an extra burden to be sure, but such is the cost of leadership. Exposing opponents' flaws and failings is key to the political process. Yet we must be keenly aware of the dividing line between exposing our opponents' failings and exposing ourselves and our party to legal action. In addition, we all have too much to do, too many people to see, and far too little time in which to see them, and so it is essential that we tap into and apply the skills and techniques that those in our position all around the world have developed to make the unmanageable, manageable. We need to be responsible about our personal safety, Comrades, not only because we are political figures, but because we are fathers and husbands and friends. And we owe it to those in our family and social circles, as we owe it to ourselves, to be responsible in this regard. And then there is the matter of our own personal health, without which nothing we discuss or plan here will be possible. Here, too, there are crucial dos and don'ts that absolutely must be honoured and obeyed.

And then, Comrades, there is the issue of humility. Yes, Labour is this country's strongest political party. And it is indeed a fact our legacy and potential are second-to-none in this Federation. But that is precisely why it is absolutely crucial that, both at the individual and the party levels, we remain alert and responsive to those areas in which we must *do* better, *seem* better, and *be* better. Let us remember that to achieve this, we must always be able to speak frankly and openly with each other as we strive to improve ourselves and our party, confident always that whatever is said among us will always be received in the spirit in which it was intended. We truly are one here. That is the source of our strength. And this is what will keep Labour moving forward. The road ahead will call for the very best that is within us.

Because what began as a problem has now become a unique and historic opportunity, an opportunity for us to be great as individuals and as a party. 'Great' not in the sense of arrogance and egotism, but 'great' in the sense of soberly demonstrating astute, resilient, and visionary leadership at a pivotal moment in our nation's history, in the sense of defending the primacy of the ballot, and in our ability to sensitise the public to the dangers of parliamentary manoeuvres designed for personal gain being sold as acts of political principle. This, as I said, will be no ordinary election.

Let us make certain, then, that in the years ahead we will be able to look back with gratitude and pride, and the history books will record, how we in this room today went forth to meet the challenges of our time and in the process affirmed, once and for all, that in St Kitts and Nevis, the will of the people shall be neither trampled nor subverted.

30TH ANNIVERSARY OF INDEPENDENCE MESSAGE TO THE DIASPORA

September 19, 2013

My Fellow Nationals –

I wish you health, peace, and happiness on this thirtieth anniversary of our nation's independence.

Our country is one of the smallest in the world. Indeed, it is the smallest in the entire western hemisphere. Yet, our people have shown time and again that neither land mass nor population size is the key determinant of sound economic management, upward social mobility, or sound, responsible governance.

Low man on the Eastern Caribbean totem pole, where size and population are concerned, our extraordinary planning and effort has placed St Kitts and Nevis in the number one position where manufactured exports are concerned; number one in International Monetary Fund 2013 economic growth projections; number one in foreign direct investment; 15 per cent above the region where math CXC results are concerned; 15 per cent above the region where English CXC results are concerned; a life expectancy that compares with the most powerful nations on earth; home ownership at unprecedented levels; and St Kitts and Nevis being officially classified as a high-income nation.

None of this happens by chance. On the contrary, these metrics are possible for a country as tiny as ours only as a result of extremely careful planning, a high level of expertise, and meticulous, responsible execution. Let us remember, however, that this is the St Kitts and Nevis way. Consider how our people leave home and then distinguish themselves in alien environments every day of the year. Consider the various Federation-specific targets that this association has set for itself over the years and then proceeded to meet. Focus and effectiveness are indeed a part of being Kittitian and Nevisian. While I am in no way condoning slavery or colonialism, there was something extraordinary about our islands that caused both the English and the French to make our islands the cornerstone of their New World empires, and there was certainly something extraordinary about our brave sugar worker ancestors whose actions put in motion the wave of archipelago-wide actions that led to Caribbean self-awareness, and placed one island after the other on the path to independence.

Most important of all, however, was the vision and courage of our first National Hero, the Right Honourable Sir Robert Llewellyn Bradshaw, who threw the doors of our nation's schools open wide despite so many others fighting so hard to keep education the special preserve of the select and privileged few. As a result of policies put in place by Premier Bradshaw and built on by those of us who continue his work, Kittitian and Nevisian engineers, bankers, doctors, architects, lawyers, pilots, economists, artists, politicians and others today move boldly across this land, leading lives of which their parents and grandparents could not even begin to dream.

Our thirtieth anniversary finds us with a government that continues to fulfil the mandate for which it was elected. Enjoying a majority of the seats in parliament, the government continues to formulate and pass legislation that protects and advances the interests of the nation and our people. Most importantly, we live in a country in which our government is guided in all things and at all times by the constitution.

And so, here we stand, thirty years after our exquisite St Kitts and Nevis flag was first raised, our inspiring anthem first sung, and the fate of our nation placed completely in our hands. Our nation is safe, our country is stable, and our Federation is a respected member of the world community of democratic nations.

May God continue to guide and bless us all.

Burning of Venezuelan Embassy and Attempts at Political Destabilisation
January 6, 2014

My Fellow Nationals –

St Kitts and Nevis ended 2013 on a highly positive note. With much of the region and the world in crisis, the socio-economic needs of Kittitians and Nevisians were being met. The international financial community have lauded all that we – the government and the public working together – have achieved. The country's business community recorded strong sales in December and throughout the Christmas and carnival seasons, nationals, residents, and visitors alike had walked, danced, and mixed in our streets at all hours of the day and night without tension or incident. The New Year dawned to find in our country a spirit of grateful optimism as we readied ourselves for the responsibilities in the year ahead. More importantly, my government is determined and equipped to ensure that in 2014 and beyond this spirit prevails.

On the evening of Saturday, January 4, 2013, an illegal night-time demonstration was held by PAM politicians and associates Lindsay Grant, Eugene Hamilton, Timothy Harris, and others. Around midnight that same night, a fire was set at the Organisation of American States building and extinguished by our nation's fire services. A few hours later, the Embassy of Venezuela burned to the ground. And two evenings prior, PAM politicians and associates Sean Richards, Jonel Powell, Timothy Harris, and others rushed and mobbed a social gathering my deputy prime minister and I were attending at a Port Zante business place in an apparent attempt to intimidate either me and/or the business persons present.

For months, persons wishing to replace my government have asserted that we in St Kitts and Nevis are gripped by a 'crisis.' The public clearly disagrees. And the public has behaved accordingly. For this, opposition politicians have repeatedly berated Kittitians and Nevisians for not rising up like the people of Tunisia, Egypt, and Libya. It is clear, therefore, that some have decided that if there is no crisis, they will have to manufacture one.

I warn any and all persons who see it as their bounden duty to create instability, that whereas my government fully respects the right of any and all nationals to disagree strongly with any policy of my government, and while we respect the right of the public to protest and to demonstrate once the requisite permits have been granted, my government absolutely will not tolerate any operational shift from disagreement and protest to destruction and mayhem. And any person involved in fomenting mayhem and destruction in this Federation will be dealt with to the full extent of the law.

St Kitts and Nevis is a part of a globalised reality. And my government has meticulously developed a solid array of valuable bilateral relationships with nations around the world, all of which have redounded to the lasting benefit of Kittitians and Nevisians. In recent months, those who oppose my government have attempted to undermine my government and weaken our nation by attacking, in various ways, relations between St Kitts and Nevis and other nations.

My government's expression of sympathy to the government of the Republic of China on Taiwan in response to one of their fishermen being killed by the government of the Philippines, was repeatedly and publicly opposed and ridiculed by Timothy Harris and other opposition candidates. The leader and people of Cuba have been publicly ridiculed and Kittitian and Nevisian graduates from Cuban universities charged with attempting to bring so-called communism into the Federation. And now, we have the attacks on both the Venezuelan Embassy and the OAS building. The OAS representative rightly sees the attempted arson at his building as an attempt to destabilise our Federation, and we all know exactly who in our country has been trying with zero success to replicate in St Kitts and Nevis what, in their words, has been happening in Egypt, Libya, and Tunisia.

On behalf of the government and people of St Kitts and Nevis, I express to the government and people of Venezuela, and to the Organisation of American States, our heartfelt regret at the aforementioned acts. Both as minister of finance and as the minister with responsibility for our security forces, I have placed every resource at the disposal of our fire services and law enforcement in their determination to establish responsibility for the aforementioned acts at the OAS building and at the Embassy of Venezuela.

I call on all nationals, regardless of political persuasion, to condemn these acts in the strongest possible terms. Together we have created a model nation here in St Kitts and Nevis. And we, as a nation, absolutely cannot – and will not – allow any person or persons to introduce into this country, at this precarious time when it is so easy for nations to topple into social and political disarray, the types of extreme political tactics that had such tragic and tumultuous consequences in Jamaica in the '70s and '80s, in Haiti in the '90s and the early years of the twenty-first-century, and in certain other countries since then.

There are those in this country whose primary objective is to win – as they define winning – regardless of the impact on our nation. Like the Tea Party in the United States, and like some in our own country in 1967, they are energised more by what they are determined to destroy than by what they wish to build.

This government and the people of this country, on the other hand, have demonstrated, time and again what, together, we can build. And this we shall continue to do. Undeterred. The fate of this tiny country is too important for us to do otherwise.

We shall remain vigilant, government and the public alike. We shall continue to distance ourselves from those who are determined to place self above country. And, together, we shall ensure that this Federation continues to be the high-achieving, internationally regarded, opportunity-producing nation that we are. My government has an obligation to ensure the safety and stability of this country and our people. And this, without question, we shall most certainly do.

May God continue to bless and guide us all. Thank you.

Politics:
St Kitts-Nevis Trades and Labour Union (SKNTLU)

St Kitts-Nevis Trades and Labour Union (SKNTLU)

The SKNTLU had been experiencing a slow decline in membership since Lee Moore's days as leader and PAM's attempts to break the union's back after they took office in 1980. With the election of the Labour Party (SKNLP) in 1995, the union felt its time had come again and that, in conjunction with a friendly Labour government (Douglas was the first political leader of the SKNLP who was not also head of the union), it could make major strides in its continuing quest to raise the quality of life of its members.

Despite the initial euphoria of the election of a Labour government, the union did not seem to be completely committed to making the necessary changes to modernise itself and be relevant to the latest generation of potential members. Its biggest challenge, of course, came with the closing of the sugar industry in 2005. The union's member numbers were much reduced and some thought that since the union was primarily based on sugar workers, the end of sugar meant the virtual end of the union. The party refuted that notion strenuously affirming that the union was still the front-line voice for workers and their families.

SKNTLU
68TH ANNUAL CONFERENCE
Honouring Our Past – Forging Our Future

Masses House, Basseterre, October 28, 2007

Comrades. I bring you warm fraternal greetings.

Today, we are gathered together to celebrate yet another year in the life of the St Kitts-Nevis Trades and Labour Union (SKNTLU). We are gathered to celebrate the existence of an organisation that has done more to protect and uplift the masses of people in St Kitts and Nevis – and indeed, the masses of people in the entire Caribbean – than any other. We are gathered to honour those who established the St Kitts-Nevis Trades and Labour Union and, in the process, we also honour those who established some eight years earlier the St Kitts Workers League.

Today, we honour the tenacity and the vision and the courage of those who came before us. For when the grip of the colonial powers was at its most severe, these brave men – Manchester, Sebastian, Halbert, and others – gathered together to forge a new path, to usher in a new day, to create, through their unrelenting determination, a new state of being. These are the people on whose shoulders we stand. These are the people whose heirs we are today as members of the St Kitts-Nevis Trades and Labour Union, and as members of the St Kitts-Nevis Labour Party. Who else in St Kitts or Nevis, which other organisation anywhere in this land, which movement in existence today, ten years ago or fifty years ago, can claim so extraordinary an inheritance?

We have indeed inherited much. But the Good Book reminds us that from whom much has been given, much will be expected. And so, because we are the direct beneficiaries of such vision, such strength, such concern about the common good, these too must be our watchwords. And we must continue to not only follow in the footsteps of those who came before us, but also to continue and extend the journey they began, to reach milestones to which they were headed before their mortality took them away.

It took twenty-two years of determined effort for the St Kitts-Nevis Trades and Labour Union to come into being. Yet our forebears did not lose heart. The Trade Union Ordinance may not have been enacted until 1939, yet throughout all the trials and frustrations our forebears persevered. Fired by the most noble and energising of mottos, 'For The Good That We Can Do,' they moved ever onward. And in 1940 was born the St Kitts-Nevis Trades and Labour Union.

In Thomas Manchester's open letter to the people of 1932, the Workers League made it clear that the advancement of the people was its number one priority. And in that letter, the League makes clear its commitment to push for the establishment of one day every year when the sale of rosettes and other novelties can take place to provide relief for the needy. In that same letter, the League demanded that a motor ambulance be acquired to transport maternity and emergency cases from outlying and neglected districts. Finally in that letter, the League stressed the importance of a Workmen's Compensation Ordinance being introduced to protect the broad masses of people in the colony.

As we reflect upon and honour this vision, we must also ask about the path that we will now forge. What is as important to us today, as we strive to advance the common good, as the League's annual rosette sale was 1932? What, in today's terms, is the figurative 'motor ambulance' that is needed to aid those in crisis in St Kitts and Nevis? What, indeed, is as important to our well-being as a people today as workmen's compensation was in the minds of the League in 1932?

These are the questions that we must ask. For the answers to them will determine our path. And the quality of life for those who will come after us. In this challenge, and in all other challenges that may come, may the St Kitts-Nevis Trades and Labour Union, and the St Kitts-Nevis Labour Party, continue as they always have, walking side by side, each one a support and a source of strength for the other, motivated and guided by that most noble of ideals, 'For The Good That We Can Do.'

SKNTLU
73RD ANNUAL CONFERENCE
Masses House, Basseterre, October 28, 2012

Comrades, for me, as political leader of the St Kitts-Nevis Labour Party, these annual conferences of the St Kitts-Nevis Trades & Labour Union always serve as powerful, energising reminders of the historic path that our two organisations have forged together. Both of us, the Labour Party and the Labour Union, were forced onto this earth by injustices and indignities that our people simply could no longer bear. Our strength derived from a stressed and exploited people straining for a better day. And together, the Labour Union and the Labour Party have worked as one for almost a century, fought tooth and nail for the workers of this country and the people of this country, while others, you will remember, fought tooth and nail in the exact opposite direction. Together, the Labour Party and the Labour Union triumphantly delivered holiday pay, universal suffrage, free secondary education, protection of wages, social security, arbitration, expanded health care, the list goes on. You are familiar with the details – no need to list them all here. But on the matter of workers' rights, the Labour governments of this country have been relentless. You will remember that one of the first things we did after being elected in 1995 was to make St Kitts and Nevis a member of the International Labour Organisation (ILO). We had decided that St Kitts and Nevis simply had to get in synch with established international standards where worker rights were concerned. And so we moved, through this relationship with the ILO, to ensure that workers, employers, and the government alike would be aware of, and adhere to, international labour norms.

In addition to this, the St Kitts and Nevis economy, as we know, is now more diversified than ever and more complex. And in this age of globalisation, employers from all over the world are coming to the Federation. We also know that there are some practices, in some countries, with which we are unfamiliar here, like men receiving one salary and women another for the same work, for example. This, a Labour government simply would not be able to abide. And so we moved quickly to pass legislation to outlaw that practice. As a result, any foreign employer entering the Federation now knows, in advance, that in St Kitts and Nevis, there has to be equal pay for equal work.

We have also been extremely vigilant on the issue of the minimum wage, carefully monitoring the relevant economic indicators and moving promptly to protect the country's workers by repeatedly increasing the minimum wage whenever conditions indicate that this would constitute a fair and just policy. As a result, workers in St Kitts and Nevis today earn one of the highest minimum wages in the region.

This year, Comrades, you have wisely decided to focus on how you might best build on your accomplishments to date. And, as a result, you have decided to commit yourself to the question of how you might best 'Tackle the Challenges of the Future.' And the challenges are great indeed.

Anti-worker right-wing interests, both within the region as well as in the wider world, have joined forces over the past several decades to demonise, weaken, and eviscerate unions. And across the world, the consequences of this onslaught litter the landscape. In addition, this modern age pummels so many people with so many technological distractions that many matters that are essential to our individual well-being, and collective well-being, have been falling by the wayside.

This, unfortunately, is the reality within which you and unions everywhere are forced to grapple as we tackle the challenges of the future. Unions are important to economies, and they are important to societies. We know that, Comrades. Always have been, always will be. And so I urge you, as we move forward, to find innovative and imaginative ways to reach out to our young people who need to be educated on the purpose, the potential, and the importance of unions. For it is from that group that future strength and growth will come. As the old proverb reminds us, many hands make the burden light. Yours is an important burden. A large burden. And, I know, a sacred and welcome burden. Key to tackling the challenges that await, however, will be your own outreach efforts as you seek ways to find committed partners and capable Comrades capable of making your tasks more manageable, partners and Comrades who can help you to continue building on the tremendous record that will forever be the historic and incomparable legacy of the St Kitts-Nevis Trades and Labour Union.

I am very pleased to be with you today. And the St Kitts-Nevis Labour Party is tremendously proud of the path that, together, we have forged.

Long live the St Kitts-Nevis Trades and Labour Union! And long live the workers of this country without whom nothing of which we are so proud, economically, would be possible.

Minimum Wage
and Long Service Gratuity
C.A. Paul Southwell Industrial Park, Basseterre, October 29, 2014

If the Rt Excellent Sir Robert Llewellyn Bradshaw, the Rt Excellent Sir C. A. Paul Southwell, and the Rt Excellent Sir Joseph Nathaniel France were here today, they would be proud indeed. They would be proud because they would see that almost one hundred years after they began their brave and heroic battle on behalf of the workers of St Kitts and Nevis, the Federal Government of St Kitts and Nevis today, led by the St Kitts-Nevis Labour Party, remains true to the original values of those who established our party at the dawn of the twentieth century. They would see that with imagination, discipline, and unsurpassed competence, we are applying those same bedrock values but within the context of the dramatically changed, truly diversified, twenty-first century economy which we have created and which is now in our care.

We have all followed, with thanksgiving and pride, the positive reports that have been issued by international financial institutions on the macroeconomic indicators of our country. We have all been lifted by the statistics showing that our tiny country leads the entire Eastern Caribbean in economic growth, foreign direct investment, the social safety net we have created for the most vulnerable among us, in manufactured exports to the United States.

Together, the government and people of St Kitts and Nevis have sacrificed and brought the debt down. The government of this country and the people of this country have trusted each other and worked together and brought violent crime — with a few isolated exceptions — dramatically down. There is so much that together we, with God's help, have accomplished.

But through it all, my government has always remained keenly aware of those whose interests we are especially bound to protect. We have always known, to the core of our being, that there is an unbreakable link between the St Kitts-Nevis Labour Party and the workers of this country. Wherever we may be, therefore, and whatever the task at hand may be, we never forget that the St Kitts-Nevis Labour Party was conceived, established, and developed into the force that it is today precisely to lift the workers of this country up, precisely to ensure that ours is a country of fairness, and justice, and hope. Precisely, most of all, to ensure that business, labour and government all understand that in this country we are each distinct but vital parts of a very precious whole, that each of us has unique and irreplaceable roles, and that we owe it to ourselves and to our country to meet these responsibilities in a spirit of discipline, commitment, and mutual respect.

It is in light of this that my government has been so vigilant, from the moment we assumed office, about the amount that employers are able to pay their employees is concerned. And it is this vigilance which has resulted in my government increasing the minimum wage that can be paid to workers in St Kitts and Nevis not once, not twice, but three times since we assumed office. That is why, despite the fact that the minimum wage in the Federation is now higher than is paid by any other country in the region, we went into parliament and increased the minimum amount that employers are able to pay to their workers for a forty-hour work week. That is why, with the minimum wage in Barbados, for example, being $338 per week; with the minimum wage in Antigua and Barbuda being $300 per week; with the minimum wage in Grenada being $240 per week; in St Lucia, $200 per week; in St Vincent and the Grenadines, $178 per week; and Dominica $162 per week, the government of St Kitts and Nevis, your government, has once again increased the minimum wage in the Federation, this time from $320 per week to $360 per week. And we did this because we understand that in addition to creating a vibrant and healthy business environment, in addition to creating a nation that is safe and secure, in addition to ensuring that our country has twenty-first century telecommunications and transportation infrastructure, the workers of this country must be protected, they must be valued, they must be looked out for. And this is what this Labour government has always done.

But it is not only when the people of the Federation are actually on the job that they need the protection of the government, as would be the case with the legally permissible minimum wage. The government is also committed to ensuring that the people of this country are protected when they decide that the time has come to move to another company, to start their own small business, or to devote their time and energy to some matter that is of special importance to their families.

When an employee has been with one employer for ten years or more, we do not feel that they should have to walk away with only a smile and a handshake in the event that they decide to leave that employer. If they have worked for one employer for ten years or more and die in the course of their employment, we do not feel that their families should be left with no consideration *vis-à-vis* the long service that their deceased relative provided to that company. Indeed, when an employee decides to retire, having reached retirement age, we think that they should be entitled to a long service gratuity as well.

What we believe, then, is that a worker's long service with one employer must mean more than a memory. And so, on July 29, 2013, we amended this country's laws to ensure that any person who has worked for one employer for ten years or more would be entitled to a gratuity should they decide to leave that company.

May this legislation bring relief to the minds of workers all across this country. May this legislation bring greater security to families large and small. May this legislation make new starts, long hoped for but heretofore never affordable, possible.

The long service gratuity will be paid out of the Severance Payment Fund, and the Ministry of Labour is available to provide very clear guidelines as to who is eligible for the long service gratuity, and the procedure via which one applies for the long service gratuity. In all circumstances, and in all areas of life, it is important to understand the rules and regulations that pertain to the situation at hand, and I urge those workers who might be interested in benefitting from this important benefit to take the time to understand the rules, and understand the regulations, so that when you move forward you will be doing so on an informed basis.

In closing, I wish to end where I began with a discussion of the increase in the minimum wage.

Increasing the minimum wage is not something that happens with the flip of a switch. It requires careful and in-depth consultation amongst business, labour, and government. I am very pleased to be able to state, therefore, that at the end of our consultations, the government was able to arrive at unanimous agreement amongst business, labour, and government as to the appropriateness of this increase in our country's minimum wage.

There is another point that is important where the minimum wage is concerned and it has to do with the social service levy. As we know, the increase of the minimum wage from $320 per week to $360 per week will place these wage earners in a new income bracket. And under normal circumstances, this would have caused them to be subject to the social service levy. We did not wish this increase to cause wage earners to be subject to this levy and so I wish to make it clear that this increase in the minimum wage will be exempt from the social service levy.

These changes in federal policy, where the minimum wage and the long service gratuity are concerned are part and parcel of my government's ongoing and ever-expanding commitment to the protection and uplift of this country's workers. This commitment exists because we know that when a government protects and uplifts its workers, it protects and uplifts the nation.

INDEX

Ken Tilley has been a communications consultant to Denzil Douglas since 1993. He has a master's degree in political economy from the University of Toronto and provides communications counsel to political parties, governments, and corporations in Canada and the Caribbean.
Photo: Giles Dickenson

9 789768 286963